American Indian Rock Art

Volume 49

With Contributions By

Peter Anick
Carolyn E. Boyd
J. Phil Dering
Julie E. Francis
Eric C. Fuller
Michael J. Fuller
Neathery B. Fuller
Spence Gustav
David A. Kaiser
James D. Keyser
Lawrence L. Loendorf
Carolynne L. Merrell
David L. Minick
Richard A. Rogers
Karen L. Steelman
Cynthia Sturm
Walter van Roggen
Steven J. Waller
Mark Willis

American Indian Rock Art
Volume 49

Edited by Amy Gilreath, Ken Hedges, and Anne McConnell

American Rock Art Research Association

Orem, Utah
2023

Compilation Copyright © 2023
American Rock Art Research Association

c/o Troy Scotter
569 East 320 North
Orem, Utah 84097-4817

This volume is published as a compilation of papers submitted by independent researchers. All rights to the content of individual papers remain with their respective authors.

ISBN 979-8-9877906-0-1

The American Rock Art Research Association is a 501(c)(3) non-profit organization.

Printed and bound in the United States of America.

Editors: *Amy Gilreath, Ken Hedges, and Anne McConnell*
Copy Editing, Layout, and Design: *Ken Hedges and Anne McConnell*
Cover Image: *Halo Shelter, Texas, rendering by Carolyn E. Boyd (see page 135)*
Title Page Photograph: *The Black Rock site, Wyoming, photo by Mark Willis (see page 53)*
Flyleaf Photograph: *The Rattlesnake Petroglyphs site, Arizona, photo by Richard A Rogers (see page 97)*

About the cover:

Our cover image is Carolyn Boyd's digital illustration of the Pecos River style mural in Halo Shelter, created in Adobe Photoshop based on GigaPan photographs. A separate layer is created for every color of paint within each individual figure. This illustration is a composite of 647 individual layers, arranged according to the results of the stratigraphic analysis. Image © Carolyn E. Boyd.

Printed by Jostens Commercial Printing
Clarksville, Tennessee

Table of Contents

Preface vi

Northern Plains Game-Charming Shamans at Verdigris Coulee, Southern Alberta
James D. Keyser 1

Under the Alcove: Radiocarbon Dates for V-neck Anthropomorphs
Lawrence L. Loendorf, Karen L. Steelman, and David A. Kaiser 21

Echo Hawk: A Rediscovered Hoofprint Boulder on Montana's Milk River
Cynthia Sturm and James D. Keyser 31

Sacred Landscapes and Rock Art Interpretation: A Time-Sensitive Example from the Bitterroot Valley, Montana
Carolynne L. Merrell 43

The Black Rock Site: Ancient Pecked Rock Art in Southwest Wyoming
Julie E. Francis, Mark Willis, and Lawrence L. Loendorf 53

Rivers, Rocks, and Rain—Petroglyphs of Southwest Oregon
David A. Kaiser 61

Insights into the Petroglyphs at Washington State Park
Michael J. Fuller, Neathery B. Fuller, and Eric C. Fuller 79

Contextualizing Northern Sinagua Rock Drawings at the Rattlesnake Petroglyphs Site
Richard A. Rogers 97

Red Cliffs Incised: A Distinctive Style of Fine Line Art at Arizona's Palatki Heritage Site
Peter Anick, Spence Gustav, and Walter van Roggen 117

The Hearthstone Project: Applying Archaeological Science, Formal Art Analysis, and Indigenous Knowledge to Rock Art Research
Carolyn E. Boyd, J. Phil Dering, and Karen L. Steelman 135

Near-field vs. Far-field Acoustic Study of White River Narrows Rock Art
Steven J. Waller 151

Using retroReveal to Enhance Pictographs at Montana Sites
David L. Minick and James D. Keyser 159

Preface

Here we are, again, with a compilation of papers that were well-presented at a virtual ARARA Conference. For the sake of our social skills, if nothing else, we hope that this second one, held June 17–19, 2022, closes the door on ARARA's virtual-only annual conferences. Though our crystal ball is cloudy, we suspect that the future holds hybridized gatherings. Covid forced our hand to learn how to hold the event virtually, which most all of us agree is far superior to not holding it at all. There is not one of us, though, who is always able to travel to a conference no matter how appealing it is to visit friends, see rock art sites on field trips, and converse with presenters and colleagues on our research findings and interests. In our opinion, some sort of a hybrid Conference could be the best for all members: actual attendance for those able and virtual attendance for others. Technology rarely is the impediment now since most all of us find it nearly as easy to watch a Zoom presentation as a movie. Who knows, one day we might even read *American Indian Rock Art* volumes on a screen!

This Volume 49 has a strong slant towards the High Plains, and so we lead with five papers concerned with rock art in that region: James Keyser's analysis of imagery at two sites at Verdigris Coulee, Alberta, interpreted as game-drive/charming scenes; Lawrence Loendorf, Karen Steelman, and David Kaiser's study of the Alcove pictograph site in Montana, with radiocarbon dates obtained that indicate the antiquity of V-neck anthropomorph and heartline motifs; Cynthia Sturm and James Keyser's review of buffalo-shaped boulders and Hoofprint tradition petroglyphs in the upper Milk River of Montana, perceiving the hoofprint motif as negative and positive images; Carolynne Merrell's consideration of a medicine tree and pictograph associated in a traditional story, found side by side on the landscape, and revered by local Salish and Kootenai, in Bitterroot Valley, Montana; and Julie Francis, Mark Willis, and Lawrence Loendorf's documentation of the Black Rock site, Wyoming, with primarily Paleoindian-age petroglyphs.

Four additional contributions address rock art elsewhere in the lower 48 states: David Kaiser details the distribution of various rock art styles in southwestern Oregon; Michael Fuller, Neathery Fuller, and Eric Fuller revisit the petroglyphs at Washington State Park near St. Louis, Missouri, reliant on substantial archival materials; while Richard Rogers as well as Peter Anick, Spence Gustav, and Walter van Roggen give attention to Arizona sites. Rogers presents a summary inventory of the motifs documented at the Rattlesnake Petroglyphs site in the Coconino National Forest. Anick et al. continue their study of primarily incised Archaic period designs made apparent with Fine Line Analyzer, underneath more recent pictographs at Palatki Heritage Site.

Implications of the final three papers reach beyond rock art designs' style, age, or distribution. Carolyn Boyd, Phil Dering, and Karen Steelman share key components of their Hearthstone Project research designs, including documentation methods and radiocarbon dating guidelines for teasing out the many intricacies of Pecos River style rock art in Texas. Accurately documenting the polychrome murals requires meticulous study using high-resolution imagery to determine paint-application sequencing, and to identify radiocarbon sample locations that provide the most interpretive bang-for-the-buck yet also, and importantly, do inconsequential damage to the artwork. Steven Waller expands on his acoustical studies, using White River Narrows, Nevada, to marshal the argument that soundscapes deserve consideration in the contextual analyses and conservation of rock art sites. In closing this volume, David Minick and James Keyser review the pros and cons of a digital photograph enhancement tool, retroReveal, of some analytical benefit provided it is resurrected from the dustbin of abandoned computer applications.

The high quality of the papers in Volume 49 is largely to the credit of the authors, of course, but it is greatly bolstered by the insightful comments and recommendations of the reviewers. We are very appreciative of their donated time and attention. We are looking at you, Peter Anick, Wes Bernardini, Jack Brink, Todd Bostwick, Julie Francis, Mavis Greer, James Keyser, Sara Scott, and Mark Wagner. Thank you!

We hope that you enjoy reading these articles as much as we have enjoyed bringing them to print.

—Amy Gilreath, Ken Hedges, Anne McConnell

Northern Plains Game-Charming Shamans at Verdigris Coulee, Southern Alberta

James D. Keyser

Verdigris Coulee, just west of Writing-on-Stone Provincial Park, contains a large corpus of petroglyphs at two sites that shows humans and animals in structured relationships indicating the practice of shamanistic game-calling. Comparing these images to ethnographic and archaeological accounts of game calling, we see similarities in the use of ritual objects, drive-lane fences, killing weaponry, and the portrayal of supernaturally powerful shamans who are able to exercise control over several species of animals. The Verdigris Coulee images are compared and contrasted to those from two other northern Plains sites that contain similar imagery.

Northern Plains Ceremonial tradition rock art was first defined by Keyser (1977b:50–52) and later refined in a series of articles, a thesis, and two books (Keyser 1979, 1984, 1987, 2004; Keyser and Klassen 2001; Klassen 1995, 1998). Although originally based on the rock art of the greater Writing-on-Stone area,[1] comparison with earlier studies (Conner 1962; Conner and Conner 1971; Dewdney 1964; Mulloy 1958) and later research (Keyser 1984, Keyser and Poetschat 2005; Loendorf 2012) has demonstrated that this tradition was widespread across the northern Plains (Figure 1) and extended at least as far south as the central Plains (Buchanan et al. 2019:66–87; McGlone et al. 1994; Wells 1996:28). In general, Ceremonial tradition rock art is characterized by petroglyphs and pictographs of humans and animals shown in iconic poses, often juxtaposed with one another. Explicit interaction between characters is rare. Humans are primarily **V**-neck, rectangular-body, and shield-bearing warriors (many who have another body style visible through their shield). Animals are generally boat-form, but many show slightly more rounded shapes.

Humans and animals are morphologically identical across the region (Figures 2 and 3), although individuals are often highly stylized, depending on the local art style (Conner and Conner 1971; Keyser 1977b, 1984, 2004; Keyser and Klassen 2001; McGlone et al. 1994). Occasional clothing and headdresses are relatively simple but weapons such as lances and shields are quite detailed. Animals have identifying external anatomical characteristics (e.g., horns/antlers, claws, a hump), and frequently heartlines and other internal organs are shown because these were thought to be places where spirit power resided. Boat-form animals often occur as shield heraldry.

In Keyser's initial (1977a, 1977b) summary of Writing-on-Stone rock art, he described in detail the body morphology typical of Ceremonial tradition humans and animals. Specifically, these include illustration of internal organs (ribs, heartlines, and kidneys); and the typical portrayal of external genitalia—particularly males' penis and testicles for both humans and animals but also the vulva for some human females (Keyser 1977b:26–36, 51, 65, 72). Furthermore, the association of such detailed **V**-neck humans with equally

James D. Keyser
*Oregon Archaeological Society,
Portland*

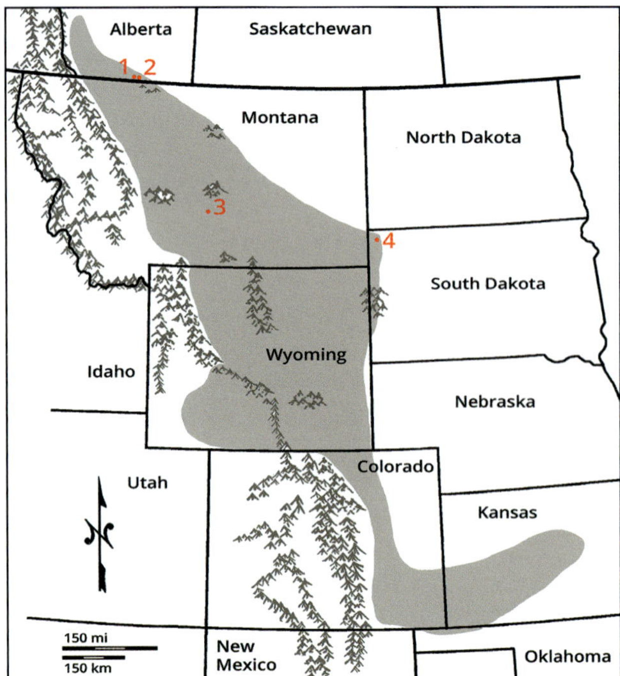

Figure 1. The distribution of the Northern Plains Ceremonial tradition. Numbered sites are 1, DgOw-28 and DgOw-29; 2, DgOv-88; 3, 24GV191; 4, 39HN219.

Figure 2. Ceremonial tradition humans are primarily shield-bearing warriors (a-f); **V**-neck humans (g-m, r), and rectangular-body humans (n-s). Note the similarities of facial features, headdresses, and internal organs for all of these. a, b, g, Alberta; c-e, h-j, Montana; f, k-m, South Dakota; n, Wyoming; o, p, Colorado; q-s, Kansas.

detailed boat-form animals was suggested to indicate vision-quest art; at least in the style common to Writing-on-Stone (Keyser 1977b:46–57). He also noted that some compositions he called visionary included rake-like forms used as ritual wands and headdress elements, leading him to speculate they were feather fans. Interestingly, although Dewdney (1962a:15, 1964:25–27) had previously recorded some of these compositions and commented on them in passing, he offered no detailed thoughts about any of them—in contrast to his focused interest on **V**-neck horsemen and their boat-form mounts.

At the time of my original definition of what was to become documented as a region-wide rock art tradition, I assumed that additional examples of these compositions, involving ritually displayed rake-like wands or batons would be found. However, this has not been the case, even though **V**-neck or rectangular-body humans and boat-form animals, often arranged in juxtaposed compositions, have been recorded at many other Plains sites (Figure 4). Instead, after nearly 50 years of regional rock art research, and following recent re-examination of petroglyphs at Verdigris Coulee for another research project (Keyser et al. 2023), I came to realize that the imagery at two sites in the Verdigris Coulee complex (DgOw-28 and DgOw-29) shows a particular type of interaction between humans and an-

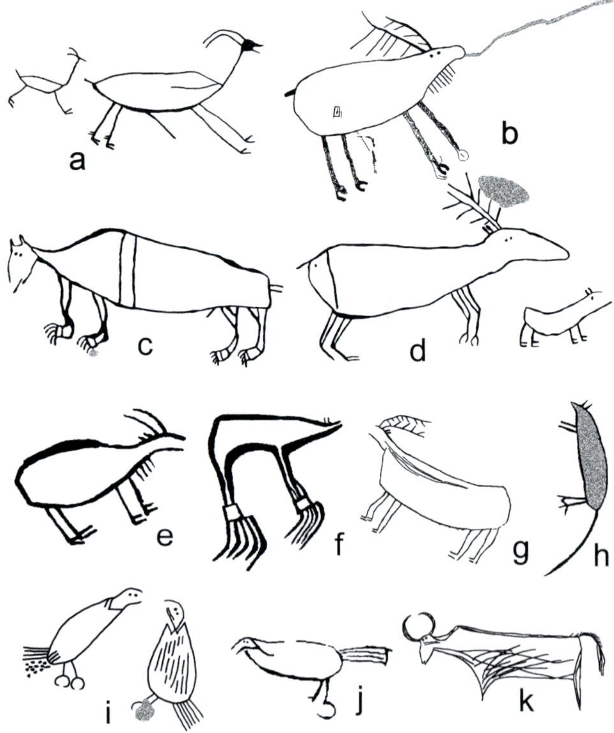

Figure 3. Ceremonial tradition boat-form animals include bighorn sheep (a, e), elk (b, d, g), bear (c, f), otter (h), sage grouse (i, j), and bison (k). a, b, Montana; c, d, South Dakota; e-j, Wyoming; k, Colorado. e, g-j are shield heraldry.

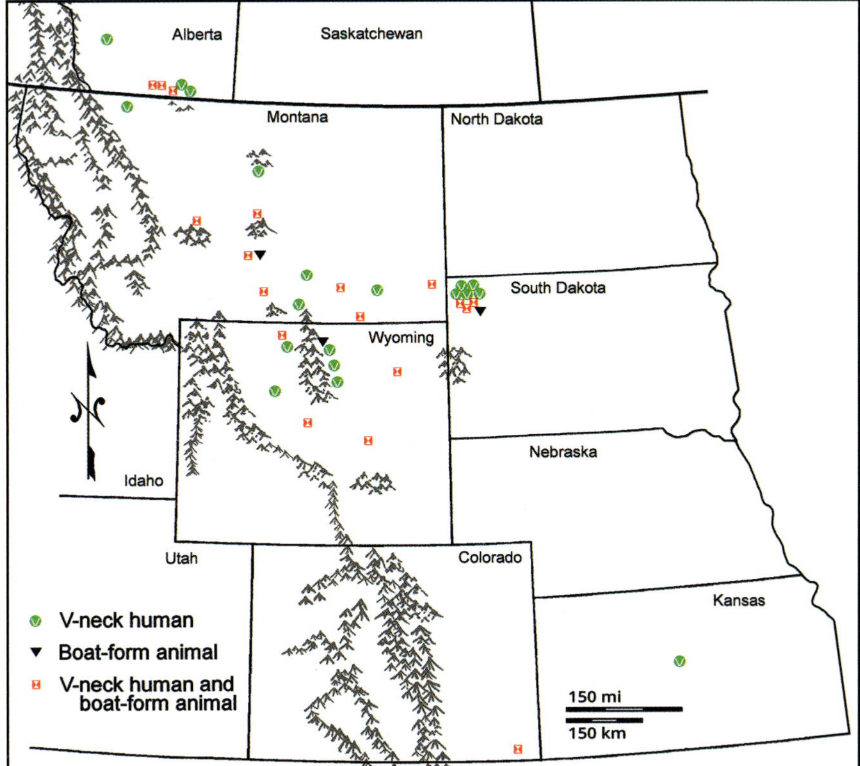

Figure 4. *Distribution of* **V***-neck humans and boat-form animals across the northern and central Plains. Most of these sites have been recorded and published since the 1976 Writing-on-Stone report (Keyser 1977a).*

imals that is different from other typical vision-quest images, and nearly unique across the northern Plains. I believe these images—and two structurally similar compositions found at other northern Plains sites—show a type of "game-calling" shaman and document the supernatural ability of these hunt shamans to control different animal species.

Petroglyphs at DgOw-28 and DgOw-29

The more than 120 representational images recorded at DgOw-28 and DgOw-29 include humans, animals, and various material culture items. In addition, there are several hundred deeply cut vertical grooves and non-representational geometric figures. Among these several hundred carvings is a constellation of approximately 50 representational images and about 25 vertical grooves that represent a series of activities that are nearly unique in Plains Ceremonial tradition rock art.

These images include almost two dozen humans, 26 animals, a single freestanding ritual wand, and a probable drive-lane fence composed of more than two dozen vertical lines. All are composed in scenes representing game calling or are individual images duplicated in such

scenes. Animals and humans are juxtaposed with one another in a dozen structured compositions, while four additional boat-form game animals and two humans (each holding aloft a ritual wand) are engraved as free-standing images.

Numerous other petroglyphs at these two sites are not part of these structured game-calling compositions. These are described and discussed in other publications (Keyser 1977a, 1977b, 1979; Keyser and Kaiser 2023; Keyser and Poetschat 2014). The images related to game calling are described below.

Humans

Twenty-three humans include a single shield-bearing warrior and 22 **V**-neck style people. These latter are separated into primary and secondary categories. The shield-bearing warrior is a simple legless figure but based on width and depth of line and its position adjacent to two **V**-neck humans engaged in sexual intercourse it appears to be part of the small scene. It is the only one of seven shield bearers at DgOw-29 that appears to be related to the game-calling imagery.

Primary **V**-neck humans are identified either because they are the only image in a composition or because they dominate a composition including multiple humans. They range from simple to highly complex. Most are explicitly men, though two are women. All but one primary figure are drawn with deep, wide, carefully controlled lines evidencing a high level of technical skill in incising petroglyphs, and each is obviously the focal point demanding the viewer's attention. Arms are held out away from the body in a typical supplicatory posture with elbows bent and hands—usually showing three to five splayed fingers—upraised. For those holding a wand, often one finger is elongated to form the wand's stem.

Primary human figures are usually very detailed (Table 1), notably more than the secondary ones (Figure 5). Heartlines and genitalia are often carefully executed, and two men have kidneys illustrated as dots in or just outside the lower torso. Facial features and ribs are occasionally drawn. Ten primary **V**-neck hu-

Table 1. Humans in Verdigris Coulee scenes.

	Wand	Headdress	Earrings	Facial Features	Hands	Heartline	Ribs	Penis	Testicles	Vulva	Kidneys
Scene 1											
Primary V-Neck	X+	X			X	X		X	X		X
Secondary V-Neck					X			*	*		*
Secondary V-Neck											
Secondary V-Neck											
Scene 2											
Primary V-Neck					X	X		*	*		*
Scene 3											
Primary V-Neck	X	X		X	X			X	X		
Scene 4											
Primary V-Neck					X			X			
Scene 5											
Primary V-Neck	X	X			X						
Scene 6											
Primary V-Neck	X+	X			X	X		*	*		*
Secondary V-Neck						X					
Scene 7											
Primary V-Neck					X	X		X	X		X
Scene 8											
Primary V-Neck	X	X		X	X	X		X	X		
Primary V-Neck	X	X		X	X	X				X	
Secondary V-Neck										?	
Secondary V-Neck						X		X	X		
Secondary V-Neck					X			?		?	
Humans holding wand											
Primary V-Neck **	X	X		X	X	X	X				
Primary V-Neck **	X	X	X		X						
Primary V-Neck	X				X	X					
Primary V-Neck	X				X			X			
Sex scene											
Primary V-Neck					X			X	X		
Primary V-Neck										X	
Shield-bearing warrior		X									

X+ Human holds wand in each hand
* Erosion has removed lower body
**Both humans jointly hold one wand

mans hold aloft one or two ritual wands, and eight wear headdresses.

Secondary humans are much simpler, usually smaller, and often more lightly incised than primary ones when they occur in the same scenes (Figure 5). Several of these are quite sketchy; often just a simple **M**-shape with a neck and head and sometimes feet, but none is as detailed as most primary humans. None wears a headdress or has facial features. Their overall simplicity makes them appear subordinate to the primary figures where they occur together.

Headdresses

Headdresses, worn by six primary humans and three others holding ritual wands, range from a short, straight line to an erect, rake-like fan, to a relatively long drooped-over branching line (Figures 5 and 6). One "fan" headdress is five lines rising directly from atop one man's head, but the likelihood that this scene and another with a distinct fan headdress were drawn by the same artist (cf. Figures 5 and 6) is strong support for this being a fan headdress. One figure in a pair jointly holding aloft a fan-type wand wears a striking combination of "floppy" earrings or earbobs paired with an erect, tree-like headdress (Figure 7a). Clearly, for the game callers at these sites, a headdress was nearly as important a piece of ritual paraphernalia as was their wand.

Wands

A dozen ritual wands are illustrated at these two sites, eleven held aloft by ten humans, and another free-standing example. Ten are tall, rake-like implements showing a long vertical stem topped by a comb-like cross piece perpendicular to the main stem (Figures 5–7). Two headdresses show this same form, and two others show a somewhat drooped-over version. These wands were originally identified as feather fans—a still valid suggestion. The remaining two wands include one straight stem with a short, downward projection at its midpoint and another scepter-like implement whose T-shaped stem is topped by a bisected oval (Figure 7b). The wand resembling a scepter has some formal similarities to the Cheyenne "Antelope Arrow" used in that tribe's antelope-charming ceremonies (Cowdrey 1999:140–142; Grinnell 1972:V.1:284).

Boat-form Animals

An extensive menagerie of boat-form style animals populates the petroglyphs of DgOw-28 and DgOw-29 (Figures 5, 6, and 8). In fact, examples of nearly half the animals identified at the genus level in all Writing-on-Stone sites are carved at these two sites, including the only pronghorn antelope, bighorn sheep, and skunks in the greater Writing-on-Stone area.[2] Among the 25 animals of interest to this research (23 recorded in situ and two others apparently stolen from DgOw-29) are four skunks, six pronghorn antelope, two elk, seven bighorn sheep, a bird, and five specifically unidentified quadrupeds. One of these latter is almost certainly a female (pronghorn or elk), two others are "fantastic" creatures with horns/antlers resembling no recogniz-

Figure 5. *The main game-caller panel at DgOw-29 contains four separate scenes (numbered). Two Historic period combat scenes superimposed over the elk and human in Scene Four are removed from this illustration. The circular shield scratched on the large central human is also an Historic period addition. Vertical grey lines are saw cuts done by thieves who stole the far-right section sometime between 1962 and 1976. They were unable to remove the center section. The squared grey area at the far left may also result from site theft. Light grey at neck of large human in Scene One is defacement.*

Figure 6. *Scene Five at DgOw-29 is so strikingly similar to Scene One, that I believe they were carved by the same artist. Photograph courtesy of Michael Klassen.*

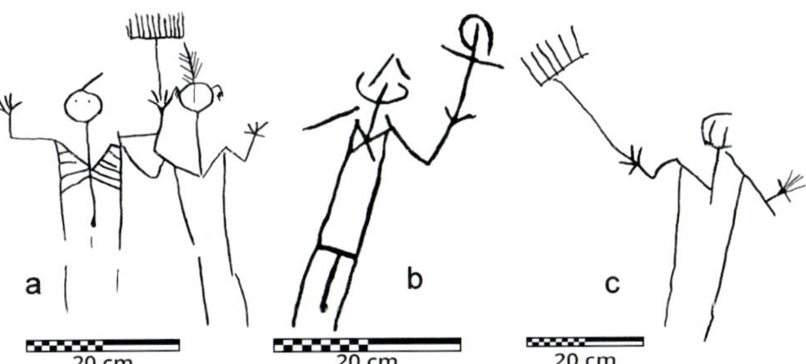

Figure 7. **V**-*neck humans holding ritual wands at DgOw-29. Note the elaborate headgear of the right-hand human in a.*

able configuration, and two are simply drawn without any identifying anatomy. In addition to the stylized boat-form body, most of these animals have "galloping" legs bent backward in the front and forward in the back to resemble a set of quotation marks.

Finally, one vertically oriented boat-form shape is carved in Scene One (Figure 5). This form is exactly the same size and shape as the boat-form bodies of other animals and has what might be a short tail and one hind leg. Unfortunately, no other anatomical details identify it, so it remains enigmatic, especially considering the exquisite detail typical of most boat-form animals.

Pronghorn Antelope. Six pronghorn antelope are found at DgOw-29; five recorded in situ (Figures 5 and 8) and a sixth (Figure 9a) that was sawn off the cliff and stolen from somewhere in the greater Writing-on-Stone area by thieves in the 1960s (Anonymous 1980:70). I identify it as coming from DgOw-29 because the only major saw damage known in the area is at this site (Keyser 1977a). Pronghorns are recognized by their characteristic long, lyre-shaped horns each with a short straight prong just above its base where it attaches to the skull, and/or a series of short vertical lines across the neck and a line across the rump. These body lines mark the pronghorn's distinctive white rump patch and broad white neck stripes. One pronghorn doe, whose real-life short horns are knobs that cannot be seen at any distance, has the characteristic neck lines and rump patch. Individual animals also have a heartline with ribs, a penis, and kidney dots. One animal has a single inverted **V**-shape rear hoof. Three pronghorns are drawn in an orthograde position, two with head down and one with head up. Two paired orthograde pronghorns each has an extraneous, deeply grooved line crossing its head.

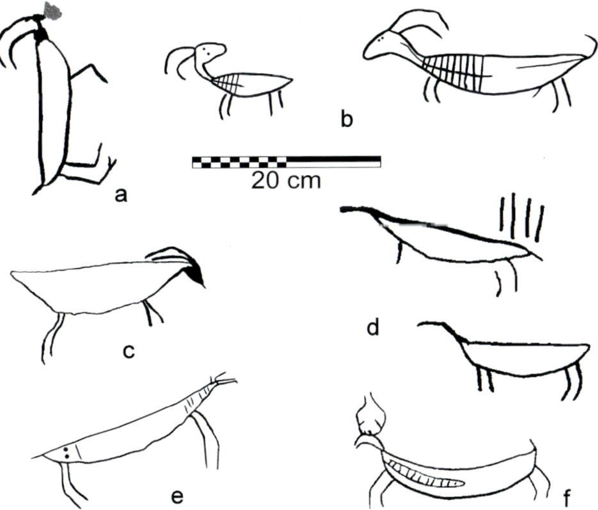

Figure 8. *Other boat-form animals at DgOw-29. (a-c) bighorn sheep; (d) species unidentified; (e, f) pronghorn antelope. Grey blob on a is defacement. All images to the same 20-cm scale.*

Figure 9. Slabs probably removed from DgOw-29. (a) A prong-horn identifiable by horn configuration, but there is no indication of the orientation of the original image. (b) A skunk and circle. Several panels at the site have extensive areas where saws were used to remove slabs in the 1960s. Photographs by Lawrence Halmrast, courtesy Royal Alberta Museum.

Skunk. Three carved skunks form a group on an extensive game-calling panel at DgOw-29 (Figure 5), and a fourth is on a sandstone slab that was almost certainly stolen from the site by cutting it away with a saw (Figure 9b). I do not know exactly which panel originally had this stolen skunk. All four animals have an elongate, banana-shaped body, short legs, a small head, and an outsized pinnate tail arched up and over their back all the way forward to the head. Legs and head of two skunks are damaged by a saw cut that fortunately did not remove that part of the panel, but the rear legs of one animal are simply missing. A longitudinal line running the length of the body on two skunks indicates their characteristic striped pelt.

Elk. Two elk are identified at DgOw-29 by massive, stylized antlers showing main branches with shorter spikes branching off to the interior (Figures 5 and 6). Both animals also have a line across the rump above the rear legs demarcating the characteristic buff-colored rump patch. The elaborate elk has a heartline with a triangular terminus, ribs, and dot kidneys. The simpler animal was stolen from site DgOw-29 sometime between 1962 when the site was first recorded by Dewdney (1962a, 1962b) and 1976 when it was recorded by Keyser (1977a). Fortunately, there is a pre-damage photograph of the entire panel taken by Lawrence Halmrast (Anonymous 1980:24; Gasser 2001:21); and a photograph of part of the stolen block showing the elk was published by the Archaeological Society of Alberta, Lethbridge Centre (Anonymous 1980:70). We also have Dewdney's 1962 drawing of this elk and associated human in situ.

Bighorn Sheep. Bighorn sheep are carved at both sites. All three at DgOw-28 are carved on the same extensive panel (Figure 10). Two right-facing bighorns loosely follow one after the other at the panel's left side. Their size and shape and near identical curl of their horns suggest they were both drawn by the same hand. To the right of these figures is a much larger sheep with a deeper body form and a larger, more realistically drawn head. This figure has seven vertical lines marking its neck and upper chest. This bighorn's lower body and legs were heavily eroded by cattle rubbing against the bottom edge of this cliff by 1976, but an earlier photograph (Anonymous 1980:29) shows it originally had the typical "quotation mark" legs.

Four bighorn sheep are carved at DgOw-29; two composed in a scene where a large ram with a visible penis follows a smaller ewe who looks back over her shoulder (Figures 8b and 11). The lead animal is identified as a ewe by three criteria. Initially, she has no genitalia displayed and a gracile form with a body less than half the size of the explicitly male animal. Additionally, although the heads of these animals are almost the same size, the horns of the lead animal are significantly

Figure 10. The largest panel at DgOw-28 shows this extensive composition (Scene Eight) involving bighorn sheep, various humans, and a series of vertical lines that I interpret as representing drive-lane fences. Note the larger humans at right center who hold rake-like feather fans. Scattered dark grey blobs around bighorn at left are defacement.

6

Figure 11. *This pair of bighorn sheep illustrates a ram's pursuit of a receptive ewe during the rut, at DgOw-29.*

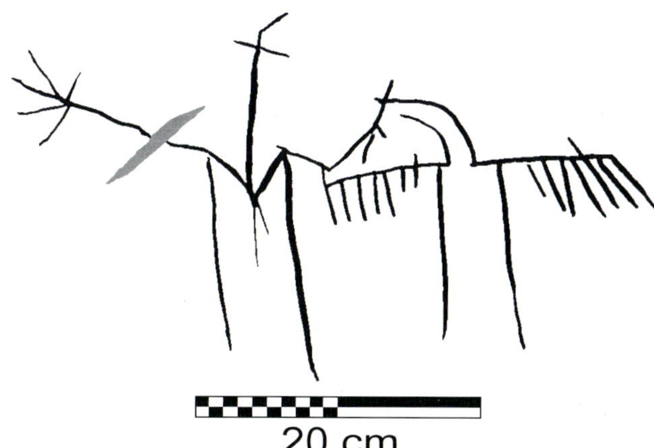

Figure 12. *In this scene the human at left touches the beak of a large bird with a ritual wand, at DgOw-29.*

smaller, showing only 70 to 80 percent of the horn length of the larger ram. Both sheep have heartlines and ribs in the chest region and the ram has a short upcurved tail. Both animals have two eyes—a unique example of twisted perspective at these two sites.

Two other more crudely rendered bighorn sheep are identified by their characteristic large, curved horns. One is drawn in a pronograde pose (Figure 8c) while the other is in orthograde position (Figure 8a). To the right of the orthograde animal a large section of the cliff has been sawn away and stolen. I suspect there may well originally have been a human interacting with this animal in a composition similar to others at the site.

Bird. A single upright, front-view bird in a "thunderbird" pose with a wing outstretched to each side, is paired with a **V**-neck human (Figure 12). The bird has neither claws nor tail and its head is turned to the left toward the human who reaches out to touch the bird's beak with a short wand. Both the bird and man have no lower margin to their body, but this area has been heavily eroded by animal rubbing. The symbolism of some sort of power-sharing between these two beings was originally instrumental in leading me to view the pairings of humans and animals at these two sites as documenting vision-quest experiences.

Unidentified Quadrupeds. Six boat-form quadrupeds at DgOw-29 cannot be specifically identified. Two are drawn as an isolated pair, one above and a little ahead of the other (Figure 8d). Two others have fantastic horns or antlers, but these are not sufficiently detailed to identify the species. It is tempting to identify one, in a pronograde position on the extensive panel filled with game-calling imagery (Figure 5), as a pronghorn based on the exag-

gerated lyre-shaped horns but there are no prongs on these nor are there body markings. Another animal, drawn in an orthograde pose is juxtaposed with a man and woman coupling in a sexual scene, but it is unclear whether the humans and animal are integral parts of a single composition. Another animal is a crude vertical representation with a vestigial head showing short ears but neither horns nor antlers (Figure 5, Scene 3). For this animal the "boat form" is inverted, with the curved line representing its back and a straight line for the belly. It has two long, straight front legs and a short line projecting to the left of the body, just before the shoulders. Rear legs and tail are broken away.

The final unidentified quadruped is a long, sleek, well-drawn animal with a body morphology like both elk and pronghorn (Figure 13). It has short ears but no antlers, an inverted **V**-shaped hoof on its rearmost leg, and a heartline. Males of all large Plains ungulates have horns or antlers, but only cervid does (deer or elk) have no antlers and pronghorn does have horns that are just small bumps. Thus, in light of these sites' typical bestiary, this is almost certainly a pronghorn doe or cow elk.

Other Imagery

A few other images are parts of game-calling scenes at these two sites. At DgOw-28 more than two dozen vertical grooves are incised into the main panel and

Figure 13. *Scenes Five and Six are carved adjacent to one another at DgOw-29.*

scattered among these grooves stand five humans (Figure 10). In addition, two bighorn sheep appear to run between two rows of these vertical lines, both of which have a human stationed at one end. The layout of this panel mimics ethnographic reports of drive-lane fences with people positioned along them to help herd the animals toward a controlling shaman who lures the animals into a trap for a communal kill.

Three other grooves are part of one scene. In this scene two vertically oriented pronghorns have a deep groove across their head and another vertical animal has a groove into its back. These appear to represent floating weapons used to dispatch the animals.

Compositions

Fourteen compositions at DgOw-28 and DgOw-29 document a complex of related ritual activities. Eight compositions juxtapose animals with humans in a stylized way showing ritualized game calling. The other compositions are not explicit scenes relating humans and animals, but they appear to show individual humans' ritual actions or the actions of animals that relate to game-calling symbolism. One of these juxtaposes a pair of copulating humans with a shield-bearing warrior and a boat-form animal, two show paired animals of the same species, and three show humans holding aloft ritual wands. One scene shows two people standing side by side while jointly holding aloft a single rake-like wand between them. In another, two bighorn sheep are engaged in a graphic depiction of courtship behavior.

Human-Animal Interactions

Six of the eight compositions involving humans and animals show the human appearing to exercise control over the animal to bring it closer, while in two others the human stands next to vertically posed animals that can reasonably be interpreted as dead. In each composition one or more humans is illustrated in such a way that the human(s) dominate the scene. In some, this dominance is indicated by the human's superior position or larger size, and sometimes also by the depiction of anatomical details indicating points of power in the body. In others, dominance is shown by the human's supplicatory pose or the animal's unnatural orthograde position, and in still others it is the exaggeratedly large hands held far above the head or out away from the body. In four scenes the human(s) hold one or two rake-like feather fans and in another scene the human reaches out to touch the beak of a large bird

with a shorter, simpler wand. In five scenes the primary human(s) wears a headdress, sometimes a notably elaborate one. The most graphic scenes simultaneously show several of these characteristics.

Four scenes (numbered for descriptive purposes) are carved adjacent to one another on a single large, smooth cliff face (Figure 5). Several of the lower images on this panel are truncated by natural block erosion where sections have fallen from the cliff, but at the panel's extreme left a suspiciously "square-cut" edge suggests a "saw-cut removal," even though this was not recognized as such in Keyser's 1976 recording. If true, this implies there originally were other animals and humans carved on the panel's left side.[3]

About five meters to the left of this large panel is another cliff face showing two scenes (numbered Five and Six on Figure 13) that are similar to Scenes One through Four. Like the larger panel, a section of this one to the left of these scenes has been chiseled out and pried off, but I have no idea what image(s) were stolen. Scene Five on this panel shows such close correspondence in specific details and structure to Scene One on the neighboring panel that I suspect they were drawn by the same artist (compare Figure 6 to Figure 5, Scene 1). These two panels contain more than half of all the game-calling images portrayed at Verdigris Coulee.

Scene One. Scene One contains four humans, a pronghorn buck, and a possible second boat-form animal (Figure 5). The primary human is the largest figure in the composition and shows the most elaborate anatomical detail of any human at either site. In addition to his anatomical detail, he holds a feather fan upright in each hand and wears a headdress of five upright feathers resembling his feather fans. He is "presenting" to a vertically oriented, head-down pronghorn buck who is likewise one of the two most-detailed animal figures drawn at either site. Surrounding this pair of obviously interacting figures are three much smaller, less detailed, **V**-neck humans who are clearly subordinate to the larger one. Just left of the antelope and parallel with its orientation is a boat-form shape that may be a very simple animal. The scene clearly expresses the idea of the pronghorn approaching the primary human who exercises control over it. The animal's orthograde position implies it is dead or soon will be.

Scene Two. Just to the right of Scene One is a human with the most exaggeratedly long arms and large hands of any in this study. He interacts with a specifically unidentifiable quadruped and three skunks (Figure 5). Of all the Verdigris Coulee scenes, this one is the most ambiguous and open to multiple interpretations. Initially, it is possible that these five images and the four images in Scene Three could all be part of a larger entity, but I argue that the emphasized hands on this human indicate he is more than a subordinate person to the larger, rectangular-headed man, so I consider these as two separate scenes. Likewise, animals in Scene Two are different from those in any other scene. The three skunks are clearly not large herd ungulates as are those in other scenes, but skunks were eaten and their pelts were used for pipe bags, medicine bundles, and other items by groups across North America (Kuhnlein and Humphries 2017). The other animal is a very detailed but unidentifiable quadruped whose only distinguishing characteristics are exaggerated horns and a horizontal line running the length of its body. The big-hands human appears to be most directly interacting with this quadruped, and his hand is superimposed on one skunk, so it seems likely that the skunks form their own freestanding group or are related to Scene One to their left. The relationship between the human and ungulate in this scene mimics those in several other scenes.

Scene Three. Scene Three shows the largest human on the panel juxtaposed with three vertically oriented animals (Figure 5). Two are pronghorn bucks but the other is specifically unidentifiable. The two pronghorns are similar enough in form that they appear to be drawn by the same hand. All three animals have short, but distinctly cut lines piercing their body or hitting their head. The human has facial features, external genitalia, and wears a long bent-over headdress with a comb of short lines extending from its top. In his hand facing the animals he holds a large feather fan. The circular shield crudely scratched and superimposed on his body is a later addition like another example on a **V**-neck human elsewhere on this panel.

Scene Four. Scene Four is one of the simplest human/animal juxtapositions at these sites. Here a relatively plain **V**-neck human with raised hands stands next to a bull elk posed in a vertically oriented head-up position (Figure 5). The human has a long penis, and the elk has large antlers, rear hooves, and a line marking its buff-colored rump. The animal's orthograde position, implying death, is what informs this scene as something more than simply "man and animal."

Scene Five. Scene Five (Figure 13) is carved about three meters west of scenes One through Four. This composition is so similar to Scene One in size, structure, and detail that I am confident both were carved by the same artist. In this scene the human also holds

feather fans in both hands and wears a feather fan headdress. His lower body is destroyed from the waist down by the collapse of a block long since fallen from the cliff, and not present when the site was first recorded. A very detailed elk—one of the most detailed animals at the site—is shown walking up to the human. Between the two is a sketchy **V**-neck human showing only the shoulders/arms, neck, and head, positioned relative to both principal actors much like one subordinate human illustrated in Scene One.

Scene Six. Just half a meter to the right of Scene Five is another composition showing a female animal approaching a man standing slightly above it and to the right (Figure 13). The man carries no ritual paraphernalia but has a heartline and external genitalia clearly portrayed. The scene's structure is nearly identical to Scene Five, though mirror imaged. Stylistic differences for both the human and animal strongly suggest it was drawn by a different artist than scenes One and Five.

Scene Seven. Scene Seven shows a large, simple **V**-neck human figure with one outsized, outstretched hand. With his other hand he touches a short wand to the beak of a large bird (Figure 12). The interaction between bird and human is explicit but its meaning is ambiguous. It might indicate control of eagles, which were sought for their feathers in elaborate eagle-trapping rituals, but it might also simply represent the transfer of spirit power. About half a meter to the right of these two figures is a vertically oriented, head-up bighorn sheep (Figure 8a). On this panel deep saw cuts just to the right of the sheep frame a stolen section of cliff, so we have no idea what images may originally have been juxtaposed with this animal. Given other scenes at site DgOw-28, however, I suspect there was a **V**-neck human associated with this bighorn.

Scene Eight. Scene Eight, carved at DgOw-28, is the most extensive composition at either site (Figure 10). Incised across 2.5 meters of cliff surface, the composition's focal point is a large man and woman, each holding aloft a feather-fan and standing side by side just above a large left-facing bighorn sheep (Figure 14). Just left of the man is a third feather fan that appears to be freestanding, but which might instead be held by an eroded human now represented only by vertical lines and possibly a pecked circular head. These outsized humans and animals are positioned among a **V**-shaped cluster of vertical grooves with a very simple **M**-shaped human just to the right (Figure 10 and 15b). Both primary humans have facial features, heartlines, and genitalia, and both wear headdresses. The woman's headdress resembles both a feather fan and the headdress worn by the human in Scene Three. Together, these three main actors and the freestanding feather fan form a typical composition for these two sites, showing a man and woman with ritual paraphernalia exercising some influence on the bighorn ram.[4]

Were this composition the only one on the panel it would still be impressive; but, in fact, when viewed in light of several scenes at DgOw-29 this appears to be part of a more extensive scene that includes two other bighorn sheep, several **V**-neck humans, and a series of prominent vertical lines that appear to represent drive-lane fences. Starting at the left of the panel there are at least two obvious humans, one each standing above and below two bighorn sheep walking single file between these people toward the larger humans. To the right of each human is a row of vertical lines and in the upper row there appear to be one or two very sketchy human figures standing among the verticals.

To the right of the lead bighorn, the upper row of vertical lines nearly merges with the freestanding feather fan and two large humans. A few other vertical lines are placed in front of the larger bighorn. Viewed as a whole, this entire composition is easily seen as a drive-lane fence complex (composed of rows of vertical grooves) with people standing

along the fences to drive the animals toward the waiting couple holding the feather fans (Figure 15). Similarly illustrated and also—at first glance—apparently "haphazardly" arrayed arrangements of lines have been recognized as game-drive fences at other rock art sites where they depict game-trapping operations (Keyser 2016).

Given the different styles of bighorn sheep in this composition it seems likely to represent two separate drawings, probably utilizing the fan-holding humans in both. The main composition including the two feather-fan-holding humans and large bighorn was apparently re-used by a second artist who added the left half of the larger composition. This composition uses the two outsized humans, but the artist drew two smaller bighorns being driven toward them between parallel drive-lane fences.

Other Compositions

Six other compositions of interest include a sex scene, humans holding a feather fan or similar ritual wand, and two pairs of interacting animals.

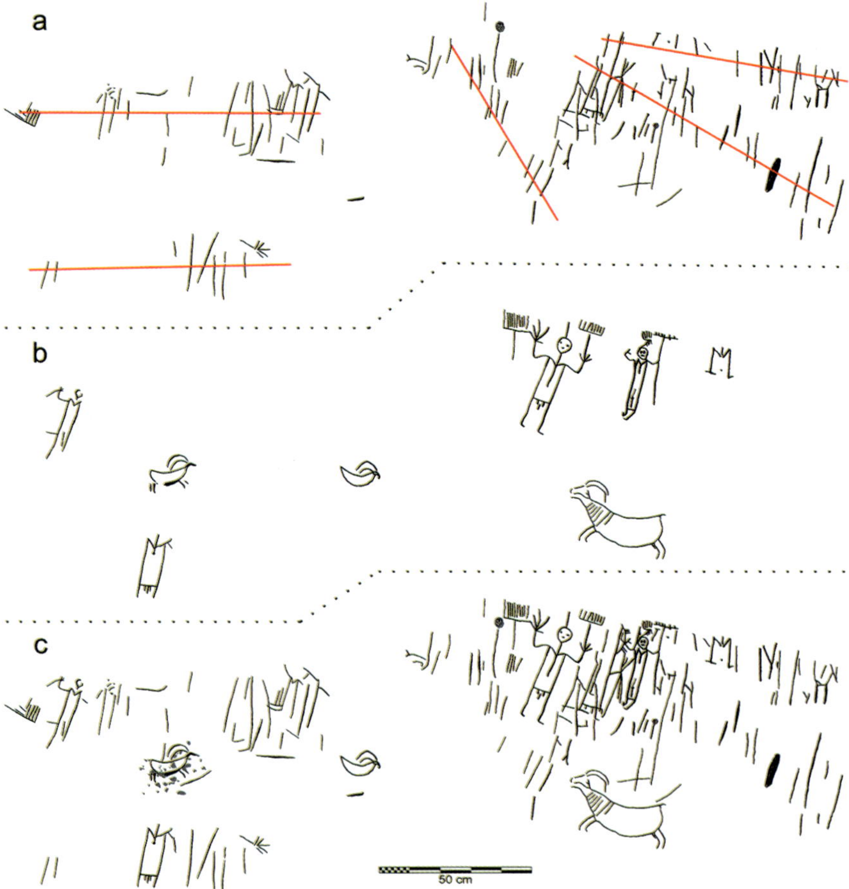

Figure 14. The primary actors at DgOw-28 show genitalia, facial features, and heart-lines. Note the figure on the right is a woman who wears a feather fan headdress.

Figure 15. Deconstructing Scene Eight enables us to more readily identify the drive-lane fences: (a) only the fence structure—red lines show the **V**-shape and parallel rows; (b) position of humans and animals; (c) composite scene.

Sex Scene. A stylized sex scene is paired with a boat-form animal and a shield-bearing warrior on one DgOw-29 panel (Figure 16). The man is positioned above the woman but his elongated penis loops down and enters the woman's body at the position of her genitalia. A shield-bearing warrior is next to the woman and a vertically oriented animal is directly above her. Showing sexual intercourse in this way is common in Ceremonial tradition rock art, and sexual activity associated with either hunting (the vertically oriented animal) or warfare (the shield bearer) fits easily into northern Plains cultural practices having to do with the acquisition, transfer, and exercise of supernatural power (Kehoe 1970).

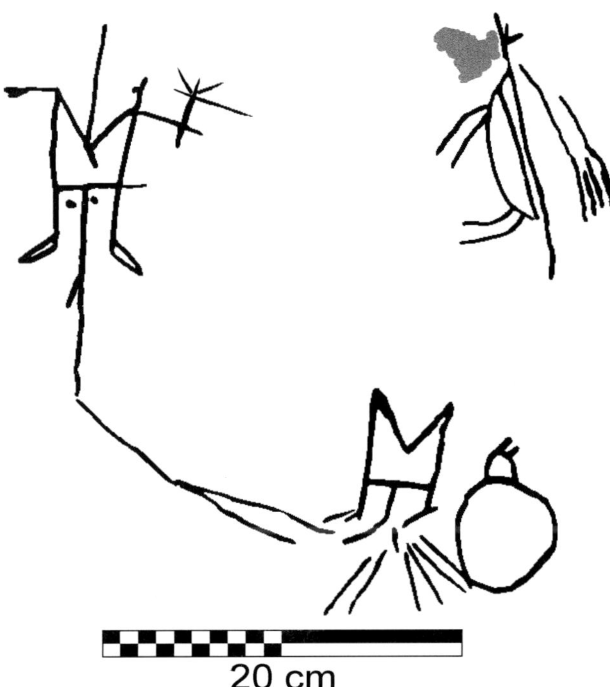

Figure 16. A sex scene at DgOw-29 is juxtaposed with a simple shield-bearing warrior and a boat-form animal with exaggerated antlers. The grey blob at the animal's head is defacement.

Humans with Ritual Wands. Four humans hold up ritual wands. One pair holds a feather fan between them, each grasping the stem with one hand (Figure 7a). One of these has eyes, ribs, a heartline, and a single-line headdress while the other wears a complex headdress with earbobs. Their lower extremities have been nearly erased by animal abrasion. Two other **V**-neck humans are drawn as freestanding figures holding ritual wands. One lightly incised example holds a feather fan out at about a 45-degree angle (Figure 7c). This poorly drawn figure has an incomplete body with no anatomical detail. A second, more precisely incised

figure, is obviously male and holds aloft a scepter-like wand (Figure 7b). His head is oddly formed and may show a conical headdress or hairdo.

Paired Animals. Three sets of paired animals and a trio of skunks are carved at DgOw-29. The skunks are discussed as part of Scene Two (Figure 5) and one pair of bighorn sheep are discussed as part of Scene Eight (Figure 10). The other pairs include two specifically unidentified animals and two bighorn sheep. The unidentifiable animals (Figure 8d) are drawn one above the other in the center of a small, sparsely incised panel. Other nearby lines may be associated faded figures.

The pair of bighorns (Figures 8b and 11) forms its own composition showing a bighorn ram trailing a bighorn ewe. Both are carefully incised with curved horns, a heartline, ribs, and two eyes shown on one side of the head. The ram has an erect phallus and short upcurved tail, while the ewe looks over her shoulder at her pursuer. This composition captures in a very life-like manner a bighorn ram's pursuit of a receptive ewe during the rut, as is seen in numerous videos of bighorn mating behavior (Hamilton and Hamilton 2021). The only aspect of the drawing not true to life is the male's upraised tail.

Regional Comparisons

When I first recorded the Verdigris Coulee petroglyphs the only previous record of them was the then unpublished photographs of Lawrence Halmrast (Anonymous 1980) and sketches by Selwyn Dewdney (1962b). The scenes involving game calling and ritual paraphernalia had never been published and essentially were unknown to rock art scholars. At the time, though no other comparable images were known (Keyser 1977b:46), I thought it was likely that additional scenes showing similar actions and ritual objects awaited discovery elsewhere in northern Plains rock art. This belief was bolstered by the fact that site DgOv-88, approximately 10 km downstream from Verdigris Coulee, in Writing-On-Stone Provincial Park, had both humans with ritual wands and boat-form animals (Figure 17)—though they are not juxtaposed in scenes like those at DgOw-28 and DgOw-29 (Keyser 1977a:96, 1977b:46, 66).

The DgOv-88 images show one well-drawn boat-form animal and a second sketchy one with no head and two humans holding wands. Neither animal can be specifically identified. The very large rectangular-body human has facial features, an exaggerated penis with a crosspiece for testicles, and ribs and kidneys

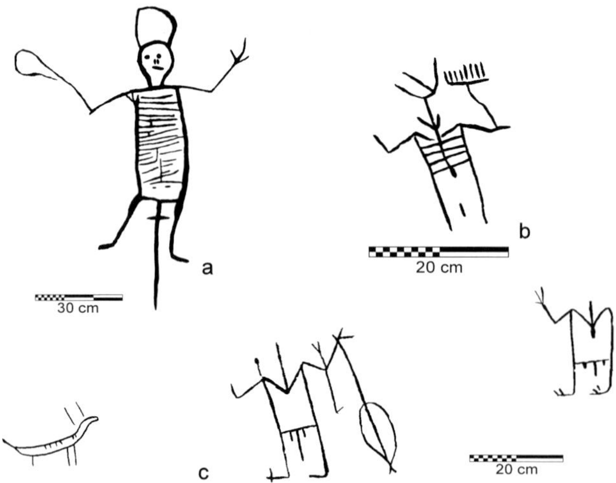

Figure 18. *Game-calling composition at 24GV191. No scale available.*

Figure 17. Game-calling imagery from DgOv-88: (a) note facial features, genitalia, internal organs, and crookneck wand; (b) note feather fan, internal organs, and genitalia; (c) possible composition with boat-form animal and two male "sitting" humans, one of whom may hold an atlatl and dart.

drawn inside his body. His ritual wand is a relatively short crookneck staff, and he wears a buffalo-horn headdress. The second human is much smaller with an incomplete head but a **V**-neck body with ribs and a heartline scribed in the upper torso. A short vertical line just below the waist could be either a penis or vulva. In one hand this figure holds up a rake-like feather fan identical to those illustrated at Verdigris Coulee.

Since that 1976 fieldwork at Writing-On-Stone, however, hundreds more sites have been located, recorded, and published throughout the Plains, and while **V**-neck humans and boat-form animals are common, and often have the same suite of anatomical characteristics discussed here (Figures 2g–s, 4), no other known example uses ritual paraphernalia like this in scenes similar to these at Verdigris Coulee. In fact, I know of only two other examples across the entire northern Plains where a **V**-neck human appears in a similarly structured relationship with boat-form animals.

The first of these is a lightly incised scene drawn high on a cliff at 24GV191 on the Musselshell River in central Montana (Figure 18). This scene shows a man with facial features, an odd hairdo, a heartline, and emphasized genitalia standing in a hands-up pose confronting an elk and a large bighorn sheep who has a smaller bighorn sheep within its body. All three animals are drawn in the classic boat-form style, with a unique gooseneck configuration indicating they were drawn by the same artist. The bull elk has a heartline, an erect phallus, and four hooves. The front two-thirds of its body is crossed by oblique, roughly parallel lines

that could represent ribs, or indicate a darker coat color contrasting to his blank (light-colored) rump. A large arrow or dart sticks in his back.

The bighorn sheep has four hooves and a smaller bighorn sheep positioned inside the rear one-third of its body. The smaller sheep has no hooves and short head projections that appear to be horns at first glance. However, a newborn bighorn lamb has notably outsized ears (nearly as large as its mother's) so the "horns" may actually represent ears. One's first impression is that the smaller sheep inside the larger one illustrates a pregnant ewe, though in the real world this would not be the case if the interior animal's head projections were horns. There is considerable debate about "pregnant bighorns" in Great Basin rock art (Culley 2008; Garfinkle and Austin 2011; Grant et al. 1968; Whitley 2005:47)—especially that of the Coso Range—but that argument involves numerous issues not pertinent to this discussion. Instead, it seems to me, given the reasonable interpretation that this scene depicts game calling, and the presence of rutting behavior imagery at DgOw-29, that this image may well represent fertility and fecundity as they relate to desired game animals.

Although the man in this scene does not hold obvious ritual paraphernalia, his upraised right and left hands show significant differences. Possibly the simpler, four-fingered left hand represents a feather fan, but it is equally plausible that the detailed, five-fingered right hand was intended to represent something more than just his hand. The dart/arrow indicates a killed animal. This scene is structurally almost identical to Scene Six at DgOw-29, and very similar to Scenes One and Five (with the exception of involving multiple animals). Were it carved at Verdigris Coulee, I would have no problem classifying it as a game-calling composition.

A second similar scene is at site 39HN219 in the North Cave Hills of South Dakota (Figure 19). At this

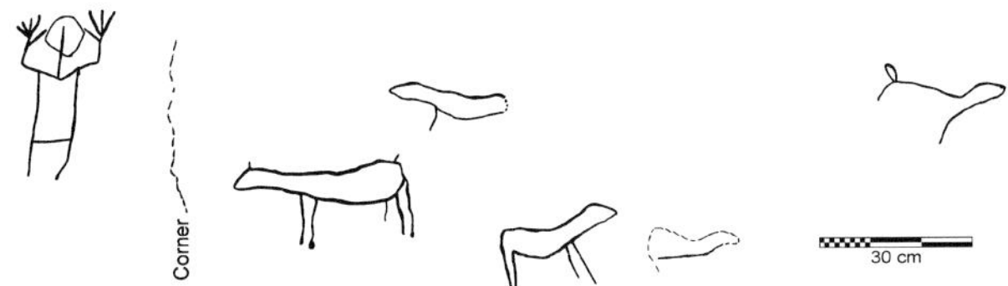

Figure 19. Game-calling composition at 39HN219. Corner is an approximate 90-degree change in orientation of cliff face so that human faces herd of animals. Dashed-line animal is heavily eroded.

site a **V**-neck human with hands upraised is carved on a surface facing a group of five boat-form animals carved on a second surface oriented perpendicular to the human. The animals are unidentifiable, and three turn back away from the human. Cowdrey (1999:141–142) first suggested these animals were part of a game-charming scene, but he conflated them with some nearby (but much older) geometric abstract images and the wrong human. Why some of these animals are shown "turned back" is not readily evident unless this grouping represents animals milling around at the finale of a successful game drive (see below).

It seems likely that both scenes at 24GV191 and 39HN219 represent the same sort of ritual activity as the Verdigris Coulee scenes, even though neither includes ceremonial paraphernalia like that illustrated at DgOw-28 and DgOw-29. Clearly, such images are not anywhere near as common as I originally thought they would be.

Discussion and Interpretation

The Verdigris Coulee scenes, and probably those at 24GV191 and 39HN219, illustrate humans exercising control over various animals and beg the question of what ritual is actually being illustrated. Human participants include both men and women, and more than half of those at Verdigris Coulee hold aloft ritual feather fans or other wands. Animals being controlled include pronghorn, bighorn sheep, elk, skunks, a bird, and unidentified species. Other images show only animals—sometimes interacting with one another—or isolated humans holding a ritual wand. In one composition two figures jointly hold the feather fan aloft. One other scene shows a man and woman in sexual union with an adjacent shield-bearing warrior all juxtaposed with a boat-form animal. Finally, one other site—DgOv-88—in Writing-on-Stone Provincial Park has boat-form animals and shows two humans holding such ritual wands.

When these scenes were first recorded, I interpreted them as vision-quest symbolism, wherein the artist portrayed his or her acquisition of spirit power from the associated animal (Keyser 1977b:51–52). This interpretation was strongly influenced by the occurrence of similar juxtapositioning of humans and animals in Columbia Plateau tradition rock art found at many sites just west of Writing-on-Stone. Notably, however, typical Columbia Plateau vision-quest scenes do not include such explicitly ritual paraphernalia as headdresses or wands, or explicit anatomical detail for either humans or animals.

Since that early interpretation, I have come to understand these scenes as something quite different than vision quest imagery. Initially, it became apparent that shamans were often the artists who made rock art (Keyser and Klassen 2001:213–221), and several years later evidence accumulated that some groups in both the Plains and Columbia Plateau made rock art as part of ritual hunting magic (Keyser and Whitley 2006). Finally, after a full recording of site DgOw-32, just upstream from DgOw-28 and DgOw-29 (Keyser et al. 2023), it became evident just how unusual these Verdigris Coulee images actually are.

Game Calling Among Northern Plains Tribes

To interpret the Verdigris Coulee images, and by extension two other similar Plains images, I summarize the practice of game calling as reported ethnographically in both Columbia Plateau and Plains cultures. On the Columbia Plateau, magic was routinely used in several ways by hunters to control and kill various game animals. Deer, elk, bighorn sheep, and mountain goats were all pictured in hunting-magic rock art, and ethnographic accounts show that various Salishan tribes resorted to several different ritual behaviors to supernaturally control at least some of these animals (Keyser and Whitley 2006:9–18). Teit (1930:243–245) describes a communal bighorn sheep hunt in which two hunt shamans (one a woman) used ritual costumes and the assistance of a dog to control the animals and drive them toward waiting hunters. This behavior is shown in Columbia Plateau rock paintings.

On the Plains, pronghorn antelope charming is well documented ethnographically. Both Grinnell (1972:V.1:277–290) and Mooney (1898:288–289) describe detailed rituals wherein an antelope shaman uses wands—called "antelope arrows"—to lure a pronghorn herd into a trap (Figure 20). Constructed drive-lane fences and an excavated pit were sometimes used in these efforts, and large contingents of women, children, and old men helped drive the animals into the

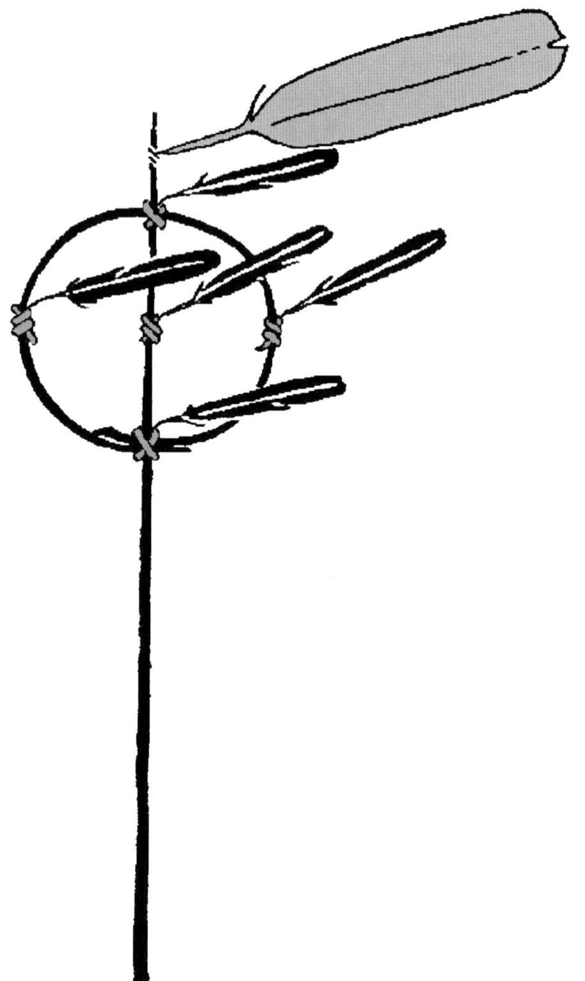

Figure 20. Reconstructed Cheyenne "Antelope Arrow" based on figure in Grinnell (1972:V.1:284) with additions by Cowdrey (1999:140–142). Note prominent feathers.

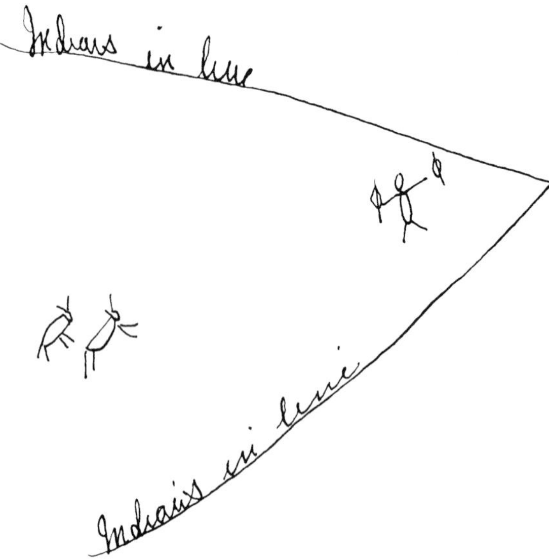

Figure 21. This drawing by George Bent diagrams a Cheyenne antelope drive he witnessed in 1853 (after Hyde 1968; see also Cowdrey 1999). Note the structural similarities to several Verdigris Coulee scenes.

trap to be killed at close quarters with clubs. In both the Cheyenne and Kiowa tribes, antelope shamans were assisted by women and during special parts of the ceremony the shaman and one or two helpers jointly held the antelope arrows and transferred them from one person to another.

We even have a schematic sketch (Figure 21) of the layout of such an antelope drive, drawn by George Bent, a biracial Cheyenne,[5] in a letter he wrote to George Hyde sometime before 1918. In his letter, Bent describes an antelope drive he witnessed in about 1853 (Hyde 1968:18–20). His drawing shows the drive lanes, the antelope shaman holding aloft his "medicine sticks" (antelope arrows), and the animals approaching him by entering the **V** formed of "Indians in line." Bent's drawing is stunningly similar to four Verdigris Coulee compositions and makes it much easier to envision the other humans in these scenes as helping with the drive,

and to see the rows of vertical grooves in the DgOw-28 scene as drive-lane fences.

There is ample ethnographic and archaeological evidence that many different Plains tribes conducted communal hunts of the three main game animals— pronghorn, bighorn sheep, and elk—depicted at Verdigris Coulee. In addition to detailed Cheyenne and Kiowa accounts (Grinnell 1972, Mooney 1898), ethnographic references show Lakota, Crow, Blackfoot, Mandan, Arapaho, Arikara, and Hidatsa all conducted communal antelope drives (Sundstrom 2000:124). For bighorn sheep, extensive archaeological evidence of communal trapping by Sheepeater Shoshones is almost as well documented as Plains bison drives (Frison 1991:246–258; Keyser 1974). Finally, Grinnell (1972:V.1:276) reports that elk were killed in communal game drives and an explicit game-drive petroglyph at 48SW85 in the Green River basin of southwest Wyoming includes elk along with bighorn sheep and bison as the quarry for different drives (Keyser 2016).

Both ethnographic and archaeological evidence indicates shamans were key to driving pronghorn and bighorn sheep, and I have no reason to believe their services would not have been used in much the same way for hunting elk. Probably the best evidence is the first-hand reports of knowledgeable Cheyenne, Kiowa, and Shoshone as to how antelope shamans conducted hunts (Grinnell 1972:V.1:277–290; Hyde 1968:18–19; Steward 1941:218–220), but archaeological evidence includes shamans' structures built into bighorn sheep traps (Frison 1991:253) and what has been interpreted as a shaman directing operations in the rock art game-driving scene at 48SW85 (Keyser 2016:53).

Correspondence Between Ethnography and Rock Art

There is a strong correspondence between the key elements of game calling in ethnographic accounts and the Verdigris Coulee petroglyphs. Similar elements shared by the two data sets range from general activities and beliefs to specific items used by principal actors (Table 2). The following attributes are most relevant:

- **Game callers were supernaturally powerful**: This is indicated in the ethnographic descriptions of their actions and indicated in rock art by the emphasis on showing "power places" (heartline, kidneys, genitals, and facial features) in the bodies of the game callers.
- **Use of ritual wands to control animals**: The ethnographic game caller uses a pair of ritual wands (called "antelope arrows") that have the express purpose of luring animals into a trap. Both double and single wands are shown in the petroglyphs.
- **Participation of women**: At certain points in the game-calling ritual, ethnographic reports indicate women participated to assist the game caller. One Verdigris Coulee petroglyph shows a woman assisting a man in using ritual wands.
- **Simultaneous manipulation of ritual wands**: In parts of the game-calling ritual, ethnographic reports indicate two people would simultaneously hold and manipulate the ritual wand. One Verdigris Coulee petroglyph shows this action.
- **Special headgear**: Special headdresses were worn and used in game-calling rituals. Ethnographically such headdresses are known for bighorn sheep drives in the Columbia Plateau but are not specifically mentioned in Plains antelope drives, although specific body-painting designs are mentioned. The Verdigris Coulee petroglyphs show an emphasis on headdresses for the game caller but not the subordinate humans.
- **Drivers help maneuver the animals**: Ethnographic reports show that drivers were used to "herd" animals into the trap. In the rock art, these drivers appear as the subordinate V-neck humans.
- **Drive-lane fences were constructed and used**: Ethnographic and archaeological evidence indicates that fences were constructed to control the movement of the animals, and ethnographic re-

Table 2. Comparison of Cheyenne antelope trapping with Verdigris Coulee game-charming scenes.

Attributes	C	V
Game caller is supernaturally powerful	X	X
Use of ritual wands ("antelope arrows")	X	X
Two individuals hold wand simultaneously	X	X
Women assist game-caller shaman	X	X
Drivers "herd" animals into trap	X	X
Use of drive-lane fences	X	X
People stationed along fences	X	X
Animals killed with clubs	X	X
Pit trap used with fences	X	
Shaman's body painting	X	
Other animals also trapped		X
Game caller wears headdress		X

C = Cheyenne Antelope Trapping
V = Verdigris Coulee Rock Art

ports indicate people were stationed along these fences. One Verdigris Coulee scene shows drive-lane fences with people standing along them.

- **Killing the corralled animals**: Ethnography indicates animals lured into a trap or surround were killed with clubs. There is an archaeological example of such a club used for bighorn sheep. Three animals in one Verdigris Coulee scene are shown in a vertical "dead" position and all are struck by "floating" clubs represented by short, deeply incised lines. However, at 24GV191 an elk is pierced by a dart or arrow suggesting that elk (being much larger) were killed in a different manner than pronghorns and bighorn sheep.

The only major discrepancies between the Verdigris Coulee imagery and ethnographic accounts are the inclusion of a sexual-intercourse scene in the rock art and the inclusion of a bird and skunks in the petroglyphs.

In sum, the Verdigris Coulee compositions strongly imply the actions of shamans/game callers. In seven separate scenes, one or two humans, whose supernatural powers are often evidenced by their depicted anatomical details, appear to exercise control over elk, pronghorn antelope, and bighorn sheep. In four scenes the protagonists utilize feather-fan wands and fancy headdresses as part of their ritual effects. But not just these explicit scenes suggest game calling. Two other single individuals hold aloft a feather fan and another type of ritual wand and in a third scene a pair of humans jointly holds a feather fan, mimicking the documented ethnographic behavior of a game-calling shaman who elicits the help of another person to hold, manipulate, and carry the ritual wands. Finally, the inclusion of a scene showing sexual coupling is consistent with ethnographic reports indicating ceremonial sexual intercourse used to transfer supernatural power, and rock art showing sexual coupling associated with game trapping (Keyser 2016:53). Other scenes explicitly showing the rutting behavior of a bighorn ram just prior to mating and a probable pregnant bighorn ewe at 24GV191 seem likely to reflect both the concepts of fertility and of sexual potency that imbue this entire game-calling activity.

The inclusion of skunks in these game-calling scenes and a scene pairing a man and bird seem slightly different but may well be related. Certainly, skunks have their own potency and controlling those animals is akin to being able to lure game animals into a trap. Additionally, skunks were eaten by many groups and their pelts were used for various items. Controlling an animal who could so readily "fight back" would be a very important ability. Likewise, eagle trapping was an activity fraught with the same sort of supernatural aspects that a game caller would need (Murray 2011).

Chronological Assessment

Based on the general chronology developed for Writing-on-Stone imagery (Keyser 1977b; Keyser et al. 2023; Klassen 1998; Magne and Klassen 1991) the game-calling petroglyphs at DgOw-28 and DgOw-29 date to the Late Prehistoric period. No game caller is associated with any Historic period indicator (e.g., metal projectile points, horses, or guns). Furthermore, only a single **V**-neck horseman and a single shield-bearing warrior capturing a gun at these sites suggest the limited extension of Ceremonial tradition art there into the Protohistoric and Historic periods. Later Historic period imagery at both sites is dominated by mature style horses and small rectangular- and triangular-body humans very different from these game-calling images. On the large DgOw-29 panel containing Scenes One through Four, these Historic period figures are superimposed over the animal in Scene Four. This chronology is further borne out by extensive analysis of the imagery at nearby DgOw-32 (Keyser et al. 2023).

Dating these images to the Late Prehistoric period is consistent with the rest of the archaeological record in this area of the northern Plains. Communal bison killing has a long history in the region (Brink 2008:18–23; Frison 1991:158–237), so we know such hunting practices would have been a normal component of the cultures who could have carved these images. In addition to bison killing, antelope procurement also has a long history in the area (Brumley 1986; Davis et al. 2000; Keyser et al. 1984:34–40), and bighorn sheep trapping was certainly practiced back into the late prehistoric past (Frison 2004:155–165; Keyser 1974). In short, the Late Prehistoric period inhabitants of this area of southern Alberta would have been prime candidates to have carved these game-calling images.

Conclusion

The complex of game-calling petroglyphs at two Verdigris Coulee sites—DgOw-28 and DgOw-29—stands out as nearly unique since they were first recorded and published (Keyser 1977a, 1977b). Their association with game calling is strongly supported by the detailed correspondences between the imagery and ethnographic and ethnohistoric reports of such activities; and, as such, they provide a Plains example of hunting-magic rock art. The fact that these images are found concentrated at two sites and at least two drawings at DgOw-29 appear to be the work of the same artist provide a strong positive answer to a test recently proposed (Keyser and Whitley 2006:16) to assess the validity of rock art hunting magic.

Three other sites, nearby DgOv-88, 24GV191 located on the Musselshell River more than 300 km to the south, and 39HN219 located more than 700 km to the southeast in South Dakota, have images that appear formally and structurally similar to those at the Verdigris Coulee sites. DgOv-88 has petroglyphs of humans holding aloft a feather fan and a long crook-neck wand, along with two boat-form animals, neither identifiable as to species. Although these figures are not composed in scenes like the Verdigris Coulee imagery, none of them would be out of place were they carved at either DgOw-28 or DgOw-29. Both humans have the typical genitalia and internal organs, and one has facial features just like those at Verdigris Coulee. The proximity of DgOv-88 to Verdigris Coulee argues that these four figures carved there were done as part of the same game-calling ceremonialism evident at DgOw-28 and DgOw-29.

The scenes at 24GV191 and 39HN219 are unique at those two sites, and stylistically both differ slightly from those at Verdigris Coulee. Neither human in these scenes wields a ritual wand, and both are portrayed with less detail than are most Verdigris Coulee examples. However, structurally the compositions very closely mimic several at DgOw-29, and were either scene carved at Verdigris Coulee, they would readily be classified as game-calling compositions. Possibly additional scenes like these will be found to help shed light on their distribution and function.

In sum, the Verdigris Coulee images, some at DgOv-88, and the scenes at 24GV191 and 39HN219 show that some northern Plains artists documented their abilities as game callers in rock art. From the Verdigris Coulee images, we have good evidence of the sorts of ritual paraphernalia (headdresses, feather fans, and at least one other type of wand) used in these activities in southern Alberta. We can also draw close parallels with the ethnographically documented game-calling activities of several different groups.

Notes

1. The greater Writing-on-Stone area extends along the Milk River in southern Alberta from Coffin Bridge to just downstream from Writing-on-Stone Provincial Park. It includes major site concentrations at Verdigris Coulee, Haffner Coulee, Wier Ranch, and Writing-on-Stone Provincial Park itself. Nearly 200 sites containing more than 5000 painted and carved images are found in this area.

2. One skunk and a probable antelope photographed in the collection of someone who sawed them off the cliff and stole them—presumably from sites at Verdigris Coulee—are shown in photographs in *Story On Stone* (Anonymous 1980). There is no information as to the site from which these panel sections were taken, but large areas of cliff face on several DgOw-29 panels show where extensive parts have been removed by sawing and chiseling. Given the minimal evidence of such removal anywhere else at Writing-on-Stone, and the recording of what was removed at those places, I am reasonably confident that this skunk and antelope were originally at DgOw-29.

3. The fallen blocks were not present in 1976 when Keyser recorded the site, and Dewdney does not mention them in his 1962 fieldwork. They may have been long destroyed, but it is possible that at least one of the "broken away" slabs published in 1980 (Anonymous 1980:70) naturally fell from this panel.

4. When he originally recorded this panel, Dewdney (1962a:15) suggested that the bighorn was "clearly by [a different] hand" than the **V**-neck humans above. While he did not give a reason for this opinion, it may have been due to the appearance of the bighorn as less deeply incised. However, after recording this animal and then later observing photographs of the panel, it appears that the difference in depth of line between the bighorn and other images above it is that the lower

parts of the panel show significant abrasion from animal rubbing. That would also explain the apparent "erasure" of the lower ends of the vertical neck and chest lines. It seems highly likely that the same artist carved all three figures.

5. George Bent was the son of William Bent, founder of Bent's Fort on the Santa Fe trail, and Owl Woman, the daughter of Cheyenne chief White Thunder.

Acknowledgments. Several people assisted in my research. Susan Ashley was field assistant during my Writing-on-Stone fieldwork. Michael Klassen has always been generous in sharing his photographs and field notes from his work at Writing-on-Stone. Jack Brink and David Kaiser helped obtain copies of Dewdney's original Verdigris Coulee site tracings and Jack assisted in obtaining the Halmrast photographs of slabs removed from DgOw-29. George Stoll, Mavis and John Greer, and Larry Loendorf provided photographs from 24GV191 that I used to make my photo-tracing of that panel. Amanda Castañeda shared her photo-tracing of that panel and discussed it with me at length. Linea Sundstrom provided photographs of 39HN219 and discussed that site with me at length. Tracings of images at DgOw-28 and DgOw-29 are reductions of my 1976 originals (provided courtesy of Alberta Archaeological Survey) augmented by reference to photographs by Lawrence Halmrast and Michael Klassen.

References Cited

Anonymous
  1980 *Story on Stone*. Archaeological Society of Alberta, Lethbridge Centre, Lethbridge, Alberta, Canada.

Brink, Jack W.
  2008 *Imagining Head-Smashed-In: Aboriginal Buffalo Hunting on the Northern Plains*. AU Press, Athabaska University, Edmonton, Alberta, Canada.

Brumley, John H.
  1986 A Radiocarbon Date from the Laidlaw Site, DlOu-7. In *Archaeology in Alberta, 1985*, edited by John W. Ives, pp. 205–206. Archaeological Survey of Alberta Occasional Paper 29, Edmonton.

Buchanan, Rex C., Burke W. Griggs, and Joshua L. Svaty
  2019 *Petroglyphs of the Kansas Smoky Hills*. University Press of Kansas, Lawrence.

Conner, Stuart W.
  1962 *A Preliminary Survey of Prehistoric Picture Writing on Rock Surfaces in Central and South Central Montana*. Billings Archaeological Society Paper 2, Billings, Montana.

Conner, Stuart W., and Betty Lu Conner
  1971 *Rock Art of the Montana High Plains*. The Art Galleries, University of California, Santa Barbara.

Cowdrey, Mike
  1999 *Arrow's Elk Society Ledger*. Morning Star Gallery, Santa Fe, New Mexico

Culley, Elisabeth V.
2008 Supernatural Metaphors and Belief in the Past: Defining an Archaeology of Religion. In *Belief in the Past: Theoretical Approaches to the Archaeology of Religion*, edited by David S. Whitley and Kelley Hays-Gilpin, pp. 67–83. Left Coast Press, Walnut Creek, California.

Davis, Leslie B., John W. Fisher, Jr., Michael C. Wilson, Stephen A. Chomko, and Richard E. Morlan
2000 Avonlea Phase Winter Fare at the Lost Terrace Site, Montana: The Vertebrate Fauna. *Plains Anthropologist* 45(174):53–70.

Dewdney, Selwyn
1962a Pictograph Recording Project: Alberta and Saskatchewan, 1962. Manuscript Report M-9286-49. Electronic document, https://www.glenbow.org/collections/search/FindingAids/archhtm/dewdneys.cfm accessed January 27, 2022.

1962b Rock Art Recordings Made at Fifteen Sites. Photographic reductions of original 24 x 30-inch sheets with full size and scale reproductions, in watercolor, line drawing, and conté chalk, of rock art at Writing-on-Stone and Verdigris Coulee. Copies on file with author.

1964 Writings On Stone Along the Milk River. *The Beaver,* Winter 1964:22–29.

Frison, George C.
1991 *Prehistoric Hunters of the High Plains.* Second Edition. Academic Press, San Diego, California.

2004 *Survival by Hunting: Prehistoric Human Predators and Animal Prey.* University of California Press, Berkeley, California.

Garfinkle, Alan P., and Donald R. Austin
2011 Reproductive Symbolism in Great Basin Rock Art: Bighorn Sheep Hunting, Fertility and Forager Ideology. *Cambridge Archaeological Journal* 21:453–71.

Gasser, Ellen
2001 *Lawrence D. Halmrast: Guardian of the Milk River.* Provincial Museum of Alberta, Special Publication No. 8. Edmonton, Alberta, Canada

Grant, Campbell, James W. Baird, and J. Kenneth Pringle
1968 *Rock Drawings of the Coso Range.* Maturango Museum Publication 4. Maturango Museum, China Lake, California.

Grinnell, George Bird
1972 *The Cheyenne Indians: Their History and Ways of Life.* Two Volumes. University of Nebraska Press, Lincoln. Reprint edition, originally published 1923, Yale University Press, New Haven.

Hamilton, Paul, and Coral Hamilton
2021 Bighorn Sheep Rut—The Mating Chase. WildlifeOnVideo (YouTube channel). Electronic document, https://www.youtube.com/watch?v=Fec565nciE8, accessed June 22, 2022.

Hyde, George E.
1968 *Life of George Bent: Written from his Letters.* University of Oklahoma Press, Norman.

Kehoe, Alice B.
1970 The Function of Ceremonial Sexual Intercourse Among the Northern Plains Indians. *Plains Anthropologist* 15:99–103.

Keyser, James D.
1974 The LaMarche Game Trap: An Early Historic Game Trap in Southwestern Montana. *Plains Anthropologist* 19(65):173–179.

1977a The Rock Art of Writing-On-Stone. Manuscript on file at Alberta Recreation and Parks, Edmonton, Alberta, Canada.

1977b Writing-On-Stone: Rock Art on the Northwestern Plains. *Canadian Journal of Archaeology* 1:15–80.

1979 The Plains Indian War Complex and the Rock Art of Writing-On-Stone, Alberta, Canada. *Journal of Field Archaeology* 6(1):41–48.

1984 Rock Art of the North Cave Hills. In *Rock Art of Western South Dakota*, pp. 1–51. Special Publication 9. South Dakota Archaeological Society, Sioux Falls.

1987 A Lexicon for Historic Plains Indian Rock Art: Increasing Interpretive Potential. *Plains Anthropologist* 32:43–71.

2004 *Art of the Warriors: Rock Art of the American Plains.* University of Utah Press, Salt Lake City.

2016 Site 48SW85: A Hunting Magic Petroglyph on the Green River. In *American Indian Rock Art, Volume 42*, edited by Ken Hedges, pp. 41–59. American Rock Art Research Association, San Jose, California.

Keyser, James D., and David A. Kaiser
2023 *War Stories: Reading Plains Indian Biographic Rock Art.* Berghahn Books, New York (in press).

Keyser, James D., and Michael A. Klassen
2001 *Plains Indian Rock Art.* University of Washington Press, Seattle.

Keyser, James D., and George Poetschat
2005 *Warrior Art of Wyoming's Green River Basin: Biographic Petroglyphs Along the Seedskadee.* Oregon Archaeological Society Publication No. 15, Portland.

2014 *Northern Plains Shield Bearing Warriors: A Five Century Rock Art Record of Indian Warfare.* Oregon Archaeological Society Press Publication 22, Portland.

Keyser, James D., and David S. Whitley
2006 Sympathetic Magic in Western North American Rock Art. *American Antiquity* 71(1):3–26.

Keyser, James D., Carl M. Davis, Bob Alex, Therese Chevance, and Thomas Haberman
1984 Lightning Spring: 4,000 Years of Pine Parkland Prehistory. *Archaeology In Montana* 25(2–3):1–64.

Keyser, James D., David A. Kaiser, and Stephen J. Lycett
2023 *"War is Their Sole Delight": Blackfoot Petroglyphs at DgOw-32, Verdigris Coulee, Alberta.* Oregon Archaeological Society Press Publication 28, Portland (in press).

Klassen, Michael A.
1995 *Icons of Power, Narratives of Glory: Ethnic Continuity and Cultural Change in the Contact Period Rock Art of Writing-on-Stone.* Master's Thesis, Trent University, Peterborough, Ontario, Canada.

1998 Icon and Narrative in Transition: Contact-period Rock Art at Writing-On-Stone, Southern Alberta, Canada. In *The Archaeology of Rock Art,* edited by Christopher Chippindale and Paul S. C. Taçon, pp 42–72. Cambridge, University Press, Cambridge, United Kingdom.

Kuhnlein, Harriet V., and Murray M. Humphries
2017 Skunk. In *Traditional Animal Foods of Indigenous Peoples of Northern North America* (online) by Harriet V. Kuhnlein and Murray M. Humphries. Centre for Indigenous Peoples' Nutrition and Environment, McGill University, Montreal, Quebec, Canada. Electronic document, http://traditionalanimalfoods.org/mammals/furbearers/page.aspx?id=6377, accessed December 30, 2022.

Loendorf, Lawrence L.
2012 *Three Rock Art Sites on the Musselshell River, Montana.* Sacred Sites Research, Albuquerque, New Mexico.

Magne, Martin, and Michael Klassen
1991 A Multivariate Study of Rock Art Anthropomorphs at Writing-On-Stone, Southern Alberta. *American Antiquity* 56(3):389–418.

McGlone, Bill, Phil Leonard, and Ted Barker
  1994 *Petroglyphs of Southeast Colorado and the Oklahoma Panhandle*. Mithras, Kamas, Utah.

Mooney, James
  1898 *Calendar History of the Kiowa Indians*. Seventeenth Annual Report of the Bureau of American Ethnology 1895-'96, pp. 129–445.

Mulloy, William T.
  1958 *A Preliminary Historical Outline for the Northwestern Plains*. University of Wyoming Publications, Laramie.

Murray, Wendi Field
  2011 A Contemporary Analysis of the Eagle as a Cultural Resource in the Northern Plains. *Plains Anthropologist* 56:143–153.

Steward, Julian H.
  1941 Culture Element Distributions XII: Nevada Shoshoni. *Anthropological Records* 4(2):209–359. University of California Berkeley.

Sundstrom, Linea
  2000 Cheyenne Pronghorn Procurement and Ceremony. *Plains Anthropologist* 45(174):119–132.

Teit, James A.
  1930 *The Salishan Tribes of the Western Plateaus*. Forty-fifth Annual Report of the Bureau of American Ethnology 1927-1928, pp. 23–396.

Wells, Nova
  1996 *The Petroglyphs of Saline River Valley, Kansas*. Monograph 2. American Rock Art Research Association, San Miguel, California.

Whitley, David S.
  2005 *Introduction to Rock Art Research*. Left Coast Press, Walnut Creek, California.

Under the Alcove: Radiocarbon Dates for V-neck Anthropomorphs

Lawrence L. Loendorf, Karen L. Steelman, and David A. Kaiser

At the Alcove site (24JT87) in central Montana, dry applied charcoal pictographs of anthropomorphs and zoomorphs are found primarily on the ceiling of a long rockshelter. In 2021, Sacred Sites Research, Inc., completed a comprehensive documentation of the site utilizing photography, illustrations/tracing, photogrammetry to create a 3D model, and drone aerial mapping. In addition, two V-neck anthropomorphs were selected for plasma oxidation and AMS radiocarbon dating. Old wood and old charcoal effects are considered unlikely. Tracing the imagery on transparent film for documentation prior to radiocarbon analysis did not appear to impact results, as background controls of unpainted rock had negligible contamination. Maximum ages for the pictographs determined by radiocarbon dating underlying oxalate minerals are consistent with the direct ages. Results on charcoal pigment are 950±50 and 1050±100 RCYBP, corresponding to the oldest dated depictions of V-neck anthropomorphs and the heartline motif.

The **V**-neck anthropomorph is a common motif at northern Plains rock art sites. William Mulloy (1958:122) was the first to describe the figure type at Pictograph Cave, near Billings, Montana, although he did not use the term **V**-neck. Mulloy emphasized the straight lines for the figure's body sides with shoulders formed by oblique lines extending down medially. This has led some to refer to the figures as **V**-shouldered rather than **V**-neck, although the latter term is more ingrained into the literature.

In order to learn more about the distribution of **V**-neck rock art figures, Lawrence Loendorf and Marion de Cruz compiled a list of all the known sites from published sources and site forms, constituting about 200 **V**-neck figures. They are most common in southern Alberta, eastern Montana, western South Dakota, and eastern Wyoming. There are a few examples in western Kansas, eastern Colorado, and northern New Mexico.

Incised petroglyphs are the most common form of the motif, constituting about 80% of the Loendorf-de Cruz sample. Additional methods of **V**-neck image creation include 4% made by pecking their outlines, and 16% are pictographs made with liquid paint or dry applied with pieces of charcoal or ochre. It is generally believed that the pecked figures are oldest, but there is little data to support that claim.

In 2021, Sacred Sites Research, Inc., (SSR) conducted a field session at Painted Canyon in central Montana. The goals of the documentation research were to (1) record the sites in Painted Canyon and (2) collect paint samples for radiocarbon dating. As the canyon rock substrate is limestone, the pictographs at these sites are good candidates for plasma oxidation and accelerator mass spectrometry (AMS) radiocarbon dating. This paper presents the results of recording at the Alcove site (one of several sites within Painted Canyon) and the successful effort to date two of the **V**-neck anthropomorph figures there.

Lawrence L. Loendorf
Sacred Sites Research, Inc.,
Albuquerque, New Mexico

Karen L. Steelman
Shumla Archaeological Research &
Education Center,
Comstock, Texas

David A. Kaiser
Oregon Archaeological Society,
Portland

American Indian Rock Art, Volume 49. Amy Gilreath, Ken Hedges, and Anne McConnell, Editors. American Rock Art Research Association, 2023, pp. 21–30.

Alcove Site

The Alcove site (24JT87), also known as the Painted Alcove site, is one of nine documented sites in the Painted Canyon complex. Painted Canyon is located in the foothills/transition zone on the northern side of the Little Belt Mountains about 60 km southeast of Great Falls, Montana. The Painted Coulee site (24JT86) and the Alcove site (24JT87) are the largest and most significant sites in the complex. The Alcove site was assigned a site number by James Keyser in 1977, and subsequently revisited by John and Mavis Greer in 1993.

Douglas fir and ponderosa pine are the dominant trees on the slopes above the canyon, while willow, chokecherry, and wild currants with a variety of grasses grow along the canyon floor. It is prime territory for deer and elk, black bears, and grizzly bears today. Bison were found in the area in the past. There is an excellent freshwater spring in the canyon.

The canyon walls are limestone with some overhangs that offer protection from rain and snow. The alcove is at the head of a small side canyon where it is tucked in the curved canyon wall, near the caprock, about 25 m above the main canyon floor (Figure 1). The long, low, sheltered area measures about 40 m across its widest dimension by 4 m at its deepest and 1.0 to 1.5 m high. The pictographs, which are mainly on the ceiling, would have been made by lying down and drawing with a somewhat long stick or crouching in an awkward position to draw directly on the ceiling. Most of the figures are in black charcoal with a few in red ochre and all appear to have been dry applied. The Alcove's limestone floor is exposed bedrock that is strewn with sharp-edged stones that make it an unpleasant place to spend much time. No artifacts or evidence of former fires were seen in the alcove which is important to note when dating charcoal drawings.

Figure 1. Aerial view of the Alcove site. Photo by Mark Willis.

With the first documentation efforts, Keyser traced most of the figures, as they fit on a single piece of available plastic, and then published the collage of images as they were recorded (Keyser and Klassen 2001:220). However, the images were not initially attributed to the Alcove site and were simply presented as a group of **V**-neck figures and associated animals. In a later publication, the figures were separated with an explanation for why they were originally arranged in a group (Keyser et al. 2012:369, note 39).

The Greers assigned figure numbers to individual images that were identified on a site map (Greer and Greer 1993:2). This allowed for linking the drawings to photographs of the ceiling. SSR personnel made panels around the figures or groups of figures and plotted them in relationship to one another. These are labeled A through P and plotted on a schematic of the rockshelter (Figure 2).

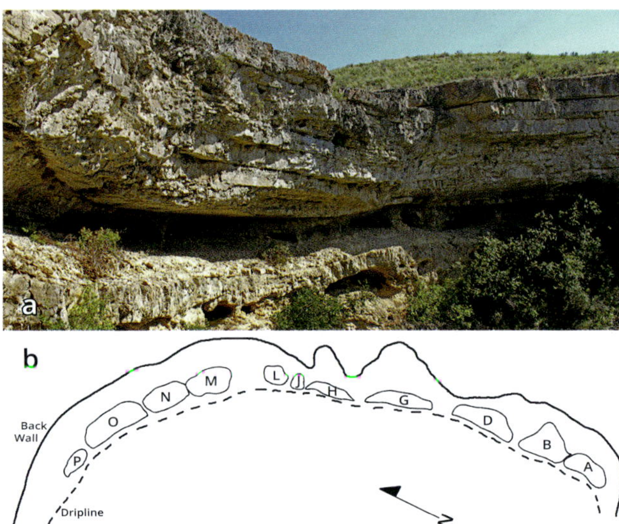

Figure 2. (a) The Alcove rockshelter. (b) Panel arrangement in the Alcove site ceiling. The other panels are on the back wall and floor. Drawing by Amanda Castañeda.

There are groups of figures on the ceiling that have anthropomorphs with feet toward the back wall adjacent to other anthropomorphs with heads to the back wall. This random arrangement suggests the figures were not intended to be shown interacting with one another and likely placed on the ceiling by more than a single artist. While most are on the ceiling, three or four figures in charcoal are found on the back wall of the alcove. They are badly eroded, but one retains a large circle area of charcoal pigment which is suggestive of a shield figure, but the image is too fragmentary to confirm that identification.

Two areas of incised line patterns are found on the rockshelter floor very close to where it joins the wall. Both sets are parallel linear incised lines with cross-cut lines that create crude grid-like patterns (Figure 3). Although they have not been consistently reported, these sorts of incised patterns are common at regional sites. Stuart Conner (Conner and Conner 1971) called them helter-skelter lines which is an apt descriptor.

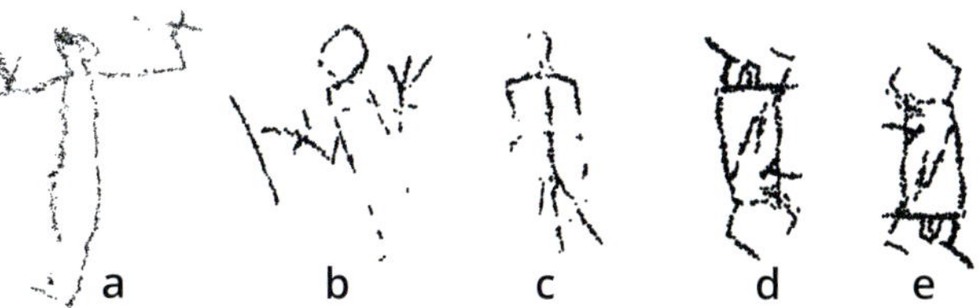

Figure 5. Other charcoal-drawn human figures at the Alcove: (a) Panel P; (b-e) Panel B; (d, e) show the same image with different orientations.

Figure 3. Incised "helter-skelter lines" on the floor of the shelter.

V-Neck Anthropomorphs

Anthropomorphs dominate the site with nine definite (Figure 4) and three possible **V**-neck figures. The latter include a single figure with parallel side for its body (Figure 5a), a figure with a straight-line body (Figure 5c), and a possible shield-bearing warrior (Figure 6). Archaeologists have recognized, since the initial recording of the Alcove, that the site contains some complex drawings of **V**-neck anthropomorphs.

Several of the Alcove **V**-neck anthropomorphs have the typical round head set atop a long neck but two have half-circle heads directly connected to their

Figure 6. Possible shield-bearing warrior on Panel E, drawn on the back wall of the shelter.

shoulders on Panels A and G (Figures 4g and i). This is an unusual trait. In the Loendorf-de Cruz compilation of about 200 **V**-neck rock art figures found at sites in Alberta, Montana, Wyoming, South Dakota, Colorado, and Kansas, there are no similar figures, and it may represent the style of an individual artist at this site.

Another unusual depiction of a **V**-neck anthropomorph on Panel N shows the top of the torso with the lines of the V extending beyond the neck to the far side of the torso, creating an **X**-shape (Figure 4a). Similar compositions have been found on Late Prehistoric and Historic art at the Rocky Coulee battle scene at DgOv-57 (Keyser 1977:22) and at DgOw-32 (Keyser and Kaiser 2023) in the greater Writing-on-Stone area of Alberta. Another example is found at Bear Gulch (Keyser et al. 2012:63). These variations of **V**-neck figures could simply be the result of individual artistic styles. However, all these examples occur in traditional Blackfoot territory, or are associated with other art identified as Blackfoot. This is further supported by the same stylistic depiction being

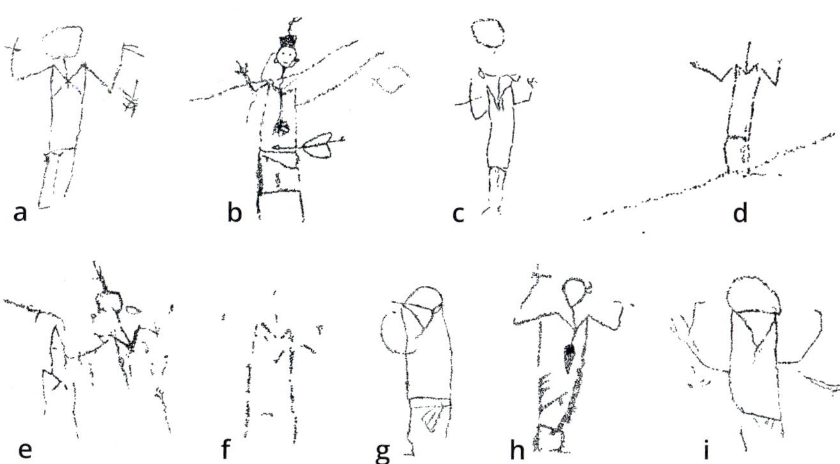

Figure 4. Charcoal drawn **V**-neck figures at the Alcove site: (a) Panel N; (b-e) Panel M; (f) Panel H; (g) Panel G; (h) Panel D; (i) Panel A.

used on a Blackfoot robe photographed at Red River by Humphrey L. Hime in 1858 (Dempsey 2007:49). Such compositional style may therefore be diagnostic of Blackfoot artists; however, more study is needed to determine if such style is also found in the art of other groups.

All **V**-neck figures, when clearly depicted, stand with their arms raised. Two anthropomorphs on Panels D and M have distinct heartlines (Figure 4b and h). The heartline motif is a name given to a line extending from the mouth to the interior of an animal or human figure, generally ending in the abstract depiction of the heart or other internal organ. This is a symbolic feature combining the windpipe and the heart, thus not conforming directly to a singular organ. The motif occurs at dozens of rock art sites across the northern Plains, and it is also found on catlinite tablets from North Dakota and Manitoba (see below).

The detail on the Panel M figures is remarkable (Figure 4b–e). Two humans wear a headdress and have earrings (Figures 4b and e), one of which also has a heartline, wears a sash, and is struck by an arrow (Figure 4b). The other could hold a bow or a spear, but it is too eroded and interconnected with another figure to be certain (Figure 4e). In Keyser's original 1977 tracing, this figure is shown holding a triangular tipped spear. It is unclear whether this detail was mistaken in the first recording due to the inferior, somewhat opaque plastic available at the time, or if these details have now eroded making such identification impossible. Another **V**-neck figure on Panel N might be holding an unknown object (Figure 4a). The lines coming from the hand could be fingers, but a cluster of lines near the figure's elbow could be part of a larger object. Additionally, one **V**-neck figure on Panel M shows its long neck crossed with a barbell shape (Figure 4c). However, it is unclear what this signifies.

Other Anthropomorphs

Anthropomorphs other than those with a **V**-neck include a large parallel-sided figure on Panel P with arms that cross the upper torso and turn up (Figure 5a). The figure has no base body line, but one leg has a flat foot. The head is open and connected to the shoulders via a short two-sided neck. On Panel B a somewhat eroded figure with a rectangular body and upraised arms may have been a **V**-neck human, but details are now lost which might confirm this (Figure 5b). A vertical line floating near the figure's hand might be a spear or other object. Another anthropomorph on

the same panel has a stick body of a straight vertical line, crossing arms that turn down, and splayed legs. Its round head is featureless. The figure appears to be phallic (Figure 5c).

At least two of the **V**-neck figures are also clearly male, with pendant phalluses shown (Figures 4a and c). Three other human figures could be female, but each is unclear. The orientation of a small anthropomorph with a rectangular body split by a diagonal line on Panel B is somewhat ambiguous. It possibly shows a bowlegged figure with arms above its head both bent to one side (Figure 5d). No neck is shown, and the "head" is a **U**-shape, with a line down the middle, which could depict face paint. However, more likely, if the figure is oriented the other direction, similar to the other humans shown on the panel, the bent legs form a now eroded round head (Figure 5e). What would be the legs now end in plantigrade feet, and the former "head" becomes a vulviform depicted below the torso. Two other **V**-neck images on Panels G and M could also be seen as female (Figures 4b and g). Each appears to have a belt or sash around their waist, below which either additional fabric hangs, or a vulva is depicted. The Panel M human shows a vertical line within the body immediately above the lower line of the torso. The other image shows a split triangular shape immediately below the sash marking the bottom of the torso. However, the narrow side of the triangle connects with the torso, widening below. This is the reverse of most pubic triangular depictions. While women are often shown wearing belts around their waist, additional biologically determinate details remain unclear in all three examples at this site. Another anthropomorph on Panel A shows a trio of lines below the torso (Figure 4i). While these lines likely indicated gender, details are no longer clear enough to make a determination as to which is shown.

The possible shield-bearing warrior on Panel E has a round shield that may have horizontal stripes or bars of black charcoal as its design (Figure 6). The head is atop a neck, and legs that are very hard to see appear to have flat feet. The figure may have a feather or other projection from the top of its head. There is additional charcoal to the right of the figure that may have once been a second shield figure.

Animals

Three zoomorphs are found on the Alcove ceiling (Figure 7). Like the human figures, all were drawn in a black pigment assumed to be charcoal. One that may be emerging from a crack on Panel N has an oval body,

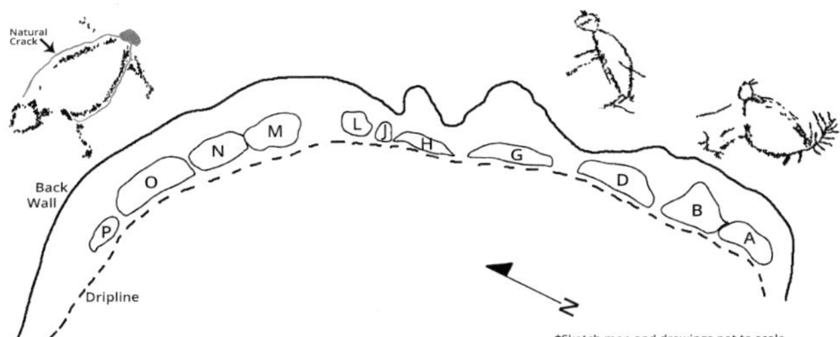

Figure 7. Placement of quadrupeds at the Alcove site. From left to right: a possible bison surrounded by a natural crack on Panel N; an unidentified quadruped and a skunk on Panel B.

roundish head, and two legs. Bounded within the confines of the natural cracks, this is the only incorporation of natural features identified at the site. It may be a bison although that identification is tenuous. The other two animals, both on Panel B, have more boat-shaped bodies and round heads. An unidentified quadruped is pierced by a line in its side, possibly indicating a spear or arrow in its side. The other animal has a raised, bushy tail that is suggestive of a skunk. Skunks are rare in rock art, but other examples have been found at DgOw-29 at Writing-on-Stone (Keyser 1977:37, 74) and another drawn in charcoal at Bear Gulch (Keyser et al. 2012:91).

Dating Methods

To learn if we could obtain an age for the **V**-neck anthropomorphs at the Alcove site, Steelman collected two paint samples and two control samples of the limestone rock for analyses. She utilized the plasma oxidation method followed by accelerator mass spectrometry (AMS) radiocarbon dating to directly date the organic material in the samples (Rowe 2009). X-ray diffraction (XRD) and Fourier transform infrared (FTIR) spectroscopies confirmed the presence of calcium oxalate coatings in the samples. In addition to the two direct ages, we were able to radiocarbon date this oxalate carbon to obtain maximum ages for the paintings that are consistent with the direct ages.

Prior to sampling, it is important that proper documentation of pictographs is conducted. Sacred Sites Research, Inc., utilized figure photography, tracing/illustration, and site mapping to document the drawn figures. Below, we describe the two panels that were sampled for dating.

Panel D is on a narrow strip of ceiling to the south of a deeper portion of the alcove. The panel area measures 4.5 m north to south by 70 cm east to west.

The south half of Panel D contains sparse imagery including some parallel lines but no discernible figures.

The density of imagery increases on the northern end. There is a fairly large element consisting of parallel and perpendicular lines (about 50 cm long), but it was not possible to sort out what it represents. There are two **V**-neck figures on the northern end, one of which is poorly preserved, but the bent arms, part of the torso, and the neck and head are visible. The clearest figure on this panel is another **V**-neck anthropomorph that has its head pointing south (so that its body length is parallel to the back wall). This anthropomorph has a heart line and some diagonal lines on the lower part of the torso (Figure 8). Paint sample 2 was collected from the heart area of this anthropomorph for dating.

Figure 8. Drawing of Panel D. This figure was sampled by Steelman for radiocarbon dating—sample 2 was taken from the triangular "heart," indicated in gray.

Panel N is just north of nearby Panel M. Panel N is in an area about 170 cm by 170 cm and about 140 cm above the rockshelter floor.

Panel N has a **V**-neck figure as well as a zoomorph (Figure 9). The largest anthropomorph at the site is in this panel, measuring approximately 50 cm tall by 35 cm wide. This **V**-neck figure has a round head, up-bent arms, a phallus, and either fingers or it is holding small implements. Paint sample 1 was collected from this anthropomorph for dating.

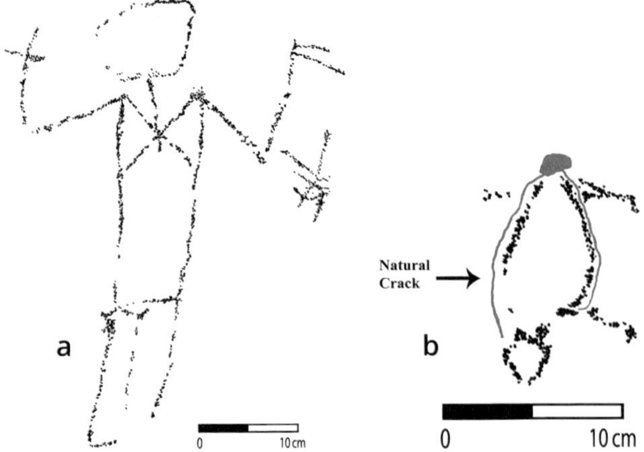

Figure 9. (a) Large Panel N **V***-neck. (b) Quadruped on Panel N.*

Sample Collection

We selected a **V**-neck anthropomorph from Panel D and another from Panel N for dating because of their diagnostic attributes and the archaeological information that would be obtained from knowing their chronology. When possible, sampling for radiocarbon dating is done in a manner that minimizes the impact of collection on pictograph images and to some extent this influences the figures chosen because the analyst is looking for places to collect samples where the paint/pigment is naturally exfoliating and would eventually be lost due to weathering. At the Alcove site, we were able to sample two **V**-neck figures, one with a heartline, which is what we wanted to date.

In the field, photographs were taken before and after collection to clearly establish and document sampling locations. Steelman wore latex gloves and used individual sterile surgical scalpel blades to remove black pigment onto sterile aluminum foil. Control samples were collected from adjacent unpainted rock to investigate levels of organic contamination in the rock substrate background. Samples were placed in pre-baked (550°C) folded aluminum foil squares, which were then stored in labeled plastic bags until laboratory analyses. Black pigment samples suspected to be made with charcoal were ~1 cm^2 in surface area with a mass of 4.8 and 5.5 mg. Control samples of unpainted rock ranged in size from 3 to 4 cm^2 with masses of 17.0 and 23.6 mg (Table 1).

Laboratory Analyses

We followed the methods of Steelman et al. (2021a, b) for the laboratory processing and radiocarbon measurement of pictograph and oxalate samples. Additional information on the dating process can be found in an online blog at https://shumla.org/shumla-chem-lab-part1/. For these Alcove site samples, no visible contaminants (e.g., plant fibers, rootlets, or spider webs) were observed at X40 magnification under a stereoscope. For the pictograph and background samples, we used plasma oxidation to convert organic material to carbon dioxide for AMS radiocarbon dating. Afterwards, we used the remaining mineral powder from the background samples (Alcove 1b and 2b) for XRD and FTIR analyses to confirm the presence of oxalate minerals, which can be radiocarbon dated to provide indirect ages for pictographs. We then used the remaining mineral powder from the paint samples (Alcove 1 and Alcove 2) for oxalate dating. After washing the Alcove 1 and Alcove 2 samples in phosphoric acid, we employed FTIR to confirm the complete removal of the carbonate minerals and the continuing presence of oxalate minerals. We then utilized the plasma oxidation technique (again) to completely remove organic contamination that might have been included in the mineral samples (Alcove 1 and Alcove 2) either due to environmental or laboratory handling. The purified oxalate samples from Alcove 1 and Alcove 2 were ultimately combusted for AMS measurement to obtain maximum ages.

Results and Discussion

Radiocarbon dates are reported in Tables 1 and 2. For the pictograph samples, the $\delta^{13}C$ value was assumed to be -25‰, as no split of the carbon dioxide was sampled for stable carbon isotope measurement due to the small sample size. During plasma oxidation, the black pigment turned white, converting to ash and indicating that the pigment is organic charcoal or soot. Oxalate radiocarbon ages were calculated using a stable carbon isotope value of -11‰, the average value measured for oxalate samples associated with pictograph sites (Russ et al. 2000). Radiocarbon results were calibrated using the OxCal computer program version 4.4.4 (Bronk Ramsey 2009, 2022) with IntCal20 curve data from Reimer et al. (2020).

Importantly, the surface of the unpainted rock substrate has negligible organic contamination. Control

Table 1. Sample information and pictograph radiocarbon results.

Sample	Sample Type	Mass (mg)	µg C	µg/mg	Shumla ID	CAMS ID	^{14}C Date (RCYBP)	Cal AD (95.4%)
Alcove 1	black paint	5.5	30	5	N39	188166	950±50	990–1220
Alcove 1b	control	17.0	0.3	0.02				
Alcove 2	black paint	4.8	20	4	N40	188167	1050±100	700–1300
Alcove 2b	control	23.6	0.6	0.03				

Table 2. Maximum ages from oxalate radiocarbon dating.

Sample	Sample Type	µg C	CAMS ID	¹⁴C Date (RCYBP)	Cal AD (95.4%)
Alcove 1	oxalate	70	181602	1400±50	560–780
Alcove 2	oxalate	80	188603	1200±40	680–975

samples of the unpainted rock were processed in the same manner as the paint samples. They contained less than 0.03 µg of carbon per milligram of solid material. This corresponds to less than 1% contamination from the rock substrate in the paint samples. This is especially important at these sites as tracing on transparent film was conducted prior to sampling. This documentation technique did not appear to impact radiocarbon dating of the images, but we were able to collect samples away from areas where adhesive tape had been attached to the wall, as we worked in tandem with the documentation team.

From Panel D, paint sample 2 from the anthropomorph with a heartline returned a radiocarbon date of 1050±100 RCYBP (radiocarbon years before present) corresponding to a calibrated age of cal A.D. 700–1300. Oxalate minerals in the underlying rock have a radiocarbon age of 1200 ±40 RCYBP, providing a maximum age of cal A.D. 680 for the pictograph. The ages are stratigraphically correct.

From Panel N, paint sample 1 from the large **V**-neck anthropomorph returned a radiocarbon date of 950±50 RCYBP corresponding to a calibrated age of cal A.D. 990-1220. Oxalate minerals in the underlying rock have a radiocarbon age of 1400±50 RCYBP, providing a maximum age of cal A.D. 560 for the pictograph. Again, the ages are stratigraphically correct.

Kibbey Alcove Style

Researchers have identified a dozen charcoal figures at two other sites, Bear Gulch (24FR2) and Atherton Canyon (24FR3), that look like the charcoal figures at the Alcove site. These two sites with similar imagery are near one another in central Montana. Based on similarities, primarily with the boat-body animal figures, Keyser et al. (2012:224) created the Kibbey Alcove style designation. Several of the animals have horns that make them appear to represent bighorn sheep, but the animal represented at Bear Gulch with a direct comparison at the Alcove site is a skunk with a boat-shaped body and a bushy tail (Keyser et al. 2012:91). Although there are only two to three examples from Bear Gulch or Atherton Canyon, the style includes **V**-neck figures with one that has an arrow entering its body at a side angle, like the Alcove figure on

Panel M. One shield-bearing warrior at Atherton Canyon resembles the possible shield warrior at the Alcove.

Dating Charcoal V-neck Anthropomorphs

Both radiocarbon-dated figures at the Alcove site were made with dry-applied charcoal pigment so there is concern about old wood/charcoal affecting interpretation of the ages due to the possibility that charcoal from an old fire was used to create images much younger than the date measurements (Bednarik 1994; Schiffer 1986). Radiocarbon dates on charcoal pictographs should be considered maximum ages for painted images unless the effects of old wood and old charcoal can be ruled out. Maximum ages for pictographs tell us that the images cannot be older than the date measured. Based on the charcoal dates, the **V**-neck anthropomorphs are not older than cal A.D. 700 and cal A.D. 990. However, based on the fact that there is no evidence of fires or hearths in the shelter, we posit that the charcoal/soot used for pigment was carried into the shelter and most likely contemporary with the creation of the pictographs.

Several factors suggest these ages are correct. One, there are no cultural deposits in the cave, so it was not possible for someone to pick up a lump of charcoal from an older fire to use to draw the figures. They had to carry the charcoal to the cave which increases the chances it came from a fire they made. Two, the two dates are close to one another, overlapping at one standard deviation. If they were the product of old wood charcoal, there is a better chance they would be from lumps of differing ages. Of course, the same artist could have drawn both figures with the same lump of charcoal, but the figures are some distance apart on the ceiling, decreasing the chances that that is what happened.

Finally, there are the oxalate dates. During the formation of oxalate coatings, biological sources (bacteria, fungi, lichen, microbes, etc.) incorporate carbon from the atmosphere into oxalic acid which then forms calcium oxalate on the rock surface. Radiocarbon ages of oxalate minerals date the formation of mineral accretions on the rockshelter surface. However, as multiple formation layers could be included, a radiocarbon determination for an oxalate accretion is a weighted average of the deposited layers' ages. Even so, underlying oxalate layers will provide maximum ages for rock paintings as the mixture of the underneath layers is still older than any overlying paint. At these sites, there was negligible accretion formation overlying paintings. Thus, the majority of oxalate minerals in the collected powdered samples would be from underneath the paintings and provide maximum ages for the pictographs (Table 2). The two dates of 1400±50 RCYBP (max cal A.D. 560) and 1200±40 RCYBP (max cal A.D. 680) are older than the charcoal in the drawings. The dates are in the correct stratigraphic order. The variation seen in oxalate ages from the Alcove site is typical of the variation seen in Spain and Texas for oxalates at similar rockshelter sites (Steelman et al. 2021b). Most importantly, these oxalate dates are older than the associated direct paint dates, showing consistent chronology of the underlying minerals and paint layers in the correct stratigraphic order. This is a good check of our laboratory techniques to ensure that we are obtaining accurate and reliable results.

If the oxalate date had been younger than the dated charcoal sample, it would have indicated that old wood or old charcoal was present and affecting results. Unfortunately, we are not able to obtain a minimum oxalate age in this case as there was insufficient oxalate coating the pictographs. The charcoal figures at the Alcove site are the oldest directly dated examples of V-neck anthropomorphs in North America with ages of 950±50 RCYBP (cal A.D. 990–1220) and 1050 ± 100 RCYBP (cal A.D. 700-1300).

The only other charcoal V-neck that has been dated is in Little Canyon Creek Cave, Wyoming (Figure 10a), with an age of 550 ±40 RCYBP (cal A.D. 1305–1440) (Francis and Loendorf 2002:52). The Little Canyon Creek figure was originally thought to be lines associated with a shield and possible lance, but a revisit to the cave revealed the figure is a V-neck anthropomorph (Loendorf and Newman 2006). This figure was dated using plasma oxidation; however, no oxalates were dated with the figure.

Previous attempts to establish a chronology for V-neck anthropomorphs relied on the Little Canyon

Creek date as a beginning age of circa A.D. 1400 (Loendorf et al. 2013), about a century older than the estimate offered for the Bear Gulch and Atherton Canyon Blackfoot style V-neck figures of A.D. 1550 (Keyser et al. 2012:234). It is clear from examples on painted robes that V-neck figures continued to be made into the 1800s (Brownstone 2001), so the age-range estimate for V-neck figures was A.D. 1400 to an ending date in the 1800s. The Alcove site's radiocarbon dates push back their beginning to circa 1000 years ago.

It should be noted that the Kibbey Alcove style has charcoal dates for a skunk at 1615±35 RCYBP (cal A.D. 335-540), an abstract design at Bear Gulch at 900±35 RCYBP (cal A.D. 1040–1215), and a shield-bearing warrior at Atherton Canyon at 650±35 RCYBP (cal A.D. 1280–1395), all dated using plasma oxidation (Keyser et al. 2012:176–177). It is clear there is no correspondence between the ages. No oxalates were dated.

It is also important to note that even though V-neck anthropomorphs are considered as part of the style, none were dated at the Bear Gulch or Atherton Canyon sites. To identify a style, it is essential to assign a date range and a distribution for the figures in the style. With this caveat, an immediate question is, Does the charcoal figure in Little Canyon Creek Cave fit in the style? The site is more than 600 kilometers south of the Painted Canyon sites and without more examples from in-between sites, it would seem foolish to include the figure in the style.

On the other hand, two charcoal V-neck figures in Lookout Cave (24PH402), Montana, are about 130 kilometers north of Bear Gulch, so they might fit in a style (Figure 10b). However, the Lookout Cave figures have an estimated age of post-A.D. 1400, which does not fit well with the age of the Alcove site.

The following admonition is found with the description of the Kibbey Alcove style: "Currently, a better definition of this style, or verification that these similar appearing images truly represent a style, awaits further research" (Keyser et al. 2012:226). It is not clear that the dates for the Alcove V-neck figures have added much to the definition of the proposed style.

The dated V-neck figure on Panel N was eccentrically composed with an X-shape at the top of the torso. This same stylistic element is found at other sites attributed to and associated with Blackfoot rock art. If this is a diagnostic feature, or a more widespread variation, rather than a quirk of individual artists, it shows this drawing style to have been used over a long period. The dating from the Alcove site indicates this style

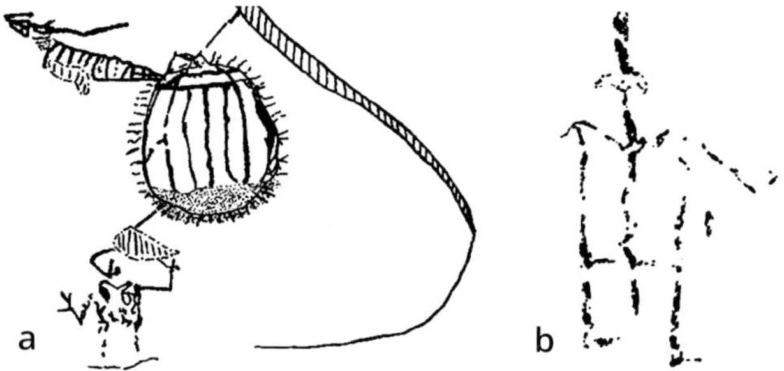

Figure 10. (a) Charcoal drawing of a **V**-neck figure at the Little Canyon Creek site, Wyoming; the figure dates 550±40 RCYBP. (b) Charcoal **V**-neck from Lookout Cave, Montana; the figure has an unknown age but is suspected to date circa 500 B.P.

was in use a thousand years ago, but we have examples of similar depictions on nineteenth century robe art as well as Historic period rock art featuring guns and horses (Keyser 1977:22; Keyser and Kaiser 2023).

Another important point regarding the age of the Alcove **V**-neck figures is the age of the heartline motif. It is recognized at rock art sites across the northern Plains, but the heartline motif does not occur at sites on the Plateau or the Northwest Coast. It is found in the Southwest after A.D. 1500 (Baldwin 1997:28; Schaafsma 1980:307) and it is generally accepted that the motif was introduced to the Pueblo tribes by Athapaskan-speaking Navajo and Apache when they moved into the Southwest.

The motif is thought to have its origins in the Midwest or the northeastern Plains. There are petroforms of humans and turtles with heartlines that are difficult to date, but several catlinite tablets having incised animals with heartlines, often bison, on them have been recovered from Devil's Lake-Sourisford sites which date from A.D. 900 to 1400 (Baldwin 1997; Syms 1979). Other examples from Oneota sites date from A.D. 1400 to 1600 (Figure 11).

Figure 11. Catlinite tablet with a bison and heartline from an Oneota site, dated to A.D. 1400–1600.

In the nineteenth century, Walter Hoffman (1891) was told by Algonkian-speaking Ojibwa sources that the heartline was used in conjunction with hunting magic. A shaman or medicine person would draw a picture of an animal, indicating the heart with a small drop of red paint. Stabbing the drop of paint, the shaman explained, was a very effective way to capture the animal because of the power of the color red: "Frequently the heart is indicated by a round or triangular figure, from which a line extends toward the mouth, generally designated the lifeline, i.e., that magic power

may reach its heart and influence the life of the subject designated" (Hoffman 1891:222).

The heartline motif may not have been used for magical purposes by all tribes. Blackfoot sources have explained that when a bear heartline was painted on a tipi cover, the figure was related to a vision experienced by its owner. The spiritual nature of the image was indicated by the combination of the heartline with marks representing the kidneys and joints, body parts that are believed to be sources of supernatural power (Brasser 1978:12). In either example, the goal was to obtain power.

Conclusion

Stylistic features such as the **X**-shape at the top of the torso on some **V**-neck figures has been recognized at other sites associated with the Blackfoot and may indicate members of this group as creators of the art found at the Alcove. Additionally, the 1000-year-old dates for the **V**-neck figures at this site are the oldest dated depictions of **V**-neck anthropomorphs and the accompanying heartline motif, showing the significant age of this style as well as the use of the heartline. Additional dating will hopefully reveal where the Alcove figures fit in the wider chronology and distribution of the **V**-neck motif and associated imagery.

Acknowledgments. We thank the additional members of the 2021 field crew: Cobe Chatwood, Mark Willis, Laurie White, Amanda Castañeda, Charles Koenig, Susan Hovde, and Garth Bontrager. KLS thanks Dr. Joseph Reibenspies of the X-ray Diffraction Laboratory at the Department of Chemistry, Texas A&M University, for assistance collecting XRD data. We thank the ranch family, especially Harry, Carol, and Sandra, for their willingness to let us access and study these important sites on their land.

References Cited

Baldwin, Stuart J.
  1997 Apacheans Bearing Gifts: Prehispanic Influence on the Pueblo Indians. *The Arizona Archaeologist* 29. Arizona Archaeological Society, Phoenix.

Bednarik, Robert G.
  1994 Conceptual Pitfalls in Dating of Paleolithic Rock Art. *Préhistoire Anthropologie Méditerranéennes* 3:95–102.

Brasser, Ted J.
  1978 Tipi Paintings, Blackfoot Style. In *Contextual Studies of Material Culture,* edited by David Zimmerly, pp. 7–18. Mercury Series Paper No. 43. Canadian Ethnology Service, National Museum of Man, Ottawa.

Bronk Ramsey, Christopher
2009 Bayesian Analysis of Radiocarbon Dates. *Radiocarbon* 51: 337–360.

2022 OxCal version 4.4.4 (online). Electronic document, https://c14.arch.ox.ac.uk/oxcal.html, accessed on March 10, 2022.

Brownstone, Arni
2001 The Musee de L'Homme's Foureau Robe and its Moment in the History of Blackfeet Painting. *Plains Anthropologist* 46(177):249–267.

Conner, Stuart W., and Betty Lu Conner
1971 *Rock Art of the Montana High Plains.* The Art Galleries, University of California, Santa Barbara.

Dempsey, L. James
2007 *Blackfoot War Art: Pictographs of the Reservation Period, 1880–2000.* University of Oklahoma Press, Norman.

Francis, Julie E., and Lawrence L. Loendorf
2002 *Ancient Visions: Petroglyphs and Pictographs from the Wind River and Bighorn Country, Wyoming and Montana.* University of Utah Press, Salt Lake City.

Greer, Mavis, and John Greer
1993 Addendum to Site 24JT87. On file with the SHPO Office, Helena, Montana.

Hoffman, Walter J.
1891 *The Midewiwin or "Grand Medicine Society" of the Ojibwa.* Seventh Annual Report of the Bureau of Ethnology 1885-'86, pp. 143–300. Washington D.C.

Keyser, James D.
1977 Writing-On-Stone: Rock Art on the Northwestern Plains. *Canadian Journal of Archaeology* 1:15–80.

Keyser, James D., and David A. Kaiser
2023 *"War is Their Sole Delight": Blackfoot Petroglyphs at Verdigris Coulee.* Oregon Archaeological Society Press, Publication 28, Portland (In Press).

Keyser, James D., David A. Kaiser, George Poetschat, and Michael W. Taylor
2012 *Fraternity of War: Plains Indian Rock Art at Bear Gulch and Atherton Canyon, Montana.* Oregon Archaeological Society Press, Publication 21, Portland.

Keyser, James D., and Michael A. Klassen
2001 *Plains Indian Rock Art.* University of Washington Press, Seattle.

Loendorf, Lawrence L., and Bonita Newman
2006 The Tensleep Rock Art Survey. Report on file with the Bureau of Land Management, Worland, Wyoming.

Loendorf, Lawrence L., Laurie White, and Greg White
2013 *Lookout Cave and Its Rock Paintings.* Report submitted to Bureau of Land Management, Havre, Montana. Sacred Sites Research, Inc., Albuquerque.

Mulloy, William T.
1958 *A Preliminary Historical Outline for the Northwestern Plains.* University of Wyoming Publications, Laramie.

Reimer, Paula J., William E.N. Austin, Edouard Bard, Alex Bayliss, Paul G. Blackwell, Christopher Bronk Ramsey, Martin Butzin, Hai Cheng, R. Lawrence Edwards, Michael Friedrich, Pieter M. Grootes, Thomas P. Guilderson, Irka Hajdas, Timothy J. Heaton, Alan G. Hogg, Konrad A. Hughen, Bernd Dromer, Sturt W. Manning, Raimund Muscheler, Jonathan G. Palmer, Charlotte Pearson, Johannes van der Plicht, Ron W. Reimer, David A. Richards, E. Marian Scott, John R. Southon, Christian S.M. Turney, Lukas Wacker, Florian Adolphi, Ulf Büntgen, Manuela Capano, Simon M. Fahrni, Alexandra Fogtmann-Schulz, Ronny Friedrich, Peter Köhler, Sabrina Kudsk, Fusa Miyake, Jesper Olsen, Frederick Reinig, Minoru Sakamoto, Adam Sookdeo, and Sahra Talamo
2020 The IntCal20 Northern Hemisphere Radiocarbon Age Calibration Curve (0-55 cal kBP). *Radiocarbon* 62(4):725–757.

Rowe, Marvin W.
2009 Radiocarbon Dating of Ancient Rock Paintings. *Analytical Chemistry* 81(5):1728–1735.

Russ, Jon, David H. Loyd, and Thomas W. Boutton
2000 A Paleoclimate Reconstruction for Southwestern Texas using Oxalate Residue from Lichen as a Paleoclimate Proxy. *Quaternary International* 67(1):29–36.

Schaafsma, Polly
1980 *Indian Rock Art of the Southwest.* School of American Research, Santa Fe, and Museum of New Mexico Press, Albuquerque.

Schiffer, Michael B.
1986 Radiocarbon Dating and the "Old Wood" Problem: The Case of the Hohokam Chronology. *Journal of Archaeological Science* 13(1):13–30.

Steelman, Karen L., Carolyn E. Boyd, and Trinidy Allen
2021a Two Independent Methods for Dating Rock Art: Age Determination of Paint and Oxalate Layers at Eagle Cave, TX. *Journal of Archaeological Science* 126:article 105315.

Steelman, Karen L., Carolyn E. Boyd, and Lennon Bates
2021b Implications for Rock Art Dating from the Lower Pecos Canyonlands, TX: A Review. *Quaternary Geochronology* 63:article 101167.

Syms, Leigh
1979 The Devil's Lake–Souriisford Burial Complex on the Northeastern Plains. *Plains Anthropologist* 24(86):283–308.

Echo Hawk: A Rediscovered Hoofprint Boulder on Montana's Milk River

Cynthia Sturm and James D. Keyser

Following a lead from the estate of John Brumley, the Oregon Archaeological Society rock art group relocated and recorded the Echo Hawk petroglyph boulder located on the Milk River northwest of Havre, Montana. In addition, the group also recorded the hoofprint boulder at Wahkpa Chu'gn bison kill in Havre. With these two sites as a basis, we summarize a small group of six Hoofprint tradition sites found in the upper Milk River drainage and compare and contrast them to Hoofprint tradition sites downstream. Finally, we examine the Gestalt symbolism of the bisected oval motif, found at several of these sites.

As characterized by Sturm and Keyser (2020:148) "Hoofprint tradition art is composed primarily of very clearly depicted ungulate hoofprints, simple grooves (which, when parallel, are interpreted as representing the bison's ribs), bearpaws, human faces, cupules, bisected ovals, and vulviforms of various shapes and sizes. It also contains a few other human and animal figures, including bison and bison heads, outsized elk, and occasional complete human representations. Some boulders have primarily geometric imagery composed as cupules and meandering lines." Sturm and Keyser (2020:136) provide a distribution map for this tradition, with it occurring from southern Alberta and southern Saskatchewan as far southeast as inland Georgia. To the 32 Northern Plains Hoofprint tradition sites that Sturm and Keyser list (2020:144–145), this paper adds one newly rediscovered site (24HL404, Figure 1), and summarizes the information known on five other sites in the upper Milk River drainage, only one of which has previously been the subject of extensive study.

Cynthia Sturm
Oregon Archaeological Society, Portland

James D. Keyser
Oregon Archaeological Society, Portland

Figure 1. *Myron Echo Hawk poses with the small petroglyph boulder at Echo Hawk (24HL404) in this 1965 photograph. View looking north into Canada provides excellent impression of Northern Plains in this area.*

Our paper begins with a review of recently completed site record updates for two sites in the upper Milk River drainage, each with a Hoofprint tradition boulder—Echo Hawk (24HL404) and Wahkpa Chu'gn (24HL101).

Three other sites in the upper Milk River drainage containing this same rock art petroglyph tradition are reviewed, and a fourth site only provisionally considered to have Hoofprint tradition rock art is also mentioned. Shared characteristics of the group of six sites are summarized to help us better understand what is more-or-less typical of this tradition. Though Hoofprint tradition rock art has been identified at sites from the far northwestern Plains into the southern Appalachians, our emphasis here is on these known manifestations in the upper Milk River drainage.

The Echo Hawk Site (24HL404)

In December of 2020, Patrick Rennie, archaeologist with the Montana Department of Natural Resources and Conservation (MT-DNRC), was given a box of slides from the estate of John Brumley, an archaeologist who grew up in Havre, Montana, and who was a long-time member of the now-defunct Milk River Archaeological Society (MRAS). In that box were five slides of a small petroglyph boulder, 24HL404 (Figure 1). Rennie sent digital versions of those slides to Keyser, but at that time all we knew of the site was that it was on the Milk River, east of the Sweetgrass Hills.

Consultation with Mavis Greer led us to a 1965 site form and a one-sentence published reference (Stallcop and English 1969:40) simply noting that the site is a petroglyph boulder near the Canadian border (Figure 2). The names Echo Hawk and Deadfoot were attached to the site, but we have elected to use Echo Hawk to commemorate Myron Echo Hawk, one of the people who first recorded the site.[1] Unfortunately, neither a legal location nor directions to the site are provided on the original site form. We contacted a former spouse of Brumley, Laurie Milne, and while she had a copy of one

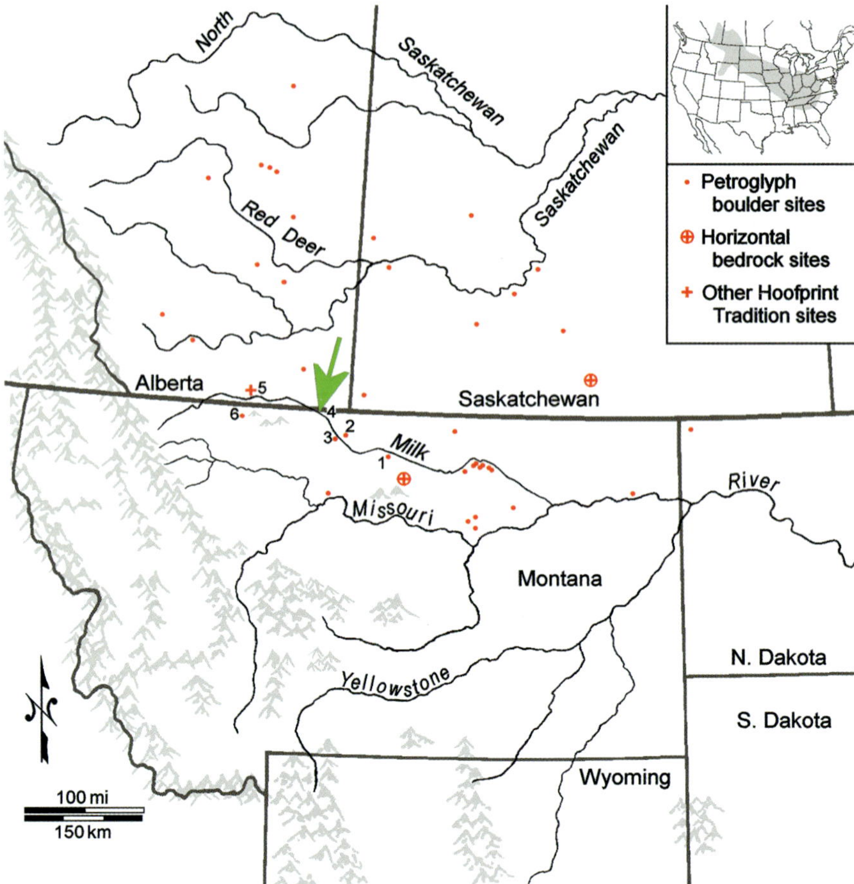

Figure 2. Petroglyph boulder sites of the Hoofprint tradition are scattered north of the Missouri River. There are also a few horizontal bedrock sites and Thunderbird Cave. Almost all Hoofprint tradition sites south of the Missouri River falling within this map area are on vertical cliff faces. LEGEND: 1. Wahkpa Chu'gn (24HL101); 2. 24HL635; 3. Donovan Site (24HL91); 4. Echo Hawk Petroglyph Boulder (24HL404, at arrow); 5. Thunderbird Cave (DgOv-88); 6. Samsal Petroglyph Boulder (24TL959).

of the same color slides we did, she had not visited the site and knew little about it other than that it is very close to the Canadian border. With a bit more sleuthing, Rennie was able to locate Rick Lieberg, a friend of Brumley and member of the MRAS, in Havre, Montana, who had visited the site with Brumley. Rennie then discovered that the boulder was on state land administered by Montana Fish, Wildlife, and Parks (not MT-DNRC), but that the legal rights to the archaeological resources on the land were retained by the lessee, a local rancher named William "Bim" Strauser. Rennie visited the site with the Strauser family, who have a deep interest in the region's archaeology, and the Strausers agreed to have our crew come to record the site. In July 2021 a five-person field crew from the Oregon Archaeological Society (OAS) travelled to the site with the Strauser family and recorded the boulder by direct tracing.

The Echo Hawk petroglyph boulder is part of a small, prehistoric rock cairn (Figure 3) constructed atop a low rise in the glacial till-capped rolling prairie stretching north of the Milk River far into Canada. The site overlooks the Lost River badlands about 3 km (2 mi) north of the Milk River and 11 km (7 mi) east of where the Milk River enters Montana from Canada. Lost River is a short segment of a periglacial meltwater channel carved at the end of the Pleistocene when the Milk River carried much greater quantities of water from melting continental glaciers. Quartzite cobbles and boulders composing the cairn range from fist-sized to more than 60 cm across. Both are common in the glacial till that caps the prairie across northern Montana, southern Alberta, and southern Saskatchewan.

Figure 3. *View looking northeast at Echo Hawk petroglyph boulder situated in the cairn in center of photo. Senior author and Strauser family approaching the small cairn. Photograph by David Minick.*

The petroglyph boulder itself has the form of a small reclining bison (Figure 4) and is embedded in the soil on the south edge of the cairn. It measures about 60 cm in maximum dimension and the part that projects up above the prairie sod is just over 35 cm tall. Its main carved surface faces almost directly south. A few shal-

Figure 4. *This view of the Echo Hawk petroglyph boulder emphasizes its bison form. Three hoofprint designs are across the lower half of the boulder. Photograph by David Minick.*

lower, upward-facing petroglyphs are carved on the top and sloping back side of the boulder.

The designs on the boulder are shallowly pecked and include four hoofprints, three irregular cupules, and an indecipherable curvilinear line abstract. Three hoofprints are pecked side by side to span the lower half of the south side of the boulder (Figures 4–6). On the left is a hoofprint formed of two facing crescents, the left one nearly destroyed by a large spall. Just to the right of this is a bisected oval measuring 11 cm across, whose negative space forms a classic two-toed

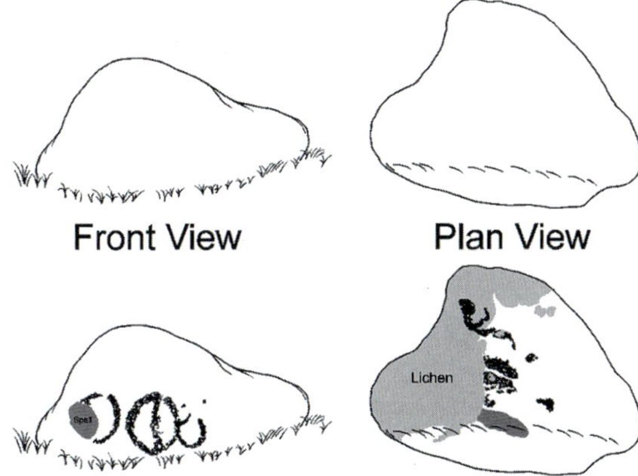

Figure 5. *Sketches of profile and plan view of the Echo Hawk petroglyph boulder from the original 1965 site form show its bison-form shape is visible only when viewed facing north. The lower views show the petroglyphs placed on the outline sketches.*

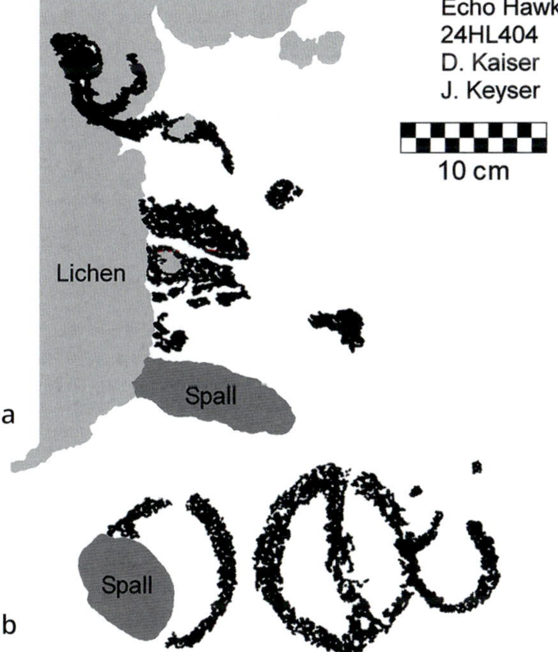

Figure 6. *The 2021 tracing of the petroglyphs on the Echo Hawk petroglyph boulder. (a) Images on the sloping back of the boulder; (b) images on the south-facing bison-form face.*

hoofprint (see discussion of Gestalt perception below). Contiguous on its right and slightly superimposing this two-toed print is the smaller third hoofprint formed of an ovoid **U**-shape with dot dewclaws at the upper ends of the **U**. In the field it was not obvious which designs superimposed the other, but the slightly fresher appearance of the **U**-shaped track suggests it was added later than the bisected oval.

The five remaining designs are on the top of the boulder: the fourth hoofprint formed by two slender halfmoon-shaped crescents; three small, rough cupules; and a curved pecked line. These images are not recorded on the original site form, but obviously were present then. They are revarnished and parts of the hoofprint and pecked line are covered by a hard, crustose, grey-green lichen.

Wahkpa Chu'gn (24HL101)

During our fieldwork in northern Montana, when we recorded the Echo Hawk boulder, the OAS crew visited the Wahkpa Chu'gn bison kill (24HL101), located on the west edge of Havre, and recorded the petroglyph boulder associated with it since the image on that boulder had not been fully documented previously. Access to the bison kill and petroglyph boulder there was provided by Emily Mayer-Lossing, Historic Preservation Officer for Havre, and Kelly and Judy Jones, who are the volunteers at the Wahkpa Chu'gn Buffalo Jump. Lela Patera, chairperson of the Board of Directors of the nearby H. Earl Clack Museum, facilitated and observed the recording project.

Wahkpa Chu'gn is a well-known, large, multicomponent bison kill and processing site excavated in the early 1960s by the MRAS (Davis and Stallcop 1966) and later in 1970 by John Brumley working for the H. Earl Clack Museum (Brumley 1971). Dating from the Besant through the Old Women's phases (Figure 7), Wahkpa Chu'gn shows a complex stratigraphic sequence of multiple bison-kill episodes spanning from about 2000 years ago to A.D. 1700. One feature of the site that has been reported (Brumley 1976; Greer and Greer 2002; Jones and Jones 2012:65) but never formally documented is a petroglyph boulder that originally sat on the bluff above the site. Emmett Stallcop showed it to Keyser in 1974. Interestingly, this boulder now sits just below the Wahkpa Chu'gn visitor center—between it and the main covered bison pound excavation in site area A—but originally it was located near where the Holiday Village Shopping Mall now sits. In the early 1970s during site preparation for the mall,

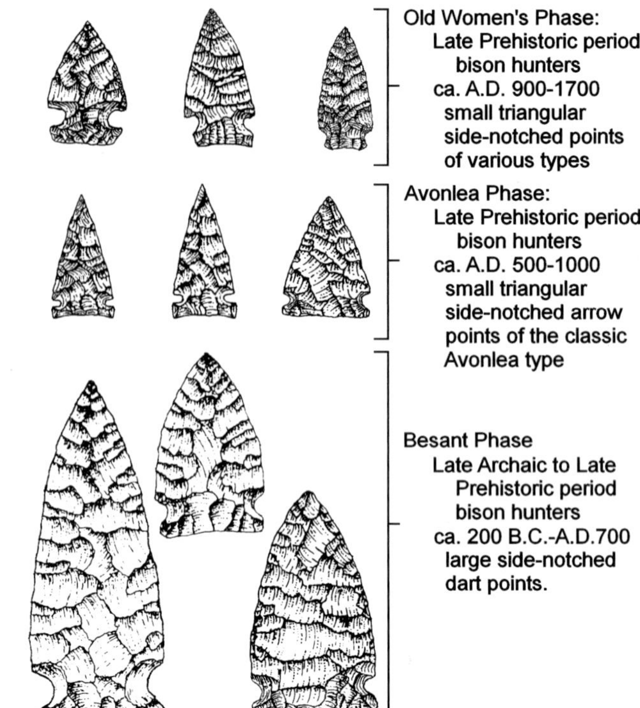

Figure 7. Late Archaic/Late Prehistoric period cultural sequence from the upper Milk River drainage. People during all three phases were excellent hunters who utilized a variety of bison jumps and pounds to slaughter herds each year. Hoofprint tradition ceremonialism could be associated with any of the groups.

the construction company was given specific instruction not to move or disturb the boulder, but that word apparently did not reach the heavy equipment operator, who bulldozed it into a shallow coulee, which he then filled in. Emmett Stallcop, who oversaw Wahkpa Chu'gn at the time, learned of this and insisted that the boulder be recovered (Greer and Greer 1993). When that was done, Stallcop then had it relocated where it could be protected from future damage. It was later moved again, downhill to its present position within the fenced Wahkpa Chu'gn site compound.

The boulder itself is a medium-sized, granite glacial erratic, light purple in color. It measures just more than a meter in maximum dimension and about 60 cm high and 45 cm wide. Shallowly abraded into its broadest face is a large ungulate hoofprint measuring approximately 12 cm across at its widest point, and now facing almost straight up. However, since the boulder has been moved at least twice from its original position, we have no way of knowing the original orientation of the carved hoofprint. At present the carving is nearly invisible until raking light strikes the boulder at a very low angle, so it was necessary for us to use artificial light to illuminate the image during our work (Figure 8).

Figure 8. *The petroglyph boulder at Wahkpa Chu'gn has a single large hoofprint visible in the center right. The lighter scrapes just below the hoofprint are damage caused by heavy machinery when the boulder was inadvertently buried and re-excavated in the early 1970s. Photograph by David Minick.*

The Wahkpa Chu'gn hoofprint is a classic bison track, formed by two toes, each in a teardrop shape separated by a raised median ridge (Figures 8–10). No dewclaws are carved. The image is very shallowly abraded into the surface of the stone, less than one cm deep. Given the stone's hardness, it seems almost certain that the hoofprint was first pecked into the rock—as are nearly all such images on harder quartzite and granitic boulders in this area of the Plains. But the smoothness of the image indicates it was abraded and refreshed—possibly several times—after it was originally pecked, so that no trace of the original pecked dints remains. Abrading the image in this way would have refreshed it by microscopically crushing the surface mineral grains and leaving a white "streak"[2] within the abraded area that would have contrasted markedly to the light purple surface. The result would have rendered the hoofprint visible from a considerable distance, especially if the face on which it is carved were positioned more vertically. Unfortunately, we will likely never know whether this was the case.

Other Petroglyph Boulders in the Upper Milk River Drainage

There are three other petroglyph boulder sites and one site where a hoofprint is carved on the wall of a shallow rockshelter located in the upper Milk River drainage. These are the Samsal petroglyph boulder (24TL959), the Donovan site (24HL91), 24HL635, and Thunderbird Cave (DgOv-88).

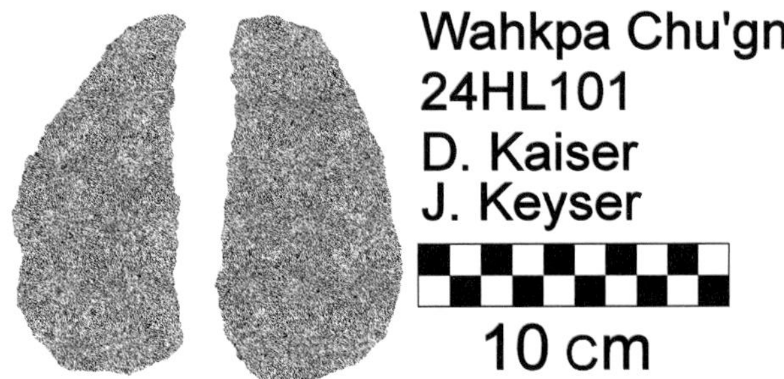

Figure 9. *The 2021 tracing of the hoofprint on the boulder at Wahkpa Chu'gn.*

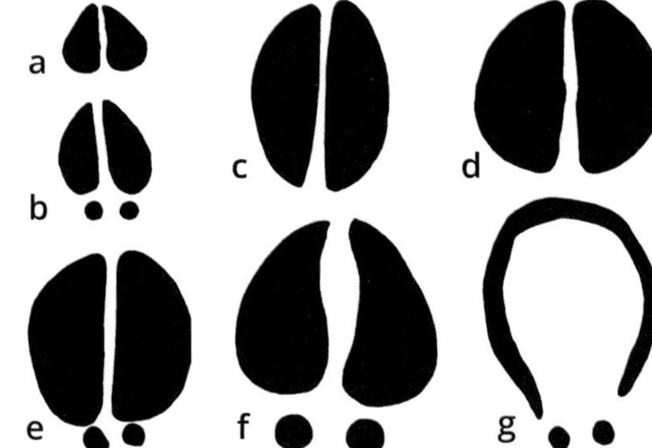

Figure 10. *Hoofprints take a variety of forms. (a, b) Probable deer tracks with teardrop-shaped toes and dewclaws on (b). (c–e) "Facing half-moon" type bison tracks; note dewclaws on (e). (f) Realistically depicted twisted teardrop-shaped toes with ovoid open space between them and dewclaws. (g) Horseshoe-shaped hoofprint with dewclaws.*

Samsal Bison-form Petroglyph Boulder (24TL959)

The Samsal petroglyph boulder is an isolated sandstone erratic in the form of a massive slab measuring 2.8 m long, reaching 1.5 m above the current ground surface, and ranging from about 20 cm to more than 50 cm in thickness. Located 120 km (75 mi) west of Havre, on the west flank of the Sweetgrass Hills, the site was first reported by Brumley and Johnson (2012) but more completely described and analyzed by Sturm and Keyser (2020). The boulder itself shows 45 pecked elements, most of which are Hoofprint tradition motifs, though a Biographic tradition combat scene involving pedestrian warriors and an 1894 graffito are also present. A combination of several of the pecked designs was used to enhance the reclining bison profile of the boulder by providing it with horns, nostrils, and kidneys. The Hoofprint tradition art on the boulder apparently dates to the Late Prehistoric period.

Donovan Site (24HL91)

A small petroglyph boulder measuring about 60 cm wide and more than a meter long has been recorded at the Donovan site along the shoreline of Fresno Reservoir (Keyser 1979:48–55). The boulder is a large, roughly rounded chunk of local sandstone eroded from its parent deposit exposed in several areas higher in the badlands above the site. It sits on the beach below the reservoir high-water line and directly below a Besant-phase bison processing area exposed as the only cultural level in two excavation units in this area of the site. Apparently, this boulder eroded from its original position somewhat higher in the cut bank by reservoir wave action. Such sandstone boulders are relatively common in the badlands' coulee mouths along this stretch of the Milk River.

There are no recognizably representational or abstract motifs carved on this boulder (Figure 11). Instead, the carvings are approximately 30 lines and small cupules, and two large, flat, smoothed areas. Some lines and cupules are as much as 2 cm deep and 2.5 cm wide, but most are shallower and narrower. A few lines appear to be paired, but not in any regular pattern. They make no discernable design, and because there are no hoofprints or other identifiable representational motifs, the marks were dismissed as tool-sharpening grooves in the original investigation (Keyser 1979:53).

Figure 11. Two views of the petroglyph boulder at the Donovan site, a bison pound and processing site. Note the absence of representational motifs.

An extensive Besant-phase bison pound and processing area are spatially associated with the petroglyph boulder (Keyser 1979:48–55). However, there is also an ephemeral, later occupation found in one area of the site, located farthest from the boulder. Although we cannot be sure the boulder is associated with this Besant-phase bison pound and processing area or with a much later transient occupation, the number of grooves, dots, and smoothed areas corresponds best with the intensity of the Besant-phase use of the site, and suggests they are

both of that age. Although there is no evidence that this boulder belongs to the Hoofprint tradition—and it may, in fact, simply be a very large whetstone—we include it in this analysis because we infer that it is associated with a Besant-phase bison pound.

24HL635

This site is located atop a large butte on the north side of the Milk River approximately midway between Wahkpa Chu'gn and Echo Hawk. Found in 1986 by an Ethnoscience field crew working on a survey for the Bureau of Reclamation (Ethnoscience 1986), the site consists of two medium-sized petroglyph boulders that are part of a group of rock cairns strung out along the top of a low ridge system on the north side of the large butte. Two outsized "tipi" rings are also in the same area as the alignment of rock cairns, but their temporal and functional relationships to the cairns and the petroglyph boulders have not been demonstrated. The butte is actually a segment of the rolling prairie in this area, cut off from the main prairie by the Milk River to the south and a tributary coulee system to the north that appears to be an ancient river course, much like Lost River adjacent to the Echo Hawk petroglyph boulder.

The two petroglyph boulders are situated near a large cairn (unfortunately disturbed by site looters). One boulder has two bison hoofprints pecked into a west-facing vertical surface, while the second boulder has a single hoofprint and a female stick-figure human pecked into a vertical north-facing surface (Figure 12). Both boulders are fine-grained quartzite glacial erratics measuring 65 to 85 cm high, and they are the only ones in the immediate vicinity both large enough and sufficiently fine-grained to be suitable for petroglyphs (Ethnoscience 1986:1). The images are very shallowly pecked, no more than one to two mm deep, and are readily visible only when sunlight rakes across the boulders at an optimum angle.

The three hoofprints at 24HL635 are classic bison tracks, all formed by two toes, each showing a "twisted teardrop" shape separated by an unpecked median ridge. The unpecked area tends to be slightly wider in the tracks' approximate center, mimicking the actual natural form of a real bison track. Paired dewclaws shown as small, pecked, circular forms are positioned behind each

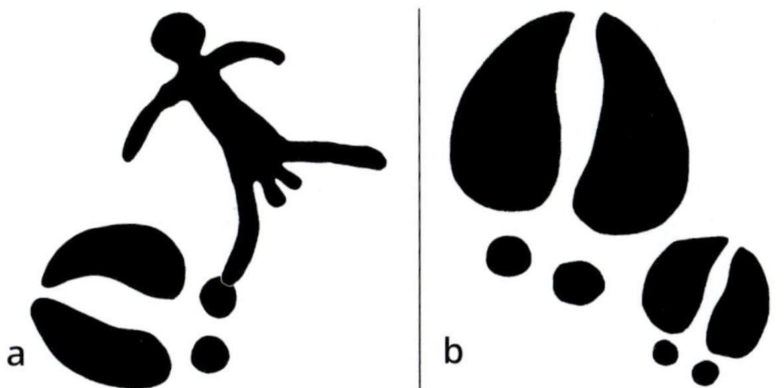

Figure 12. *Hoofprints and female human on two separate boulders at 24HL635, taken from Ethnoscience site form. Group at (a) is on one boulder, (b) is on second boulder. No scale available.*

track. The two paired tracks on one boulder are vastly different in size, with one half the size of the other.

On the second boulder, the single bison track is superimposed by a female stick-figure with a vulva shown by pendant labia between splayed legs. One leg just barely superimposes one dewclaw of the bison track. Without personally examining the images we cannot say for sure but, as drawn in the site form (Ethnoscience 1986:7), the shape of the labia mimics the form of a bison track.

Thunderbird Cave (DgOv-88)

Located in Writing-on-Stone Provincial Park, Thunderbird Cave is a relatively large but shallow rockshelter high on the canyon wall on the south side of the Milk River. The rockshelter contains approximately 250 petroglyphs and pictographs on its ceiling, walls, and rear floor. The images include a single bison hoofprint, 18 human figures, 6 animals, 4 freestanding items of material culture, 2 possible (but very sketchy) vulviforms, a dozen rectilinear geometric forms, and more than 200 carved lines and deep grooves. Dozens of the grooves are arranged in long rows of tally marks. The imagery ranges from classic Ceremonial tradition V-neck style humans, a shield-bearing warrior, and boatform animals, to Biographic tradition tipis and small rectangular-body humans. On the ceiling is painted the eponymous Thunderbird (Figure 13), one of the most iconic and widely published images from the site (Keyser 1977:74, 2004:28; Keyser and Klassen 2001:213).

The only indisputable Hoofprint tradition art element at the site is a single bison track with dewclaws, which is ground high onto the side wall of the rockshelter just above the head of a tall human (Figure 14). Although two incised images below and to the left of this image appear to be simple vulviforms, and there is a crude incised human handprint petroglyph found at the rear of the rockshelter, none of these can be temporally or functionally associated with the hoofprint

Figure 13. *The namesake thunderbird from Thunderbird Cave. Note hailstones covering body and lightning extending from tips of both wings. Trident form held in beak probably represents sound of thunder. DStretch enhancement LRE. Photograph by Mike Taylor, DStretch by David Minick.*

Figure 14. *The single bison hoofprint at Thunderbird Cave is deeply ground into the rockshelter wall just above the head of this deeply incised human figure.*

or the Hoofprint tradition. This is the only hoofprint found in the more than 200 sites in the greater Writing-on-Stone area, and vulviforms (if these are, in fact, that motif) and petroglyph handprints are exceedingly rare at Writing-on-Stone sites.[3] Therefore, we suspect that these putative vulviforms and the one handprint might be part of the Hoofprint tradition, but with so much other rock art at the site it is unlikely that we will ever be able to verify this. Nonetheless, the unique hoofprint itself is strong evidence that the rockshelter was known and used by artists of the Hoofprint tradition.

Summary Characteristics of Upper Milk River Hoofprint Tradition Rock Art

Currently five Hoofprint tradition sites and a sixth petroglyph boulder that we infer to be associated with the Hoofprint tradition have been confirmed on the upper Milk River, which we delineate as extending from Wahkpa Chu'gn to its headwaters. Four of these sites (Echo Hawk, Wahkpa Chu'gn, 24HL635, and Thunderbird Cave) are quite small; only the recently reported Samsal petroglyph boulder (Sturm and Keyser 2020) has more than half a dozen Hoofprint tradition images. The small sites reported here in detail for the first time (Echo Hawk, Wahkpa Chu'gn, and 24HL635) all have fewer than half a dozen petroglyphs, and Hoofprint tradition art in Thunderbird Cave consists of a single bison track with dewclaws and possibly a few other incised images. The enigmatic petroglyph boulder at the Donovan site may or may not relate to the Hoofprint tradition.

Other than their small size, the first thing that one notes about the upper Milk River petroglyph sites is that they all seem to have very strong bison associations. The boulders at Echo Hawk (Figures 4 and 5) and Samsal are themselves bison-form stones, mimicking a reclining bison, and the arrangement of images on the Samsal boulder shows horns, kidneys, and nostrils in the correct anatomical position to reinforce its bison-form aspects (Sturm and Keyser 2020:146–147). The fact that Echo Hawk is such a relatively small bison-form boulder is perfectly consistent with the small size of several other bison-form petroglyph boulders across the Northern Plains (Freeman and Freeman 1996) and the size of typical *iniskim* stones (Peck 2002) which are small bison-shaped fossils that fit in the palm of a hand. Clearly, shape is important; size is not.

A second shared attribute of these sites is that four (Wahkpa Chu'gn, Donovan, Samsal, and 24HL635) are closely associated with known bison kills and one other (Echo Hawk) likely is. The boulders at Wahkpa Chu'gn and the Donovan site are both actually part of a kill-site complex. John Brumley (1976:11), who was intimately involved in the investigation of Wahkpa Chu'gn for many years, reported that he felt the boulder was

associated with the kill site, and in a later oral interview (Greer and Greer 1993:2), he expanded on this to indicate he thought it most likely was associated with the Avonlea-phase component of the site (Figure 7), given the ceremonialism he believed was associated with Avonlea-phase peoples. However, there is widespread evidence that Besant-phase people, who used Wahkpa Chu'gn earlier than Avonlea, had equally impressive ceremonialism associated with their bison killing operations (Frison 1971). So, it seems to us that either the Besant or Avonlea phase kill operations could reasonably be associated with the petroglyph boulder. For that matter, it is certainly possible that such hoofprint ceremonialism could have been associated with the latest Old Women's phase use of Wahkpa Chu'gn.

For the Donovan site, we are reasonably certain that the boulder is associated with the Besant-phase bison kill, but whether it represents ritual or simply tool sharpening cannot be determined.

Less direct, but very suggestive associations with bison kill sites are present for the Samsal boulder and site 24HL635. Additionally, we believe it is quite likely that there are bison kills near the Echo Hawk site. At Samsal a nearby bison kill was reported to the authors the year after we recorded the site, but we have been unable to visit and evaluate it. Site 24HL635 sits directly across the Milk River from the Besant-phase Donovan site bison pound and there are two other large-scale bison kill and processing complexes dating to the Besant and Old Women's phases within two kilometers of the site upstream and downstream (Keyser 1979). In all, more than a dozen recorded bison kills and other drive-lane complexes spanning the last 2000 years of Plains prehistory are found within an 8 km (5 mi) stretch of the Milk River—one of the richest areas of bison kills known in northern Montana (Keyser 1979)—all overseen by the butte topped by 24HL635, directly across the river.

Additionally—although we know of no organized survey of the Milk River and Lost River valleys near the Echo Hawk petroglyph boulder—examining the terrain immediately below the site using Google Earth, Keyser was immediately struck by how suitable it is for the implementation of all manner of bison pounds and jumps. Based on the different hoofprint forms and the superimposition of one over the other on the Echo Hawk boulder, we know that the site was repeatedly visited and used. It would not surprise us if it functioned similarly to site 24HL635, as an adjunct to one or more kill sites in the valleys below.

Finally, although there is no direct association of a bison kill site with Thunderbird Cave and its single Hoofprint tradition element (an abraded hoofprint) among many others, this small but very prominent rockshelter is on the south side of the Milk River just across from the "main site" (DgOv-2) in Writing-on-Stone Provincial Park (Figure 15). Its notable location, eroded in an upper level of sandstone cliffs, is unique for the Writing-in-Stone area. That, coupled with it having the only known hoofprint found at more than 200 sites in the Writing-on-Stone area, caused Keyser and Poetschat to suggest that the rockshelter may have been viewed as a "Buffalo Home" cave, where various Northern Plains tribes believed the buffalo had originally come up from the underground (Keyser and Poetschat 2009:81).

Figure 15. *Thunderbird Cave (arrow) is situated high on the bluffs at Writing-on-Stone, in a position that dominates the river valley. Photograph by Jack Brink.*

The Bisected Oval/Hoofprint and Gestalt Perception

The largest and most central pecked image on the south face of the Echo Hawk boulder is a vertically bisected oval. This motif occurs occasionally on Northern Plains petroglyph boulders (Hoy 1969:50; Park 1990:47; Sturm and Keyser 2020:144), but it is absent at other Northern Plains Hoofprint tradition sites (e.g., Fredlund 1993; Keyser 1984, Keyser and Poetschat 2009; Sturm and Keyser 2020:145; Sundstrom 2004). When such images occur on Northern Plains petroglyph boulders, they are often reasonably interpreted as vulviforms (Greer and Greer 2000:5; Sturm and Keyser 2020:142–143), which research has shown are metaphorically related

to hoofprints based on a strong linkage between women, bison, and fertility in Northern Plains cosmology (Sundstrom 1993, 2002a, 2002b, 2004, 2006).

However, as we recorded and later analyzed the site's images, it struck us that this bisected oval is more than simply a circular design with a line running through it. Although easily recognized as such, while in the field Sturm noted the three-dimensional quality, which highlights the hoofprint shape contained within the lines. In fact, the figure itself is an example of the Gestalt principle of "figure-ground" perception (Rodríguez Martínez and Castillo Parra 2018). Visually, our most common perception of a petroglyph like this is as a "line" or "lines" pecked into an essentially featureless rock surface (Figures 4, 5, and 16a). The stone surface, then, is perceived as the background or "ground" when we "see" this figure; much like the canvas is recognized but dismissed for a painting. Hence, with the surface of the stone as "background," the observer naturally perceives a shape formed of lines that create an oval bisected by a vertical line.

But we know that petroglyph artists also occasionally created bas-relief images where the intended form was created by removing the area surrounding a desired shape with scraping and/or abrading to highlight a raised area as the primary design feature. Sundstrom (2004:133–137, 164) illustrates various examples of such bas-reliefs associated with the Hoofprint tradition in Ludlow and Medicine Creek caves. Perceiving this bisected oval in a slightly more complex manner, the image can also be seen as a very shallow bas-relief if we instead focus our visual attention on the background rather than the pecked lines. If we do this, our perception shifts, and we see the inner shapes within those lines (Figure 16b) and can immediately recognize a classic "facing half-moon" bison track form contained within the contours of the bisected oval when the lines

Figure 16. *The bisected oval on the Echo Hawk petroglyph boulder illustrates very well the Gestalt principle of "figure-ground" perception, wherein you see one form (a) if you focus on the carved lines and a different form (b) when you shift your focus to the shapes contained by the carved lines. Rubin's vase-face illusion (c) is a classic example of "figure-ground" perception used in modern-day psychological studies.*

that bound the internal image become the "ground." Thus, the image becomes a bisected oval/hoofprint—two simultaneous designs, one abstract, one representational and realistic. However, the observer cannot perceive them both simultaneously, since they are a "bistable image" in Gestalt terminology, so the viewer must mentally switch from one to the other—just as we must with Rubin's classic vase-face illusion (Figure 16c).

But this is not just an interesting visual perceptual phenomenon. The importance is that the link between the bisected oval/vulviform and the hoofprint is now not reliant solely on metaphor; instead, it is real—all it requires is a slight change in how we see the figure, and the observer can flip between one and the other. Certainly, this would have been understood by the prehistoric artists, who were undoubtedly impressed with this realization, just as we are when we see the vase-face illusion, or any of several other similar ones.

Our discovery of this bisected oval/hoofprint form led us to review a similar image from the Samsal petroglyph boulder (Sturm and Keyser 2020:143). Similarly categorized in our previous work as a bisected oval but referred to as both a vulviform (which is being grabbed by a handprint in an example of sexual capture) and a hoofprint, we realized why we struggled to decide clearly on one or the other identification. It is not one or the other—it is both at the same time! In fact, our previously published pairing of a photograph of the image with a tracing of it (Sturm and Keyser 2020:Figures 15, 16) is a classic example of how one can see both entities under different perceptual conditions, since the lighting of the photograph essentially reduces the pecked image to background for the viewer (Figure 17), while the two-dimensional tracing shows the pecked lines and shapes as primary.

In short, this bisected oval/hoofprint image relies not on cultural metaphor to see the linkage of vulviform and ungulate hoofprint. Rather, that linkage is hardwired into the human brain—it is there for anyone to see.

In our table of petroglyph boulder motifs (Sturm and Keyser 2020:144), we reported several additional sites with bisected ovals. For these, a photograph of the Herschel boulder (Schneider 2003:122) shows two bisected ovals with internal hoofprint shapes, similar to those on Echo Hawk and Samsal. For others, we have only inconclusive photographs or line drawings that do not permit us to determine the true visual nature of the images, thus leaving an opportunity for further investigation as to whether they also illustrate this same Gestalt perception.

Figure 17. This bisected oval/hoofprint on the Samsal petroglyph boulder is another example of seeing one or the other depending on the viewer's focus on the carved lines or the alternate image created within the bisected oval. In this view the raking sunlight is such that the hoofprint appears in low bas-relief. Photograph by David Minick.

Conclusions

The Hoofprint tradition petroglyphs in the upper Milk River drainage form a relatively distinctive subset of those found across the Northern Plains. All of the sites are small and feature only a very few images attributed to the Hoofprint tradition. Samsal has the largest corpus of imagery with about two dozen images, but more than half of these are cupules. Samsal and 24HL635 have the only humans that are part of the Hoofprint tradition—two faces and a single shaman holding a probable rattle and feather fan at Samsal, and a woman at 24HL635. The sites other than Samsal all have only one to eight images. The Donovan site boulder has no recognizable representational elements, only lines, cupules, and smoothed areas.

Both Samsal and Thunderbird Cave were extensively used by artists carving and/or painting images attributed to other rock art traditions. The other four sites considered here have only motifs that we regard as part of the Hoofprint tradition. A very strong association with bison kills accompanies the bison track symbolism of these sites, and two of the boulders are integral features within large bison-kill sites.

None of the sites is a ribstone or has ribstone elements, like Hoofprint tradition sites common to the north and east. Such ribstones used pecked parallel grooves to mimic a bison's ribcage structure, which further enhances the association with that animal. In fact, the entire repertoire of Hoofprint tradition imagery at these sites is far more limited than occurs at sites downstream in the Milk River drainage and elsewhere to the east. For instance, with the exception of single handprints at Thunderbird Cave and Samsal (both possibly attributable to other art traditions), there are no penisforms, bear paws, handprints, footprints, nucleated circles, or circles with interior crosses, all of which are common at downriver sites. Likewise, none of these sites is anywhere near as large as several of those found to the east such as Snake Butte, St. Victor, the Indian Lake Medicine Boulder, or the Simonton site. And while several of the sites on the lower Milk River may be near bison kills, there is not the intimate association that occurs on the upper reaches of the river.

Notes

1. Myron "Hobe" Echo Hawk, a member of the Pawnee Tribe from Oklahoma, worked with the Bureau of Indian Affairs in Montana on various road projects. In the early 1960s he became friends with Paul English, who worked for the Montana State Highway Department, and given their mutual interest in archaeology, they made a trip with other members of the MRAS to do the initial recording of this petroglyph boulder in 1965 (English et al. 1965).

2. The formal geological definition of streak is "the color of the powder produced when a mineral is dragged across an unweathered surface" (Wikipedia 2022) However, the same principle applies to produce the grey-white "powdery" color caused by the crushing of mineral grains in the "canvas" stone when a petroglyph is made by lightly pecking or abrading the stone surface. The result is an image that is notably lighter in color than the surrounding rock surface, especially if that surface has a naturally darker hue. Thus, when the petroglyph is freshly made—and for many years afterward until the modified surface begins to weather back to the original color of the stone—it stands out to the eye much more than its depth of cutting would suggest.

3. Newly discovered Foothills Abstract tradition pictographs at DgOv-2, directly across the valley from Thunderbird Cave, contain several handprints (Turney et al. 2021), but these are much older than most of the rock art at Writing-on-Stone.

Acknowledgments. Many people shared in the success of our recording effort for the Echo Hawk and Wahkpa Chu'gn petroglyph boulders. Without Patrick Rennie's help from start to finish, the project would have never happened. Likewise, the Strauser family exhibited typical Montana hospitality in making us welcome on their state lease and assisting us in accessing the Echo Hawk boulder. Dave Aagesen was also helpful in our effort to locate the site. Staff at the Wahkpa Chu'gn site and the H. Earl Clack Museum in Havre were very gracious and supported our work at Wahkpa Chu'gn. David Minick took the photographs used in this report and managed to resurrect the photographs of the Donovan site. George Shannon searched the Bureau of Reclamation's Missouri Basin Region archive in vain for original photographs of the Donovan site petroglyph. Mavis Greer provided the original Echo Hawk site form and the only previously published reference for that site and helped figure out approximately where it had to be located. She also shared her site form update for Wahkpa Chu'gn, which provided invaluable information about the petroglyph there. David Kaiser assisted with the tracing of both sites.

References Cited

Brumley, John
  1971 Preliminary Report on Area A Wahkpa Chu'gn Site (24HL101): Results of the 1970 Field Season. *Archaeology in Montana* 12(1):11–39.

  1976 *The Wahkpa Chu'gn Archaeological Site: A Bicentennial Project.* H. Earl Clack Museum, Havre, Montana.

Brumley, John H., and Ann M. Johnson
  2012 Samsal Ranch Petroglyph Boulder and Adjacent Sites in Toole County. *Archaeology in Montana* 53(2):39–50.

Davis, Leslie B., and Emmett Stallcop
  1966 The Wahkpa Chu'gn Site (24HL101): Late Hunters in the Milk River Valley, *Archaeology in Montana*, Memoir 3, Volume 7.

English, Paul, John Brumley, Myron Echo Hawk, and Rick Lieburg
  1965 Archaeological Survey Site Form for 24HL404. On file with the Montana State Historic Preservation Office, Helena, Montana.

Ethnoscience, Inc.
  1986 Site Form for 24HL635. On file with Montana State Historic Preservation Office, Helena, Montana.

Fredlund, Lynn
  1993 *Archaeological Investigations and Rock Art Recordation at Recognition Rock (24RB165), Rosebud County, Montana.* GCM Services Inc., Butte, Montana.

Freeman, Gordon R., and Phyllis J. Freeman
1996 Sacred Rocks of Alberta: Descriptions of Eleven Glyphed Boulders, a Meteorite, and Their Sites. Manuscript on file in Provincial Archives of Alberta, Royal Alberta Museum, Edmonton, Alberta, Canada.

Frison, George C.
1971 The Buffalo Pound in Northwestern Plains Prehistory: Site 48CA302, Wyoming, *American Antiquity* 36:77–91.

Greer, John, and Mavis Greer
1993 *1993 Site Visit Record for Rock Art Boulder at Site 24HL101, Wahkpa Chu'gn Bison Kill*. Report on file with the Montana State Historic Preservation Office, Helena, Montana.

Greer, Mavis, and John Greer
2000 Boulder Rock Art of Montana. Paper Presented at the 58th Annual Meeting of the Plains Anthropological Society, St. Paul, Minnesota. Electronic document, https://www.greerservices.com/Assets/publications_pdfs/2000_Greer_Plains_NE_MT_BoulderRA.pdf, accessed February 22, 2022.

2002 Rock Art and Bison Kills on the Northwestern Plains. Paper presented at the 60th Annual Meeting of the Plains Anthropological Society, Oklahoma City, Oklahoma. Electronic document, https://www.researchgate.net/publication/344398788_Rock_Art_and_Bison_Kills_on_the_Northwestern_Plains#fullTextFileContent, accessed February 22, 2022.

Hoy, Judy
1969 Petroglyph Boulders in Phillips County, Montana. *Archaeology in Montana* 10(3):45–65.

Jones, Tim E. H., and S. Louise Jones
2012 *St. Victor Petroglyphs: The Place of the Living Stone*. The Friends of St. Victor Petroglyphs Cooperative Ltd., Assiniboia, Saskatchewan, Canada.

Keyser, James D.
1977 Writing-On-Stone: Rock Art on the Northwestern Plains. *Canadian Journal of Archaeology* 1:15–80.

1979 Late Prehistoric Period Bison Procurement on the Milk River in North-Central Montana. *Archaeology in Montana* 20(1):1–241.

1984 Rock Art of the North Cave Hills. In *Rock Art of Western South Dakota*, edited by L. Adrien Hannus, pp. 1–51. Special Publication 9, South Dakota Archaeological Society, Sioux Falls, South Dakota.

2004 *Art of the Warriors: Rock Art of the American Plains*. University of Utah Press, Salt Lake City.

Keyser, James D., and Michael A. Klassen
2001 *Plains Indian Rock Art*. University of Washington and UBC Press. Seattle and Vancouver.

Keyser, James D., and George Poetschat
2009 *Crow Rock Art in the Bighorn Basin: Petroglyphs at No Water, Wyoming*. Oregon Archaeological Society Press, Publication 20. Portland, Oregon.

Park, John A.
1990 The Simanton Petroglyph Hill Site (24PH2072): A Ceremonial Complex in Northern Montana. *Archaeology in Montana* 31(2):41–19.

Peck, Trevor R.
2002 Archaeologically Recovered Ammonites: Evidence for Long-term Continuity in Nitsitapii Ritual. *Plains Anthropologist* 47:147–164.

Rodríguez Martinez, Guillermo Andrés, and Henry Castillo Parra
2018 Bistable Perception: Neural Bases and Usefulness in Psychological Research. *International Journal of Psychological Research* 11(2):63–76.

Schneider, Erinn Dayle
2003 *Rock Art in Southern Saskatchewan*. Master's Thesis, Department of Archaeology, University of Saskatchewan, Saskatoon, Saskatchewan, Canada.

Stallcop, Emmett, and Paul English
1969 A Summary of Known Archaeological Sites in North Central Montana. *Archaeology in Montana* 10(3):35–44.

Sturm, Cynthia, and James D. Keyser
2020 *Samsal: A Bison-form Petroglyph Boulder Near the Sweet Grass Hills, Montana*. In American Indian Rock Art, Volume 46, edited by Richard A. Rogers, Evelyn Billo, and Robert Mark, pp. 135–155. American Rock Art Research Association, San Jose, California.

Sundstrom, Linea
1993 *Fragile Heritage: Prehistoric Rock Art of South Dakota*. South Dakota Historical Preservation Center, Vermillion.

2002a Steel Awls for Stone Age Plainswomen: Rock Art, Women's Religion, and the Hide Trade on the Northern Plains. *Plains Anthropologist* 47:99–119.

2002b Prayers in Stone: Hoofprint-Vulva-Groove Rock Art in the Context of Northern Plains Indian Religion. In *Rock Art and Cultural Processes*, edited by Solveig Turpin, pp. 1–26. Special Publication 3, Rock Art Foundation, San Antonio, Texas.

2004 *Storied Stone: Indian Rock Art of the Black Hills Country*. University of Oklahoma Press, Norman.

2006 Reading Between the Lines: Ethnographic Sources and Rock Art Interpretation Approaches to Ethnography and Rock Art. In *Talking with The Past: The Ethnography of Rock Art*, edited by James D. Keyser, George Poetschat, and Michael W. Taylor, pp. 49–72. Oregon Archaeological Society Publication 16, Portland.

Turney, Michael, Landon Bendiak, and Jack W. Brink
2021 New Discoveries of Vertical Series and Foothills Abstract Rock Art at Writing-on-Stone, DgOv-2, Southern Alberta. *Plains Anthropologist* 66:179–216.

Wikipedia
2022 Streak (mineralogy). Wikipedia (online). Electronic document, https://en.wikipedia.org/wiki/Streak_(mineralogy), accessed January 4, 2023.

Sacred Landscapes and Rock Art Interpretation: A Time-Sensitive Example from the Bitterroot Valley, Montana

Carolynne L. Merrell

A Medicine Tree in the Bitterroot Valley of Montana has long been a favored stopping point for people passing through the valley. Few visitors know that high on the cliff behind the tree a pictograph remains, one elusive element among the cultural aspects of the site sacred to the Bitterroot Salish peoples. Today as local stories about the Medicine Tree become less familiar, the once-living tree is in its final stages of disappearing completely from the land. Researching the legends and compelling ethnographic histories of the tree have contributed information leading to the identification and the understanding of a nearby, associated pictograph site and its major elements that are an integral part of this sacred location.

As much as rock art researchers hate to admit it, the pictographs and petroglyphs at a site may not always be its most significant feature. This is the case for the subject of this paper, which relates the history of a Medicine Tree in the southern Bitterroot Valley of Montana and how a pictograph feature is but one contributing component that enhances the narrative for the sacredness of the location by the Salish (Flathead) people. The natural decay and final disappearance of this tree over the next few years will leave little physical evidence to remind people of the contextual history of this site. Although its location on the Bitterroot Valley landscape will remain sacred to the Salish, who continue to hold the story relevant in their cultural traditions, those not familiar with or sensitive to the Native ethnographic information regarding this location, may view the pictographs and assign unrelated interpretations to them.

History of the Medicine Tree (24RA513)
Known in Salish as *Chi-eh, eh*

From the time Euro-Americans first entered the land along the eastern flank of the Rocky Mountains, forming the border between Montana and Idaho, there have been stories about a few select trees that were adorned with offerings left by the local Indians (Weisel 1951). When questioned, the Native Americans explained that these trees were a part of their sacred landscape. For lack of a better word the Euro-Americans called these trees "medicine trees" and the name stuck. Joseph Whitehouse, a member of the Lewis and Clark Corps of Discovery, described such a tree in his journals. On September 11, 1805, near Woodman's Creek, the first campsite after leaving Travelers' Rest in what is now Lolo, Montana, Whitehouse described an instance of a culturally altered tree. He "passed a tree on which was a number [sic] of Shapes drawn on it with paint by the natives. a white bear Skin hung on the Same tree.

Carolynne L. Merrell
*Archaeographics,
Hamilton, Montana*

American Indian Rock Art, Volume 49. Amy Gilreath, Ken Hedges, and Anne McConnell, Editors. American Rock Art Research Association, 2023, pp. 43–51.

we Suppose this to be a place of worship among them" (Thwaites 1905:154, capitalization in original).

A more familiar documentation for the alteration of a tree refers to placing a head or the horns of a bighorn sheep into a crotch of a live tree that then continues to grow around them. A few examples still exist (Figure 1). In 1824, Alexander Ross recorded a "Ram's Horn Tree" near Hellsgate, east of Missoula, Montana, in this description:

> ...one of the first Flathead Indians who passed this way attacked a mountain ram as large and stout as a common horse; that on being wounded, the fierce animal turned round upon his pursuer, who taking shelter behind the tree, the ram came against it with all his force, so that he drove his head through it; but before he could get it extracted again, the Indian killed him, and took off the body, leaving the head as a memento of the adventure. All Indians reverence the celebrated tree, which they say, by the circumstances related, conferred on them the power of mastering and killing all animals; hundreds, therefore, in passing this way sacrifice something as a tribute to the ram's head; and one of the Iroquois, not to

Figure 1. Example of embedded horn in tree and the complete skull of a ram.

incur the displeasure of the god of hunters, hung a bit of tobacco on the horn, to make his hunting propitious [Ross 1855:18–19].

In 1833, W. A. Ferris, an employee with the American Fur Co., wrote in his journal regarding a similar tree along the Bitterroot River that had a horn of an animal embedded in it. To quote from his journal:

> On the east side of the Bitter Root river, there is a singular curiosity, that I had not before observed, because it is situated under some rocky bluffs, almost impassable to horsemen, the proper road being on the west side of the river. It is the horn of an animal, called by hunters, the "Big-horn," but denominated by naturalists "Rocky Mountain Sheep;" of a very large size, of which two-thirds of its length from the upper end, is entombed in the body of a pine tree, so perfectly solid and firmly, that a heavy blow of an axe did not start it from its place.—The tree is unusually large and flourishing, and the horn in it some seven feet above the ground. It appears to be very ancient, and is gradually decomposing on the outside, which has assumed a reddish cast. The date of its existence has been lost in the lapse of ages, and even tradition is silent as to the origin of its remarkable situation. The oldest of Indians can give no other account of it, than that it was there precisely as at present, before their father's great grandfathers were born. They seldom pass it without leaving some trifling offering, as beads, shells, or other ornaments—tokens of their superstitious veneration for it. As high as they can reach, the bark of the tree is decorated with their trifles [Ferris 1940:232–233].

This tree and its surroundings are the main subject of this paper as they relate to a nearby pictograph site. Although the Euro-Americans' history of this tree begins in the 1833 journals of Ferris, for the Salish of the Bitterroot Valley, it figures into tales of Coyote. The Salish have a series of Coyote stories that incorporate certain landforms that are still evident in Bitterroot Valley. One of these tales relates the creation of the Medicine Tree. Although versions of this story vary with each narrator, the basic components remain the same. After reviewing several of these, I found the version related by Salish elder Peter Pichette (1920) to be the most authentic in its description of this Medicine Tree site:

One day while the Coyote was traveling, he accidentally stepped on something which cried out '"Oh! you have broken my leg. I was just about to warn you of some great danger of which is very near, but as you have injured me I will not." As the Coyote looked down, he saw a poor little lark on the ground suffering with a broken leg. "Oh!" Said the Coyote pitifully, "I did not mean it. Do not worry, l will heal it for you," so he did it magically. "Well now listen" said the lark. "A little farther on you will hear some one [sic] calling you. It is the wicked mountain sheep ram who kills everyone who goes by. He is very quick and powerful and when you meet him you must be very watchful for he may kill you." "Thank you," said the Coyote, "I will see if I can put an end to that wicked beast," so the Coyote went on and soon he heard some one [sic] calling: "Coyote come right this way." The Coyote went along until he saw the Ram coming to meet him. They walked up to each other until they were very near, then stood watching each other very closely. "Oh!" said the Coyote to himself, "You do look awfully fierce and wicked with those great big ugly horns, but I must kill you some way or other." After gazing at each other awhile, the Ram said in a roaring voice, "What right have you to trod over my private land without my consent? Whoever does it only at the cost of his life." "Is that so!" said the Coyote, "Have you killed many already?" "Certainly," said the Ram, "Countless numbers." "Is that so?" said the Coyote, "You must be very powerful." "Certainly, I am," said the Ram. "Well," said the Coyote, "Let me see how powerful you are with those horns. Strike this pine tree and let me see how deep they will penetrate it."

During all this time, the Coyote had his eyes on him. "Alrite" said the Ram, and suddenly jumping, struck the tree high in the trunk, burying one of his horns deep into the tree. Before he could release himself, the Coyote drew his great flint knife and cut the head from the ram which fell to the ground. Then he cut the head from the horn which was stuck into the tree, then the head dropped to the ground. Then he cleaned out the horn, took the head and body and threw them on the mountain side. The blood splashed upon the rocks which left an imprint or carving on the rocks, looking very much like [a] human face which looks toward the horn in the tree. This is the only remains of this wicked mountain sheep. After all was done the Coyote stood by the tree and said: "In the future generations this tree will be a Medicine Tree to all tribes" and it surely was, for every lndian who passes by Medicine Tree is bound to stop and leave an offering and make a request for what he wishes or prefers and surely the wish will be granted some day.

Following this review of the traditional story, we can look at the geographic location for the story at the southern end of the Bitterroot Valley and see that the evidence of Coyote's adventure is supported. There is a mature ponderosa tree containing a bulge in the midsection, located east of the Bitterroot River at the base of a steep rocky outcrop (Figure 2). The second component from the Coyote story is found on the steep rocky hillside that rises directly behind the tree. From one viewpoint a very clear profile of a face looks out from the rocks toward the tree (Figure 3). Two other aspects of the location are found high along the steep cliffs behind the Medicine Tree now protected by an active den of rattlesnakes.

Figure 2. Medicine Tree over the last 30 years: (a) circa 1994, (b) 1998, (c and d) 2002 post fire and winter storm, (e) July 2022.

Figure 3. Rock face (in center of photo) looking out toward the Medicine Tree.

Near the top of the cliffs a break in the climb provides a viewpoint that looks across the valley to the West Fork of the Bitterroot River and the traditional southern Nez Perce Trail. Looking south, the East Fork of the Bitterroot River is seen as it flows north from Sula and Ross's Hole. Turning from these viewpoints back toward the base of the exposed cliff there is a small, one-person alcove with a partial stacked rock wall (Figure 4). Several yards beyond and around

Figure 4. Alcove with stacked rock at viewpoint above the Medicine Tree.

a sharp turn in the cliff is the pictograph panel on an exposed section of rock (Figure 5). It faces south and toward Lost Trail Pass at the end of the valley.

Figure 5. Area overview of pictograph panel taken from upslope looking down.

The Pictograph Panel (24RA503)

The pictograph panel occupies about a three-foot wide by five-foot tall section of the exposed, fractured, rock surface (Figure 6). The central figure that clearly dominates the space is a quadruped (Figure 7). Other elements of the panel include vertical tallies, and on the lower right are two smaller unidentifiable figures (Figure 8). The lower section of the panel below the animal is covered with a spatter of random red pigment flecks that were likely applied by either blowing or spattering pigment on the rock wall and down onto the horizontal flat rock shelf below the panel (Figure 9).

Montana State Archaeological Survey Records note that May Vallance (1960) was the first to record

Figure 6. Pictograph panel. Enhanced in Photoshop.

Figure 7. *Quadruped above scale and tally strikes above the ram. Enhanced.*

Figure 8. *Two very faint zoomorphs on shelf below main panel. Enhanced.*

Figure 9. *Spattered pigment. Enhanced.*

the site, although general local lore suggests that the site was known by early Bitterroot Valley residents exploring the land around the Medicine Tree. One observation made during a review of the many site records from the files reviewed by this author over the years and casual conversations held with those familiar with the pictograph site is that no one noted a possible relationship between the Medicine Tree and the pictograph other than to use the tree's place on the landscape as a point of departure for locating the pictograph (Keyser

and Knight 1976; Malouf 1961; Ward 1973). Random comments gleaned from a study of the various site forms and photographs of the panel suggested that the extent of the red-orange pigment was often difficult to identify because of deteriorating conditions related to pigment loss, fading over time, and the deposit of some areas of pigment over dark grey sections of the base rock. This was especially true for the main figure of the quadruped. These problems were also evident in some of my photographs taken when I recorded the panel, where I could see the likely problem was that dark rock behind a section of the head paint was concealing the fact that a gap in the paint showed that the head area was intentionally detached from the body.

Working with my photographs in about 1994, prior to DStretch, I was able to apply computer digital enhancement techniques to scanned colored slides and negatives. The separation of the head from the neck became most evident when I enhanced my images by lightening the rock color, saturating the red ochre pigment, then increasing the contrast between the two colors. When this was done, the break between the body and the head could be seen, with the head appearing as described in the legend, in which Coyote removed it before throwing it against the cliff face. These results allowed me to see the animal and the pigment clearly enough to identify it as a bighorn sheep ram with a detached head (Figure 10), an identification reinforced by the structure and physical characteristics of a big-

Figure 10. *Close-up of bighorn with semi-detached head.*

horn sheep ram (Figure 11). The body in the photograph of the ram can be described as robust with solid legs and body and a well-formed head with large horns. The tracing of the animal in the pictograph (Figure 12) shows a clear, well-defined body with the head appearing in fragmented applications of pigment that are not easily described. Earlier sketches of the animal on site forms show it with an attached head, likely because the dark rock behind the head masks the break or gap in the pigment. Linda Ward (1973:30) described it as "an animal figure, apparently with antlers." It is important to note here that this pictograph panel does not appear to have been intended to be a detailed painting of the entire story, but rather portrays the essence of the moment when the wicked ram is destroyed. That is the reason the ram is central to the panel.

The portrayal of the bighorn sheep pictograph at this particular location on the landscape was not a random choice. Wildlife biologists claim that the few bighorn *(Ovis canadensis)* here today are remnants of the several much larger bands that once occupied the entire Bitterroot Range (Buechner 1960). The Salish had a deep expert knowledge of their environment and moved through their landscape harvesting the resources that became available with the seasons. The hunters knew when and where they would find game animals including the bighorn sheep of the Bitterroot Mountains (Cross 1996:38). The identification of the quadruped in the pictograph as a ram appears to fit with the killing of the ram in the Coyote Story. This returns us to the remains of the Medicine Tree and the concern for the future identification and significance of this pictograph and its location on this sacred Salish ground.

Even after the Bitterroot Salish, led by Chief Charlo, were pressured to leave the Bitterroot Valley by the United States government and move north to the Jocko Reservation in 1891, they continued to return to the upper end of Bitterroot Valley where they had always peacefully coexisted with the Euro-American settlers. When they returned, they camped and held pow wows at Medicine Tree Flat. On one occasion in 1923, local resident Bertie Lord recorded the event with a photograph (Figure 13). The original photo is held in the archives of the Darby District Office of the Bitterroot National Forest. All of the people in the photo are identified and the Medicine Tree behind them looks very much like the same tree I photographed in 1993,

Figure 11. A Rocky Mountain bighorn sheep.

Figure 12. Tracing of bighorn sheep ram pictograph.

Figure 13. Copy of historic photo of Salish members standing in front of the Medicine Tree during a visit to the Bitterroot Valley about 1923. Photo by Bertie Lord, 1923, courtesy of the archives of the Darby District Office of the Bitterroot National Forest.

with the same bulge in the midsection that is thought to be the tree's accommodation for the horn.

From the 1920s until 2004, the development of the land surrounding the Medicine Tree placed pressure on its natural environmental setting and put its health at increasing risk, threatening its health and safety. As the Bitterroot Valley has grown in popularity and population, the Montana Transportation Department had attempted on several occasions to remove the tree. Ever vigilant, the Salish Tribe and those who recognized the value and significance of the Medicine Tree have repeatedly fought to protect its location. Even with added support of the ground around the tree, the proximity of the highway continues to take its toll on the health of the tree (Figure 2a). The highway department was not the only threat to the tree. Not all people who knew about the tree treated it with respect. History describes a few malicious isolated acts that placed the life of the tree in jeopardy; but through them all, it continued to survive into the 1990s. Although the top of the tree was dying by 1998, the midsection continued to hang on to life, still extending its "feeble arms" to accept the offerings tossed onto the upper branches (Figure 14a) even as the green foliage faded to brown (Figure 2b). Thus,

festooned with offerings, the tree faced the tremendous fires that burned much of the upper Bitterroot Valley in 2002. It did not emerge from the fires unscathed, yet still afforded a noble perch for the osprey (Figure 2c). The bark split with the heat of the fire and fierce winter winds eventually cracked off the top 80% (Figure 2d). Finally, in 2004 a piece of good news offered hope for its future. The Confederated Salish and Kootenai Tribes purchased the property that contained the Medicine Tree and the pictograph on behalf of the history and culture of the Salish people (Merrell 2004). The tribes also settled their discussions with the State Highway Department in favor of preserving the Medicine Tree easement property. But that is not the end of the story. The deterioration of the tree continues. In honoring the tree, visitors have nearly loved it to death with their offerings around its base and in its branches, but also poked into the remaining bark of the aged ponderosa (Figure 14b). Today the tree stands as a broken memorial on sacred ground (Figure 2e). Still, the people continue to come and leave their tokens and prayers for this broken giant (Figure 15). These people include not only the Salish, and other Native Americans, but also non-Indians who respect the tradition or are just curious about items placed at the site. However, the time is

Figure 14. Offerings left at the Medicine Tree in the form of (a) bundles of beads, feathers, and cloth thrown into the branches, and (b) coins inserted into the tree bark .

Figure 15. Examples of offerings left at the Medicine Tree.

coming when this tree will disappear altogether. What then will become of the pictograph site that no longer has its totem to identify the place on the landscape?

Summation and Future Consideration

The future for the Medicine Tree's geographic location and its history related to the life lessons taught by Coyote stories from the Bitterroot Valley will remain embedded in Salish culture and under their protection. But what are the lessons or takeaways for rock art researchers who approach a rock art site without considering why it may have been created at that select location on the landscape? This raises further questions regarding how the Medicine Tree pictograph site will be viewed in future years without its landmark tree, how it will be described by those unaware of the ethnographic information that supports the story the pictograph represents, not to mention why the pictograph is placed where it is. Would this panel have ever been created had not this geographic location been chosen as the setting for the Medicine Tree story by the Bitterroot Salish people?

The story related to this pictograph site is just one example among many in the literature that are based on ethnographic analogies and stories related to certain geological landforms that inspired the creation of pictographs and petroglyphs related to a specific culture (Hann 2013; Kaiser 2017; Merrell 2005; Patterson 2022). The major difference between the increased sensitivity for the location of the Medicine Tree pictograph and others based solely on geological comparisons is that the relationship that likely inspired the Medicine Tree pictograph was not based just on geological features but rather on a living tree and an embedded ram's horn as the major features. These features combined to provide the inspiration for the creation of the pictograph.

To the ever-expanding list of geological/geographic-related observations that may be noted when recording pictograph and petroglyph sites, we should add the consideration for physical, living entities in the vicinity in light of any ethnographic stories and history that may be related to those attributes as they might influence the interpretation of the rock art. Natural features often affect the location and subject matter selected by the original creators of rock art. These are often landscape features like cliffs, crevices, or watercourses. However, sometimes the natural features are biota—living animals, the horns of a once-living animal, or vegetation such as a tree—like the subject in this paper. These living features should inform rock art archaeology at every stage of our work.

Acknowledgments. From 1994 to 2000 I worked as a volunteer with the Bitterroot National Forest, monitoring and updating the files on record for all of the known rock art in the Bitterroot Valley. During that time, I visited the Medicine Tree and pictograph site on several occasions, photographing and taking notes. A part of this work over the years entailed consulting with the Flathead Salish Culture Committee regarding their history as it related to the more than 15 pictograph sites in their Bitterroot Valley homeland. I especially valued my time spent with Marcia Pablo, archaeologist and Flathead Salish tribal member, and Tony Incashola, Director of the Flathead Salish Culture Committee (deceased March 2022).

References Cited

Buechner, Helmut K.
  1960 *The Bighorn Sheep in the United States, its Past, Present and Future.* Wildlife Monograph 4. The Wildlife Society, Bethesda, Maryland.

Cross, Marcia Pablo
  1996 *Bighorn Sheep and the Salish World View: A Cultural Approach to the Landscape.* Master's thesis, University of Montana.

Ferris, Warren A.
  1940 *Life in the Rocky Mountains: A Diary of Wanderings on the Sources of the Rivers Missouri, Columbia, and Colorado from February 1830, to November, 1835.* Edited by Paul C. Phillips. The Old West Publishing Company, Denver. Originally published in a series of installments in the Western Literary Messenger, J. S. Chadbourne & Co., Buffalo, N. Y, from July 13, 1842, to May 4, 1844.

Hann, Don
  2013 Implied Narrative: Rock Art, Landscape, and Myth at Picture Gorge, Oregon. In *American Indian Rock Art, Volume 39,* edited by William D. Hyder, pp. 101–113. American Rock Art Research Association, Glendale, Arizona.

Kaiser, David A.
  2017 Cannibal Woman on the Columbia—Exploring a Mythological Motif. In *American Indian Rock Art, Volume 43,* edited by Ken Hedges and Mark A. Calamia, pp.1–9. American Rock Art Research Association, San Jose, California.

Keyser, James D., and George C. Knight
  1976 The Rock Art of Western Montana. *Plains Anthropologist* 21(71):1–12.

Malouf, Carling
  1961 Pictographs and Petroglyphs. *Archaeology in Montana* 3(1):1–13.

Merrell, Carolynne L.
  2004 History of the Medicine Tree. Conference: Honoring the Heritage of the Plateau People: Past, Present, and Future. Washington State University. Pullman.

  2005 Location, Location, Location: Rock Art as Sacred Geography. In *Making Marks: Graduate Studies in Rock Art Research at the New Millennium,* edited by Jennifer K. K. Huang and Elisabeth V. Culley, pp.183–196. Occasional Paper No. 5. American Rock Art Research Association, Tucson, Arizona.

Patterson, Carol
2022 Athapaskan Social Imagery in the Uinta Basin: Interpretation through Ethnographic Analogy. *Expression* 35:51–58.

Pichette, Pierre
1920 Legend of Medicine Tree and the Medicine Face Twelve Miles South of Darby, Montana at the Upper Part of the Bitter Root Valley as Related by Peter Pichette. Pamphlet on file at the Ravalli County Museum, Hamilton, Montana.

Ross, Alexander
1855 *The Fur Hunters of the Far West: A Narrative of Adventures in the Oregon and Rocky Mountains*. Volume 2. Smith, Elder and Co., London. Electronic document, https://archive.org/details/cihm_40229/mode/2up, accessed August 17, 2022.

Thwaites, Reuben Gold (editor)
1905 *Original Journals of the Lewis and Clark Expedition 1804–1806*. Volume 7. Dodd, Mead & Company, New York. Electronic document, https://archive.org/details/originaljournals07lewiuoft/mode/2up, accessed August 17, 2022.

Vallance, May
1960 Report for Site No. 24RA503, Ravalli County. River Basin Survey, Montana State University. Smithsonian Institution, Washington, D.C.

Ward, Linda
1973 *Prehistory of the Bitterroot Valley*. Master's Thesis, University of Montana.

Weisel, George F., Jr.
1951 The Ram's Horn Tree and Other Medicine Trees of the Flathead Indians. *The Montana Magazine of History* 1(3):5–13.

The Black Rock Site: Ancient Pecked Rock Art in Southwest Wyoming

Julie E. Francis, Mark Willis, and Lawrence L. Loendorf

The Black Rock site (48SW5952) contains two panels of fully pecked representational figures and abstract images. It is one of the few pecked rock art sites known from southwestern Wyoming, with the oldest imagery dated to Paleoindian times. Tratebas (1999, 2018) has interpreted one panel at Black Rock as a single, Late Pleistocene age composition depicting a mountain sheep surround and a hunt shaman. However, recent recording indicates multiple manufacturing episodes created over the course of the Holocene.

Pecked rock art is ubiquitous across the Great Basin and the entire Intermountain West of the United States. What Whitley (2018:22–23) has termed the Great Basin Tradition (GBT) extends into portions of western Wyoming (Francis and Loendorf 2002; Walker 2018) and perhaps as far east as the Black Hills (Tratebas 2018:73–74). However, pecked rock art is not particularly common in southwestern Wyoming due, in large part, to the predominance of soft, easily eroded, Late Cretaceous and Tertiary sandstones in the region. Of the nearly 100 known rock art sites from Lincoln, Sublette, and Sweetwater counties in the database of the Wyoming State Historic Preservation Office (SHPO) Cultural Records Office (CRO), most are incised and scratched sites of Late Prehistoric and younger age, with pecking documented at fewer than 15 localities. Of these, most are known from the vicinity of Flaming Gorge Reservoir near the Utah/Wyoming state line (Keyser and Fossati 2014). At these sites, pecked Uncompahgre style Archaic figures (Cole 1990:82–96) underlying younger Fremont and incised images are frequently so eroded that they appear as indecipherable vestiges.

The Black Rock site (Figure 1) stands out as an extremely well-preserved site in southwestern Wyoming containing fully pecked rock art. One of two

Julie E. Francis
Department of Anthropology, University of Wyoming, Laramie

Mark Willis
Sacred Sites Research, Inc. Albuquerque, New Mexico

Lawrence L. Loendorf
Sacred Sites Research, Inc. Albuquerque, New Mexico

Figure 1. Overview of 48SW5952, the Black Rock site, looking north. All photos by Mark Willis.

American Indian Rock Art, Volume 49. Amy Gilreath, Ken Hedges, and Anne McConnell, Editors. American Rock Art Research Association, 2023, pp. 53–60.

pecked panels contains an array of well-defined abstract/geometric figures, two large anthropomorphic depictions, at least 10 much smaller humanlike figures, two mountain sheep, and an elk (Figure 2). The abstract/geometric imagery in conjunction with representational anthropomorphs and mountain sheep clearly link this site to the GBT. Nearly all figures are almost completely revarnished to the hue of the surrounding sandstone, and one anthropomorph returned an AMS age in excess of 11,000 RCYBP (Liu and Dorn 1996, see below). Earlier published references to Black Rock (Francis 2018:160–162; Francis and Loendorf 2002:65; Keyser and Klassen 2001; Tratebas 1999, 2018) have been brief and based upon minimal recording. In this article, we present the results of more detailed recording of Black Rock completed in 2018 and offer new insights into what is a far more complex site than previously recognized.

Figure 2. Panel 1 at the Black Rock site.

Background

The Black Rock site has been included in the CRO database maintained by the Wyoming SHPO for nearly 40 years. The late Joe Bosovich, a longtime member of the Wyoming Archaeological Society, happened upon Black Rock in 1968 (Tanner et al. 1995). Recognizing its significance and desiring to protect it, he kept its location confidential. Eventually, Bosovich took Dudley Gardner of Western Wyoming College to the site. They plotted its location on a 15′ USGS quad map, made a brief set of notes, and obtained a site number (48SW5952) from the CRO. The site form (Gardner and Bosovich 1984) describes the best-preserved

panel as containing at least six anthropomorphic stick figures, at least two mountain sheep, a possible bear, and a horizontal ladderlike image. The second panel is described as containing only one stick figure and slash marks. The site form notes that the figures were pecked through desert varnish with heavy patina in the pecking. No photographs or drawings are included with the site form.

Sometime later, Bosovich showed Black Rock to Russ Tanner, then of the BLM Rock Springs office (Tanner et al. 1995). Tanner recognized that the rock art could be quite old, and he contacted Julie Francis and Larry Loendorf about including the site in a then-ongoing dating study. As a result, Ron Dorn of Arizona State University visited the site with Francis, Loendorf, Tanner, and Bosovich to collect samples in August 1995. The investigators were unaware of the Smithsonian site number assigned to the site but took a few 35 mm color slides and made a rough sketch and notes showing Dorn's sampling locations. Results returned a Paleoindian age (Liu and Dorn 1996) and are discussed in more detail below. Black Rock was then visited and photographed by Alice Tratebas (1999:18–20) shortly after publication of the Liu and Dorn age estimates to compare the site with other Paleoindian/Early Archaic rock art at the Legend Rock site (48H04) and in the Black Hills. Jim Keyser also visited the site with Russ Tanner and mentioned the site as an example of the Early Hunting Tradition in 2001 (Keyser and Klassen 2001:82, 84).

In preparation for the 2016 Dinwoody Dissected workshop (Walker 2018), Francis began researching the location of Black Rock. She was able to identify a general location using Google Earth and her 1995 color slides, researched the SHPO CRO database in that area, and discovered that a site form had been on file since 1984. From the 15′ topographic map with the site form and using Google Earth, she was able to plot the exact site location. During the workshop, at least two participants mentioned that they had unsuccessfully tried to locate the site and speculated that it may have been destroyed. This served as impetus to return to the site and more fully record it. On August 19, 2018, Francis and Mark Willis successfully relocated Black

Rock, discovering it to be in much the same condition as observed in 1995. The site has now been recorded to current standards, with site forms, maps, and photographs on file at the CRO in Laramie. In addition, a photogrammetric model of the rock surface was created. Approximately 400 photographs were taken with a professional grade Canon 5DS R DSLR. The images were collected from varying distances and angles around the rock art panels and later imported into Agisoft Metashape photogrammetry modeling software. The software produced a point cloud of about 30+ million points that represent the surface of stone. Ambient occlusion enhancements were applied to the digital model to exaggerate minute details. Creating such a model allows for additional study and examination away from the site. It also creates a digital record of the site that may prove important should the actual rock art be vandalized or damaged in some other way.

Setting

The Black Rock site is situated at the extreme northwestern margin of the Great Divide Basin on the west slope of one of the outermost hogbacks of the Rock Springs Uplift (Figure 3). To the west and north, the basalt-capped mesas of the Quaternary age Leucite Hills volcanic field punctuate the low ridges of the uplift. Extending for over 88 km (55 mi) from west to east, the well-known Killpecker dune field, also of Quaternary age, lies only about 5 km (3 mi) north. Vegetation is dominated by sagebrush, with sparse grasses. With no nearby permanent water sources, and at an elevation of 2175 m (7135 ft), Black Rock sits in a high desert.

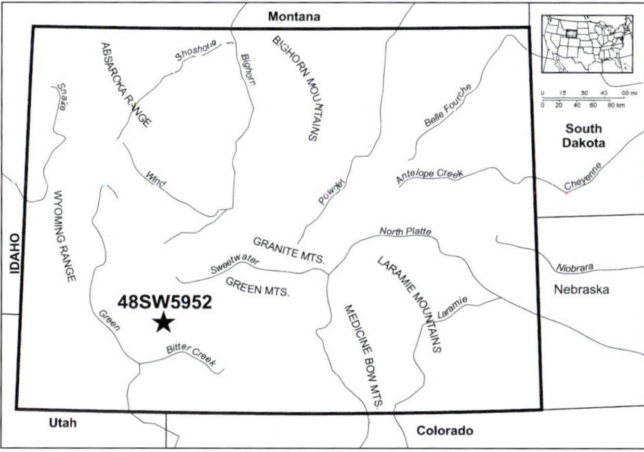

Figure 3. General location of the Black Rock site.

On the western slope of the hogback, differential erosion has created an unusual, thumb-shaped outcrop (Figure 1) jutting out from a bed of resistant, grey sandstone in the Late Cretaceous age Lance formation (Love and Christiansen 1985). Remnant patches of reddish hued varnish on the southwest side of the outcrop suggest severe erosion from the strong prevailing westerly winds which formed and continue to shape the Killpecker dune field (Ahlbrandt 1974). The two panels, designated 1 and 2 from left to right, occur on perpendicular sides of a niche at the eastern end of this outcrop. Only by virtue of the protection afforded by the ceiling of the niche and the larger overhang at the top of the outcrop have these survived. Panel 1 is in much better condition than Panel 2 and is the primary subject of this article. Erosion has undercut the lowest portion of the outcrop beneath the panels. As a result, both are stranded, with the bottom edges of each roughly 2 m above the present ground surface.

The 1995 Dating Project

During the 1995 visit, a trilobed headdress anthropomorph and mountain sheep with well-preserved varnish in the upper portion of Panel 1 were considered the best candidates for dating (Figure 4). The anthropomorph was the only element that was able to be dated. Liu and Dorn (1996) used two independent techniques to arrive at a Late Pleistocene age estimate for this figure. The first was AMS radiocarbon dating of weathering rind organic materials (WROs). This yielded an age of 11,650 ± 50 RCYBP (Liu and Dorn 1996). In addition, analysis of varnish microlaminations (VMLs) using backscatter electron microscopy showed stratigraphy consistent with that from well-dated volcanic landforms of Late Pleistocene age, specifically the Younger Dryas time frame (Liu and Dorn 1996), consistent with the Late Pleistocene AMS age estimate.

Figure 4. Upper portion of Panel 1 at the Black Rock site, showing abstract and representational elements thought to be of early Paleoindian age.

After publication by Liu and Dorn (1996), questions concerning the accuracy of "bulk" samples of WROs embedded in rock varnish became apparent

(Francis and Loendorf 2002:52–65). Dorn (1998) issued strong cautionary notes about using AMS ages from bulk WROs, due to a mixture of older and younger carbon in sandstones. Thus, there is some error factor associated with the AMS age estimate. Under any circumstance, the imagery is extremely ancient. Given the VML stratigraphy, Tratebas (2018:73) considers the date to represent a firm Late Pleistocene age.

Evidence for Paleoindian occupation near Black Rock is abundant. Tanner reports surface finds of Clovis, but more commonly Goshen, points (Tanner et al. 1995) from the area, and the Killpecker dune field, well-known for the occurrence of intact Paleoindian sites, can be reached in an hour's walk. Early Paleoindian materials, roughly contemporaneous with the AMS age estimate for Black Rock, have been found in the Killpecker dunes about 35 km west of the site. The Krmpotich waterhole sites include one locality (48SW13621) with camel bone possibly associated with chipped stone, a Goshen occupation at 48SW13619, and a Folsom occupation at 48SW9826 (Kornfeld et al. 2010:409–412; Smith and Miller 2016). Slightly younger than the Black Rock AMS age is the Finley site (48SW5), the type site for the Cody Complex (Laughlin 2010), also within a two-day walk of Black Rock. Roughly 20 km northwest and also in the Killpecker dunes is the Larson cache or possible burial (48SW1121), containing 40 Scottsbluff points (Kornfeld et al. 2010:383). Folsom and Cody Complex materials have been recovered from the Joe Bosovich site complex (48SW5950), only a 30-minute walk from Black Rock (Kautzman and Pastor 2002:27 Murray and Thompson 1999:3). Given the abundant evidence for Clovis, Goshen, and Folsom near Black Rock, as well as the VML stratigraphy, we consider a general early Paleoindian age range as defined by Kornfeld et al. (2010:73–84) for the trilobed anthropomorph to be reasonable.

The Rock Art

Panel 1 (Figure 2) contains over 30 elements, of which the vast majority are completely revarnished. Based upon superimpositions and formal variation, rock art on Panel 1 was created numerous times. Evident on the 3D model of Panel 1 (Willis 2018) is the superimposition of the right foot (from the perspective of the viewer) of the dated anthropomorph over some heavily varnished pecking. There also are other areas of what may be heavily varnished, random pecking, particularly in the lower left portion of Panel 1. These cannot be associated with other imagery and may be

older than the dated anthropomorph.

The dated anthropomorph, three zoomorphs, and abstract/geometric figures (Figure 4) appear to represent a roughly contemporaneous and complex scene of likely early Paleoindian age. The fully pecked mountain sheep in the upper center portion of the panel stands out. It faces left, measuring roughly 20 cm from nose to the end of a short, stubby tail. The front legs show faint indications of ball-shaped hooves. Emerging from the creature's back is a horned, triangular head sitting atop a narrow neck. The right horn recurves inward. The left horn curves nearly 30 cm to the right across the top of the panel. The dated anthropomorph stands to the right of the emergent head and measures about 20 cm tall. It presents as a frontal view with a rectangular body and round head topped by a three-lobed headdress resembling a modern cowboy hat. This headdress appears to be unique and so far has not been documented at other sites in the region. Legs and arms are outstretched, with a variable number of oversized fingers and toes. The fingers on the right end at a heavily varnished vertical crack or V-shaped incision which has been enhanced by pecking. Two other fully pecked zoomorphs (Figure 5) occur in the lower half of the panel. Below the upper mountain sheep is a left-facing elk. It sports an impressive rack of branching antlers, and the hind legs appear to end in ball-shaped feet. Peck marks on the front legs appear to have been smoothed and are not well defined in the body, suggesting that the image has been reworked. A second left-facing mountain sheep is to the right of the elk. The horns, head, and withers have been pecked around an enhanced natural feature, and a short stubby tail is discernible to the right of a superimposed anthropomorph. Individual peck marks in the recurved horns have been smoothed, suggesting later reworking of this figure.

Physically connecting the representational images are abstract/geometric elements and enhanced natural

Figure 5. Lower portion of Panel 1 at the Black Rock site. The fully pecked elk and lower mountain sheep are thought to be of early Paleoindian age.

features (Figure 4). The left horn of the head emerging from the back of the upper sheep becomes the upper side of a ladderlike image which is directly connected to an unusual, elongated element. A curvilinear abstract element emerges from the lower portion of the elongate figure. This intersects the vertical crack/incision, which in turn, is intersected by the right hand of the anthropomorph. Thus, all these images are actually one complex element. To the left of the upper sheep is a "trident-like" design (Figure 4). Recent exfoliation (Figure 5) along a prominent crack has truncated the base of this element and the tines of the elk's right antler directly below. Though it cannot be demonstrated, it is possible that the two elements were once connected, and that the "trident" represents an exaggerated extension of the elk's antlers. Similarly, a thick pecked line truncated by exfoliation may have once connected the upper sheep and elk. Several abstract elements at the extreme left and right sides of the panel are not physically connected to the remainder of the images but, based upon similarity in pecking techniques, are considered associated.

The incorporation/enhancement of natural features into these images stands out. Several natural holes/voids which dot the surface of Panel 1 have been enlarged by pecking and quite possibly drilling, for example, at the nose and above the back of the upper mountain sheep and at the end of the right horn of the emergent head (Figure 4). Two other natural features have been modified by pecking to form elongated cigar-shaped elements. The larger of these (Figure 4) is about 13 cm long and has been formed by pecking an elongated area around a concretion with a narrow, longitudinal depression. The lower mountain sheep has been pecked around a similar figure (Figure 5).

One large and ten smaller anthropomorphic images have been added to the lower portion of Panel 1 (Figure 6). The most prominent is a tall (ca. 35 cm) figure which mostly obliterates the hind quarters of the lower sheep. This image exhibits a long rectangular torso, with short upstretched arms lacking hands or fingers. Legs are short in comparison to the torso and lack any indication of feet or toes. It has a long neck topped by a round head with a single feather. An irregular pecked area occurs to the immediate right of the head, suggesting some type of substance emerging from a presumed mouth. This also suggests that the figure is represented in profile view.

The smaller (ca 10 cm or less in height) anthropomorph-like images have been placed across the lower

Figure 6. Lower right portion of Panel 1 at the Black Rock site, showing feathered anthropomorph (superimposed on the lower mountain sheep) and smaller birdlike human figures. Several more recent (unvarnished) pecked areas also occur at the lower left and right side of the photograph.

portion of the panel and may be associated with the feathered anthropomorph. The small figures are quite simple, with narrow bodies. When defined, heads are round with no facial features. Torsos occasionally end in stubs. Legs, when present, lack feet and toes. Arms are outspread and tend to be long in proportion to the length of the torso with no hands or fingers depicted. All impart an abstract quality, and several of the smaller figures resemble birds as much as humans. The right arm of one partially superimposes the front leg of the elk, and the horns of the lower mountain sheep may be partially superimposed by the right arm of another (Figure 6). Another may superimpose the body of the feathered anthropomorph (Figure 6). However, the superimposition may be the result of reworking this figure by smoothing and incising, rather than the original pecking.

Near-complete revarnishing suggests roughly similar ages for the feathered anthropomorph and small humanlike images superimposed on the sheep and elk associated with the early Paleoindian anthropomorph. Unfortunately, there is no way to determine the actual time difference between manufacture of the superimposed images. However, formal characteristics of the two large anthropomorphs may offer some clues. When viewed from a typological perspective, the two large anthropomorphs share no formal characteristics. They differ with respect to their overall dimensions, posture, proportional relationships between the length of appendages and torsos, presence or absence of digits, and headdress type. Had these figures been found on different panels or at different sites, they would likely be considered different descriptive types (Loendorf and Porsche 1985) or styles, perhaps dating to different time periods. These dissimilarities suggest a fair amount of age difference between the early Paleoindian trilobed anthropomorph and the feathered figure. Based upon the heavy varnish development, a middle or late Paleoindian or Early Archaic age estimate for the feathered anthropomorph and smaller figures seems reasonable.

Five other pecked elements exhibit little to no varnish development in comparison to immediately adjacent figures, indicating still yet more recent additions to Panel 1. One, at the lowest edge of the panel, resembles a bird, and a second (Figure 6) behind the elk's rear legs may be what Gardner and Bosovich (1984) identified as a bear. The other elements consist of random pecked areas, of which one has obliterated an abstract/geometric image and possibly a quadruped. Given the near complete lack of varnish development on these images, a rough age estimate of no older than 1000 years is reasonable.

The most recent addition to Panel 1 consists of scratches above the horizontal ladder design at the top of the panel (Figure 7a and b). We could not closely study this portion of the panel in the field due to the lack of a ladder. The fine scratches include an unknown elongated figure and a dome-shaped image, as well as other lines. The fine scratching manufacturing technique is typical of Biographic Tradition (Keyser and Klassen 2001) and may suggest that these specific Black Rock images are of Protohistoric or Historic age.

Interpreting Black Rock

Tratebas (1999:19–20, 2018:73) interprets Panel 1 at Black Rock as a single contemporaneous hunting scene depicting at least one "surround" by pedestrian hunters. As she describes the panel (1999:19–20), the dated anthropomorph with the trilobed headdress is likely the game-calling shaman. The tallest anthropomorph and an unspecified number of small "stick" figures are positioned in front of and below the lower mountain sheep in what Tratebas considers to be a trap. Although superimpositioning is a rare characteristic of Paleoindian age pecked rock art in the Black Hills, she considers the superimposition of the feathered anthropomorph on the lower mountain sheep to be an intentional part of the composition. Furthermore, "stick humans are also in front of and below the wapiti, as if positioned in another surround" (Tratebas 1999:20). Tratebas (2018:73) also interprets the upper mountain sheep to have been speared. Presumably, this is the long thick line extending downward from the figure's chest.

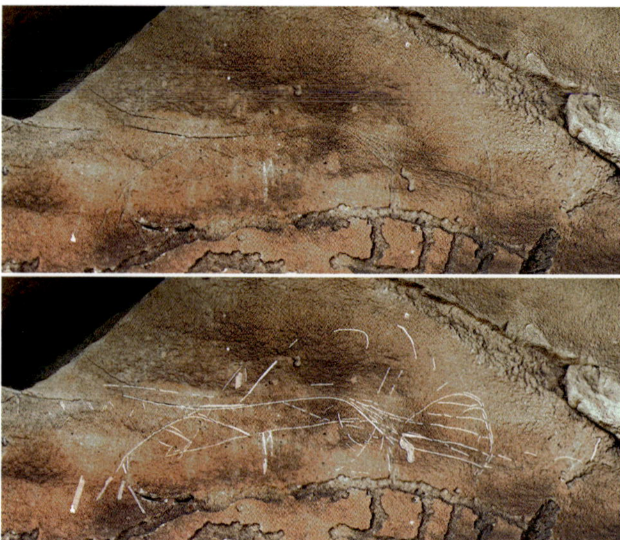

Figure 7. (a) Recent scratched imagery, likely of Protohistoric or Historic age, at the top of Panel 1, the Black Rock site. (b) Overlay tracing of scratched lines. Tracing by Ken Hedges.

How the abstract and geometric imagery fits into this scenario is not discussed.

Contemporaneity aside, Tratebas's interpretation raises several questions, the first of which is her identification of the dated anthropomorph as a "game-calling" shaman (Tratebas 1999:19). In contrast to other regional sites, the zoomorphic images face away from this figure, rather than being called towards it. Although younger, several panels at Rocky Ridge (42DA14), near the Wyoming/Utah state line, contain human figures facing and which appear to be beckoning or calling to groups of elk or sheep (Loendorf and Castañeda 2021:35,43,69). Tratebas (1999:20) also infers that the tallest anthropomorph represents a "similar ceremonial figure." However, this figure also appears to be facing the opposite direction from the animal images. Furthermore, how the superimposition of this figure on the lower mountain sheep relates to game-calling is unclear.

A second question is the notion of a human "surround" without the aid of traps, corrals, or weaponry. Intensive utilization of mountain sheep in the Absaroka Range north of Black Rock dates as old as Cody times (Page 2016), and evidence for Late Prehistoric, Protohistoric, and Historic use of deadfall drive lines, catchpens, and nets to trap mountain sheep is abundant (Eakin 2005; Francis et al. 2022; Frison et al. 1986; Kornfeld et al. 2010:304–312; Scheiber and Finley 2017; Sundstrom and Walker 2021). Similar hunting techniques are described in the ethnographic literature (Fowler 1986:79, 81; Steward 1933:253; Thomas et al. 1986:267) and are replicated in the regional rock art, most notably in Paleoindian age rock art at Whoop-up Canyon (48WE60) (Tratebas 2018). There, several panels clearly depict animals impaled from above being driven into nets or enclosures by humans (see illustration in Kornfeld et al. 2010:314). Similar scenes occur at Rocky Ridge along with a few scenes of humans prodding animals with some type of implement (Loendorf and Castañeda 2021:49, 54, 63, 74, 98, 99). Little on Panel 1 at Black Rock suggests functional traps or enclosures, weaponry, or humans actively pursuing or dispatching game, as is seen at other sites. The ladderlike design could possibly represent a net or fence. However, its position, above and slightly right of the dated anthropomorph, with the elk and two sheep at some distance left and below of, and facing away from a possible net or fence, does not suggest an active hunting scene. That, and the physical continuity between all the pecked elements on the upper part of the panel, suggests a symbolic, if not metaphorical, nature for the ladderlike motif, as well as complex spiritual relationships between humans and animals.

Rather than a contemporaneous scene, Black Rock represents a palimpsest of images and scenes with changing meanings and understanding to different visitors to the site over time. The integration of abstract imagery with the early Paleoindian trilobed anthropomorph and mountain sheep conveys the impression of visionary experience and the acquisition or expression of supernatural power from powerful animals (Whitley 2000:58, 89). The feathered anthropomorph conveys a much different spiritual nature. The feathered headdress of the tall anthropomorph and human/birdlike images may be a metaphorical expression of the taller figure's power. The substance emerging from the head of the tall figure evokes accounts of the shaman's healing rituals, which can include blowing tobacco smoke (Zigmond 1986:406). The near obliteration of the mountain sheep by the feathered figure literally suggests imposition of one type of power over another. Minor enhancements through smoothing and incising of some images attest to later visits to the site. The unvarnished pecking has generally been placed in open areas, as if to fill in empty space on the panel, and only one older image has been defaced by more recent pecking. Furthermore, in contrast to many sites where scratching superimposes older petroglyphs, the most recent scratched images have been placed above the pecked images. This suggests that the spiritual power of the ancient imagery was recognized by more recent site visitors.

Concluding Thoughts

Black Rock has been considered in a somewhat monolithic manner by all who have previously mentioned or reported on the site. Despite having an age estimate for only one image, the heavy varnish development has resulted in a presumption of great antiquity and stylistic similarity for all imagery at the site (see Francis 2018:160; Tratebas 1999, 2018). Indeed, the site as a whole has been characterized as "Paleoindian" rock art sometimes lumped within the Early Hunting Tradition (Keyser and Klassen 2001:82). Tratebas (2018:73–74) correctly points out considerable differences between Black Rock, the Early Hunting petroglyphs of the Black Hills, and the Legend Rock Outline Complex of Paleoindian/Early Archaic age of the Bighorn and Wind River Basins (Francis 2018:162–165). Black Rock highlights the diversity of Paleoindian and more recent belief systems, and it is a complex, "multicomponent" site where, beginning in Paleoindian times, rock art has been created over the course of the entire Holocene.

Acknowledgments. We wish to thank the late Joe Bosovich for finding Black Rock, recognizing its importance, and diligently protecting it for so many years. Thanks also go out to Dudley Gardner for filling out the first site form and to Russ Tanner for encouraging us to include Black Rock in the 1990s dating studies. Ron Dorn, and his tireless research on rock coatings, is also deeply appreciated for his interest and curiosity about Wyoming rock art. We also very much appreciate Jack Brink for his insightful comments and meticulous editing.

References Cited

Ahlbrandt, Thomas S.
  1974 Dune Stratigraphy, Archaeology, and the Chronology of the Killpecker Dune Field. In *Applied Geology and Archaeology: The Holocene History of Wyoming*, edited by Michael Wilson, pp. 51–57. The Geological Survey of Wyoming Report of Investigations No. 10, Laramie.

Cole, Sally J.
  1990 *Legacy on Stone: Rock Art of the Colorado Plateau and Four Corners Region.* Johnson Books, Boulder, Colorado.

Dorn, Ronald I.
  1998 Age Determination of the Coso Rock Art. In *Coso Rock Art: A New Perspective*, edited by Elva Younkin, pp. 67–96. Maturango Press, Ridgecrest, California.

Eakin, Daniel H.
  2005 Evidence for Shoshonean Mountain Sheep Trapping and Early Historic Occupation of the Absaroka Mountains of Northwest Wyoming. In *University of Wyoming, National Park Service Research Center 29th Annual Report*, edited by Henry J. Harlow and Maryanne Harlow, pp. 74–86. University of Wyoming, Laramie.

Fowler, Catherine S.
1986 Subsistence. In *Handbook of North American Indians, Volume 11: Great Basin*, edited by Warren L. D'Azevedo, pp. 64–97. Smithsonian Institution, Washington, D.C.

Francis, Julie E.
2018 Age Estimates and Classification of Pecked Rock Art. In *Dinwoody Dissected: Looking at the Interrelationships between Central Wyoming Petroglyphs*, edited by Danny N. Walker, pp. 159–184. Wyoming Archaeological Society, Casper.

Francis, Julie E., and Lawrence L. Loendorf
2002 *Ancient Visions: Petroglyphs and Pictographs of the Wind River and Bighorn Country, Wyoming and Montana*. University of Utah Press, Salt Lake City.

Francis, Julie E., Lawrence L. Loendorf, Marcel Kornfeld, Mary Lou Larson, and James M. Adovasio
2022 Down the Rabbit Hole: Comment on Sundstrom and Walker (2021). *American Antiquity* 87(3):620–622.

Frison, George C., Rhonda L. Andrews, James M. Adovasio, Ronald Carlisle, and Robert Edgar
1986 A Late Paleoindian Animal Trapping Net from Northern Wyoming. *American Antiquity* 51:352–361.

Gardner, Dudley, and Joseph Bosovich
1984 IMACS site form, 48SW5952. On file at the Wyoming SHPO Cultural Records Office, Laramie.

Kautzman, Matthew, and Jana Pastor
2002 *The Bosovich Site Complex: Archaeological Investigations at the North and South Table Mountain Site*. Report prepared by Archaeological Services of Western Wyoming College for the Bureau of Land Management, Rock Springs. On file at the Wyoming SHPO Cultural Records Office, Laramie.

Keyser, James D., and Angelo Eugenio Fossati
2014 Pecked Petroglyphs at the Gateway Site: The Uncompahgre Style in the Green River Basin. *The Wyoming Archaeologist* 58(2):13–28.

Keyser, James D., and Michael A. Klassen
2001 *Plains Indian Rock Art*. University of Washington Press, Seattle.

Kornfeld, Marcel, George C. Frison, and Mary Lou Larson
2010 *Prehistoric Hunters-Gatherers of the High Plains and Rockies*. Third edition. Left Coast Press, Walnut Creek, California.

Laughlin, John P.
2010 National Register Nomination Form, 48SW5, the Finley Site. On file with the Wyoming SHPO Cultural Records Office, Laramie.

Liu, Tanzao, and Ronald I. Dorn
1996 Understanding the Spatial Variability of Environmental Change in Drylands with Rock Varnish Microlaminations. *Annals of the Association of American Geographers* 86(2):187–212.

Loendorf, Lawrence, and Amanda Castañeda
2021 *Rock Art Recording at the Rocky Ridge Site (42DA14), Manila, Utah*. Prepared by Sacred Sites Research, Albuquerque, New Mexico.

Loendorf, Lawrence L., and Audrey Porsche
1985 *The Rock Art Sites of Carbon County, Montana*. Contribution No. 224. Department of Anthropology, University of North Dakota, Grand Forks.

Love, J. D., and Anne Coe Christiansen
1985 *Geological Map of Wyoming*. United States Geological Survey, Denver.

Murray, Susan, and Kevin W. Thompson
1999 *The Bosovich Site Complex Status Report*. Western Wyoming College Contributions to Archaeology No. 14, Rock Springs.

Page, Michael K.
2016 *The Goff Creek Site (48PA325): Prehistoric Bighorn Sheep Procurement in the Absaroka Mountains of Northwestern Wyoming*. Cultural Resource Series No. 3, Office of the Wyoming State Archaeologist, Laramie.

Scheiber, Laura L., and Judson Byrd Finley
2017 Mountain Shoshone Technological Traditions Across the Great Divide. In *Across a Great Divide: Continuity and Change in Native North American Societies, 1400–1900*, edited by Laura L. Scheiber and Mark Mitchell, pp. 128–152. University of Arizona Press, Tucson.

Smith, Gene, and Thomas Miller
2016 Wyoming Cultural Properties Form, 48SW13618. On file with the SHPO Cultural Records Office, Laramie.

Steward, Julian H.
1933 *Ethnography of the Owens Valley Paiute*. University of California Publications in American Archaeology and Ethnology 33(3):233–350. Berkeley.

Sundstrom, Linea, and Danny N. Walker
2021 The Sheep Mountain Animal Net Revisited. *American Antiquity* 86(4):833–844.

Tanner, Russel, Joseph Bosovich, Julie E. Francis, and Ronald I. Dorn
1995 The Black Rock Petroglyph: A Possible Clovis-age Rock Art Site. Paper presented at the 52nd Annual Plains Conference, Laramie, Wyoming.

Thomas, David Hurst, Lorann S. A. Pendleton, and Stephen C. Cappannari
1986 Western Shoshone. In *Handbook of North American Indians, Volume 11: Great Basin*, edited by Warren L. D'Azevedo, pp. 262–283. Smithsonian Institution, Washington, D.C.

Tratebas, Alice M.
1999 The Earliest Petroglyph Traditions on the North American Plains. In *Dating and the Earliest Known Rock Art*, edited by Matthias Strecker and Paul Bahn, pp. 16–27. Oxbow Books, London.

2018 Distinguishing the Early Hunting Tradition from Other Regional Petroglyph Styles. In *Dinwoody Dissected: Looking at the Interrelationships between Central Wyoming Petroglyphs*, edited by Danny N. Walker, pp. 59–76. Wyoming Archaeological Society, Casper.

Walker, Danny N. (editor)
2018 *Dinwoody Dissected: Looking at the Interrelationships between Central Wyoming Petroglyphs*. Wyoming Archaeological Society, Casper.

Whitley, David S.
2000 *The Art of the Shaman: Rock Art of California*. University of Utah Press, Salt Lake City.

2018 Early Northern Plains Rock Art in Context. In *Dinwoody Dissected: Looking at the Interrelationships between Central Wyoming Petroglyphs*, edited by Danny N. Walker, pp. 21–34. Wyoming Archaeological Society, Casper.

Willis, Mark
2018 48SW5952 Panel 1—Enhanced. Sketchfab.com (online). Electronic document, https://sketchfab.com/3d-models/48sw5952-panel-1-enhanced-144ab7490947478fa03854764937f273, accessed July 30, 2022.

Zigmond, Maurice L.
1986 Kawaiisu. In *Handbook of North American Indians, Volume 11: Great Basin*, edited by Warren L. D'Azevedo, pp. 398–411. Smithsonian Institution, Washington, D.C.

Rivers, Rocks, and Rain—Petroglyphs of Southwest Oregon

David A. Kaiser

Rock art is common in the eastern half of Oregon, but relatively rare west of the Cascade Mountains. While the handful of sites found in the Willamette Valley and the Cascade foothills are relatively well known, a cluster of little-studied rock art exists in southwestern Oregon, where the Northwest Coast and California culture areas meet. Initial in-person investigations and a survey of the literature give context to two previously unrecorded sites as well as reexamination of the distribution patterns of Far Western Pit and Groove, Pecked Curvilinear Nucleated (PCN), and Northwest Coast rock art traditions.

Rock art in Oregon's rain-soaked western half of the state occurs much less frequently than in the drier part of the state east of the Cascade Mountains. While much of the art of the Willamette Valley and Cascade foothills has been documented and discussed (Kaiser 2016; Kaiser and Cleary 2020; Keyser 2005; Loring and Loring 1982a:152–159, 214–220; Poetschat et al. 2010), the petroglyphs of southwest Oregon have received little attention. So, a recent project set out to record two previously undocumented sites and investigate several more reported in the literature, some officially recognized and several others appearing as brief mentions in non-archaeological publications.

Elk Rock

Elk Rock, located along the South Fork of the Coos River, east of Coos Bay, has been an enigma to rock art researchers. The only published image of the site is in the region-wide rock art survey by Loring and Loring (1982b:Figure 144e). The authors include a sketchy drawing of an elk's head and neck, with a rack of antlers on top (Figure 1). The image was traced from a photograph sent to them by John O. Hess of Portland in 1965. The Lorings explain that the size and exact location of the figure were unknown to them. In Keyser's report on the rock art of western Oregon, he did not include Elk Rock in his study of known sites as it seemed "unlikely to be of native origin" (Keyser 2005:73, Note 2). In addition to the general paucity of rock art west of the Cascades, representative, non-geometric rock art is even more rare in the area.

However, the existence of several references to Elk Rock in non-archaeological contexts, including historical mentions, pointed to its early existence and Native origin. Along the Coos

Figure 1. Elk Rock as sketched by Loring and Loring (1982b) from a photograph provided by John O. Hess in 1965.

David A. Kaiser
Oregon Archaeological Society, Portland

River an early schoolhouse was established around 1884 which was nicknamed "Quin College" after a local landowner, but its official name was Elk Rock School (Mahaffy 1965:40). In a letter describing her teaching days in the early twentieth century, Smith (1963:4)[1] explains that the name was "derived from a flat-faced rock bluff overhanging the river just above and across from the schoolhouse. On this rock was drawn an elk's head said to be the work of an Indian, many years ago." There was also mention of a home along the South Coos River named "Elk Rock Lodge" (Coos Bay Times 1914). Prior to extensive road building, the rivers were the primary means of transport in the area, and it is said that "riverboat passengers traveling on the South Fork were familiar with the picture of an elk's head painted on a flat-faced rock" (Mahaffy 1965:2).

In addition, "The Legend of Elk Rock" was published in a local journal in 1906.[2] The story was written by Agnes Sengstacken, a prominent local woman, under her maiden name, Agnes Ruth Lockhart (1906). It told the tragic tale of two Indian lovers who courted near a prominent rock along the river and were married. One day, years later, the man went hunting elk near this same rock, but, unbeknownst to him, this time his wife went looking for him. Unsuccessful in the hunt, the man was just about to leave when he saw movement in the woods nearby. Loosing an arrow, his sure aim hit the mark, but was accompanied by a terrible human cry. He had shot his wife, who died in his arms. Her body was found near this riverside stone, and she was buried nearby. Her husband disappeared, never to be seen again; only his broken bow was found floating in the river.

The tale goes on to describe that when the members of the tribe returned to the location they "were amazed and terror-stricken to see upon the front of the rock where it faced the river, the glowing figure of an elk! Dignified and beautiful, tinted with the ruddy hue of nature, the image of the noble creature stood out bold and clear upon the rough surface, as though instinct with life. How and when the majestic animal was pictured there, no human tongue can tell, for the mystery of its appearance has never been solved" (Lockhart 1906:15).

A resident of the city of Coos Bay (then known as Marshfield), Agnes Sengstacken, née Lockhart, was a lecturer, writer, and poet, as well as collector of Native basketry and clothing. In the same year she published "The Legend of Elk Rock" she also published *A Legend of the Coos*, a short book poetically telling another tragic story of other Indian lovers (Lockhart 1909b). But

how authentic were these legends? Typical of much pioneer "fakelore" these romantic legends use prominent landscape features and names, and often tell tales of heroic Indian braves and their princess brides—just such characters occur in her stories. The lack of supernatural figures and elements is also unlike other authentic indigenous lore in the region (e.g., Jacobs 1940; St. Clair and Frachtenberg 1909). However, the description of the elk carving on the rock is certainly based on a real image.

More reliably, Joseph Maloney, an ethnographer from the University of California, visited the area in 1931. His notes describe him camping near Elk Rock on July 27th of that year. While there he "took daylight and flash light [sic] pictures of elk rock, hoping to get trace of traditional carving. No results" (Maloney 1931). While supporting the existence of the carving, this points to its poor condition at the time. Furthermore, 25 years earlier, at the end of "The Legend of Elk Rock," the state of the image is described. "Summer's heat and winter's frost have worked their will upon the sandstone rock, dimming the natural color of the elk and almost obliterating its rugged outlines" (Lockhart 1906:15). Additionally, it was reported that "during strong feeling against the Indians a renegade white man took a chisel and tried to obliterate the picture. An attempt to restore it was made by Susie Quist (Hanson) and her sister Charlotte (Baer)" (Smith 1963:4). So, between the early and mid-twentieth century the image had been variously reported faded, destroyed, and restored.

Taking the various descriptions, tales, and reports in mind, the author set out to see if the site still existed. An initial survey of the area was conducted on land, but nothing could be found matching the descriptions. I later took to the water, paddling a kayak along the lower Coos River searching for the elusive image. Apart from various reports of its poor condition, I was discouraged by the sheer lack of rock faces of any size along this portion of the river.

However, I eventually came across a large, vertical rock surface jutting out of the river, with a prominent overhang protecting the surface. Now somewhat hidden by a thick growth of ivy hanging from above, a large image of an elk stood out prominently (Figure 2). Deeply carved in profile, the image shows the animal's back, neck, and head with an eye and mouth, topped with six-pointed antlers (Figure 3). The image is approximately a meter square. The art is of a Euro-American style, particularly the overlapping perspective of the antlers. The underside of the animal's neck

Figure 2. Above the Coos River, Elk Rock is partially hidden by hanging ivy.

Figure 3. "Restored" Elk Rock petroglyph. Note the natural cracks forming the animal's rear leg.

also lacks the long hairs often shown in Native depictions of elk, differentiating them from other cervids.[3] The deep grooves of the ear and antlers are painted with a fading commercial white pigment. This paint remains only on the upper portion of the image where it is most protected by the overhang.

So, reports of its "restoration" after the chisel attack appear true. The rock surface above the elk's back and behind its head is somewhat rough and pitted, perhaps evidence of the use of such a tool to chip away the art. But how accurate was the restoration by the Euro-American women? There is no way of knowing for sure. The rough sketch of the image published in Loring and Loring (1982b:Figure 144e) bears a close resemblance to what remains there now, so it was not likely traced from a photograph of the original image.

There is also confusion in the early reports as to whether the image was a pictograph or a petroglyph. Pictographs are uncommon in western Oregon and northern California, and no remaining faded pigment

was revealed using DStretch color-enhancing software. Lockhart (1906:15) ambiguously describes the image as "tinted with the ruddy hue of nature." Maloney (1931) interviewed an old-time resident who "remembered the carving, said it was painted blue." Mahaffy (1965:2) also says the image was painted. Granted that none of these people were trained in documenting rock art, but it remains unclear if the original image was painted or carved, or both. Based on Maloney, it may well have been both, such as exists today. Equally, if it was regularly viewed by river traffic, a carving might well have been painted by early settlers to enhance visibility or during the restoration efforts. Even today, the image must be recognized by some who still use the river, as the ivy directly in front of the image had been removed. However, there is no graffiti at the site.

Taking a closer look at the image, it is possible that traces of the original image remain. Inspection of the image reveals a couple of elements that might show parts of the original carved image. Behind the neck of the animal there appears to be a ghost image of another arc showing the neck and back of an elk (Figure 3), but it is unclear. Erosion, lichen growth, and the inability to view it very close up due to its location over the water prevented determination of whether the vertical element is natural or carved, but the connecting horizontal line does appear to be human-made. This line is not in alignment with the back of the clearly visible elk carving, so it does not seem to be an extension of it.

Also of note, to the right of the carved image and aligned with the figure's back is a natural crack that curves downward, making a shape resembling the rump and back leg of an elk (Figure 3). This use of natural features is not unusual in Native rock art, particularly that with a spiritual component. So, it seems likely that if this natural shape were seen, it could have been incorporated into the creation of the original image.

While we now have an imperfect record of the image that was originally at the site, assuming the existing art is an approximation of the original in content, size, and location, it may still help reveal why it was first placed here, at a location that can only be accessed from the river. It is unlikely to be a memorial, such as that described in "The Legend of Elk Rock," but it may be noteworthy that this location is where elk were hunted in the story. Though clearly this could be extrapolated from the image itself, other sources describe how the image "marked the spot where an elk went over the cliff and into the river" (Mahaffy 1965:2). The same explanation is given in Loring and Loring (1982b:9).

Like the buffalo jumps of the Plains Indians, similar descriptions of driving game over precipices occur elsewhere in the Northwest Coast cultural area, along the Oregon coast, and into California (Anell 1969:23-34, Map 3). One of the most prominent, though historically questionable examples is another "Elk Rock," along the Willamette River across from the city of Milwaukie, just south of Portland, Oregon. Multiple early legends tell of an elk, or a herd of elk, being driven over a high cliff to plunge into the river below, where they were killed (Hillsboro Independent 1895; Shelor 1900). This was said to be supported by the discovery of antlers in the water below (Wrenn and Starkweather 1939:6). More reliably, the Kathlamat described driving elk down a cliff on Saddle Mountain near the coast in northwest Oregon, where their bones were broken on the rocks below (Boas 1901:222). Similarly, up the Columbia River, the Wanapum described a location called "Place Where Deer Fall Down" where a hunter with deer power would hunt deer by chasing them over a cliff (Relander 1956:310).

Alternately, Maloney's informant described how elk were once driven down the coulee just up-river from the carving, and into the water where they were helpless and could be easily killed (Maloney 1931). Likewise, this technique was also used at an island along the south slough at Coos Bay, where elk would get caught in the high tide and were easily dispatched (Lindsay 1995:203; Maloney 1931).[4] Moreover, a Coos legend tells how the sons of a woman who married a wolf "would drive live deer or elk down to the river, where the brothers could kill them easily" (St. Clair and Frachtenberg 1909:29–30).

As described by Maloney's informant, there is indeed a coulee just upstream and intervisible with the site (Figure 4). With its raised sides creating a funnel down to the river, this would be a perfect place to drive elk, making them easier to kill. Such water drives were frequently assisted by using dogs to frighten the animals, and watercraft were used in the killing of the mired animals (Anell 1969:100–101). The original art therefore appears connected with hunting, perhaps as a form of hunting magic to attract the animals or ensure success of the hunt. As described in the Wanapum description above, such hunters were often thought to have special animal powers. This idea may have been reinforced if the natural shape of the rump and legs of the elk were recognized and enhanced. Furthermore, when the river is high the elk image would be partially submerged, as evidenced by the discoloration of the ivy surrounding it (Figure 2). This recurring submersion of the lower half of the image, just as the real animals would be during the hunt, indicates a form of sympathetic magic (Keyser and Whitley 2006) in which the repeated manipulation of this motif (the natural submersion in water) is believed to cause similar actions in the physical world (the driving into and killing of elk in the river).

The original art was likely the product of the Hanis- or Miluk-speaking Coos Indians who lived in the area along the rivers and around Coos Bay. An early resident of the area reported that a village site formerly existed along the river below Elk Rock (Maloney 1931). The age of the art is now impossible to determine. Lockhart (1906:15) describes it as faded around the turn of the last century and thought it possibly a hundred years old. It seems unlikely that it could have been significantly older, considering the damp climate and the erosive effects of the river in flood.

So, while disappointingly corrupted by vicious attack and well-meaning restoration, Elk Rock still has things to tell us. Highlighting Native hunting practices, it is also a rare example of representational rock art in the region, though its original details are now lost to us. Unique in this area of Oregon, this representational art appears to originally have been part of a wider indigenous carving tradition in southwest Oregon more commonly finding expression in portable objects (Aikens 1993:178–180; Pullen 2010).

Pit and Groove Rock Art in Southwest Oregon

Only a handful of rock art sites have previously been reported in southwest Oregon (Keyser 2005:3, 5; Loring and Loring 1982b:2), the majority of which consist primarily of cupules, grooves, and geometric shapes. These carvings are classified as Northern Variants of

Figure 4. Coulee leading to river, just upstream from Elk Rock.

the Far Western Pit and Groove tradition (Whitley 2000:47–50) found primarily in California, north of San Francisco, but extending into southern Oregon.

For this project, existing reports, historical accounts, and grey literature were surveyed for other mentions of rock art in southwest Oregon, and limited investigations were conducted as time allowed. Additional sites were discovered, all occurring along rivers, giving a clearer picture of the art and its distribution in the study area. However, to set these in context, I wish to look at the largest assemblage of rock art previously known in the area.

Twomile and the Rogue River

The Rogue River flows from the High Cascades, through several counties in southwest Oregon, before finally reaching the ocean at Gold Beach. Multiple petroglyph sites are known along its course, possibly due to the large size of the sites as well as the heavy river rafting traffic that brings many people into remote areas of the officially designated wild and scenic river.

Petroglyphs along the river have been recognized near Gleason Bar and Brushy Bar, but little information has been published on these sites. Consisting largely of cupules and zigzags, they are characteristic of rock art in the area, exemplified by the Twomile site (35CU66) further downstream. This site is both the largest and best-documented site in the region, consisting of more than 60 carved sandstone boulders at a traditional Tututni fishing and eeling location.

In the early twentieth century, the rapids at Twomile were dynamited to aid river traffic (Beauchamp 2015; Bureau of Land Management and U.S. Forest Service 2004:47), but many carved boulders along the shore remain. Now somewhat overgrown with brush and moss, some of the art can be difficult to locate, while other boulders still stand out prominently (Figure 5). The site has been well known for many years. Elements of the art were sketched and mapped in 1964 by Stephen Dow Beckham (Beauchamp 2015), with more detailed drawings of 29 boulders made by Loring and Loring (1982b:13–15).

In 1977, despite the strong objection of local Native Americans (Curry Coastal Pilot 1977; Kocher 1977), seven of the carved boulders were removed from the site by the Curry County Historical Society to protect the carvings from erosion due to yearly flooding as well as vandalism and theft which had occurred (Burgess 1976). These large rocks were moved to the Curry County Museum at the fairgrounds in Gold

Figure 5. Cupule boulder at Twomile, along the Rogue River.

Beach, about 56 km (35 mi) downstream. These boulders were then moved in 2002 to a museum in Agness, a town near the Rogue River closest to where the rocks originated. This museum closed in 2010, and the boulders were again moved nearby to Agness Park where they are now displayed (Figure 6). While divorced

Figure 6. Petroglyph boulders from Twomile now displayed at Agness Park.

from their original environment, these boulders still clearly reveal their geometric carvings, though some of the designs on boulders placed under tree canopies are beginning to be concealed beneath moss.

The remaining in situ boulders were the focus of a recording project led by Forest Service archaeologist Janet Joyer (Joyer 1996; Joyer and Leen 1996; Leen 1994). Rocks were cleaned of moss and designs were painted with aluminum oxide for photography (Figure 7). Reports reveal art representative of that scattered throughout the region but found here in a large concentration, with approximately 900 cupules, over 30 zigzags, nine triangular vulviforms, and various grooves and other shapes (Joyer and Leen 1996:4–5). Largely lacking representational elements, these designs, with a predominance of cupules, are typical of the Far Western Pit and Groove tradition.

Figure 7. Designs were painted with aluminum oxide for photography during the 1994 recording at Twomile. Note the natural vulviform shape of the rock. Image courtesy of Dan Leen.

Similar sites found in northern California are commonly associated by numerous tribes with rain making and weather control (Driver 1939:421; Heizer 1953) and are commonly known as "rain rocks." Through analogy, the art at Twomile has been interpreted along the same lines (Joyer 1996; Joyer and Leen 1996). Many carved boulders at this site and others are situated between low and high waterlines, being periodically inundated. Rituals would help to bring rain to raise water levels and wash away silt at the mouths of rivers, allowing fish to return upstream. According to Kathy Leep, a Native woman who volunteered in the 1994 recording project, the petroglyphs were there to "scare away 'Apitiwa,' the Indian fish devil, who kept the fish away" (Joyer 1996:33), and she recalled her grandfather burning offerings in the cupules at the site. While clearly connected with fish runs, such art has also been associated with human fertility (Whit-

ley 2000:98–101), as evidenced by the vulviforms at Twomile (Figure 7).

Beyond their ritual function, one of the large stones at Twomile was associated with a mythical story. Describing a smooth river rock, Waterman (1925:541) reported, "This rock was once, in the Indian belief, a person. On the face of this rock, near the river, are some petroglyphs, covered with patches of moss." It is unclear which exact rock this is, or other details, but it was described as located along the river near the town of Agness. However, this adds the witnessing of traditional stories in the landscape as another function of the rock art in the region.

In addition to the previously recognized petroglyphs on the Rogue, another site further upstream has been reported below Winkle Bar, near Zane Grey's historic cabin. This panel consists of at least two ovals[5] pecked into a vertical rock face rising out of the water, as shown on various river rafting websites (e.g., Van Marmot and Van Marmot 2016). This site has not been recorded, but it indicates the likelihood of other sites along the river that have not been recognized.

Coquille River

Between the Rogue and Coos rivers to the north, the Coquille runs through Coos County and into the Pacific Ocean at Bandon. Three pecked petroglyph boulders with Northwest Coast tradition images were reported on the South Fork of the Coquille above Powers (AP News 1990). Discovered in 1987, the site was recorded, and replicas were made to allow campers to make rubbings at Daphne Grove Campground nearby (Forest Service 1989:Siskiyou National Forest). These images included a large, stylized fish (Figure 8).

However, once this discovery became newsworthy, Jeff Kerker of Bandon came forward claiming to have carved them about fifteen years earlier (AP News 1990). Producing photographs of the newly completed images, he was able to prove that he created the carv-

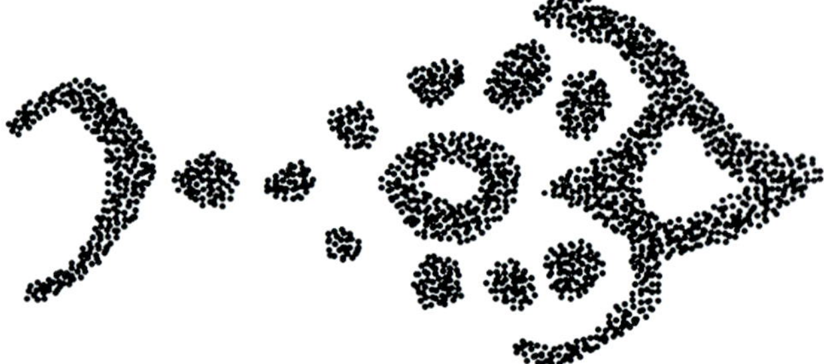

Figure 8. Tracing of a Northwest Coast style fish, one of the fake petroglyphs found along the Coquille River.

ings. This was embarrassing to the professionals involved in verifying the images. To make matters worse, a syndicated article describing the error was published around the country (AP News 1990) and the case was later included in the book *Dumb History: The Stupidest Mistakes Ever Made* (Green 2012).

It is interesting to note that avocational rock art recorders Malcolm and Louise Loring, who extensively documented the rock art of the Northwest (Loring and Loring 1982a and b), lived in Coquille, a town along the river between Powers and Bandon. In addition to documenting rock art, they also created replicas of various images to use for education. Could they have inadvertently inspired Kerker to experiment with making his own art?

While some of the criticism leveled at the archaeologists was justified, it highlights the difficulties encountered when verifying indigenous rock art. The art found near Powers did not consist of copies of specific known images, which would have been recognized. They were original designs but echoed the style of Northwest Coast art, and were also eroded, as they were below the high waterline of the river. It is therefore understandable how mistakes in authentication such as this could occur. Another outlying but genuine Northwest Coast tradition image is found in southern Oregon at Medicine Creek Rockshelter (Keyser 2005:58), so it was not beyond the realm of possibility to find similar images here. However, in the case of the Coquille petroglyphs, the investigators failed to take the large flood of 1964 into account, which would have displaced or destroyed the rocks. Lessons were learned about the process of verification of Native art, but it has led to ongoing confusion about the existence of petroglyphs along the Coquille in this area (e.g., Pullen 2010:337).

Another petroglyph found by the river was incised on a flat rock discovered near the Johnson Mill Pond (or Log Pond) just south of the city of Coquille (Dunn et al. 2018:14). Consisting of a handful of incised rectilinear geometric shapes (Figure 9), it is unclear if the carving originated in the Coquille Valley. The designs and technique are unlike other known petroglyphs in southwest Oregon, but comparisons are limited to a relatively small sample. The rock with the carving was given to James Metcalf, chairperson of the Coquille Indian Tribe at the time,[6] and is now believed to reside with the tribe.

Umpqua River

Further north, along the Umpqua River, a large fishing site was located at the rapids near Scottsburg,

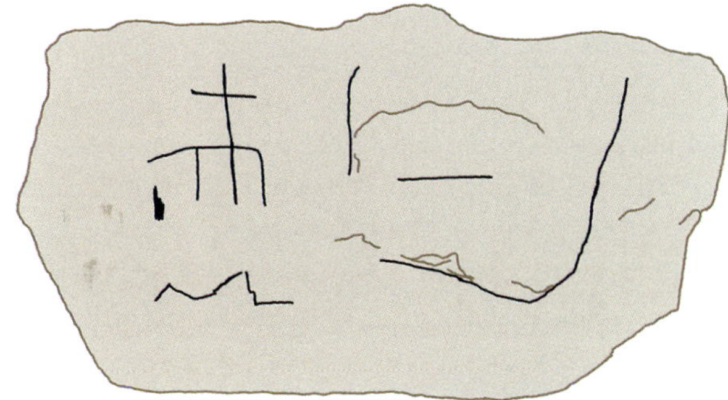

Figure 9. Photo-tracing of incised stone found along the Coquille River.

as illustrated by Captain Albert Lyman around 1850 (Whereat Phillips 2017:7). Like Twomile on the Rogue River, this area was dynamited to aid river navigation. While the rapids were destroyed, Scottsburg remained the headwaters of navigation on the Umpqua, acting as a transfer point between stage lines and steamboat traffic on the river.

Despite the changes made to this portion of the river, petroglyphs have been reported on the bed of the Umpqua nearby. These are said to be visible only for a few months of the year when the river is low (Smoke Signals 2001:5). Undocumented, these images are said to be rapidly eroding in the flow of the river. A carving of a water beetle is reported at the site (Aikens 1993:180). Water beetles were considered good luck amongst the Coos, and this beetle may have been an attempt to ensure successful fishing at the site (Pullen 2010:335).

These carvings were not discovered during a limited preliminary investigation of the area via kayak. However, a more thorough search is likely to reveal these locally known images. What was found was a large cupule-covered boulder, near the former rapids (Figure 10). This 1.2-meter boulder has more than 30 cupules scattered across its surface, some quite large and deep,

Figure 10. Recently identified cupule boulder along the Umpqua River.

while others are shallow and largely eroded. Also nearby, hidden beneath snags of trees along the river, are what appeared to be additional cupule-marked stones, but these could not be verified due to their inaccessibility. Formal recording of this boulder and verification of other nearby imagery awaits further fieldwork.

The area was traditionally used by the Penutian-speaking Kalapuyans, the Siuslaw-speaking Lower Umpqua, as well as Athapaskan speaking Upper Umpqua. This boulder located along the river and covered in cupules is typical of many other sites in the region. Most probably associated with weather control, this site is likely another example of a "rain rock."

Further upriver, at the Bottle Creek Site (Loring and Loring 1982b:3) red painted abstract geometric shapes juxtaposed with stick figure anthropomorphs are found in small rock cavities near the Umpqua River. Such images are typical of vision quest imagery throughout the Columbia Plateau (Keyser 1992). This art is classified as part of the High Cascade style generally found in the Cascade Mountains (Keyser 2005:54–56).

Smith River

Elizabeth Morrissey's family lived in Douglas County along the Smith River, a tributary of the larger Umpqua River. She described a rain rock in the river near Spencer Creek. "We were told never to beat on that rock. The Indians used to come up and camp near the falls in the summer, catch eels and smoke them for winter. When they headed back down the river in the fall, they stopped at the rock. They held their ceremony to bring the fall rains, beating on the rock with sticks" (Whereat Phillips 2017:7). Morrissey does not specifically describe any rock art, but the tradition of cupule stones and "rain rocks" are common throughout southwest Oregon and northwest California, and this appears to be such a site. I was unable to examine the river in the area to confirm this petroglyph or assess its condition due to access issues across surrounding private land.

Siuslaw River

An intriguing possibility for the northernmost extent of the rain rock tradition in the study area is found along the Siuslaw River in Lane County, running from the central Oregon Coast Range to the coastal town of Florence. About 32 km (20 mi) upstream is an area known as Rainrock. Named by H. L. Walter for a stop on the Southern Pacific railway, he claimed the appellation was "arbitrary and it has no particular significance"

(McArthur 1927:78–79). However, considering the rock art associated with weather control traditions found along the rivers to the south, it bears investigation. There is significant exposed rock along the river in this area, but no in-person examination was made as part of this project.

Distribution

With the exceptions of the incised stone along the Coquille, and the reported but undiscovered water beetle carving on the Umpqua, all the newly identified sites are classified as Northern Variants of the Far Western Pit and Groove tradition. The inclusion of these new sites helps build a better picture of the distribution of this art tradition in the region (Figure 11).

An isolated cluster of four Pit and Groove sites has been previously identified in the lower Willamette

Figure 11. Rock art sites in western Oregon showing rivers discussed in the text.

Valley, associated with southern Kalapuyan groups (Keyser 2005:5, 52; Loring and Loring 1982a:218–219, 1982b:4–5). Another cluster of three other sites was noted along the Rogue River, as discussed above, and a final small cupule site near the head of the Rogue River, lies just north of the California border by Emigrant Creek (Keyser 2005:5, 52). However, with the addition of these newly recognized and probable sites, the gaps in the distribution of these previously isolated sites begins to fill in. A fuller constellation of Pit and Groove sites extends from northern California along the coastal rivers in southwest Oregon and into the southern Willamette Valley. The outlying cupule site at Emigrant Creek might be associated with the Klamath rock art tradition, which also associated cupule creation with weather control (Spier 1930:21, 141). Future investigation is likely to reveal even more sites in the region, further completing this distribution pattern.

PCNs at 35CU142

A related but different style of art is found at the base of a steep incline leading to the ocean, south of the town of Port Orford in Curry County. A horizontal boulder about two meters wide is covered in cupules, circles, and other geometric shapes (Figure 12). Site 35CU142 is on a remote area of State Park land and sits near the outlet of a small ephemeral stream. The petroglyph boulder sits on the edge of the sandy beach, and is regularly inundated by higher tides, as is evident from the abundant tidal debris further up the hillside. Nearby is a series of small rockshelters and a large midden containing shell and fire-cracked rock. While previously reported, the rock art at the site had never been fully documented.

All petroglyphs at 35CU142 are pecked. Circular shapes dominate the art (Figure 13). There are 18 small cupules scattered across the rock; most are quite circular, but one is rather elongated, and another has a short "tail" appended. Larger circular and oval shapes dominate the art, with 19 circles ranging from 8 cm to 39 cm across. Seven of the circles are nucleated, one made with a wide, deeply carved oval around a large, bas relief protrusion in the center. Another deeply pecked, large circle surrounds a broken, jagged scarred center. A pair of circles and a circle and cupule are each joined by a thin line connecting them, creating barbell shapes. Another shallow line or groove occurs near the largest nucleated circle. Two arcs might also be incomplete or eroded circles. Two areas also have small clusters of scattered peck marks.

Figure 12. Seaside petroglyph boulder at 35CU142.

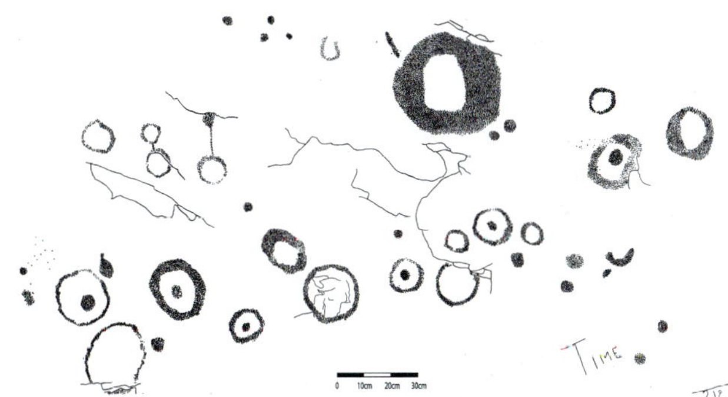

Figure 13. Tracing of designs at 35CU142.

While somewhat eroded, the art is in good condition. There are small scratches across the boulder likely occurring from ocean debris washing across the rock. However, despite its remote location and the difficulty accessing the site, there is graffiti on one corner of the rock. The word "Time" is incised in large letters, and nearby in smaller letters is what appears to be the number "21" and a tailed circle, possibly intended to be a balloon. The site was first described in the literature in 1982 by Reg Pullen, who noted "shallow circular depressions that appear to be petroglyphs."[7] It was more fully described by Rick Minor (1986:96–97) as part of a survey of archaeological sites on State Park land along the coast. In addition to the cupules, he also describes four large "vulviforms" carved on the rock. While there are no shapes at the site that would generally be identified as vulviforms, there are four large, nucleated circles. Minor associates the art with the "rain rocks" and "baby rocks" of northern California, with their noted fertility associations. It is therefore likely that he interpreted these nucleated forms to be vulva shapes. Further north, also in Curry County at the Twomile site, the large assemblage of cupule boulders includes what would more traditionally be identified as vulviforms.

It wasn't until 1994 that two of the large circular shapes were identified as part of the Pecked Curvilinear Nucleated (PCN) tradition,[8] found in northern California (Fentress 1994:2). Occurring in the North Coast range of California, PCNs (Figure 14) were first defined by Teresa Miller (now Saltzman) as consisting primarily of "circles and ovals, which have nuclei that appear raised. They seldom occur in any discernable pattern. The elements are pecked into the surface of the rock" (Miller 1977:44). PCNs are frequently carved into chlorite schist boulders (Gillette 2011; Miller 1977:44), as is the case at 35CU142 where it occurs on a large, flat blueschist metavolcanic rock.

Figure 14. *PCNs at the type site on Ring Mountain in Marin County, California. Image courtesy of Ken Hedges.*

The large PCN at the site is pecked 5 cm deep around the perimeter, giving the center a distinctly raised appearance (Figure 15). With a diameter of 39 cm this is one of the largest PCN carvings reported, Gillette and Miller Saltzman (2003:106) reporting that "PCN elements range in size from 3 cm to as large as 25 cm." The second PCN identified at the site is now damaged. The outer circle is pecked 4 cm deep, but the remaining interior protuberance has

Figure 15. *Large PCN at 35CU142 with bas-relief nucleus on right. Broken PCN on left of image.*

been removed (Figure 15). Such "missing" nucleated PCN centers are noted at many other sites. While some researchers have hypothesized that the centers of the carvings were damaged or removed by a later culture group (Parkman 1993), others have put forward the idea that the centers were removed to create charmstones (Parkman 1993; Rhode 1991). However, when performing replication experiments, Gillette (2011:63) discovered that "a misplaced hammerstone, while pecking, would result in the abrupt removal of the nucleated portion." Therefore, the missing nuclei here and at other sites are most likely the result of an accident in their initial creation.

The PCN art at 35CU142 marks the northernmost example of this tradition, primarily located along the coast range north of San Francisco, in Marin, Sonoma, and Mendocino counties (Gillette 2011:3) (Figure 16). A possible second far north example in Oregon has been reported near the Umpqua River, based on a single photograph (Gillette 2011:62), but its exact location is unknown, and it has not been verified.

There are numerous factors that make the art at 35CU142 difficult to date with certainty. Several researchers estimate the age of manufacture of PCNs between 5000 and 8000 years B.P. (Gillette 2011; Miller 1977; Parkman 1993), without much supporting empirical data, apart from their consistent occurrence as the oldest motif in superimposition sequences. However, no such superimpositions exist at this site. On the other hand, Heizer and Clewlow (1973:29–31) include PCNs as part of California's North Coast petroglyph style, which they estimate began "no earlier than the late 1500's or early 1600's." Whitley (2000:47–50) calls this style the Northern Variant of Far Western Pit and Groove Tradition. He points out that we have significant ethnology on the creation of Far Western

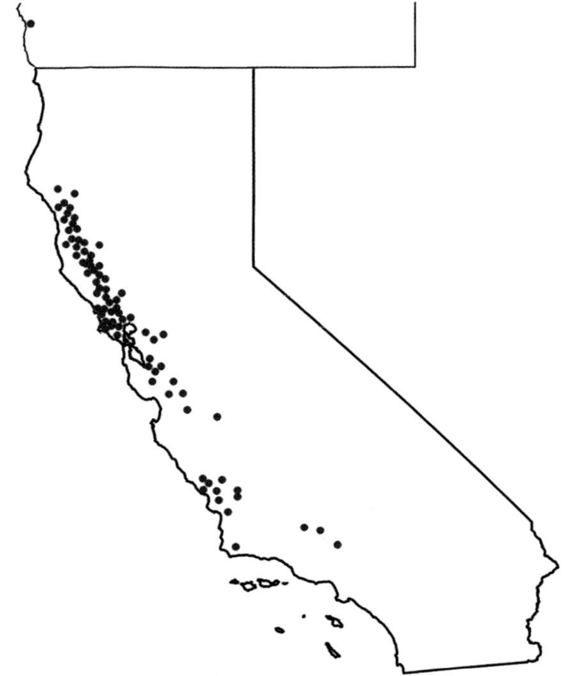

Figure 16. Distribution of PCN rock art in California (after Gillette 2011:3), and the outlying site at 35CU142 in Oregon.

Pit and Groove art, and much of it must be of relatively recent manufacture.

It is just possible that the boulder is not in its original position. The rock could have moved into its current position during a landslip event, or have been buried in a landslide, protecting the carvings, and only recently been exposed again due to coastal erosion. However, the placement of the art only on the upper face of the horizontal rock does not lend credence to the idea of significant movement of the stone.

A nearby shell midden was radiocarbon dated to 1050 ± 70 years old (Erlandson 2021), showing activity in the area about a thousand years ago. While not necessarily directly associated with the rock art, it indicates a time when the area was in use and may indicate a similar early date for the petroglyph's manufacture. Most significantly, however, the degree of erosion at the 35CU142 site does not indicate great age, especially considering the erosive action of the waves and debris that routinely wash over the boulder.

The Northern Variant of the Far Western Pit and Groove tradition includes cupule boulders described as rain rocks in Tolowa, Karok, and Hupa tribal areas, and as baby rocks in the area occupied by the Pomo in northern California. While both traditions had to do with renewal and fertility, rain rocks focused primarily on weather control and the increased rain swelling the rivers allowing the passage of fish, whereas baby rocks had more to do with human reproductive fertility. A majority of PCN carvings occur in the Pomo tribal area, and therefore such art has generally been interpreted through their ethnographic traditions. Indeed, some PCN carvings have direct ethnographic description of their creation and functions (Gillette 2011:90–95; Hedges 1983; Marymor 1998).

Baby rocks were visited by both Pomo men and women to cure sterility. Various rituals were performed including cutting the rock (Loeb 1926:247–248) or making "upon the surface of the stone a large carving representing a genital" (Barrett 1952:387). The PCNs therefore might be vulviform representations.[9] The dust from such carvings was often ground to a paste and used to paint the body, as well as inserted into a woman as medicine to increase fertility (Barrett 1908:175, 1952:387; Loeb 1926:247). Several of these descriptions specifically mention the bluish rocks associated with PCN carvings. Rather than applying to all cupule carvings, Hedges (1983:20) limits the Pomo baby rock analogy to cases when "1. the rock is chlorite schist, serpentine, or some other soft material which can be reduced to a powder. 2. The site consists of deeply incised grooves, with or without cupules and/or pecked oval forms." Such a description matches both PCNs in general and, with the exception of incised grooves, also describes the art found at 35CU142.

Another beachfront petroglyph located just south of the California border, also washed by the changing tide, was used for weather control and had possible fertility associations. Anthropologist Melville Jacobs interviewed a Coquille-Tolowa Native who described a rock on the beach near the Smith River. "When the tide is up, the ocean hits it. When a child is born, some make it rain, some will make good weather. If one wants to make good weather, one picks up a beach rock and hammers, saying a formula, and then he throws the hammer rock into the ocean, and then you get it" (Joyer 1996:32).

Additionally, a huge blueschist monolith once stood overlooking the sea at the mouth of the Coquille River in Bandon. Known historically as Tupper Rock after the local landowner, but traditionally referred to as Grandmother Rock, the monolith was said to be a woman and her granddaughter huddled under a blanket and turned to stone (Jacobs 1940:141). It is reported that pounding on this rock could calm the ocean (Hall and Hall 1995:84). It is unknown if this great Medicine Rock had petroglyph carvings on it, but the weather control function as well as the rock's blueschist composition leaves this as an intriguing possibility. However, this landmark was unfortunately blown apart with dynamite and used to build the south jetty at the mouth of the river in the 1880s.

So, the petroglyphs carved on the beach at 35CU142 might have had a weather control function but more likely represented a baby rock or similar fertility-related carving, though these functions are not mutually exclusive. The carvings may have been made approximately a thousand years ago when the site was being used for gathering shellfish but are probably significantly later based on the lack of erosion on the beachside boulder.

Like the Northwest Coast tradition face painted at Medicine Creek Rockshelter, the PCN art at 35CU142 could simply be an extreme outlier in the distribution of PCNs (Figure 16). However, this site may indicate further PCN sites yet to be found in northern California or southern Oregon. While located in historical Tututni territory, well beyond the traditional area of the Pomo, the art is clearly part of a wider-spread Pecked Curvilinear Nucleated tradition covering much of the coastal range of northwestern California and now known to extend northward into southern Oregon. As the most northerly example of this tradition, it highlights a region where California culture areas intersected with that of the Northwest Coast.

Oregon Seashore Rock Art

Rock art on the beach and in tidal zones is common in Northwest Coast rock art, from Alaska to the state of Washington (Lundy 1974), but petroglyphs along the beach in Oregon are rare (Figure 11). The recording of 35CU142 led to additional investigation of the only two other rock art sites reported along the Oregon coastline, at Ecola State Park and at Pitcher Point along Tillamook Bay (Keyser 2005:5; Loring and Loring 1982a:152–153). Both of these sites remain questionable, identified as part of the Northwest Coast tradition based primarily on their locations on the northern Oregon coast.

Ecola (35CTL65)

A petroglyph at Indian Beach in Ecola State Park was first illustrated by Loring and Loring (1982a:153). They made multiple searches of the beach looking for two petroglyphs originally reported to them by Gale Dale of Portland, but these could not be located. What they did find in 1970 was an isolated panel that consisted largely of vertical grooves and a connecting

diagonal line (Figure 17), approximately 18 x 30 cm. The site was assigned a number (35CTL65) by Minor (1986:10) based on the description by the Lorings. However, neither this petroglyph nor the original panels reported by Dale have been relocated in any subsequent searches (Deur 2016:403; Minor 1986:20; Moss and Erlandson 1995, 1996:20).

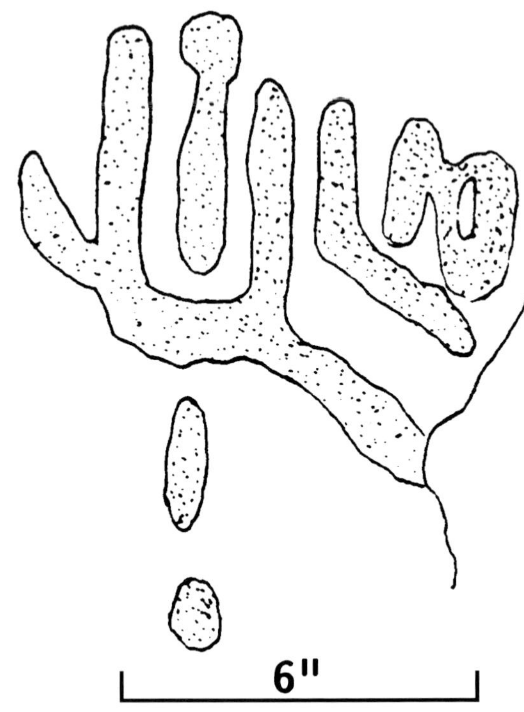

Figure 17. Drawing of reported petroglyph at Ecola (Loring and Loring 1982a:153).

Oral history from the Nehalem Tillamook tells of a village at Ecola Point, where they would hunt sea lions on the rocks below. Handholds were once carved in the cliff leading to the beach, but these have now eroded (Deur 2016:403). Additionally, "some singular carving upon the ledges, resembling more the hieroglyphics of the Chinese" were seen in 1846 [10] (Palmer 1906:196–197), hinting of a petroglyph tradition in the area, but also likely lost to erosion.

Loring and Loring (1982a:153) describe the grooves in the rock at Ecola as "weathered the same color as the stones." In addition, they describe how they also "found several conglomerate rocks with grooves where the softer rock had eroded more rapidly than the hard portions. These, at first, gave an impression of carving." These grooved rocks were also encountered by the present author when attempting to relocate the petroglyphs reported at this site.

It is possible that this site has either been eroded or lost due to the actions of the sea. However, while there was a village nearby, and other petroglyphs may possibly have occurred at this location, the inability of any further surveys to rediscover the carving, as well as non-representational images conforming to the natural grooves eroded in other rocks on the beach, point to this site likely being a misidentified natural feature.

Pitcher Point

Another petroglyph on the north coast was also reported by Loring and Loring (1982a:152–153) along Bayocean Spit at Tillamook Bay. On the east side of the peninsula between the ocean and the bay, a sandstone bolder with carvings was reported to the Lorings in 1977 by Carol O'Gara of the Oregon Archaeological Society. The Lorings subsequently documented it (Figure 18a) and describe "two circles, each 5 inches in diameter and with a pit in the center.…Below the circles, a point on the rock and a deep gash resemble a mouth so that, viewed in profile, the carving has the appearance of a seal or sea lion head" (Loring and Loring 1982a:152).

The boulder's location was relatively easily relocated (Figure 18b). While Loring and Loring (1982a:152) describe the pecking as "waterworn and not easy to see," on close inspection the image, while somewhat visible, showed no signs of pecking or other human manufacture, even using a hand lens. The reported carving of eyes and a mouth consisted only of natural spalling, folds, and circular erosion around vugs in the rock. It appears to be a case of pareidolia, a function of the mind where recognizable images, particularly faces, are seen where none exist.

Moreover, the location of this site makes this image additionally suspect. The Bayocean Peninsula, separating Tillamook Bay from the ocean, was the site of a large resort community in the early twentieth century. A town, with houses, shops, a large swimming pool, and a dancehall, once existed on this now unpopulated area of land. But due to the construction of the north jetty at the entrance to Tillamook Bay, the spit began to rapidly erode, endangering the community built there. Despite various attempts to hold back the encroachment of the sea, during a series of storms in 1952 a mile-wide breach occurred in the spit, leaving the northern portion an island (Terich and Komar 1973:70–75). This breach was closed by the Army Corps of Engineers in 1956 using rock from nearby quarries, as well as sandstone from a ridge along the bay southeast of the site (Terich and Komar 1973:78).

The image reported by Loring and Loring is located where the breach occurred and is likely on one of the sandstone boulders used for riprap to repair the spit. Therefore, this site should also be removed from future surveys of coastal rock art in Oregon, being another case of misidentification.

Thus, previously identified sites at both Ecola State Park and Pitcher Point at Tillamook Bay appear to have been misidentified natural features. While there may once have been a rock art tradition among the indigenous communities along the northern Oregon coast, no evidence now remains. Therefore, 35CU142 along the southern Oregon coast stands as a unique example of coastal rock art in the state.

More significantly, removing these sites from the southern distribution of Northwest Coast tradition rock art (Keyser 2005:3,50) shows that while coastal communities along the Oregon coast were part of the wider Northwest Coast culture, the rock art tradition does not appear to have continued down the coast. Instead, makers of this art turned up the Columbia River and moved inland. Carvings of Northwest Coast tradition faces occur at Willamette Falls along the Willamette River, a tributary of the Columbia (Kaiser 2016:18). Moreover, further east, the Northwest Coast influences mixed with inland Plateau traditions, creating the Columbia River Conventionalized, or Long Nar-

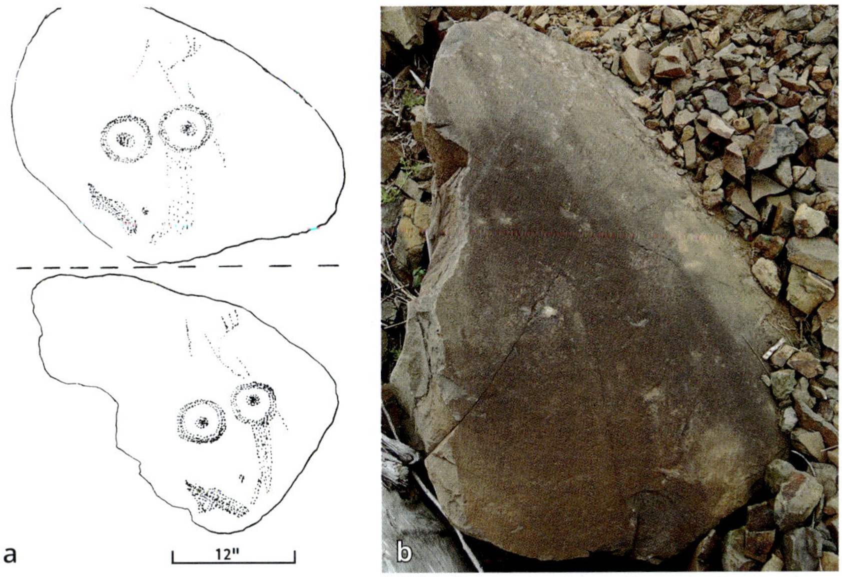

Figure 18. (a) Drawings of Pitcher Point image along Tillamook Bay (Loring and Loring 1982a:153). (b) Pitcher Point rock, showing only natural features.

rows style, art found along the mid-Columbia (Keyser 1992:96–97; Lundy 1983; Wellmann 1979).

Conclusions

A closer look at the understudied art of southwest Oregon shows that the region possesses a richer tradition of rock art than previously recognized (Table 1), with most occurring along most major waterways in the area.[11] The majority of the art is abstract or geometric, but rare examples of representational art occur, such as that found at Elk Rock and reported along the Umpqua River. Much of the art appears associated with hunting and fishing, as well as weather control. In addition, reevaluation of the distribution patterns of neighboring art styles more fully shows the Northern Variant of the Far Western Pit and Groove tradition extending north from California and into Oregon as far as the southern Willamette Valley (Figure 11). Likewise, the Pecked Nucleated Curvilinear style is shown to extend into southwest Oregon as well. Conversely, the reevaluation of other coastal art in the state

Table 1. Rock art sites in southwest Oregon.
See Loring and Loring (1982a, b) and Keyser (2005) for
descriptions of Far Western Pit and Groove sites and other
regional sites not discussed in this paper.

Location (North to South)	Confirmed	Unconfirmed
Petersen Ranch	FWPG	
Rainrock		FWPG
Briley Ranch	FWPG	
Hadleyville Pitted Boulder	FWPG	
Smith River		FWPG
Scottsburg	FWPG	
Scottsburg (Water Beetle)		R
Umpqua River (location unknown)		PCN
Yoncalla Boulder	FWPG	
Bottle Creek	HC	
Elk Rock	R	
Coquille	U	
Tupper Rock (destroyed)		FWPG
35CU142	PCN	
Twomile	FWPG	
Brushy Bar	FWPG	
Gleason Bar	FWPG	
Upper Rogue		FWPG
Indian Rock	U	
Emigrant Creek	FWPG	

FWPG = Far Western Pit and Groove　　HC=High Cascade
PCN = Pecked Curvilinear Nucleated
R = Representational/Undetermined　　U = Undetermined

redraws the southern extent of the Northwest Coast art tradition only as far as the Columbia River and its tributaries. This report is only an initial survey of the area, and further, more detailed study should prove productive and enlightening.

Acknowledgments. Special thanks to the following for helping to make this project happen: The Oregon Archaeological Society for the Loring Grant to help fund the fieldwork; Susan Caisse and Brad Stiener for their assistance in the field; Rick Minor and Dan Leen for providing me with reports and images of Twomile; Ken Hedges for the PCN image from California; and James Keyser for his helpful review of this paper.

Notes

1. Republished in Oregon Historical Quarterly (Smith 1965).

2. First published in 1906, the story was republished in a statewide journal three years later (Lockhart 1909a).

3. While acknowledging this image could therefore be a deer, in deference to over a century of it being referred to as an elk, the image is thus referred to in this report.

4. Rather than plunging elk over a very high cliff into the river at Elk Rock into the Willamette River, as described above, the existence of Elk Rock Island (a peninsula in the summertime) in the river opposite this precipice could be the source of the name, indicating the trapping of elk on an island and driving them into the water to hunt them.

5. River guides reportedly describe these shapes as turtles, but there are no clear details in the online photographs to support this identification.

6. It is unclear exactly when this petroglyph was discovered, but James Metcalf was chair of the Coquille Indian Tribe from 1992 to 2012.

7. Quoted in Minor 1986:96, citing Pullen 1982b. However, while the site was first noted by Pullen, the correct citation is 1982a.

8. Debate continues whether Pecked Curvilinear Nucleated art is an independent tradition, or a style that is part of the wider Far Western Pit and Groove tradition.

9. As identified by Minor (1986:96–97).

10. The site is described as being at Cape Lookout (Palmer 1906:196). This name was frequently attributed in historical descriptions to what is now Tillamook Head, just north of Indian Beach in Ecloa State Park, rather than the promontory south of Tillamook Bay which now bears this name.

11. A previously unknown petroglyph site with two elements—possible turtle-like and insect-like images—was recently discovered on the Winchuck River in the extreme southwestern corner of the state. As of this writing, a paper describing the new find is in press in *Rock Art Papers* (Merlin 2023).

References Cited

Aikens, C. Melvin
  1993 *Archaeology of Oregon.* U.S. Department of the Interior, Bureau of Land Management, Oregon State Office, Portland.

Anell, Bengt
  1969 *Running Down and Driving of Game in North America.* Studia Ethnographica Upsaliencia 30. Berlingska Boktryckeri, Lund, Sweden.

AP News
  1990 Artist Claims "Ancient" Petroglyphs His Own Work. AP News, Syndicated, October 24 (online). Electronic document, https://apnews.com/article/3496ae34af8ec9de7f068534d74 3d814, accessed July 20, 2022.

Barrett, Samuel Alfred
  1908 *The Ethno-geography of the Pomo and Neighboring Indians.* University of California Publications in American Archaeology and Ethnology 6(1).
  1952 *Material Aspects of Pomo Culture.* Bulletin of the Public Museum of the City of Milwaukee, Volume 20. In two parts.

Beauchamp, Douglas
  2015 Petroglyph Boulders on the Rogue River at Two Mile Creek: Intentions and Actions, 1974–2015. Paper presented at the Northwest Anthropological Conference, Eugene, Oregon. Electronic document, https://www.academia.edu/35537431/ Petroglyph_boulders_on_the_Rogue_River_at_Two_ Mile_Creek_Curry_County_Oregon_Intentions_and_Actions_1974_2015, accessed February 17, 2022.

Boas, Franz
  1901 *Kathlamet Texts.* Bureau of American Ethnology Bulletin 26.

Bureau of Land Management and U.S. Forest Service
  2004 Rogue River Float Guide. Bureau of Land Management, Department of the Interior and U.S. Forest Service, Department of Agriculture.

Burgess, F. W.
  1976 "Twomile Petroglyphs." Letter to Ted Long, May 26, 1976. In Twomile Petroglyphs (35CU66) Letters and Photos – From 1976–1977, Curry County, Siskiyou National Forest, on file with State Historic Preservation Office, Salem, Oregon.

Coos Bay Times
  1914 Informal Chat. *Coos Bay Times,* June 20, 1914, p. 10. Marshfield, Oregon.

Curry Coastal Pilot
  1977 Native Americans Protest Removal of Valued Relics. *Curry Coastal Pilot,* August 11, 1977, p.8. Brookings, Oregon.

Deur, Douglas
  2016 *Empires of the Turning Tide: A History of Lewis and Clark National Historical Park and the Columbia-Pacific Region.* Pacific West Region: Social Science Series, Publication Number 2016-001. National Park Service, U.S. Department of the Interior.

Driver, Harold E.
  1939 *Cultural Element Distributions X: Northwest California.* University of California Anthropological Records 1(6).

Dunn, Bert, Andie E. Jensen, Yvonne-Cher Skye, and the Coquille Valley Museum
  2018 *Coquille.* Arcadia Publishing, Charleston, South Carolina.

Erlandson, Jon
  2021 United States / OR / Curry County / 35CU142 / Beta-66899. Electronic document, https://www.canadianarchaeology.ca/samples/15581, accessed February 25, 2022.

Fentress, Jeffrey
  1994 A Glimpse of Oregon Rock Art. *Bay Area Rock Art News* 12(1):2. Bay Area Rock Art Research Association, San Francisco.

Forest Service
  1989 *Windows on the Past: Interpretive Guide to Pacific Northwest History.* U.S. Forest Service, Department of Agriculture.

Gillette, Donna Lee
  2011 *Cultural Markings on the Landscape: The PCN Pecked Curvilinear Nucleated Tradition in the Northern Coastal Ranges of California.* Ph.D. thesis, Department of Anthropology, University of California, Berkley.

Gillette, Donna, and Teresa Miller Saltzman
  2003 So What's a PCN? In *American Indian Rock Art, Volume 29,* edited by Alanah Woody and Joseph T. O'Connor, pp. 105–109. American Rock Art Research Association, Tucson.

Green, Joey
  2012 *Dumb History: The Stupidest Mistakes Ever Made.* Plume, New York.

Hall, Roberta L., and Don Alan Hall
  1995 Changes. In *People of the Coquille Estuary,* edited by Roberta L. Hall, pp. 81–90. Words & Pictures Unlimited, Corvallis.

Hedges, Ken
  1983 A Re-examination of Pomo Baby Rocks. In *American Indian Rock Art ,Volume 9,* edited by Frank G. Bock, pp. 10–21. American Rock Art Research Association, El Toro, California.

Heizer, Robert F.
  1953 Sacred Rain Rocks of Northern California. Paper on California Archaeology 22. *Reports of the University of California Archaeological Survey* 20:33–38.

Heizer, Robert F., and William W. Clewlow, Jr.
  1973 *Prehistoric Rock Art of California.* Ballena Press, Ramona, California.

Hillsboro Independent
  1895 Tragedy of Elk Rock. *Hillsboro Independent,* September 27, 1895, p. 4. Hillsboro, Oregon.

Jacobs, Melville
  1940 Coos Myth Texts. *University of Washington Publications in Anthropology* 8(2):127–260.

Joyer, Janet E.
  1996 Messages In Stone. *Southern Oregon Heritage* 2(2):30–34.

Joyer, Janet E., and Daniel Leen
  1996 Twomile: A Petroglyph Site in Southwest Oregon. Paper presented at the Society for American Archaeology Meeting, New Orleans. Paper on file with Siskiyou National Forest.

Kaiser, David A.
  2016 Willamette Falls: Rock Art at the End of the Oregon Trail. In *American Indian Rock Art, Volume 42,* edited by Ken Hedges, pp.15–24, American Rock Art Research Association, San Jose.

Kaiser, David A., and Julia Cleary
  2020 Image Rock—Rediscovering a Petroglyph in the High Cascades. *Journal of Northwest Anthropology* 54(2), pp.165–174.

Keyser, James D.

1992 *Indian Rock Art of the Columbia Plateau.* University of Washington Press, Seattle.

2005 *Pictographs of the High Cascades: Rock Art of Western Oregon.* Umpqua National Forest. Heritage Report 1, United States Forest Service.

Keyser, James D., and David S. Whitley

2006 Sympathetic Magic in Western North American Rock Art. *American Antiquity* 71(1):3–26.

Kocher, Charles

1977 Indians Protest Rock Removal. *The World,* August 9, 1977. Coos Bay, Oregon.

Leen, Daniel

1994 *The Twomile Petroglyphs—1994 fieldwork.* Report on file with Siskiyou National Forest.

Lindsay, Lee W. Jr.

1995 Native Use of Resources on the Oregon Coast. In *People of the Coquille Estuary,* edited by Roberta L. Hall, pp.191–210. Words & Pictures Unlimited, Corvallis.

Lockhart, Agnes Ruth

1906 Legend of Elk Rock. *The Coos Bay Monthly* 1(2):12–15, October 1906.

1909a Legend of Elk Rock. *Oregon Teachers Monthly* 14(2):70–73.

1909b *A Legend of the Coos.* Philoplis Press, San Francisco.

Loeb, Edwin M.

1926 *Pomo Folkways.* University of California Publications in American Archaeology and Ethnology 19(2).

Loring, J. Malcom, and Louise Loring

1982a *Pictographs & Petroglyphs of the Oregon Country, Part 1: Columbia River & Northern Oregon.* Monograph 21. Institute of Archaeology, University of California, Los Angeles.

1982b *Pictographs & Petroglyphs of the Oregon Country, Part 2: Southern Oregon.* Monograph 21. Institute of Archaeology, University of California, Los Angeles.

Lundy, Doris

1974 *The Rock Art of the Northwest Coast.* Master's thesis, Simon Fraser University, Burnaby, British Columbia.

1983 Styles of Coastal Rock Art. In *Indian Art Traditions of the Northwest Coast,* edited by Roy L. Carson, pp. 89–97. Archaeology Press, Simon Fraser University, British Columbia.

Mahaffy, Charlotte L.

1965 *Coos River Echoes.* Interstate Press, Portland, Oregon.

Maloney, Joseph

1931 Extract from a report of J. L. Parrish, Indian Agent, in a census of the To-To-Tin Indians; and other southern Oregon coast bands identified as Coos, July 10, 1854 [unpublished ethnographic research notes]. Ethnological documents of the Department and Museum of Anthropology, University of California, Berkeley, item no. 22, unpaginated.

Marymor, Leigh

1998 Pomo Baby Rock. *Bay Area Rock Art News* 16(1):3–4. Bay Area Rock Art Research Association, San Francisco.

McArthur, Lewis A.

1927 Oregon Geographic Names. *Oregon Historical Quarterly* 28(1):65–110.

Merlin, Peter W.

2023 Along Chetco Trails: An Unrecorded Petroglyph Site in Southwestern Oregon. In *Rock Art Papers, Volume 20,* edited by Ken Hedges. San Diego Rock Art Association (in press).

Miller, Teresa A.

1977 *Identification and Recording of Prehistoric Petroglyphs in Marin and Related Bay Area Counties.* Master's thesis, Department of Anthropology, San Francisco State University.

Minor, Rick

1986 *An Evaluation of Archaeological Sites on State Park Lands along the Oregon Coast.* Report 44. Heritage Research Associates, Eugene, Oregon.

Moss, Madonna L., and Jon M. Erlandson

1995 *An Evaluation, Survey, and Dating Program for Archaeological Sites on State Lands of the Northern Oregon Coast with Reports on Archaeological Surveys of South Slough (Coos Bay) and Intertidal Fishing Sites.* Report submitted to the Oregon State Historic Preservation Office, Salem.

1996 *Native American Archaeological Sites of the Oregon Coast— Multiple Property Submission.* The Historical Context for the Nomination to the National Register of Historic Places, United States Department of the Interior, National Parks Service.

Palmer, Joel

1906 *Journal of Travels over the Rocky Mountains—To the Mouth of the Columbia River, Made During the Years 1845–1846.* Arthur H. Clark, Cleveland.

Parkman, E. Breck

1993 The PCN-Style Petroglyph. In *There Grows a Green Tree: Papers in Honor of David A. Fredrickson,* edited by Greg White, Pat Mikkelsen, William R. Hildebrandt, and Mark E. Basgall, pp. 351–371. Publication 11. Center for Archaeological Research, Davis, California.

Poetschat, George, James D. Keyser, David A. Kaiser, Robin Harrower, and Anthony Farque

2010 Interpreting Cascadia Cave: An Upstream Struggle. *American Indian Rock Art, Volume 36,* edited by Ken Hedges, pp. 59–70, American Rock Art Research Association, Glendale, Arizona.

Pullen, Reginald J.

1982a Archaeological Site Record, 35CU142. Site form on file, Oregon State Historic Preservation Office.

1982b *The Identification of Early Prehistoric Settlement Patterns Along the Coast of Southwest Oregon: A Survey Based Upon Amateur Collections.* M.A. thesis in Interdisciplinary Studies, Oregon State University, Corvallis.

2010 Spiritual and Ritual Origins and Practices. In *Our Culture and History: The Confederated Tribes of Coos, Lower Umpqua and Siuslaw Indians,* by Don Whereat, pp. 330–337. Privately published. Electronic document, https://shichils.files.wordpress.com/2017/10/our_culture__history.pdf, accessed March 5, 2022.

Relander, Click

1956 *Drummers and Dreamers.* The Caxton Press, Caldwell, Idaho.

Rhode, P.

1991 Are Charmstones Hatched From PCNs? *Bay Area Rock Art News* 9(2):8–10. Bay Area Rock Art Research Association, San Francisco.

St. Clair, Harry Hull, and Leo J. Frachtenberg

1909 Traditions of the Coos Indians of Oregon. *The Journal of American Folklore* 22(83):25–41.

Shelor, William H.

1900 The Willamette. *The Pacific Monthly* 4(1):13–15, May 1900.

Smith, Florence A.

1963 River Days. *The World,* May 17, 1963, pp. 4, 6. Coos Bay, Oregon.

1965 Coos River School Days. *Oregon Historical Quarterly* 66(1):52–57.

Smoke Signals
2001 Federal Agencies, Tribes Work to Save Ancient Art in Umpqua River. *Smoke Signals,* January 15, 2001, p. 5. Grand Ronde, Oregon.

Spier, Leslie
1930 *Klamath Ethnography.* University of California Publications in American Archaeology and Ethnology 30.

Terich, Thomas A., and Paul D. Komar
1973 *Development and Erosion History of Bayocean Spit, Tillamook, Oregon.* School of Oceanography, Oregon State University, Corvallis.

Van Marmot, Bruce, and Linda Van Marmot
2016 Rafting Oregon's Rogue River 6/9-Jun-2016. Boots on the Trail (blog). Electronic document, https://vanmarmot.org/2016/06/11/rafting-oregons-rogue-river-69-jun-2016/, accessed September 6, 2022.

Waterman, T. T.
1925 The Village Sites in Tolowa and Neighboring Areas in Northwestern California. *American Anthropologist* (new series) 27(4):528–543.

Wellmann, Klaus
1979 *A Survey of North American Rock Art.* Akademische Druck- und Verlagsanstalt, Graz, Austria.

Whereat Phillips, Patricia
2017 Place Names of the Coos, Lower Umpqua and Siuslaw Indians: The Lower Umpqua. *The Voice of CLUSI* 10(18):7. Confederated Tribes of Coos, Lower Umpqua and Siuslaw Indians, Coos Bay, Oregon.

Whitley, David S.
2000 *The Art of the Shaman: Rock Art of California.* University of Utah Press, Salt Lake City.

Wrenn, Sarah B., and Harvey Gordan Starkweather
1939 Early Days and Ways. Oregon. [Manuscript/Mixed Material] Library of Congress, Electronic document, https://www.loc.gov/item/wpalh001988/, accessed July 24, 2022.

Insights into the Petroglyphs at Washington State Park

Michael J. Fuller, Neathery B. Fuller, and Eric C. Fuller

Sites 23WA1 and 23WA2 are protected and interpreted petroglyph sites in Washington State Park near DeSoto, Missouri. The nineteenth- and twentieth-century research at the site has generally not been fully considered in recent publications concerning the site; especially the significant artifacts recovered from the "crevice feature" at 23WA1 excavated in 1959 by a team that included Ron Wyatt and two citizen archaeologists, Leonard Blake and Robert Elgin. Woodland and Mississippian period artifacts were recovered from that feature, as well as from the surface and near-surface deposits at 23WA2. Important insights also come from an unpublished map prepared by Kent Bonar in 1970.

The Washington State Park sites (23WA1 and 23WA2) are among the most extensive and extraordinary petroglyph sites in the state of Missouri; they are situated along the Big River, which is a tributary of the Meramec River within the Mississippi River watershed (Figure 1). The sites have been discussed in numerous publications (Diaz-Granados and Duncan 2000, 2004; Diesing and Magre 1942; Duncan and Diaz-Granados 2018a, 2018b; Fuller et al 2019a, 2019b; Wyatt 1959, n.d., and more). Important aspects of the sites' discovery, mapping, and testing have largely been omitted in the published articles. The purpose of this article is to present the early Euro-American history of research at the sites as well as a few new insights. The senior author of this paper visited and photographed Washington State Park several dozen times over the past 50 years (Fuller et al. 1970). The deep petroglyphs are always visible, but many times the faint petroglyphs can only be discerned at certain times of day and certain months of the year. The original paper delivered at the ARARA Zoom 2022 conference included a third site (23WA1702); it will be considered in a future article.

The iconography at Washington State Park was linked in the 1950s with the designs on Mississippian shell gorgets, embossed copper plates, and pottery vessels. The shared design elements gave rise to the dating of the site within the time frame of A.D. 900 to 1400. Ironically, a citizen archaeologist, Frank Magre, reasoned that motifs such as thunderbirds, deer, turtles, and turkey tracks were evidence of Woodland culture traits that would become fused with the Mississippian elements (Magre 1970, 1975). His interpretation would not find support among the professional archaeologists though the recent analysis of lithic artifacts from 23WA1 suggests that his hypothesis is plausible.

Washington State Park is situated in a straight-line distance of 47.5 miles (76.5 km) south of Big Mound (23SL3)—a ridgetop mound that was the largest of the St. Louis Mound group (Chapman 1980:163–170; Conant 1879:40–46; Leach 2017:97–109). Washington State Park is within the "sphere" of direct influence of Cahokia and its daughter settlements of East St. Louis and

Michael J. Fuller
*St. Louis Community College,
St. Louis, Missouri*

Neathery B. Fuller
*St. Louis Community College,
St. Louis, Missouri*

Eric C. Fuller
*Smallin Civil War Cave,
Ozark, Missouri*

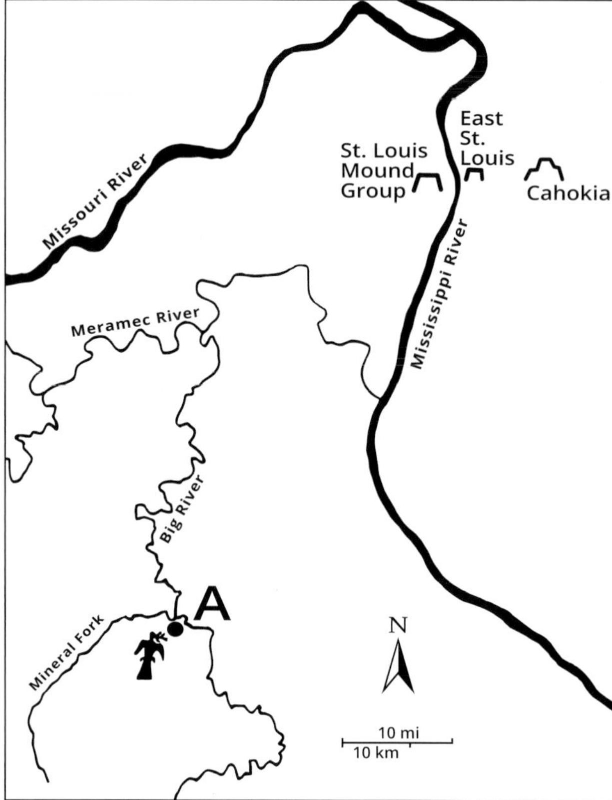

Figure 1. *Location of the Washington State Park Petroglyph Site A (23WA1) in relation to the St. Louis Mound group, East St. Louis Mound group, and Cahokia.*

St. Louis Mound groups (Pauketat 2004:Figure 1.1). The straight-line distance between 23WA1 and the central plaza of Cahokia is 52.4 miles (84.3 km).

Euro-American Interest in the Washington State Park Sites

The petroglyphs at 23WA1 were known to the Euro-American settlers as early as December 4, 1844, when Albert C. Koch attempted to acquire one or more panels (Koch 1847:86–87, 1972:74, 162; Bruce McMillan personal communication July 25, 2022). Koch was especially interested in the footprint petroglyphs (Figure 2). George Washington Higginbotham (b. 1805; d. 1863), owner of the site in the 1840s, declined Koch's request. Judge Thomas Higginbotham (b. 1835; d. 1914), son of George Washington Higginbotham, would remove several petroglyphs from the site and create his own private museum next to his home in Blackwell, Missouri. His collection was sold by his heirs, who did not find the petroglyphs, pottery vessels, and stone tools to be of any interest. It is fortunate that in the late 1930s/early 1940s, Eugene H. Diesing obtained photographs of a sun petroglyph (Figure 3) as

Figure 2. *One of the most prominent footprints at 23WA1, located in Cluster 2, is possibly one of the petroglyphs "desired" by Koch. Photograph taken by Eugene Diesing in the 1930s and published by Diesing and Magre 1942; also published in Chapman and Chapman (1964:130). Original photograph is in the Archives of the Missouri State Parks.*

Figure 3. *Sunburst petroglyph with nine arms was most likely removed from 23WA1 and displayed in the private museum of Judge Thomas Higginbotham; photograph taken by Eugene Diesing in the 1930s and published in Diesing and Magre (1942:Plate Vd). Magre (1975) recorded that the nine-armed sun measured 9 inches (22.9 cm) from arm to arm. Original photograph is in the Archives of the Missouri State Parks.*

well as a crane petroglyph (Figure 4) that were part of the Judge Higginbotham collection.

One explanation for Koch's interest in the footprint petroglyphs from 23WA1 is that he wanted to take the specimen(s) to his museum in St. Louis because of their "novelty" value. Koch's obituary (Daily Missouri Republican 1868) noted that some individuals in St. Louis considered him a "humbug," but that his death would be "severely felt in private as well as scientific circles" in the U.S.A. and Europe.

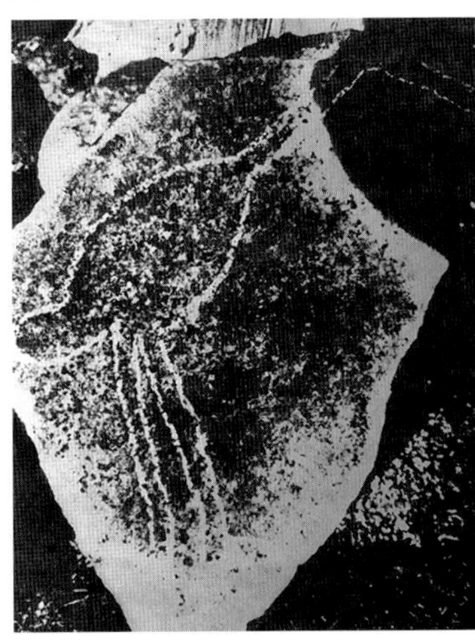

Figure 4. Crane petroglyph removed from 23WA1 and displayed in the private museum of Judge Thomas Higginbotham. Original photo from the Archives of the Missouri State Parks.

Koch did more than assemble a museum of bizarre finds—he lectured, published his results, and suffered criticism (some justified and other not). McMillan (1980:35) is more generous in assessing Koch when he acknowledges the vaudeville-like atmosphere of his museum, but also the fact that "the museum did contain a number of important natural history collections that provided substance for inquiry by scholars at the time."

Footprint petroglyphs were an issue of great interest to early natural historians—were they carved into bedrock, were they fossils, supernatural phenomena, or hoaxes? Schoolcraft (1822, 1825:171) published reports on footprint petroglyphs that had been removed by Rev. Frederick Rappe from a rock exposure along the bank of the Mississippi River at St. Louis. Almost a century later, David I. Bushnell (1913) prepared an article about footprint petroglyphs for *American Anthropologist*; he removed a footprint petroglyph from a bluff top site in Jefferson County, Missouri, on August 26, 1901, and shipped it to the Peabody Museum at Harvard University (Bushnell 1901). Koch would have realized that the footprint directly associated with unmistakably Native American petroglyphs would dispel any conjecture that the footprints were fossils or evidence of supernatural activity. The idea that footprint petroglyphs in Missouri are fossils has remained in the paranormal literature as recently as the 1970s (Corliss 1976:3–8).

The property for Washington State Park was purchased from Press Graws Higginbotham (b. 1875; d. 1952) by Albert P. Greensfelder for $7,987.50 (according to a manuscript filed by local historian, Dorothy Jean O'Brien n.d.). Press Graws Higginbotham was a grandson of George Washington Higginbotham. The property was donated to the State of Missouri on December 29, 1932. Greensfelder, a St. Louis philanthropist, served for many years as Vice-Chairman of the Missouri Conser-

vation Commission. Teams of planners and workmen began constructing gravel roads, pavilions, and other structures in the park area. Civilian Conservation Corps (CCC) crews recognized the importance of the petroglyphs by 1934 and proposed to create a roofed museum or fenced enclosure. A CCC report in 1936 conjectured that the Washington State Park petroglyphs are "thousands of years old" (Teasdale 1936).

A letter prepared by Paul V. Brown (1938) indicates that the first plan map of the petroglyphs at Washington State Park was created between 1934 and 1938 by Charles G. Wilder—a young archaeologist who participated on several New Deal archaeological projects (Dye 2016:28, Table I.2; Huddleston 2009) and served as the chairman for the Southeastern Archaeological Conference (Haag 1939:2, 23). Wilder was brought to Washington State Park from his work with the Tennessee Valley Authority; it is unlikely that he stayed very long in the park as he had pressing mound excavations awaiting along the Tennessee River. Wilder first appeared in scientific publications when he co-authored a paper about ancient climate in the *Geological Society of America Bulletin* (Hubbard and Wilder 1930); his career in archaeology would come to an end by 1942 when he was removed from a committee appointment of the Society for American Archaeology for "no longer working in the field of Archaeology" (SAA 1942:202). Wilder was sent to Washington State Park not because he had any expertise in rock art, but because he was the most junior of the team of archaeologists working on the rescue archaeological projects in the Tennessee River Valley.

The Wilder map may have been lost over the decades. Oral history at Washington State Park is that a large, elaborate map was lost in a fire that happened many decades ago—that might have been Wilder's map, but more likely it was a large version of the third map (made by Robert Elgin in 1961) of the site.

In the late 1930s/early 1940s, Eugene Diesing and Frank Magre prepared an article for the *Missouri Archaeologist* that was published in 1942. High-quality photographs for their article are preserved (Figures 2, 3, and 8) in the Archives of the Missouri State Parks in Jefferson City. Diesing and Magre (1942:15) reported that they used Kalsomine paint to make the petroglyphs discernible in their black-and-white photographs. This product is the same as whitewash, calcimine, or lime paint. By today's standards, it was a lamentable decision.

Carl Chapman (1959) visited the site sometime around 1940 when he was a graduate student at the University of New Mexico; he described the Washington State Park petroglyph sites as "one of the most outstanding of its kind east of the Rocky Mountains." Between 1941 and 1943, Frank Magre guided a University of Chicago graduate student, Robert Bell, to Washington State Park as part of a dendrochronological sampling project. O'Brien (n.d.) reports that a "Bluff Cedar" tree near the Washington State Park boundary dated to A.D. 1120 and was one of the oldest trees sampled in Bell's study.

1959 Excavation at 23WA1

Park officials realized by 1958 that it was impossible to keep visitors from walking on the petroglyphs at 23WA1. One story, told by a local resident (Patrick Howe, personal communication February 28, 2019), is that the local group of Boy Scouts began digging sediment along the edges of the bedrock exposure in 1956 to uncover more of the petroglyphs; they chalked and photographed the more-prominent petroglyphs (Figure 5).

Figure 5. *The "Mighty Thunderbird" and the lightning bolt chalked and photographed in 1956 by a group of Boy Scouts from Washington County, Missouri. Many details were not chalked. Photograph courtesy of Patrick Howe.*

Missouri State Parks decided that a viewing platform was necessary to stop visitors from walking on the petroglyphs and that some form of shelter would be useful to protect the petroglyphs against weathering. In 1959, Robert Elgin was hired to design and oversee the construction of the boardwalk and shelter; he was the perfect choice because he was a professional engineer and also a member of the Missouri Archaeological Society. It was decided that the boardwalk should

run east-west across the center of 23WA1—covering a natural crevice, devoid of petroglyphs.

Sometime before 1959 Professor Carl Chapman and Eleanor Chapman (n.d.) created the second known map of the site. It is a pencil map (Figure 6) on a rollout sheet of graph paper. They mapped select groups of petroglyphs and wrote captions that were subsequently used to create signboards (Figure 7). The Chapman map identifies seven panels that would be discussed and the critical petroglyph elements in each to illustrate. Their map was not meant to be an exhaustive catalog, but a

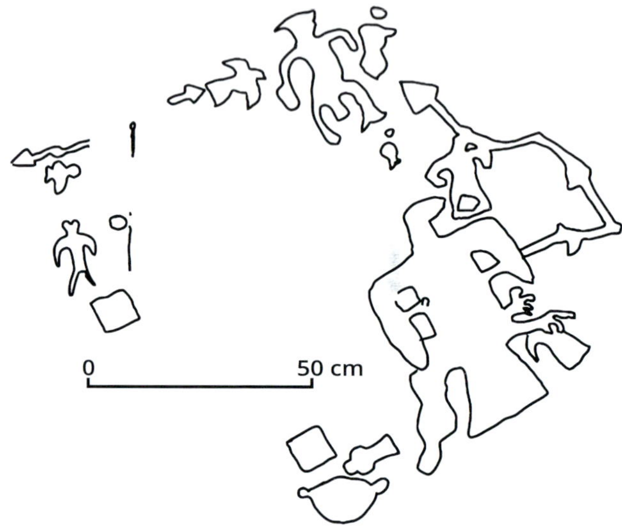

Figure 6. *Detail of the pencil drawing of Cluster 1 at 23WA1 prepared by Prof. Carl Chapman and Eleanor Chapman (n.d.), circa 1958. Redrawn by Neathery Batsell Fuller.*

Figure 7. *Interpretive sign for petroglyphs in Cluster 1 at 23WA1, circa 1959, based on the drawing of Carl and Eleanor Chapman (n.d.).*

guide for the artist creating the signboards. The drawings on their original map are very faint and the graph paper bears several wet bottle marks. The scale of the map is in feet; but unfortunately, this map is not dated. For the most part, the Chapmans' map agrees with the major details recorded by Diesing's photographs (Figure 8), though there are some differences.

Figure 8. Cluster 1 photographic image by Diesing in the Archives of the Missouri State Parks. Duncan and Diaz-Granados (2018a:Figure 2.9) identify the large bird as Hawk = Morning Star and also see "possible" symbols representing the A.D. 1054 supernova. We believe an equally plausible explanation for the large birds in Clusters 1 and 2 relates to the Osage tradition of Xu-tha'gthe-zhe (Mottled or Immature Golden Eagle) who carefully carried the Osage ancestors to safety in the branches of a large oak tree (Bailey 2010:21).

Robert Elgin was intrigued by the petroglyphs and decided to create his own map. This third map for 23WA1 was completed in 1961. He established a 1x1-ft chalk grid system and took a series of tiled photographs in order to create a mosaic. Examples of Elgin's original photographs are kept in the Archives of the Missouri Department of Natural Resources, Division of State Parks (hereafter referred to as Missouri State Parks) and the Archives of the Rolla Research Center of the State Historical Society of Missouri (Figures 9 and 10). Elgin's map shows 188 petroglyphs. Copies are in the possession of his heirs, Washington State Park, and the Archives of the Missouri State Parks.

Dr. Carl Chapman recommended Ron Wyatt (a graduate student at the University of Missouri–Columbia) to the Missouri State Parks for the task of excavating the soil within a crevice before it was covered with the viewing platform. Wyatt had previously participated in the excavations at Modoc Rock Shelter

Figure 9. Cluster 1 as photographed by Richard Elgin in 1959 for a photomosaic from which he produced a map. Each grid square is 1 x 1 ft. From the Archives of the Missouri State Parks.

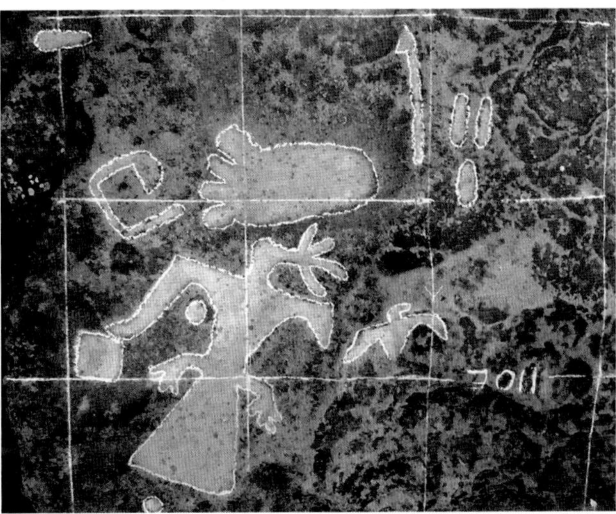

Figure 10. Cluster 2 as photographed by Richard Elgin in 1959 for a photomosaic from which he produced a map. Each grid square is 1 x 1 ft. From the Archives of the Missouri State Parks.

in Illinois during 1955, as well as the fieldwork with R. O. Keslin at the Saline Creek salt pan sites in St. Mary, Missouri, during 1958 (Wyatt, personal communication August 27, 2018). Wyatt (Figure 11) lived at the site during the summer of 1959 and excavated with the assistance of a superb citizen archaeologist named Leonard Blake. Wyatt's salary was $225 a month; he was allowed to live in the service building at the park, and he had to purchase his meals at the park concession building (Jaeger 1959). Wyatt's wife did not join him during the excavation and his fieldwork was interrupted by the requirement of three weeks of training with the military reserves. His employment contract was very specific in that he would not be paid for the three week "leave" to participate in reserve training.

Figure 11. Excavation of the crevice at 23WA1 (Wyant 1959:17). Robert Elgin (left) outlines petroglyphs situated north of the crevice while Professor Chapman (wearing a pith helmet) sits in the crevice and discusses the site with Ron Wyatt (facing the camera), and Leonard Haslag. From the Archives of the Missouri State Parks.

The sediments excavated by Wyatt during 1959 were removed in arbitrary 6-inch layers using shovel and trowel. Wyatt's usual field methods at that time included ¼-inch-mesh hardware cloth screening, and the size-range of material in the collection appears consistent with that technique. Diagnostic cultural material was very sparse considering the amount of fill in the crevice at 23WA1 (Wyatt, personal communication July 25, 2018). After the excavation was complete, the crevice was filled with gravel and the boardwalk was built above it. A short article in the *Missouri Archaeological Society Newsletter* (Wyatt 1959) made the odd assertion that "neither Woodland nor Mississippian artifacts could be found in association with the petroglyphs." That was not true, and it was not what Wyatt had concluded.

The artifacts that Wyatt excavated during 1959 were discussed in an unpublished manuscript that he prepared while a student at Harvard University; a copy of the manuscript is kept in the museum archives at the University of Missouri–Columbia and in the Archives of the Missouri State Parks. The artifacts from the 1959 excavation at 23WA1 are curated at the University of Missouri–Columbia.

Wyatt's (n.d.:7) unpublished manuscript lists several varieties of prehistoric material culture from within the crevice:

- Numerous flint and some quartzite chips
- Unmodified iron ore
- Fire-cracked rock
- A few specks of charcoal
- A small, unmodified chunk of galena
- A small, circular, water-polished pebble
- The base to an expanding-stemmed drill
- A small circular or oval scraper
- A thick, side-notched arrowhead with straight blade-edges and a slightly convex base
- A basal fragment of a possible corner- or side-notched point
- Four other point fragments
- A short, corner-notched projectile point with a convex base
- Small sherd of Korando Cordmarked pottery

The most significant of the 1959 artifacts is the side-notched arrowpoint (Figure 12a) that was excavated in Square H at a depth of 10 inches (25 cm) beneath the surface. It is 24.5 x 14.3 x 4.1 mm and weighs 0.8 grams.

Ray (2016:53–54; personal communication June 10, 2019) places this point as a variant of the Cahokia point that is termed Cahokia Double Notched. Reber et al. (2017:224–225) use the term Cahokia Bi-Notched for this point variant. Chapman (1980:306–307) noted that Cahokia notched points are found across the Ozark Highland region in Missouri and in the St. Louis area; he reported that length ranges from 13 to 35 mm with an average of 26 mm. Side-notched arrow points appear in the lithic assemblage of Cahokia (DeMott et al. 1993:Plate 7.1; Kelly 1982:Plate 51m; Bill Iseminger, personal communication June 22, 2019), in Mississippian sites in the American Bottom (Milner 1984:95, Figures 41f-g, 42a; Milner et al. 1984:Plate 32b), at a number of sites in Missouri, and at Spiro Mound in Oklahoma (Brown 1996:445, Figure 2-63d-h).

Another significant artifact from Wyatt's 1959 excavation is a "small" body sherd of Korando Cordmarked ware. The shape and thickness of the sherd (5.3 mm)

Figure 12. (a) Cahokia side-notched projectile point discovered during Wyatt's excavation during 1959 at 23WA1 (scale in mm). (b) Resharpened/exhausted Snyders point excavated at 23WA1 (scale in cm); Wyatt's notes on the artifact bag indicate that it was discovered 10 ft northeast of the "Mighty Thunderbird" petroglyph = Cluster 1 panel.

would suggest that it had been part of a typical jar-shaped vessel. Korando Cordmarked ware was considered by Chapman (1980:284–285) as characteristic of the Late Woodland period but "may have continued to be manufactured in the Early Mississippi Period."

One of the surprises from Wyatt's excavation at 23WA1 is the presence of Woodland period lithic artifacts in the fill of the crevice. The only complete Woodland period artifact discovered in the 1959 excavation is a resharpened/exhausted Snyders point (Figure 12b) that was discovered at a depth of 9 inches in the crevice. Wyatt noted on the bag tag that this artifact was 10 feet northeast of the "Mighty Thunderbird" petroglyph.

The Snyders point is 37.6 x 30.3 x 6.7 mm at 4.5 grams. Chapman (1980:312) notes that Snyders points are found in all portions of Missouri, but with the greatest frequency in the Northeast region. Chapman associated Snyders points in Missouri with the Middle Woodland period (from 500 B.C. to A.D. 400) though he notes that a few examples appear as early as the Late Archaic period (3000–1000 B.C.). Sandstrom and Ray (2004:26) report that Snyders points are widely scattered, but uncommon in the Ozark region of Missouri. Snyders points were documented in the Cahokia vicinity during the FAI-270 excavation of Middle Woodland period features at the Holding Site (Fortier et al. 1989:Figure 125m-q, Plate i). Several Snyders points were documented at Middle Woodland sites in St. Louis County including the Creve Coeur site (Blake 1942; n.d.; Silverman 1997) and the Cowmire Creek site (Craig and Vorreyer 2004).

Two projectile point fragments discovered in 1959 are problematic in terms of their identification. We prefer to see their most likely identification as the basal portions of Steuben points; Jack Ray believes that they are so fragmentary that they should only be considered unidentifiable projectile points/knives. One fragment, manufactured out of banded chert typical of the Ozark region, was discovered 22 inches below the surface in the crevice in excavation Square F. The second basal fragment was discovered 18 to 19 inches below the surface in Square C. The second point was manufactured out of rhyolite, an igneous rock that is available in limited outcrops in southeast Missouri. If these fragments are portions of Steuben points, then they would fit into a time frame of Middle Woodland into the Late Woodland, approximately A.D. 200–700. Steuben points were recovered during the FAI-270 project near Cahokia from several sites including Leingang (Bentz et al. 1988:51, 54, Figure 15e-i) and Holding (Fortier et al. 1989:354, Plate 46n).

The number and variety of petroglyphs at 23WA1 may reflect the fact that some figures were made during the Woodland periods while others were added during the Mississippian period. In fact, there is a good possibility that ritual activity at 23WA1 began during the Archaic period. Coy et al. (1996:151–152) and Wagner et al. (2018:108–109) have argued that footprint petroglyphs in Kentucky and Illinois date to the Archaic period. Diesing (1955:Figures 7.2–7.4) noted three examples of full-grooved axes from sites in very close proximity to 23WA1; this artifact type is most often associated with the Middle Archaic period in Missouri (Chapman 1975:38; Chapman and Chapman 1964:158, Figures 7-63, 7-8, 7-13A, and 7-18) and may appear as early as 6000 B.C. at the sites in Illinois (Cook 1976; Farnsworth 1985:92). The property owner of the Three Hills Creek petroglyph site (23WA1702) discovered a full-grooved axe not far from the petroglyphs. Likewise, a significant Late Archaic site (23WA1707) is proximal to the Wallen Creek petroglyph site (23WA7). The idea of Archaic period rock art in Missouri is not implausible considering that pictographs stylistically dated to the Archaic period have been identified by Diaz-Granados and Duncan (2000:191) at two sites elsewhere in Missouri: White Rock Bluff (23TE01) and Deer Run Shelter. We have visited both of these Archaic pictograph sites and agree with the proposed dating.

The bifacial stone tools found in the crevice at 23WA1 include a small scraper manufactured out of pink, heat-treated chert. The scraper is 22.3 x 22.1 x 5.8 mm at 3.5 grams. A handwritten note on the artifact bag indicates that the scraper was excavated 17.5 inches beneath the surface; the excavation unit was not recorded on the paper bag.

Several mineral specimens recovered by Wyatt at 23WA1 are of particular interest because they are minerals of ceremonial importance during both the Woodland and Mississippian periods in Missouri. The most common mineral deposited in the crevice was druze quartz (Figure 13), which undoubtedly was collected from the ridges and stream-gravel deposits close to the site. Several dozen samples of druze quartz from the 23WA1 excavation range in size from gravel to fist-sized cobbles. The total weight of the larger pieces of druze quartz is 1.99 kg (4.38 lb). Druze quartz had many functions within the ceremonial world of Woodland and Mississippian people. In one sense, it sparkles like the stars and is often something of a "smear"—like the stars that form the Milky Way; it would be of obvious

Figure 13. Specimen of druze quartz from 21 to 25 inches below the surface of the crevice in Square B. It weighs 227.1 grams

Figure 14. Specimen of hematite from 0 to 6 inches beneath the surface of the crevice in Square D. It weighs 42.6 grams.

ritual significance in the medicine bundles of individuals belonging to the *Tsi shu* (Sky clans) of the Osage and their ancestors. Another way to conceptualize druze quartz, according to a contemporary Osage consultant, is that it is the ice crystals of the Underworld turned to stone—that would make fragments of druze quartz very significant to individuals with medicine associations with the Underworld. A third thought is that the glittering druze quartz crystals could have been seen as part of the shed skin of the *ts'a'-to(n)-ga* (Osage, Great Serpent). The Cherokee perceived that the Great Serpent (*uktena* in the Cherokee language) was a mixture of a serpent's body, horns, a bright blazing crest like a diamond, and either feathers or "glittering scales" (Beddoe 1903:208; Mooney 1902). Possessing a piece of the *ts'a'-to(n)-ga* shed skin would certainly have been powerful magic. Mooney (1889:168) reports that a Cherokee informant listed the necessary objects that had to be placed as offerings during the construction of a mound included *ulasu'ti* stone (a talismanic crystal) and the horn, tooth, or "scale" of an "enormous horned serpent with magical powers." Furthermore, Mooney (1889:167) added that Alice Fletcher witnessed a similar ceremonial mound-building with required offerings at one of the secret rites of the Ho-Chunk/Winnebago.

More than three dozen pieces of unmodified hematite (Figure 14) were excavated from the crevice at 23WA1 during 1959. The source of these would have been the ridge tops and stream gravels near 23WA1. The combined weight of the 27 largest pieces is 1.94 kg (4.27 lb). Hematite, ground into a powder, was the common source of red pigment for the ritual painting of sacred objects as well as for adorning the human body during the Mississippian period (Milner 1998:86).

Two cubes of galena (Figure 15) were recovered from 23WA1. The larger cube measures 1.29 x 1.23 x 1.02 cm and weighs 7.3 grams. The smaller cube measures 1.13 x 0.98 x 0.76 cm and weighs 2.9 grams. Galena was utilized during the Woodland, Mississippian, and Historic periods as a source of gray/white pigment (Milner 1998:86; Waltham et al. 1980:23, 39); it has been proposed that Cahokia was the hub for the trade of galena during the Mississippian period (Waltham 1981:42). Conrad (1991:145) notes that the most-elite individual buried during the Mississippian period at the Emmons site in Fulton County, Illinois, was accompanied by a wooden rattle carved out of red cedar and decorated in the form of a "well-sculpted representation of a human face with galena painted weeping eyes."

The presence of both Woodland and Mississippian period artifacts at the Boatyard site (23WA31) is not

Figure 15. Two cubes of galena from 23WA1. Left, from Square C, 14 to 20 inches beneath the surface within the crevice. Right, from Square A, 36 to 40 inches beneath the surface.

surprising considering that the petroglyphs are situated a half-day's walk from this very large village/town site that had been occupied during both the Woodland and Mississippian periods. The topography of the Boatyard site includes a large platform mound that has been almost leveled after a century of cultivation. The artifacts from the Boatyard site confirm the presence of a thriving Woodland and Mississippian community in the Big River Valley near 23WA1; Frank Magre's assertion made in 1970 at a meeting of the Mound City Archaeological Society that both Woodland and Mississippian iconography is reflected in the petroglyphs thus gains a little more traction.

Wyatt (n.d.:15) recorded the Boatyard site with the Archaeological Survey of Missouri after conducting a thorough survey and limited testing of the site; he noted that it yielded a large sample of pottery sherds of which 71% were Woodland and 29% were Mississippian. We examined the artifacts that Wyatt collected from 23WA31 and revisited the site; our conclusion is that Wyatt's assessment of the site is accurate. The Boatyard site was first described by John Thomas (1907:174). A second survey of the Boatyard site, after Wyatt's, was conducted by a cultural resources management (CRM) team from the University of Missouri–Columbia. The CRM survey recovered 99 sherds, 55% Woodland, 45% Mississippian; they specifically reported one Powell Plain sherd, one Cahokia Red Filmed sherd, and a single piece of galena weighing 1,186 grams (Ives et al. 1982:57–58). The importance of the Boatyard site in the Big River Valley was recognized by Koldehoff and Wilson (2010:240) in their study of Mississippian celts.

We believe that the mineral artifacts—druze quartz, hematite, and galena—were brought to the site for ritual purposes. Some of the other artifacts (mineral, plant, and animal) may have been left for short periods of time in the shallow basins in the bedrock on both sides of the crevice. Rainwater collects and quickly evaporates from the shallow basins, and this could have been seen as a spiritually cleansing/empowering of the offerings. Several petroglyphs surround the basins, while the majority are situated between the basins and the crevice.

We suggest that offerings of weapons were brought to the site and either left as permanent offerings or "recharged" by being dipped into the water collected in the shallow basins above the crevice. Research at 23WA1 during the solar eclipse of 2017 resulted in the unexpected discovery by Eric Fuller of a serrated Scallorn

point, manufactured out of a thin chert flake (Figure 16), that was eroding from the soil deposits at the west edge of the petroglyph panels. The undamaged condition of the Scallorn point removes the possibility that it was a chance hunting loss. Rituals involving arrows are well known among the traditions of the Osage Nation. The Rite of Vigil required a red arrow and a black arrow to represent day and night (LaFlesche 1921:Figure 7, 1925:233–234, 364–369, 1932:98).

Figure 16. *Serrated Scallorn point manufactured out of local, pinkish-white chert discovered during 2017 eroding from deposits adjacent to the west edge of the petroglyphs at 23WA1. It is 23.8 x 12.0 x 3.3 mm, and 0.9 grams. Scale in mm.*

Smallwood et al. (2018:222–223) have argued that serrated Scallorn points should be specifically associated with warfare and noted that the "serrations would have improved the shock, awe and lethalness of arrows." Indeed, the three large caches of arrows (many with serrated edges) that were placed as burial offerings at Cahokia in Mound 72 (Fowler 1999:Figures 8.1, 8.2 and 8.3; Rose 2006) carry the message of military shock and awe from the world of the living into the world of the dead. A second explanation for the purpose of serrated arrow points is that they had been dipped into a poisonous substance that would insure the death of the wounded animal or human (Prof. Leo Huff, personal communication 1974). There is an ethnographic reference to the use of poison arrows with serrated edges (called corrugated edges) by the Mattaponi tribe of Virginia (Jones 2007:34). Arrow poison was used by the Illini, Omaha, and Creek (Jones 2007)—all tribes that have been proposed as associated with Missouri prehistoric populations. Ethnographic interviews by Eric Fuller with two members of the Osage Nation have revealed that Eastern Red Cedar (*Juniperus virginiana*) was used to create an arrow poison. The root of the Eastern Red Cedar was boiled into a thick black substance and the arrowheads were dipped into the root tar toxin. An animal or human nicked by an Osage poisoned arrow would experience dizziness within an hour. Milkweed pods would be wrapped around the poison arrow tips to protect the archer against accidental injury. Both ethnographic consultants agreed that the function of the serrations on an arrow point could be to hold the poison.

1959 Excavations at 23WA2

The petroglyphs at Washington State Park B (23WA2) are located near the Ranger's headquarters at the park. Unlike 23WA1, they are not protected by an overhead canopy. The most significant motifs at this site are the ceremonial maces.

Wyatt (n.d.:10) excavated at 23WA2 and recovered pottery sherds belonging to a plate and a vertical-walled bowl. He identified the plate as Powell Plain ware (dating from A.D. 1100 to 1275); the shell-tempered sherds were found 7 inches below the ground surface. A surface survey by Wyatt around the petroglyphs at 23WA2 discovered material culture including 33 fragments of shell-tempered pottery (St. Clair ware), the tip of a projectile point, several mussel shell fragments, and numerous flint/quartzite waste flakes. We interpret the pottery sherds associated with 23WA2 as evidence of offerings brought to the petroglyph site and left on the exposed bedrock. The plate and bowl would have contained organic offerings. The plate and bowl may have been intentionally "killed" when the ritual action was completed, then covered with a thin layer of soil.

Research after 1959 Excavations at 23WA1

Study of the petroglyph panels would take place in 1960 and 1961 by a Missouri Parks ranger named Kenneth G. Middleton. He produced a two-page report in 1962 summarizing his research results. His sketches compare favorably with the drawings of Chapman and Chapman, and Elgin. He did make a significant observation when studying Cluster 7 on the north side of the crevice where he recognized an animal with a long upright tail walking along a symbolic trail or river; it strongly resembles pictographs of a puma/panther at sites in Missouri and Illinois.

A decade later, in 1970, Kent Bonar would study the petroglyphs at 23WA1 and significantly change the way the site should be perceived. Bonar, a gifted naturalist, produced a two-page handwritten cover letter and seven-page handwritten report on this mapping of the site. He studied the 1959 map prepared by Elgin and was perplexed that he could see many petroglyphs that were not recorded by Elgin. Bonar enlisted the advice of two citizen archaeologists (Frank Magre and Father Benedict Ellis) to help him determine what were natural features and what were petroglyphs. Bonar's careful study of 23WA1 would result in approximately 525 petroglyph elements (Figure 17) in contrast to the 188 mapped by Elgin. Furthermore, Bonar divided the site into seven major panels—two north of the crevice and five to the south. His map at first glance shows the overall pattern of dense petroglyphs on both sides of the crevice.

It must be remembered that even the Bonar (1970) map is incomplete because many dozens of petroglyphs were destroyed along the south edge of the site during the construction of Highway 21. A true map of the site "might" resemble an oval bisected down the middle by the crevice. The version of the Bonar map that we have published is oriented with the crevice running up and down in order to suggest that the overall distribution of the petroglyphs resembles the pattern of several vulva petroglyphs at the site. One way the site may have been perceived by the Native Americans living in the Big River Valley was that the bedrock ledges on either side of the crevice, decorated with petroglyphs, were figuratively a supernatural *mons pubis*—the rounded mass of tissue over the joint of the pelvis girdle of a female Spirit Being.

Wyatt had counted seven vulva petroglyphs (Figures 18 and 19) during his research in 1959. We have seen at least five "definite" vulva petroglyphs at 23WA1 and suspect that Wyatt's number is correct. It is interesting that Diesing and Magre (1942:11) included the vulva petroglyphs in their discussion of "indescribable types…oval or horse-shoe shaped with bisecting line ending with a cup" and clearly show two examples (Diesing and Magre 1942:Plate Vb and e).

Explanations of 23WA1 and 23WA2

Giving meaning to the petroglyphs at 23WA1 and 23WA2 is a task fraught with potential mistakes, but that has not kept various researchers from attempting. Clearly, there was an original meaning in the heart of the Native American artists, meanings in the hearts of Native Americans who visited the site and left offerings, and finally the meanings that Euro-American archaeologists have proposed.

Interpretations of some of the petroglyphs are scattered in the text of Diesing and Magre (1942:11–15). They note the presence of an oval with a bisecting line and state that "it may be compared to a horseshoe with bisecting line extending not quite to the opening at the calks." Vulva petroglyphs that Diesing and Magre called bisected ovals or horseshoe shapes appear in Clusters 3 (2 examples), 7, 8, and 11. We will never know if Diesing and Magre self-censored the term vulva from their report, or if it was done by the editor of their manuscript.

In their interpretations, Diesing and Magre (1942:13–14) noted that the two large bird figures "resemble those of a hawk or eagle, and are thought to represent the thunderbird." They noted that the hawk/eagle petroglyph in Cluster 1 had such fine detail that feathers can be recognized in the tail; those can still be seen on days when the light is at just the right angle to the rock surface. Diesing and Magre recorded the presence of a coiled snake with open jaws in Cluster 3. They noted several solid-figure squares and rectangles

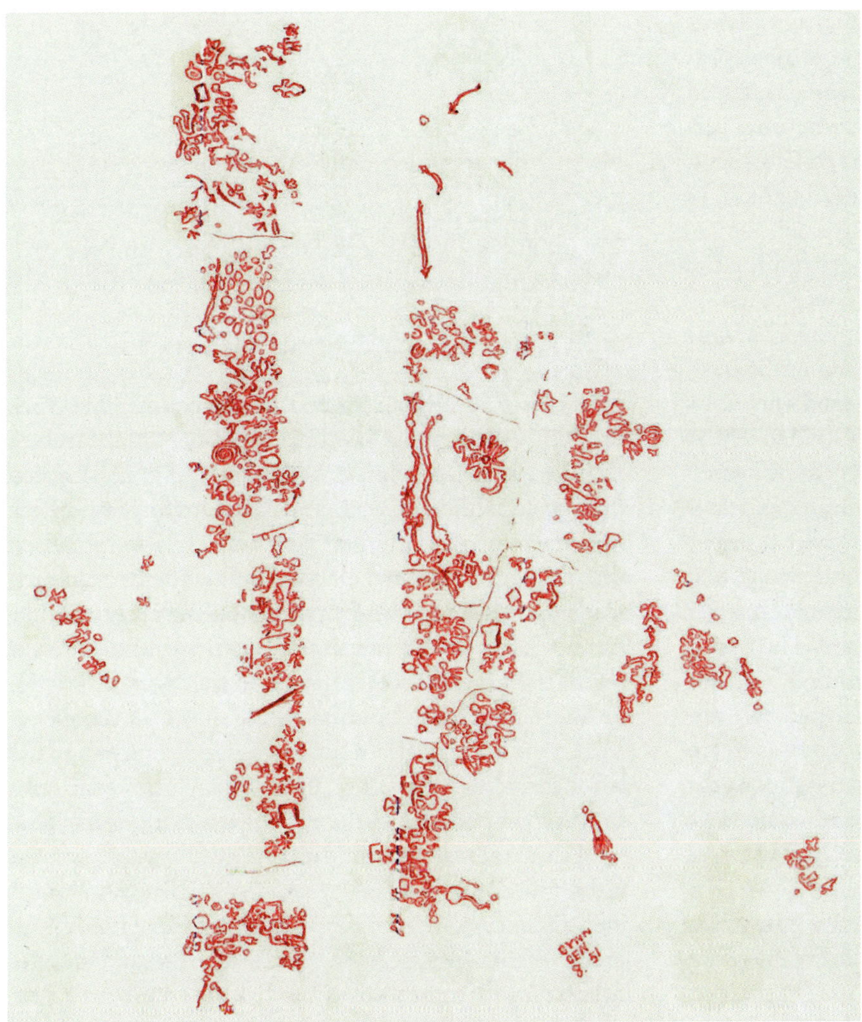

Figure 17. Bonar's map of 23WA1 showing 525 petroglyphs divided into two concentrations by the crevice that runs east-west.

Figure 18. Cluster 8 includes at least 12 petroglyphs including a round vulvar form. Duncan and Diaz-Granados (2004:205) identify this as an Ushje (female organ of the world)—the entrance to the Lower World/Underworld. Quintero (2009:219) uses the term Uze for vagina in Osage. The petroglyph measures 20 x 13 cm. Scale is 20 cm.

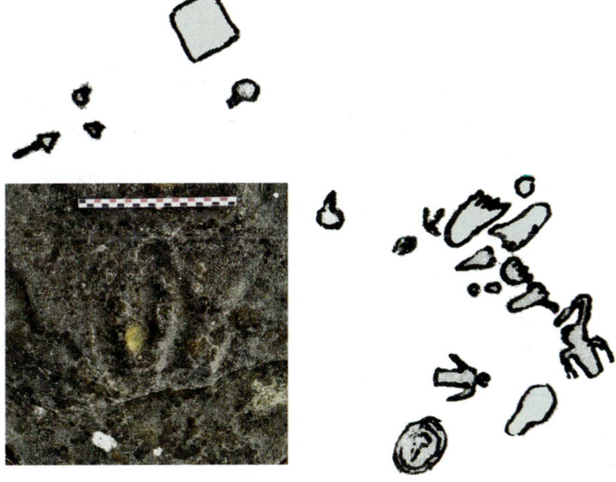

Figure 19. Elgin's (1961) drawing of a group of at least 21 petroglyphs that includes the largest vulvar petroglyph (26 x 16 cm) situated near north edge of 23WA1. The vulva petroglyph is positioned on a portion of the bedrock that dips to the north; it is not visible from the viewing platform.

89

scattered in different parts of the site (such as Clusters 1, 2, 4, 6, 8, and 10), speculating that these could represent houses or wigwams. Diesing and Magre suggested that the wavy or zigzag line petroglyphs sometimes terminate in the shape of an arrowhead (as in Clusters 1 and 4), but others have the appearance of a snake in motion (such as in Cluster 4).

The text for the interpretive signs, written for the park by Chapman and Chapman (n.d.), described how different panels portray a variety of "themes." The large bird in Cluster 1 is described by Chapman and Chapman as "the Mighty Thunderbird that sends his bolts of lightning by little birds." Cluster 2 is described by the Chapmans as "Talking Thunderbird and group of small thunderbirds." Cluster 3, which has several themes, is summed up as "Fertility and Rain—the great number of oval shaped female fertility symbols and two joined human figures probably indicate the great desire for fertility of crops, game animals, and people. The coiled rattlesnake and thunderbirds are rain symbols." Cluster 7, on the north side of the crevice, is described as "Sunburst and Mace—In the center of this group is a sun burst that has connected with it a human figure and a fertility symbol. West of it is an arrow and mace. The sun was an object of reverence by those Indians, and the mace was a symbol of authority."

Chapman and Chapman (n.d.) wrote a paragraph essay that was displayed on a large sign at the entrance to the petroglyphs:

> These petroglyphs are rock carvings believed by archaeologists to have been made by the Middle Mississippian people related to the builders of the Cahokia Mounds (Illinois) and the Mound City People who once lived in St. Louis. The figures of birds, snakes, animals, and other symbols were made for religious, ceremonial, and mythological reasons. They (the petroglyphs) are important in giving a glimpse into the psychological thoughts of the mind of early men in Missouri in his struggles to understand the universe. The people who made these symbols were Indians, the ancestors of the Indians found here when Missouri was first discovered in 1673.

Indians and Archaeology of Missouri (Chapman and Chapman 1964:79) contained only a single paragraph about the site:

> The Washington State Park petroglyph site was probably the junction of game trails and war

trails, and was possibly a consecrated spot where young men were initiated into secret society rites and were taught the mythology associated with the initiation. The rock carvings may have been memory aids for songs and rites that were part of the ceremony. The symbols probably had magical as well as religious meanings, and participation in the ceremonies at the sacred spot could have been the means of imparting the power of the symbols to the participants.

Klaus P. Wellman visited Washington State Park sites as well as the Maddin Creek site on March 9, 1970, with Frank Magre. Wellman (1979:157) noted that both Maddin Creek and Washington State Park sites have fertility-themed artwork. He also suggested that the lemon-shaped elements could be germinating seeds and that the two humans holding an arrow-like symbol between them are holding a corn husk. Wellman (1979:Figure 800) illustrated the two human figures in Cluster 2 as holding what "may be a cornstalk" and proposed that the "tailed ovoid" petroglyphs to the left and below of the left figure "may represent corn sprouts." The identification of corn as a motif in Cluster 2 was not taken from the signage and probably was not an idea volunteered by Magre. We find Wellman's identification of corn to be very convincing. Furthermore, Wellman suggested that the larger and smaller squares could represent a birth house and/or a preparatory hut—a speculation certainly not out of tune with the fertility imagery at this particular site.

We are glad to recognize the vast literature on Washington State Park written by Carol Diaz-Granados and Jim Duncan (Diaz-Granados 1993, 2004; Diaz-Granados and Duncan 2000, 2004; Duncan and Diaz-Granados 2004, 2018a, 2018b; and more). Jim Duncan's research on the site began in 1961 when he served as an interpretive ranger at the site (Duncan and Diaz-Granados 2018a:30)—his ancestral connection to the Osage Nation and status in the Osage Native American Church have led to many significant insights. They identify the vulva petroglyphs at 23WA1 as a motif associated with Old-Woman-Who-Never-Dies or First Woman (Diaz-Granados 1993:332–335; Duncan and Diaz-Granados 2004:193–195; and more)—"she is associated with the earth, lives in a square house in the south, or the Moon, and is sexually involved with the great serpent" (Duncan and Diaz-Granados 2018b:61–62, Figure 3.1). They offer an interesting perspective on the two human figures that Wellman interpreted as holding a cornstalk; Duncan and Diaz-Granados (2018a:Figure 2.19) interpret the imagery as a ritual in which medicine bundles are gathered and opened, while at another level the pair are probably also representations of the hero twins Stone and Gray Wolf, nephew of Hawk. They identify the footprint petroglyphs as symbolic of the presence of Hawk who is the same as Morning Star-Venus (Duncan and Diaz-Granados 2018a:53, Figure 2.16).

Our recent research (Fuller et al. 2019a, 2019b) was related to observing the petroglyphs during the total solar eclipse and our analysis of the artifacts excavated by Wyatt in 1959. After seeing the map made by Bonar (1970), we recognize that the entirety of 23WA1 is a large vulva and that the petroglyphs along the edge of the crevice (symbolically the *mons pubis*) portray an emergence sacred story that includes spirit beings and totemic symbols of a variety of clans. We were particularly pleased when Sean StandingBear recognized his clan symbol petroglyph—a black bear paw—in Cluster 7. We suspect that several other petroglyphs interpreted as related to hunting magic by Magre and Chapman should be interpreted in the context of the clans, subclans, and bands within the Osage Nation. For example, the bird tracks in Cluster 4 could be clan symbols for the Crane or Swan clan (Burns 1984:36; LaFlesche 1928:123), the turtle petroglyph in Cluster 4 could be a clan symbol for the Turtle clan (Burns 2001:33), and a long-tailed animal in Cluster 7 is most likely a representation of the Puma or Panther clan (Burns 1984:36; LaFlesche 1928:33). Historic records of Osage clans do not include a Beaver clan, but a beaver paw print in Cluster 6 may well represent the Beaver band noted by Matthews (1961:706). Burns (1984:29) observed that he knew of at least 84 clans and subclans, but that no "complete" list or count exists.

The presence of clan symbols and the strong association with earth fertility suggest that 23WA1 was associated with a creation story of significance to the Boatyard site, which is within view from 23WA1. This interpretation may seem somewhat hard to reconcile with the fact that the best-known Osage creation stories involve "descent" of their ancestors from the sky (Bailey 2010:46–49; Ordoes and Ortiz 1984:119, 512 based upon Fletcher and LaFlesche) and not emergence from beneath the earth. It is worth noting that one version of the Osage "descent" sacred story told by Shun-kah-mo-lah to Francis LaFlesche (Bailey 2010:59) included the detail that the *Tsi'-zhu* (Sky) People came down in the form of eagles and that two eagles could find no resting place in the branches of a large red oak tree, so they dropped to the ground. The concept of two sacred eagles somewhat echoes the two thunderbirds represented in Clusters 1 and 2 at 23WA1. The sacred story of the eagles landing in the branches of the red oak tree is still valued by the Osage Nation and a mural of this story decorates the wall of the Osage Law Court in Pawhuska, Oklahoma.

Bailey (2010:17) notes that each Osage Nation clan had its own origin story and that we have good knowledge of only two (Wolf clan and Black Bear clan) out of the 24 clan origin stories. Emergence stories are known among the Lakota Nation, who belong to the same Siouan language family as the Osage Nation. The Lakota Nation relate in their sacred story that their ancestors emerged through a hole in the ground, a cave, that is today called Wind Cave (Marshall 2001:56); they revere *Oniya Ashoka* (Lakota, "where the earth breathes inside") as their point of emergence onto the surface of the earth (Rossi 2017:4; U.S. National Park Service 2003:541). Other Siouan language Nations have emergence stories, including the Hidatsa, who emerged from the earth near a large lake; the Mandan, who emerged from a cave near the mouth of the Missouri River; and the Arikara, who lived in Mother Earth then Mother Corn brought them to the surface (State Historical Society of North Dakota 2022). The Baxoje/Iowa Nation creation story is a combination of Bear People (Earth Moiety leaders) emerging from the earth and Eagle People (Sky Moiety leaders) descending out of the sky (Lance Foster, personal communication August 7, 2022). We believe that 23WA1 could represent either an emergence sacred story or, like that of the Iowa Nation, a combination emergence/descent sacred story.

Emergence creation stories are found among several Native American Nations including the Creek, Alabama, Chickasaw, Choctaw, and Muskogee (Grantham 2002:109–133). Emergence myths are also found among many Native American nations in the Southwest and Mexico (Leeming and Leeming 1994:58). It has been reported that each Hopi clan has its own version of the Hopi emergence sacred story (Loftin 2003:131). It is interesting to think about Wellman's interpretation of corn in the petroglyphs at 23WA1, because some Native American Nations in the Southwest link the emergence from Earth Mother with receiving corn from the Corn Mother (Wiget 1996:57).

A final comparative observation, far from Missouri, is that of the vulva petroglyphs carved at the Wedding Rocks site (45CA215) along the Pacific coast of Washington. The Wedding Rocks site motifs harken to a Haida sacred story of Raven and Fungus (also called Biscuit Man) who paddle a canoe to an island where vulvas were alive on a rocky surface (Browne 2016). Raven and Fungus retrieved many of the vulvas to create women by attaching the vulvas to men—truly an innovative solution for a village populated only by men! It would be ironic if the iconography at 23WA1, like the iconography of the Wedding Rocks site on the Pacific Ocean, was not about emergence or descent but—as Frank Magre often argued—sexuality, identity, and procreation.

Acknowledgments. We acknowledge that we are describing archaeological sites situated in the ancestral and spiritual homeland of the Wahzhazhi (Osage) Nation. We all owe a debt of gratitude to the Native American artists who carved the wondrous scenes on the rocks in Missouri. It has been our great pleasure to visit these sites with Thomas Mercer, E. Sean StandingBear, and Patricia StandingBear—we have greatly benefited from their knowledge of Osage culture.

A thousand thanks to our friends in the Missouri State Parks: Sharon Hultberg, (Manager, Washington State Park), Bill Mayberry (Naturalist, Washington State Park), Michael Ohnersorgen (Director, Cultural Resource Management Program, Missouri State Parks), and Kim Dillon (Cultural Resources Management Section Lead, Missouri State Parks). Special thanks to Jeffrey S. Alvey (Archaeologist, Missouri State Historic Preservation Office) for providing access to the archival files for Washington County, and to Heather Gibb (Records Coordinator, Missouri State Historic Preservation Office) for maintaining the statewide database.

Special thanks for the help provided by our good friends at the University of Missouri–Columbia: Jessica Boldt (Assistant Curator of the Museum of Anthropology), Candace Sall (Director of the Museum of Anthropology), and R. Bruce McMillan (Director Emeritus of the Illinois State Museum and Adjunct Research Associate in Anthropology at UMC). We acknowledge information provided by Leo Huff (Professor of History at Missouri State University), Bill Iseminger (Retired Assistant Manager at Cahokia Mounds State Historic Site), Jack Ray (Center for Archaeological Research at Missouri State University) and Lance Foster (Tribal Historic Preservation Officer and NAGPRA representative for the Iowa Tribe of Kansas and Nebraska). Numerous citizen archaeologists deserve thanks for their years of assistance to us on this and many other projects: Frank Magre, Dick Elgin, Dick Martens, Doug Porter, John Northrip, Mark Leach, and Alan Westfall. Any mistakes and errors rest solely on the shoulders of the senior author.

References Cited

Bailey, Garrick
  20100 *Traditions of the Osage: Stories Collected and Translated by Francis LaFlesche.* University of New Mexico Press, Albuquerque.

Beddoe, John
  1903 Review of *Myths of the Cherokees* by James Mooney. *Man* (3):207–208.

Bentz, Charles, Dale L. McElrath, Fred A. Finney, and Richard B. Lacampagne
  1988 *Late Woodland Sites in the American Bottom Uplands.* University of Illinois Press, Urbana.

Blake, Leonard W.
  1942 A Hopewell-like Site near St. Louis, *Missouri Archaeologist* 8(1):2–7.

  n.d. The Creve Coeur Lake Hopewell Site. Unpublished manuscript in the possession of Richard Martens.

Bonar, Kent
  1970 *Petroglyph Mapping [at Washington State Park].* Manuscript on file in the Archives of the Missouri State Parks.

Brown, James A.
  1996 *The Spiro Ceremonial Center: The Archaeology of Arkansas Valley Caddoan Culture in Eastern Oklahoma.* Volume 2. Memoirs of the Museum of Anthropology 29. University of Michigan Museum of Anthropological Archaeology, Ann Arbor.

Brown, Paul V.
  1938 Letter to the Missouri Games and Fish Department (Missouri Parks) on April 22 requesting that a base chart prepared by Charles G. Wilder be sent to the National Park Service. Record Group 10 in the Archives of the Missouri State Parks.

Browne, Colin
  2016 *Entering Time: The Fungus Man Platters of Charles Edenshaw.* Talonbooks, Vancouver, British Columbia.

Burns, Louis F.
  1984 *Osage Customs and Myths.* Ciga Press, Fallbrook, California.

  2001 *Osage Indian Bands and Clans.* Clearfield, Baltimore.

Bushnell, David I., Jr.
  1901 *Fieldbook No. 2.* David I. Bushnell, Jr., collection, identifier 1.5C. Peabody Museum Archives, Harvard Library, Cambridge, Massachusetts. Details available at https://hollisarchives.lib.harvard.edu/repositories/6/archival_objects/1369612, accessed September 7, 2022.

  1913 Petroglyphs Representing the Imprint of the Human Foot. *American Anthropologist* 15(1):8–15.

Chapman, Carl H.
  1959 Manuscript prepared on March 18, 1959, excerpt from a letter written to Abner Gwinn on May 3, 1955. Archives of the Missouri State Parks, Jefferson City.

  1975 *The Archaeology of Missouri, I.* University of Missouri Press, Columbia.

  1980 *The Archaeology of Missouri, II.* University of Missouri Press, Columbia.

Chapman, Carl H., and Eleanor Chapman
  1964 *Indians and Archaeology of Missouri*. University of Missouri Press, Columbia.

  n.d. Plan and sign captions for Washington State Park Petroglyphs. Document 13.005.001, Archives of the Missouri State Parks, Jefferson City.

Conant, Alban Jasper
  1879 Archaeology. In *Switzler's Illustrated History of Missouri from 1541 to 1877*, edited by Chancy R. Barnes, pp. 3–122. C. R. Barns, St. Louis.

Conrad, Lawrence A.
  1991 The Middle Mississippian Cultures of the Central Illinois River Valley. In *Cahokia and the Hinterlands: Middle Mississippian Cultures of the Midwest*, edited by Thomas E. Emerson and R. Barry Lewis, pp. 119–156. University of Illinois Press, Urbana.

Cook, Thomas G.
  1976 *Koster: An Artifact Analysis of Two Archaic Phases in West Central Illinois*. Prehistoric Records No. 1. Northwestern Archeological Programs, Evanston, Illinois.

Corliss, William R.
  1976 *The Unexplained: A Sourcebook of Strange Phenomena*. Bantam Books, New York.

Coy, Fred E., Thomas Fuller, Larry G. Meadows, and James L. Swauger
  1996 *The Rock Art of Kentucky*. The University of Kentucky Press, Lexington.

Craig, Joseph, and Susan Vorreyer
  2004 *The Cowmire Creek Site: A Havana Tradition Middle Woodland Period Habitation Site in St. Louis County, MO (23SL1056)*. Environmental Compliance Consultants Inc., Springfield, Illinois.

Daily Missouri Republican
  1868 Dr. Albert C. Koch. *Daily Missouri Republican*, January 14, 1868, page 2, column 1. St. Louis, Missouri.

DeMott, Rodney C., Derrick J. Marcucci, and Joyce A. Williams
  1993 *The Archaeology of the Cahokia Mounds ICT-II: Testing and Lithics, Part 2*. Illinois Historic Preservation Agency, Springfield.

Diaz-Granados, Carol
  1993 *The Petroglyphs and Pictographs of Missouri—A Distributional, Stylistic, Contextual, Temporal and Functional Analysis of the State's Rock Art*. Ph.D. dissertation, Department of Anthropology, Washington University in St. Louis.

  2004 Making Stone, Land, Body, and Spirit: Rock Art and Mississippian Iconography. In *Hero, Hawk, and Open Hand: American Indian Art of the Ancient Midwest and South*, edited by Richard F. Townsend and Robert V. Sharp, pp. 138–149. Art Institute of Chicago, Chicago.

Diaz-Granados, Carol, and James R. Duncan
  2000 *The Petroglyphs and Pictographs of Missouri*. University of Alabama Press, Tuscaloosa.

  2004 Reflections of Power, Wealth, and Sex in Missouri Rock-Art Motifs. In *The Rock-Art of Eastern North America*, edited by Carol Diaz-Granados and James R. Duncan, pp. 145–158. University of Alabama Press, Tuscaloosa.

Diesing, Eugene H.
  1955 Archaeological Features in and around Washington State Park in Washington and Jefferson Counties, Missouri. *Missouri Archaeologist* 17(1):12–23.

Diesing, Eugene H., and Frank Magre
  1942 Petroglyphs and Pictographs in Missouri. *Missouri Archaeologist* 8(1):8–18.

Duncan, James R., and Carol Diaz-Granados
  2004 Empowering the SECC: The "Old Woman" and Oral Traditions. In *The Rock-Art of Eastern North America*, edited by Carol Diaz-Granados and James R. Duncan, pp. 190–218. University of Alabama Press, Tuscaloosa.

  2018a The Big Five Petroglyph Sites: Their Place on the Landscape and Relation to Their Creators. In *Transforming the Landscape: Rock Art and the Mississippian Cosmos*, edited by Carol Diaz-Granados, Jan Simek, George Sabo, and Mark Wagner, pp. 30–56. Oxbow Books, Oxford, United Kingdom.

  2018b Landscape, Cosmology, and the Old Woman: A Strong Feminine Presence. In *Transforming the Landscape: Rock Art and the Mississippian Cosmos*, edited by Carol Diaz-Granados, Jan Simek, George Sabo, and Mark Wagner, pp. 57–74. Oxbow Books, Oxford, United Kingdom.

Dye, David H.
  2016 An Overview of Federal Work Relief Projects in Tennessee and the Tennessee Valley, 1933–1942. In *New Deal Archaeology in Tennessee: Intellectual, Methodological, and Theoretical Contributions*, edited by David H. Dye, pp. 1–28. University of Alabama Press, Tuscaloosa.

Elgin, Robert L.
  1961 *Plot Plan of Petroglyph Shelter & Area at Washington State Park*. Copies on file at Washington State Park and Archives of the Missouri State Parks.

Farnsworth, Kenneth B.
  1985 Preliminary Evaluations of Bannerstones and other Groundstone Artifacts in the Wear Collection from the Bullseye Site (11-GE-127). In *Middle Archaic Investigations along the Illinois River Floodplain: Archaeological Evaluations at the Quasar (11-GE-136) and Bullseye (11-GE-127) Sites in Greene County, Illinois*, edited by Harold Hassen. St. Louis District, U.S. Corps of Engineers, Cultural Resource Management Report No. 18.

Fortier, Andrew C., Thomas O. Maher, Joyce A. Williams, Michael C. Meinkoth, Kathryn E. Parker, and Lucretia S. Kelly
  1989 *The Holding Site: A Hopewell Community in the American Bottom*. University of Illinois Press, Urbana.

Fowler, Melvin L.
  1999 *The Mound 72 Area: Dedicated and Sacred Space in Early Cahokia*. Illinois State Museum Society, Springfield.

Fuller, Michael J., Neathery B. Fuller, and Eric C. Fuller
  2019a Total Solar Eclipses and Rock Art in Missouri. *Missouri Archaeological Society Quarterly* 36(4):12–19.

  2019b Artifacts Associated with the Washington State Park Petroglyphs. *Missouri Archaeological Society Quarterly* 36(4):12–20.

Fuller, Michael J., Stan Meyers, and Don Dougan
  1970 Prehistoric Indian Folklore as Interpreted from a Study of Missouri Petroglyphs. Unpublished manuscript, copies in the possession of the author and Doug Porter, Fordland, Missouri.

Grantham, Bill
  2002 *Creation Myths and Legends of the Creek Indians*. University Press of Florida, Gainesville.

Haag, William G.
  1939 Program of the Third Southeastern Archaeological Conference. *Newsletter of the Southeastern Archaeological Conference* 2(1):1–24.

Hubbard, George D., and Charles G. Wilder
1930 Validity of the Indicators of Ancient Climate. *Geological Society of America Bulletin* 41(2):275–292.

Huddleston, Connie M.
2009 *Kentucky's Civilian Conservation Corps.* History Press, Charleston.

Ives, David J., J. Alan May, and David D. Denman
1982 *Pine Ford Lake Phase I Archeological Survey.* Manuscript on file with the Museum of Anthropology, University of Missouri–Columbia.

Jaeger, Joseph
1959 Letter defining terms of employment for Ron Wyatt on file in the Archives of the Missouri State Parks; prepared on April 8, 1959.

Jones, David E.
2007 *Poison Arrows: North American Indian Hunting and Warfare.* University of Texas Press, Austin.

Kelly, John Edward
1982 *Formative Development at Cahokia and the Adjacent American Bottoms; A Merrell Tract Perspective, Volume II.* Western Illinois University, Archaeological Research Laboratory, Macomb.

Koch, Albert C.
1847 *Reise durch einen Theil der Vereinigten Staaten von Nordamerika in den jahren 1844 bis 1846.* Arnoldische Buchhandlung, Dresden and Leipzig. Electronic document, https://archive.org/details/reisedurcheinent00koch, accessed September 7, 2022.

1972 *Journey Through a Part of the United States of North American in the Years 1844 to 1846.* Translated by Ernst A. Stadler. Southern Illinois University Press, Carbondale.

Koldehoff, Brad, and Gregory D. Wilson
2010 Mississippian Celt Production and Resource Extraction in the Upper Big River Valley of St. Francois County, Missouri. *Missouri Archaeologist* 71:217–248.

LaFlesche, Francis
1921 *The Osage Tribe: Rite of the Chiefs; Sayings of the Ancient Men.* Thirty-sixth Annual Report of the Bureau of American Ethnology 1914-1915, pp. 35–604.

1925 *The Osage Tribe: The Rite of Vigil.* Thirty-ninth Annual Report of the Bureau of American Ethnology 1917-1918, pp. 31–630.

1928 *Osage Tribe, Two Versions of the Child-naming Rite.* Forty-third Annual Report of the Bureau of American Ethnology 1925-1926, pp. 23–164.

1932 *A Dictionary of the Osage Language.* Bureau of American Ethnology Bulletin 109, pp. 1–406.

Leach, Mark W.
2017 *The Great Pyramids of St. Louis.* Privately printed.

Leeming, David Adams, and Margaret Adams Leeming
1994 *Encyclopedia of Creation Myths.* ABC-CLIO, Santa Barbara, California.

Loftin, John D.
2003 *Religion and Hopi Life.* Second edition. Indiana University Press, Bloomington.

Magre, Frank
1970 The Maddin Creek Petroglyph Site, Washington County, Missouri. Lecture given at the Mound City Archaeological Society meeting on February 3, 1970, Oak Knoll Science Museum, St. Louis.

1975 Higginbotham-Engledow Collection Notes. Unpublished manuscript in the Archives of the Missouri State Parks.

Marshall, Joseph M.
2001 *The Lakota Way: Stories and Lessons in Living.* Viking Compass, New York.

Mathews, John Joseph
1961 *The Osages: Children of the Middle Waters.* University of Oklahoma Press, Norman.

McMillan, R. Bruce
1980 Objects of Curiosity: Albert Koch's 1840 St. Louis Museum. *The Living Museum* 42(2/3):35–38.

Middleton, Kenneth G.
1962 *Summer Field Work at Washington State Park.* Manuscript on file in the Archives of the Missouri State Parks.

Milner, George R.
1984 *The Julien Site (11-S-63).* University of Illinois Press, Urbana.

1998 *The Cahokia Chiefdom: The Archaeology of a Mississippian Society.* Smithsonian Institution Press, Washington, D.C.

Milner, George R., Thomas E. Emerson, Mark W. Mehrer, Joyce A. Williams, and Duane Esarey
1984 Mississippian and Oneota Period. In *American Bottom Archaeology,* edited by Charles J. Bareis and James W. Porter, pp. 158–186, University of Illinois Press, Urbana.

Mooney, James
1889 Mound-building. *American Anthropologist* 2(2):167–171.

1902 *Myths of the Cherokee.* Nineteenth Annual Report of the Bureau of American Ethnology 1897-1898, Part 1, pp. 3–548.

O'Brien, Dorothy Jean
n.d. Washington State Park. Manuscript on file in the Archives of the Missouri State Parks.

Ordoes, Richard, and Alfonso Ortiz
1984 *American Indian Myths and Legends.* Pantheon, New York.

Pauketat Timothy R.
2004 *Ancient Cahokia and the Mississippians.* Cambridge University Press, Cambridge.

Quintero, Carolyn
2009 *Osage Dictionary.* University of Oklahoma Press, Norman.

Ray, Jack H.
2016 *Projectile Point Types in Missouri and Portions of Adjacent States.* Missouri Archaeological Society, Springfield.

Reber, Robert J., Steven L. Boles, Thomas E. Emerson, Madeleine G. Evans, Thomas J. Loebel, Dale L. McElrath, and David J. Nolan
2017 *Projectile Points and the Illinois Landscape: People, Time, and Place.* ISAS Studies in Archaeology 11. Illinois State Archaeological Survey, University of Illinois, Urbana.

Rose, Jerry
2006 Elite Burial at Cahokia. Paper presented at the Symposium on Elite Burials, St. Louis Society of the Archaeological Institute of America, September 30, 2006, St. Louis Community College–Florissant Valley.

Rossi, Adam
2017 *Where the Earth Breathes Inside: The Attitudes of Lakota People toward Wind Cave National Park.* Master's thesis, Davis College of Agriculture, Natural Resources and Design, West Virginia University.

SAA
1942 Society for American Archaeology Annual Meeting. *American Antiquity* 8(2):202–205

Sandstrom, Carl B., and Jack H. Ray
2004 *A Point Identification Guide for Southwest Missouri.* Ozarks Chapter of the Missouri Archaeological Society, Springfield.

Schoolcraft, Henry Rowe
1822 Remarks on the Prints of Human Feet, Observed in the Secondary Limestone of the Mississippi Valley. *American Journal of Science and Arts* 5(2):223–230.

1825 *Travels in the Central Portions of the Mississippi Valley: Comprising Observations on its Mineral Geography, Internal Resources, and Aboriginal Population.* Collins and Hannay, New York.

Silverman, Thomas
1997 *Lithic Analysis of the Creve Coeur Site (23SL20).* Senior Honors Thesis, Department of Anthropology, Washington University in St. Louis.

Smallwood, Ashley M., Heather L. Smith, Charlotte D. Pevny, and Thomas A. Jennings
2018 The Convergent Evolution of Serrated Points on the Southern Plains-Woodland Border of Central North America. In *Convergent Evolution in Stone-Tool Technology,* edited by Michael J. O'Brien, Briggs Buchanan, and Metin I. Eren, pp. 203–227. Massachusetts Institute of Technology, Cambridge.

State Historical Society of North Dakota
2022 *Section 3. Origin Stories.* North Dakota: People Living on the Land (website). State Historical Society of North Dakota, Bismarck. Electronic document, https://www.ndstudies.gov/gr8/content/unit-i-paleocene-1200-ad/lesson-3-building-communities/topic-1-migrations/section-3-origin-stories, accessed September 7, 2022.

Teasdale, J. W.
1936 Letter to Gordon F. Daggett, Inspector, National Park Service Office in Jefferson City, Missouri. Carbon copy of the letter in the Archives of the Missouri State Parks.

Thomas, John L.
1907 **Historic Landmarks of Jefferson County,** *Missouri Historical Review* 1(3):171–180.

U. S. National Park Service
2003 *The Black Hills as a Sanctuary and Sacred Landscape.* U.S. National Park Service Publications and Papers 157. Electronic document, https://digitalcommons.unl.edu/natlpark/157/, accessed September 7, 2022.

Wagner, Mark J., Kayleigh Sharp, and Jonathon Remo
2018 Transformed Spaces: A Landscape Approach to the Rock Art of Illinois. In *Transforming the Landscape: Rock Art and the Mississippian Cosmos,* **edited by Carol Diaz-Granados, Jan Simek, George Sabo III, and Mark Wagner, pp. 100–155. Oxbow Press, Oxford, United Kingdom.**

Waltham, John A.
1981 *Galena and Aboriginal Trade in Eastern North America.* **Scientific Papers 17. Illinois State Museum, Springfield.**

Waltham, John A., Stephen H. Stow, and Marvin J. Karson
1980 Copena Galena: Source Identification and Analysis. *American Antiquity* **45(1):21–42.**

Wellman, Klaus P.
1979 *A Survey of North American Indian Rock Art.* Akademische Druck- u. Verlagsanstalt, Graz, Austria.

Wiget, Andrew
1996 Oral Literature of the Southwest. In *Handbook of Native American Literature,* edited by Andrew Wiget, pp. 53–64. Garland Publishing, New York.

Wyant, William K.
1959 Preserving Indian Rock Carvings in the Ozarks. *St. Louis Post–Dispatch,* October 4, 1959, p. 17.

Wyatt, Ronald
1959 Summer Fieldwork at Washington State Park, Missouri. *Missouri Archaeological Society Newsletter* 134:7–10.

n.d. A Study of Three Petroglyph Sites along the Big River in the Eastern Ozarks Highland of Missouri. Unpublished manuscript, Museum of Anthropology at the University of Missouri– Columbia.

Contextualizing Northern Sinagua Rock Drawings at the Rattlesnake Petroglyphs Site

Richard A. Rogers

This paper presents the documentation and contextualization of the Rattlesnake Petroglyphs, a Northern Sinagua site located east of Flagstaff, Arizona. First, the Northern Sinagua archaeological culture and prior research on northern Sinagua rock drawings are briefly reviewed. Next, the site's local geographic and archaeological contexts are described. To further contextualize the Rattlesnake Petroglyphs, the site's inventory is compared to well-documented Northern Sinagua petroglyph sites. Certain element types are examined in more detail, including spirals and spiral variants, possible depictions of migration, human feet, variations of the "Basic Form" (figures often identified as lizards, anthropomorphs, and "lizard men"), and distinctively well-pecked lizard-like figures. Finally, the presence of "bell rocks" is briefly described, pointing to possible public, ceremonial functions of the site.

This paper presents the documentation and contextualization of the Rattlesnake Petroglyphs (AR-03-04-02-4453), a Northern Sinagua site located on an isolated basalt outcrop (Figure 1) in the Coconino National Forest (CNF), approximately 20 mi (33 km) east of Flagstaff, Arizona. I begin with a brief overview of the Northern Sinagua archaeological culture and prior research on northern Sinagua rock drawings. Next, I describe the site as a whole, including its geographic context, and establish the local archaeological context for the petroglyphs, including cultural affiliation and time frame. To further contextualize the Rattlesnake Petroglyphs, I first compare the site's

Richard A. Rogers
*Professor of Communication,
Northern Arizona University,
Flagstaff*

Figure 1. *A view of the east side of the southern portion of the basalt outcrop, which has four panels (#22–25) with nine petroglyphs.*

American Indian Rock Art, Volume 49. Amy Gilreath, Ken Hedges, and Anne McConnell, Editors. American Rock Art Research Association, 2023, pp. 97–116.

inventory to other well-documented Northern Sinagua petroglyph sites and identify potentially atypical patterns within the inventory. With that basis, certain element types are examined in more detail, including spirals and spiral variants, possible depictions of migration, human feet, variations of the "Basic Form" (figures that are often ambiguous and variously identified as lizards, anthropomorphs, or "lizard men"), and distinctively well-pecked lizard-like figures that manifest formal traits different than typical Basic Form lizard-like figures. Finally, I briefly report on the presence of "bell rocks," boulders showing evidence of use-wear from repeated striking and that ring when struck.

The Northern Sinagua Archaeological Culture

The Northern Sinagua inhabited the San Francisco Mountain Volcanic Field east of the San Francisco Peaks before and after the eruption of Sunset Crater ca. 1085–1090 C.E. (Elson and Ort 2012; O'Hara 2015). After the eruption, conditions became more favorable for agriculture and populations increased (Downum 1992). The florescence of the Flagstaff-area Northern Sinagua correlates with this period of increased habitation, ca. 1085–1250 C.E., falling within the Pueblo II–Pueblo III (PII–PIII) periods in the broader Southwest, with substantial numbers of Northern Sinagua sites ranging from the area around Walnut Canyon in the south to near Deadman Wash and Wupatki Pueblo in the north. Toward the end of their residence in the San Francisco Mountain Volcanic Field, the Northern Sinagua moved from their small settlements scattered across the landscape, clustering in a few larger sites (Downum 1992; O'Hara 2015). By the beginning of the fourteenth century, most of the Flagstaff-area Sinagua had moved south to Anderson Mesa and perhaps the Verde Valley (Downum 1992), and from there, possibly, to Homol'ovi, eventually settling at Hopi and possibly other Pueblos (Bernardini 2005; Downum 1992; Kuwanwisiwma et al. 2012).

The PII–PIII Northern Sinagua were relatively sedentary dry farmers using a mixed subsistence strategy including cultivated plants, gathered plant foods, and wild animals (Downum 1992). They engaged in extensive trading and other relationships with a variety of other archaeological cultures, including the Cohonina, Kayenta, and Hohokam. As manifested in imported items such as ceramics and shell jewelry, architectural features such as ball courts and Chaco-style wall construction, and iconographic similarities with

the decorated ceramics and rock drawings of many of these cultures (Downum et al. 2012; Hedquist 2012; O'Hara 2012; Rogers 2021), the PII–PIII Northern Sinagua appear to have been a dynamic, hybridized culture at a crossroads where multiple outside influences were operating and distinctive local traits were manifest (Downum 1992; Downum and Garcia 2012; Pilles 2017). Such hybridity makes the identification of diagnostic traits of the Northern Sinagua difficult; since the early twentieth-century work of Harold Colton, the Northern Sinagua have been primarily identified by abundant presence of the locally produced plainware, Alameda Brown Ware (O'Hara 2015).

Northern Sinagua Rock Drawings

Research on Northern Sinagua rock drawings began ca. 1918 with Harold Colton's work at Turkey Tanks (Weaver and Slominski 1992) and Picture Canyon, the latter being the largest concentration of Northern Sinagua petroglyphs. Colton's (1946, 1960) subsequent descriptions of Northern Sinagua rock drawings were based on Picture Canyon, Turkey Tanks, and Walnut Canyon, all in the Sinagua "heartland" (O'Hara 2015). To date, however, only three large concentrations of Northern Sinagua rock drawings have been both completely documented and published: Turkey Tanks (Weaver and Slominski 1992), Lizard Man Village (Weaver 1994), and the Angell Complex and other sites in Youngs Canyon (Rogers 2021), although the publication on Youngs Canyon does not include the complete documentation for every site in the canyon. Along with more scattered efforts (D'Amico 1977) and general reports on the concentrations of Northern Sinagua rock drawings in Walnut Canyon (Gearty and Purcell 2018) and Picture Canyon (Weaver 2014–2015), as well as broad characterizations of Northern Sinagua rock drawings (Colton 1946; Hays-Gilpin and Weaver 2012), the existing literature provides a foundation for contextualizing newly-recorded sites such as the Rattlesnake Petroglyphs.

Efforts to identify diagnostic traits of Northern Sinagua rock drawings that enable clear distinctions from neighboring rock art traditions are limited conceptually, empirically, and practically (Rogers 2021). One important factor is that a key trait of the Northern Sinagua rock art tradition is its participation in regional iconographic systems, an extension of the broadly hybridized nature of the PII–PIII Northern Sinagua discussed above. Defining distinct traits of neighboring rock art styles is especially challenging when much of the subject matter, not to mention many conventions (e.g., size of motifs, manner of representing certain subjects), are shared among not only neighboring traditions such as the Cohonina and Kayenta (Hays-Gilpin and Weaver 2012), but more broadly as well, from Hohokam to Chaco. Spirals, zigzag and spiral snakes, flute players, and stick-figure lizards and anthropomorphs (some with circular abdomens) are examples of such regional imagery that are found at Northern Sinagua sites. Because of this participation in regional iconographies, overlapping significantly with the traditions of other archaeological cultures such as the Kayenta and Hohokam, some of the issues I explore through the Rattlesnake Petroglyphs may be useful in the study of other rock art traditions in the region.

The Rattlesnake Petroglyphs Site

The Rattlesnake Petroglyphs are located at an elevation of approximately 5905 ft (1800 m) on a large, isolated basalt outcrop near the bottom of a valley in between two cinder cones (small volcanoes). The outcrop measures approximately 10 m east-west by 30 m north-south, with a saddle in between two higher mounds of rock. The petroglyphs are all located on the southern half of the larger, southern mound (Figures 1, 2, and 3). There are open, level areas immediately adjacent to the east and west sides of the outcrop. The ground level on the east side is substantially lower than on the west side, making the outcrop appear much larger and taller when approached from the east (Figure 1). The outcrop is surrounded by a combination of Piñon-Juniper woodland (although all the piñons are long dead) and grasslands, much of it covered in cinders. The top of the outcrop offers 360-degree views

Figure 3. A view of the south side of the southern portion of the basalt outcrop, which has six panels (#16–21) with 34 petroglyphs.

of the surrounding valley (Figure 4). Probably due to the view, some of the petroglyph panels often have long streaks of white avian excrement on them, which appear to be from large birds using the outcrop as a perch.

The vast majority of Northern Sinagua rock drawings (and all fully documented and published sites) are located along drainages such as Youngs Canyon, Walnut Canyon, the Rio de Flag, and San Francisco Wash. On initial examination, the Rattlesnake Petroglyphs site appeared to be located away from drainages, but careful pedestrian surveys of the proximate landscape and topographic maps revealed a shallow drainage just to the south. The drainage, the presence of at least two possible field houses adjacent to the outcrop, possible rock-outlined garden plots near the drainage, and a half dozen possible hoes and hoe fragments seen in the area suggest the outcrop was surrounded by agricultural areas on at least three sides.

Figure 2. A view of the inside and top of the southern portion of the basalt outcrop, which contains 15 panels (#1–15) with 54 petroglyphs.

Figure 4. This view of Panels 3, 4, 5, and the left side of Panel 7 is taken from the top of the outcrop facing east, with a small valley and a cinder cone in the background.

Archaeologically, both the immediate and general area identify the site as Northern Sinagua in the range of 1085–1225 C.E., from the eruption of Sunset Crater to the concentration of the Sinagua population into a small number of large sites in the San Francisco Mountain Volcanic Field. Alameda Brown Ware (ABW), the locally produced plainware that is the primary diagnostic marker of the Sinagua, predominates in the area; the Sunset type, which is post-eruptive (Hays-Gilpin and Downum 2012; Rogers 2021:88), predominates among the ABW sherds. Sherds observed in the immediate vicinity of the site mirror the larger pattern, being almost entirely ABW (mostly Sunset, with a much smaller amount of Angell). A handful of Tusayan Gray Ware sherds—an imported corrugated plainware and the second most common plainware in the area—have also been observed near the site, along with two sherds of San Francisco Mountain Gray Ware (Deadman Fugitive Red), a Cohonina plainware that is generally found in small numbers in the area. No identifiable decorated sherds have been found near the site itself. Decorated ceramics in the general area are predominantly the Sosi/Holbrook B and Flagstaff/Walnut types of Tusayan and Little Colorado White Wares, pointing to a heavy occupational period of ca. 1075–1225 C.E. (Rogers 2021:Table 3).

There are hundreds of Northern Sinagua sites within a mile of the Rattlesnake Petroglyphs, mostly field houses but also pit house villages, pueblos, possible ceremonial features, and other petroglyph sites, many but not all of which are in the CNF database. For example, the one-square-mile section immediately to the southeast of the Rattlesnake Petroglyphs contains 73 sites included in the CNF database. Detailed artifact inventories are available for many of these sites (Rogers 2021), virtually all of which are unambiguously Sinagua (based on the predominance of ABW), with most falling in the 1085–1225 C.E. range (based on decorated ceramics and the predominance of Sunset among the plainware sherds). The nearest relatively large (for this area) habitation site to the Rattlesnake Petroglyphs is 700 m to the northwest, which includes an L-shaped, possibly two-story surface room block, at least four pit houses, at least two field houses, and a large depression with an associated masonry structure. The sherds at this habitation site are also predominantly ABW, mostly Sunset but also including Youngs and Angell. The abundant decorated sherds include mostly Little Colorado White Wares with some Tusayan White Wares, predominantly Sosi/Holbrook B and Flagstaff/Walnut but with a few

pieces of Tusayan Black-on-white (post-dating 1225 C.E.). Overall, the ceramic inventory of this large habitation site near the Rattlesnake Petroglyphs mirrors the surrounding area, with a high occupational density during the period of 1085–1225 C.E., corresponding to the Angell-Winona-Padre and Elden phases of the Northern Sinagua (Downum 1992; O'Hara 2015).

The Rattlesnake Petroglyphs have been marked and labelled as "petroglyphs" on USGS maps for many decades, which probably explains the dearth of identifiable decorated sherds at the site itself. After visiting the site many times since the late 1990s, during 2021 and the first half of 2022 I thoroughly documented the site, identifying 25 panels and 97 elements, some of which were only seen after months of work at the site. This is a larger than average Northern Sinagua petroglyph site, but smaller than the nearby Angell Complex (305 elements, 1.7 km south-southeast) in Youngs Canyon, Turkey Tanks (281 elements, 9.3 km west-northwest), and Lizard Man Village (150 elements, 12.1 km west). Complete documentation of the Rattlesnake Petroglyphs is on file at the Flagstaff Ranger District Office, CNF.

Inventory

This section presents an overview of the inventory of the Rattlesnake Petroglyphs in relation to other documented sites, summarizing broad categories of types of images. The following percentages and the tallies they are based on should not be taken as precise—ambiguities in the imagery, indeterminate thresholds for deciding if a figure belongs in one category versus another, and the particular taxonomical biases of those who have produced these categories and counts make them useful for broad characterizations but not precise numerical comparisons.

Table 1 summarizes the inventories of zoomorphs (including anthropomorphs) at the Rattlesnake site, sites in Youngs Canyon (including the Angell Complex), Turkey Tanks, and Lizard Man Village. The Rattlesnake and Turkey Tanks inventories both have about one-half zoomorphs, while Youngs Canyon and Lizard Man Village both have about one-third. The Rattlesnake Petroglyphs site has the smallest percentage of snakes, the smallest percentage of mammalian quadrupeds, and no identifiable birds or bird tracks, which are minimally present at the other three sites. The Rattlesnake site has more possible feet and paw prints than Youngs Canyon and Lizard Man Village, but far less than Turkey Tanks, which is known for its numerous feet. Four of the six identified human feet from the

Spirals and Routes

Spirals

Rattlesnake site, however, are both small and ambiguous, possibly bear paws or something else entirely (see the section on feet below), so the Rattlesnake inventory could be more in line with the "norm" of Youngs Canyon and Lizard Man Village in this category.

I discuss the "Basic Form" in detail below, but it includes lizards, anthropomorphs, and possible tailed anthropomorphs, often called "lizard men," although some of these figures could be plants as well. This is one of the main taxonomical issues, as Weaver's counts from Turkey Tanks and Lizard Man lumped many of the possible variations of the Basic Form into a single category. Treating these as a single category, the Rattlesnake site has almost twice the percentage of Basic Form images (36.1%, with the other three areas having around 20%).

Table 2 summarizes the inventories of "geometric" images. Note that I do not assume that geometrics are necessarily "abstract" or pure design, but may also be figurative, even if I do not understand what they might represent. The overall count of geometrics at the Rattlesnake site is not substantially out of line with the other sites, representing about one-quarter of the total inventory, as at Turkey Tanks, with Lizard Man Village at about one-third. One statistical variation, but perhaps more importantly an experiential standout at the Rattlesnake Petroglyphs, is the frequency and variability of spirals.

Spirals and Routes

Spirals

Both the Rattlesnake site and Lizard Man Village have about twice the percentage of spirals and spiral variants compared to the much larger inventories in Youngs Canyon and Turkey Tanks. At the Rattlesnake site, these include simple spirals (both curvilinear and rectilinear), double intertwined spirals (both curvilinear and rectilinear), and what I am calling complex intertwined branching spiral elements (all of which are curvilinear).

There are four simple spirals (i.e., singular and unbranching) at the Rattlesnake site, including both small and medium-sized ones, and both rectilinear and curvilinear ones (Figure 5). The Panel 24 curvilinear spiral (Figure 5d) shows the only apparent instance of vandalism at the site: the panel has multiple gouges from bullets, two of which directly destroyed part of the spiral.

Turning to complex spiral forms, the Rattlesnake site has two double intertwined spirals, one curvilinear on Panel 11 and one rectilinear on Panel 16 (Figure 6).

There are two instances of complex, intertwined, branching spirals at the Rattlesnake site. I am not aware of comparable figures in Youngs Canyon or at Turkey Tanks or Lizard Man Village, although Turkey Tanks has one instance of serial spirals (Weaver and Slominski 1992:94). The first is the only petroglyph on Panel 10 and is difficult to visualize (Figure 7a). Careful observations, detailed analysis, and manipulation of photographs revealed a fairly distinct pattern, as shown in Figure 7b. Four curved lines branch off a central "trunk," one of which makes a full spiral inside of the other three "branches." Panel 10 is just to

Table 1. Inventories of zoomorphic figures at Northern Sinagua petroglyph sites.

Category/Site (total inventory)	Rattlesnake (97)	Angell/Youngs Canyon (441)	Turkey Tanks (281)	Lizard Man Village (150)
The Basic Form	36.1%	22.9%	20.0%	19.3%
Lizard	4.1%	9.1%	19.6%	19.3%
Lizard or Tailed Anthropomorph	16.5%	3.4%	(in above)	(in above)
Ambiguous Lizard, Anthro, Plant	10.3%	6.6%	(in above)	(in above)
Anthropomorph	4.1%	3.8%	(in above)	(in above) +0.4%
Foot, Hand, Paw	6.2%	2.2%	22.4%	0.7%
Snake (zig-zag or wavy line)	2.1% (with head)	3.8% (with head)	7.1% (wavy line)	6.0% (wavy line)
Quadruped (mammalian)	3.1%	6.0%	4.3%	6.7%
Bird, Bird Track	0.0%	1.9%	2.5%	0.7%
Total Zoomorphs	47.4%	36.8%	56.3%	33.3%
Sources: Rogers (2021), Weaver (1994), Weaver and Slominski (1992)				

Table 2. Inventories of "geometric" figures at Northern Sinagua petroglyph sites.

Category/Site (total inventory)	Rattlesnake (97)	Angell/Youngs Canyon (441)	Turkey Tanks (281)	Lizard Man Village (150)
Spiral & Spiral Variant	8.2%	4.4%	4.3%	10.0%
Simple Curvilinear	3.1%	Not avail.	3.2%	8%
Simple Rectilinear	1.0%	Not avail.	0.7%	0.7%
Double Intertwined Curvilinear	1.0%	0.0%	0.0%	0.0%
Double Intertwined Rectilinear	1.0%	0.5%	0.0%	1.3%
Complex Branching	2.1%	0.0%	0.0%	0.0%
Concentric Circles	2.1%	1.9%	0.0%	1.3%
Hooked Cross	1.0%	0.0%	0.0%	0.0%
Cross (simple or enclosed)	0.0%	0.9%	0.7%	4.7%
Other Geometric	12.4%	Not avail.	18.2%	21.3%
Total "Geometrics"	23.7%	Not avail.	26.8%	36.0%
Sources: Rogers (2021), Weaver (1994), Weaver and Slominski (1992)				

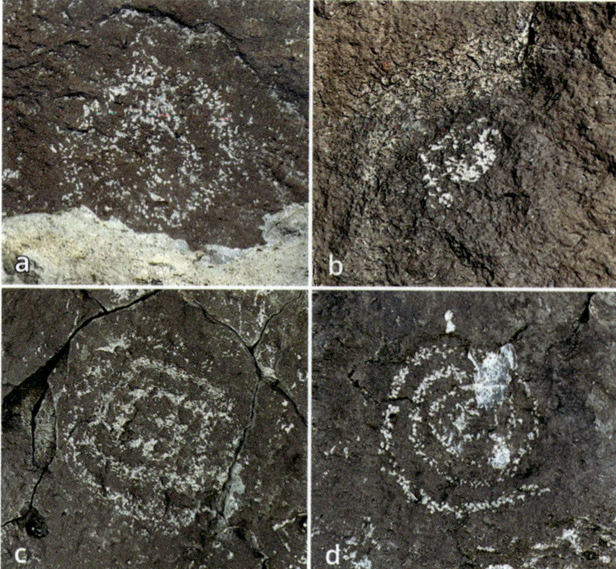

Figure 5. Simple spirals: (a) Panel 8 includes a simple curvilinear spiral (approx. 17.0 x 18.0 cm); (b) Panel 18 includes a small, simple, curvilinear spiral (approx. 5.0 x 7.5 cm); (c) Panel 19 includes a simple rectilinear spiral (approx. 13.0 x 15.0 cm); (d) Panel 24 includes a simple curvilinear spiral (approx. 16.0 x 16.0 cm), with gouges from bullets visible on the spiral.

Figure 6. Double intertwined spirals: (a) Panel 11 contains one petroglyph, a double intertwined curvilinear spiral (approx. 21.0 x 21.0 cm); (b) Panel 16 includes a double intertwined rectilinear spiral (approx. 12.5 x 18.0 cm).

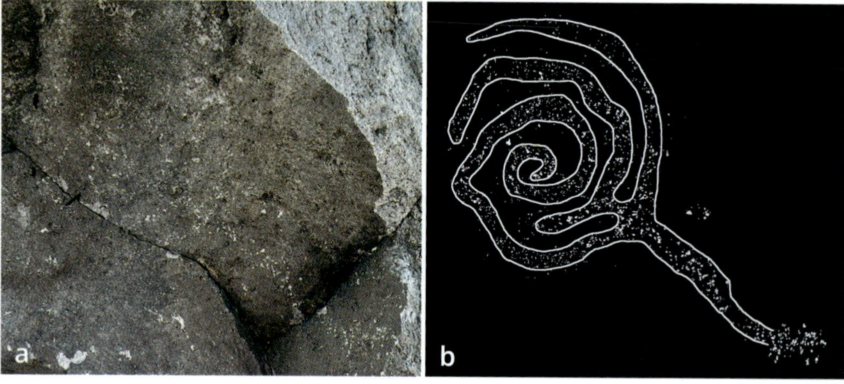

Figure 7. (a) Panel 10 is composed of a faintly pecked, complex, intertwined, branching spiral variant (approx. 21.0 x 43.0 cm). (b) This graphic interpretation of Panel 10 shows four curved lines branching off of a central "trunk," one of which makes a full spiral inside of the other three "branches."

the left of Panel 11, which contains the intertwined double curvilinear spirals described above (Figure 6a). Before parts of the Panel 11 double spiral apparently lost some of its upper edges to spalling, it is possible that the dispersed end of the "trunk" from Panel 10 (Figure 7) might have connected to the spiral on Panel 11.

The second instance of a complex, intertwined, branching spiral at the Rattlesnake site is on Panel 20. Also difficult to visualize, the central part of the panel appears to have a headless stick figure superimposed on one side of a set of intertwined, branching spirals (Figure 8). While I am unable to determine with certainty which of these images is superimposed on the other, there are two different levels of pecking evident on the spiral versus the headless stick figure and the more thickly pecked stick figure appears to be later than the complex spiral.

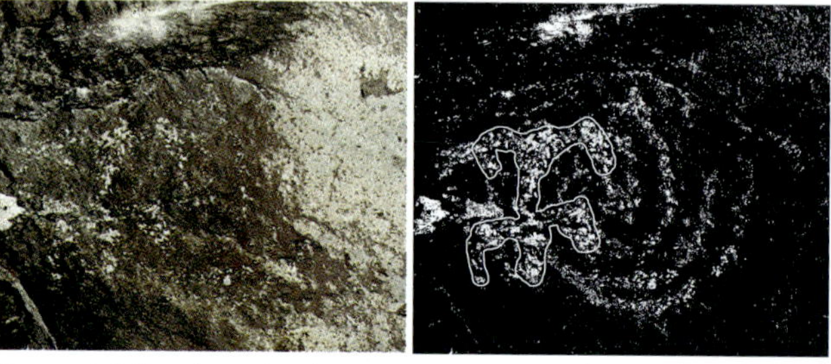

Figure 8. This digital enhancement of Panel 20 shows a sparsely pecked, complex, intertwined branching spiral (approx. 20.0 x 26.0 cm) apparently superimposed by a more heavily pecked headless stick figure.

Routes

Panel 19 (Figure 9), which contains the simple rectilinear spiral pictured above in Figure 5c, has the only two unambiguous instances of mammalian quadrupeds at the site. It also contains a long, linear, generally vertical element that I provisionally interpret as a path, trail, or route of some kind. It extends from the bottom of the main part of the panel to its top, and onto the next rock surface, with a minimum length of 95 cm. It is sparsely pecked, but in a manner that enables visualization and visual differentiation from surrounding and overlapping glyphs. There are several reasons to postulate that this long linear element could be a representation of a path, trail, or route. One is its proximity to an antlered quadruped, possibly indicating a depiction of a game trail.

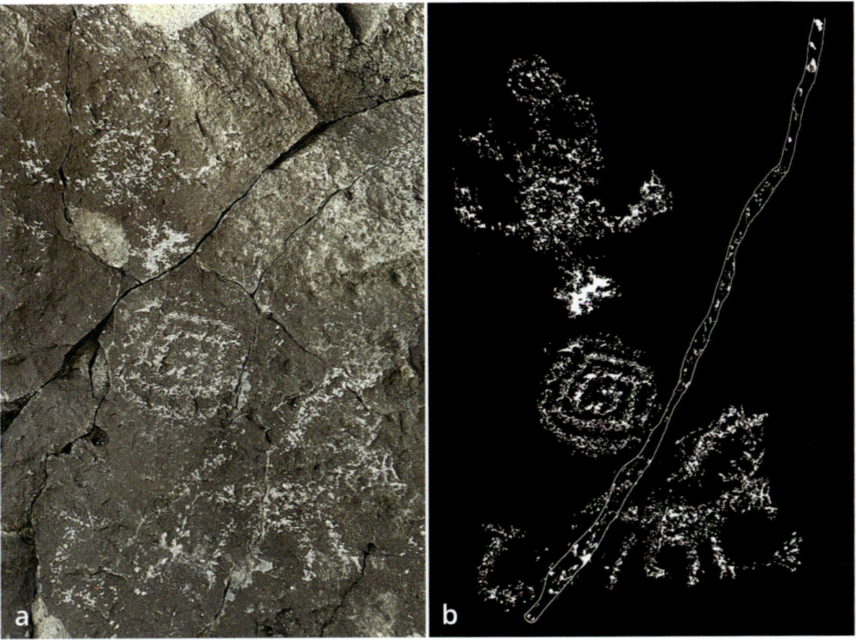

Figure 9. Panel 19: (a) The main part of the panel includes (from top left to lower right) a full-bodied tailless lizard-like figure, a small quadruped, a rectilinear spiral (see Figure 5c), a sparsely pecked linear element going from the bottom to the top of the main concentration of images on the panel, and an antlered quadruped. (b) This graphic interpretation of the main part of the panel includes the outline of a sparsely pecked, long, linear element that runs from the bottom to the top of this part of the panel, measuring at least 95 cm in length. For comparison, the antlered quadruped in the lower right is approx. 19.0 cm long by 14.0 cm high.

A different reason to interpret this as a path or route comes from the Northern Sinagua petroglyphs at AR-03-04-02-4652 in Youngs Canyon (Figure 10), a site approximately 4 km from the Rattlesnake Petroglyphs (for a more complete description and discussion, see Rogers 2021). This site has similar long, sparsely pecked "routes," though in this case there are many of them, they converge/diverge (branch) and intersect in complex ways, and they sometimes incorporate spiral patterns, not entirely unlike the two complex, intertwined, branching spirals from the Rattlesnake Petroglyphs described above (Figures 7 and 8). These "routes" are also sparsely pecked in a manner that makes them both visible and visually differentiated from surrounding and overlapping glyphs. Finally, as with Panel 19 at Rattlesnake, these "paths" are in proximity with quadrupeds and much bolder geometric elements, including spirals. While these long, linear features at AR-03-04-02-4652 are only postulated as paths or routes (Rogers 2021), not confirmed, the "trail" on Panel 19 at the Rattlesnake Petroglyphs site is reminiscent of them in terms of the style of production and appearance of the lines.

Another reason to consider the simple but long linear element on Panel 19 at the Rattlesnake Petroglyphs

site and the far more complex lines from AR-03-04-02-4652 in Youngs Canyon as routes is the relationship of both to spirals and the high percentage of spirals at both sites. A common Pueblo interpretation of at least some spirals is symbols of migration (see, e.g., Colwell-Chanthaphonh and Ferguson 2006:156). Simple spirals (i.e., singular and unbranching) are often identified in such ways, but more complex spirals, such as the double intertwined and complex, intertwined, and branching examples from the Rattlesnake site (described above), could also be representations of migration. Ancestral Hopi migrations were complex, heterogeneous, and nonlinear (Bernardini 2005; Ferguson and Colwell-Chanthaphonh 2006), with groups merging and diverging with other groups throughout migrations that eventually ended at Hopi or other Pueblos. This would be consistent with both the complex spiral forms at the Rattlesnake Petroglyphs site (Figures 7 and 8) and the complex lines from AR-03-04-02-4652 in Youngs Canyon (Figure 10), for migration routes can be marked in ways other than simple spirals. As Bernardini and Fowles (2010:253) recount,

> In the Rio Grande Gorge is a large boulder on which have been pecked two parallel rows of dots extending roughly two meters across the rock face.... A Pueblo consultant...suggest[ed] that such petroglyphs are reminiscent of the rows of corn kernels laid down on kiva floors in the recitation of group histories. With the placement of each kernel, he noted, a step in the group's travels through time and space is narrated, so one might reasonably conclude that whoever pecked the rows of dots in the past was employing a similar mnemonic device to aid in the retelling of history.

With this addition to the relationship between rock drawings and migration histories, it seems possible that even the single, simple linear pathway from Panel 19 at the Rattlesnake Petroglyphs site (Figure 9) could be such a mnemonic device, "map," or "record." That pathway in particular is pecked in such a way as to be reminiscent

Figure 10. Youngs Canyon petroglyphs at AR-03-04-02-4652: (a) This petroglyph site includes many converging/diverging, crossing, and spiraling lines suggestive of "routes" or "paths" in proximity to quadrupeds and much bolder geometric elements, including spirals. (b) In this graphic interpretation, the complexity of the intersecting, converging, diverging, and in some cases spiraling long linear elements is demonstrated (sparsely pecked meandering lines and other faint elements are outlined in red). The panel is approx. 2 m high by 3 m wide.

of the rows of corn kernels described by Bernardini and Fowles's Pueblo consultant. Future consultations with Hopi or other Pueblo groups can hopefully shed light on this possibility for the Rattlesnake site's "path" and its complex spirals, and the panel in Youngs Canyon with multiple, intersecting "paths" and spirals.

Feet

The presence of up to six petroglyphs depicting human feet (or footprints, or possibly sandals) at the Rattlesnake site may be related to both the spirals and the possible linear path or route. In their discussion of the unusually large number of petroglyphs depicting human feet at Turkey Tanks (up to 22.4% of the inventory, though some may be bear paws or human hands), Weaver and Slominski (1992:85) note that

"feet or footprint petroglyphs are easily associated with travel, journeys, migrations, or other movements," and cite Frank Waters's 1963 *Book of the Hopi*, indicating that Hopi consultants made this association. Weaver and Slominski also point out that Anglos readily make the same association, leading to their skepticism, but not outright denial, that this association was made by the Sinagua. However, given that the Turkey Tanks petroglyphs are located at one of the few permanent water sources in the area between Flagstaff and the Little Colorado River (Weaver and Slominski 1992:82), and given sources indicating that the tanks were used by both indigenous travelers and early Anglo explorers (Anonymous n.d.; Schindler and Kitt 2019:17–18), associating the very high percentage of feet at the site with travel, while by no means definitive, seems not unreasonable. The Rattlesnake site inventory's 6.2% of possible feet (some of which may be bear paws or something else entirely) is much lower than Turkey Tanks but much higher than Lizard Man Village, where none of the elements in Weaver's (1994) inventory resemble human feet, and Youngs Canyon, with four possible cases of human feet (<1% of that inventory), all of which are on a single panel (Rogers 2021).

The first foot at the Rattlesnake site is the least ambiguous at the site and is the only figure on Panel 2, located at the top of the outcrop (Figure 11a). Viewed while standing on the top of the outcrop, this is a visually very prominent petroglyph, being relatively large (roughly life-size) and fairly solidly pecked. The second clearest instance of a human foot is on Panel 8, on a horizontal surface at the top of the outcrop's southern end (Figure 11b). Half the size of the Panel 2 foot, it

*Figure 11. Likely feet: (a) Panel 2, located at the top of the outcrop (see Figure 2), contains one figure, a roughly life-size human foot (approx. 20 cm long). (b) Panel 8 includes a likely human foot (approx. 10 cm long) with apparent toes (pointing up and to the right below the dot and **U**-shaped element).*

has the general shape of a human foot, and it appears to have five fairly distinct toes despite clarity being obscured by rough pecking and abrasions on the high parts of the rock surface on its left side in particular.

Moving to less definitive instances, Panel 7 (Figure 12a) includes a small figure that is roughly the shape of a human foot or bear paw, and has indications of pecks at the top that could be claws or toes. Panel 17 includes a small, densely pecked figure (Figure 12b) that vaguely resembles a foot. However, it is so small and roughly pecked that it could be something else, such as a bear paw or plant form. Another possible foot is on the upper right of Panel 3 (Figure 12c). It is somewhat roughly pecked, and some apparent details preclude definitive identification as a foot. The top of the foot by the "toes" is exceptionally wide in comparison to the "heel" (6.0 cm versus 2.5 cm), and the top spreads symmetrically, unlike a human foot. There are somewhat distinct pecks running along the top edge of the foot, which could be claws or toes, but there are at least twice as many of these pecks as the number of claws or toes would allow. Like some other possible feet at the site (Figure 12b), it also resembles a plant form of some kind. Finally, the lower left of Panel 4 (see Figure 15) also contains a very small element that has the general shape of a human foot pointed down and to the right, but the figure is too small and rough to make more than a highly provisional identification.

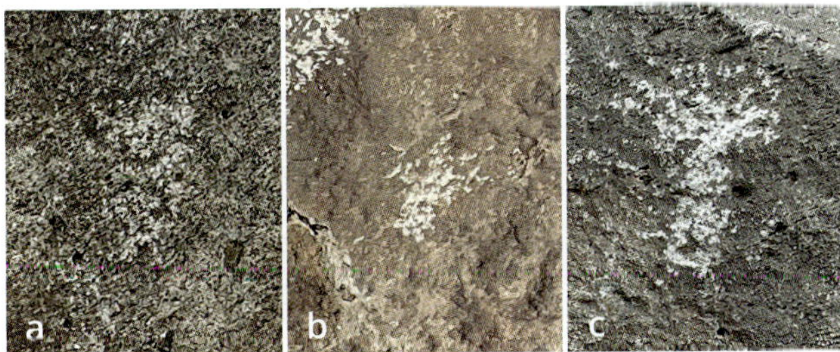

Figure 12. Possible feet: (a) Panel 7 includes a small figure (approx. 6.5 cm by 5.0 cm) that is roughly the shape of a human foot or bear paw, and has indications of pecks at the top that could be claws or toes. (b) Panel 17 includes a small, densely pecked figure (approx. 5.5 cm high by 3.5 cm wide) that could be a human foot. (c) Panel 3 includes a possible foot (approx. 8.0 cm long by 6.0 cm wide at the top) that also suggests a plant form.

Even if only the first two instances described above are actually representations of human feet, the Rattlesnake site still has a higher percentage of feet than Lizard Man Village and Youngs Canyon, and that could be correlated to the Rattlesnake site's higher concentration of spirals and spiral variants. However, the large "migration pathways" panel at AR-03-04-02-4652 in Youngs Canyon upon which my linkage of the path/route on Rattlesnake Panel 19 to migration is based has no associated feet.

The Basic Form

Setting possible representations of migration aside, I turn next to a discussion of the Basic Form, which I began exploring in the context of documenting the Northern Sinagua petroglyphs in Youngs Canyon (Rogers 2021). A substantial issue in categorizing elements in Sinagua rock drawings (and many others in the Southwest) is what I call the Basic Form and variations of it. The Basic Form at its core is a "stick figure" variously interpreted as an anthropomorph, a lizard, or a "lizard man" (tailed anthropomorph), but these types of figures could also be plants in some cases (Rogers 2021). Lack of attention to variations in the Basic Form results in different labels (different presumed referents) being attached to arguably similar images and grouping what are arguably different images into a single category.

There are several common variations in figures that manifest the Basic Form, as illustrated in Table 3. First, some of these figures are tailed, some are not, and some

Table 3. Variations of the Basic Form at the Rattlesnake site.

Figure Form	Count	Head	Rounded Abdomen	Panel Numbers (instances >1)
(figure)	1	●	None	1
(figure)	1	▲	None	3
(figure)	9	● (8) ▲ (1)	None	1 (4), 4 (3), 15, 23
(figure)	5	● (4) None (1)	None	3, 7, 14, 16, 20
(figure)	1	●	None	1
(figure)	1	●	None	7
(figure)	2	●	None	5, 6
(figure)	1	●	1	3
(figure)	1	▼	None	6
(figure)	3	●	1	1, 3, 7
(figure)	1	●	None	4
(figure)	1	●	None	1
(figure)	1	●	None	21
(figure)	1	●	None	25
(figure)	1	▼	None	4
Totals	30	Roundish 25 Triangular 3 Semicircular 1 No head 1	2	

have short tails (e.g., not extending as low as the bottom feet); such short tails are also possible penises if the figure is an anthropomorph. The "tails" could also be the bottom stalk/trunk of plants (Rogers 2021). Second, there are different orientations of the four "limbs," as shown in Table 3. Third, the "limbs" have different shapes: linear (either extending horizontally at a right angle to the body or at a diagonal), rectilinear (out then up or down at a roughly right angle), and curvilinear (downward or upward). Fourth, the head can be roundish (including oval), semicircular (the bottom of the head being flat), triangular (pointed up or down), or absent (with or without a neck). Fifth, some have a rounded abdomen ("pot belly") and some do not, a difference noted in Weaver and Slominski's (1992) documentation of Turkey Tanks, unlike most of the other variations being discussed here. For the most part, "full bodied" versions of the Basic Form also manifest these variations, but only apparently "stick figure" examples (including those with "pot bellies") will be included in this discussion.

Before discussing the potential significance of these distinctions, reviewing specific examples of these variations from the Rattlesnake Petroglyphs site will be helpful. There are 30 sufficiently visualizable stick figure variations of the Basic Form at the site: eight on Panel 1 (Figure 13), four on Panel 3 (Figure 14), five on Panel 4 (Figure 15), one on Panel 5 (Figure 16), two on Panel 6 (Figure 17), three on Panel 7 (Figure 18), one on Panel 14 (Figure 19), one on Panel 15 (Figure 20), one on Panel 16 (Figure 21), one on Panel 20 (Figure 8), one on Panel 21 (Figure 22), one on Panel 23 (Figure 23), and one on Panel 25 (Figure 24). Before moving to a formal analysis of these cases, it is worth noting that 22 of 26

Figure 13. Panel 1 includes eight variations on the Basic Form. The top part of the panel is approx. 120 cm wide.

Figure 14. The central area of Panel 3 includes four variations of the Basic Form, including a finely and solidly pecked lizard-like figure with a hooked tail and rounded abdomen (approx. 23.0 tall cm by 8.5 cm wide), as well as a possible human foot in the upper right (see Figure 12c).

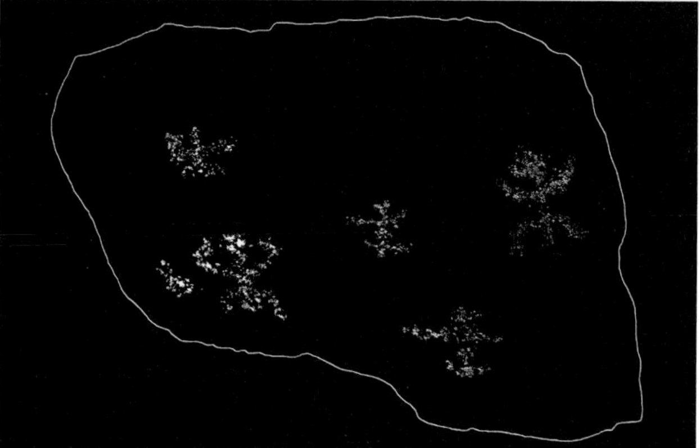

Figure 15. Panel 4 includes five variations of the Basic Form and a possible human foot on the far left (approx. 2.0 x 3.5 cm).

cases of lizard-like figures at the site are concentrated in the center of the site, inside and on top of the basalt outcrop, and all but two are generally west-facing.

Several patterns are evident in these 30 cases (Table 3). The most common variant with nine instances (30.0%, Table 3, Row 3) has the upper limbs extending out then up at roughly right angles, the lower limbs extending out then down at roughly right angles, and a tail; all such cases have heads, nine being round(ish) and one being triangular. This is the classic form often described as a "lizard man" (e.g., Kuwanwisiwma and Koyiyumptewa 2018:29), but could arguably be a mundane lizard. There is also one instance of a variation of the same form, but with a short tail (or penis); this figure has a distinctly semicircular head, the only variant with that head shape at this site (on Panel 3, Figure 14). Clearly marked as different by tail length, head shape, and especially distinctive right angles on all four limbs, the short-tailed, semicircle-headed figure

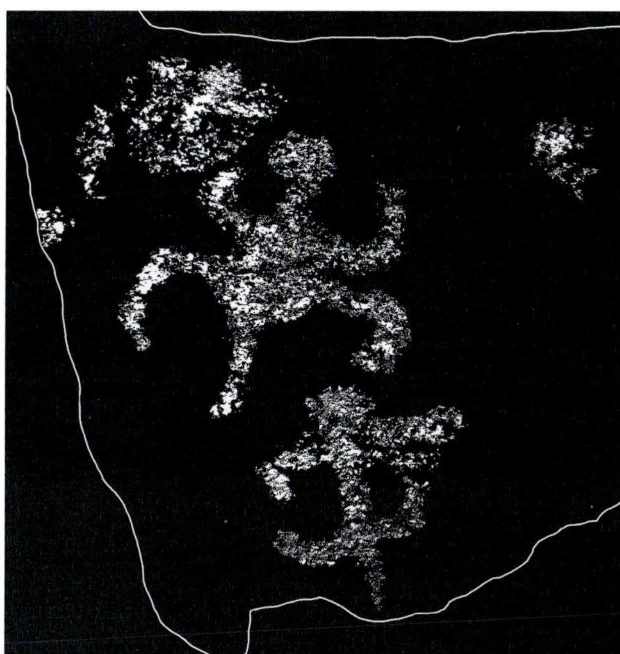

Figure 16. Panel 5 includes one variation of the Basic Form (bottom) and a large full-bodied lizard-like element (approx. 20.0 cm tall by 17.0 cm wide).

Figure 17. Panel 6 has two possible variations of the Basic Form, but they are ambiguous and may not be Basic Form figures; the right figure (approx. 8.0 cm tall by 10.0 cm wide) may be a butterfly.

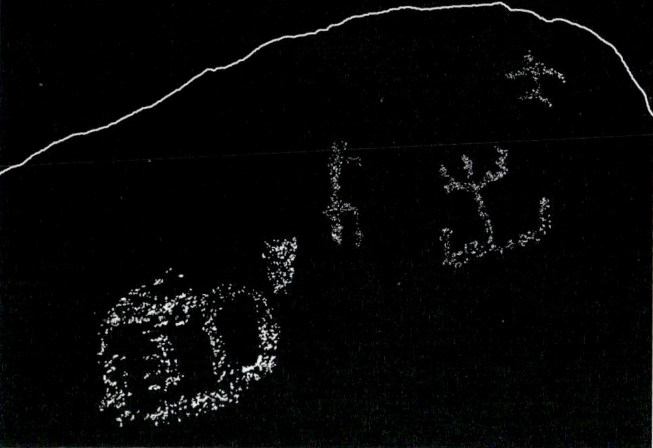

Figure 18. Panel 7 includes a three-chambered rectangular element (approx. 25.0 x 16.0 cm in total), a possible human foot or bear paw, and three variations on the Basic Form, two of which are very faint and apparently incomplete.

Figure 19. Panel 14 contains a faint, obscure variation on the Basic Form petroglyph (approx. 15.0 x 7.0 cm), on which the presence or size of a tail is uncertain.

may be a male anthropomorph as opposed to a lizard or a tailed anthropomorph.

The second most common variant with five instances (16.7%, Table 3, Row 4) has all four limbs extending out then down at roughly right angles and has a tail; four of such cases have round heads, with the fifth being apparently headless. There is only one other instance of all four limbs extending out then down at right angles at the Rattlesnake Petroglyphs site (on Panel 7, Figure 18); it has been classified in Table 3 as tailless, suggesting an anthropomorph, but the faint and possibly incomplete nature of this element makes it difficult to definitively rule out a tail.

The third most common variant with three instances (10.0%, Table 3, Row 10) has upper limbs extending out then up at roughly right angles, lower

Figure 20. Panel 15 has two roughly pecked figures; the right figure is a variation of the Basic Form (approx. 13.0 x 9.0 cm), but the lower limb positions are unusual, and the tail is uncertain. The panel shows use-wear consistent with "bell rocks" identified at the site.

Figure 21. This portion of Panel 16, just below the rectilinear intertwined spirals pictured in Figure 6b, contains a set of concentric circles and a variation of the Basic Form (approx. 14.5 cm tall by 8.5 cm wide), both of which are faint.

Figure 22. Contrast enhancement of Panel 21, lightly pecked on a lightly patinated boulder, shows a variation of the Basic Form (approx. 16.0 cm tall by 10.0 cm wide) and a large hooked cross superimposed on faint, sparsely pecked images.

limbs extending out then up in a clear curvilinear form, and no tail. There are three other instances of variants that have the distinctly curved, out-then-up lower limbs: one has purely horizontal upper limbs and no tail (on Panel 4, Figure 15), one has upper limbs that extend out then down at roughly right angles and no tail (on Panel 1, Figure 13), and one has upper limbs extending out then up in a generally curved fashion but has a tail (on Panel 21, Figure 22)—the only case of a tail on a figure with clearly upward-curving lower limbs. In total, there are five clear examples of upward curving lower limbs and no tail, all with round(ish) heads. This curved lower limb form does not appear to be a good fit for anthropomorphs given the position of what would be the legs and five of six examples be-

ing tailless does not seem to fit well with most lizards (perhaps they are frogs).

There is one clear instance of a tailless anthropomorph at the site, the only figure on Panel 25 (Figure 24), whose upper limbs extend out then up at roughly right angles, and whose lower limbs extend down and out diagonally from a common point, each composed of a single, straight line. A possible second tailless anthropomorph is a figure with four out-and-down limbs on Panel 7 (Figure 18), although, as noted above, the incomplete and faint nature of the figure makes the lack of a tail less than definitive. A third possible tailless anthropomorph is the figure on Panel 3 with upper limbs extending out then up and the lower limbs out and down, the only semicircular head, and a very short tail, possibly indicating a penis on a male anthropomorph (Figure 14).

This analysis of selected traits of Basic Form stick figures at the Rattlesnake site does not resolve, but at the very least highlights, two broad issues in identifying these variations on the Basic Form. First, the existence of "lizard men" (apparently tailed anthropomorphs)

Figure 23. Panel 23 includes a long, narrow, well pecked lizard-like Basic Form (approx. 23.0 cm tall by 7.0 cm wide).

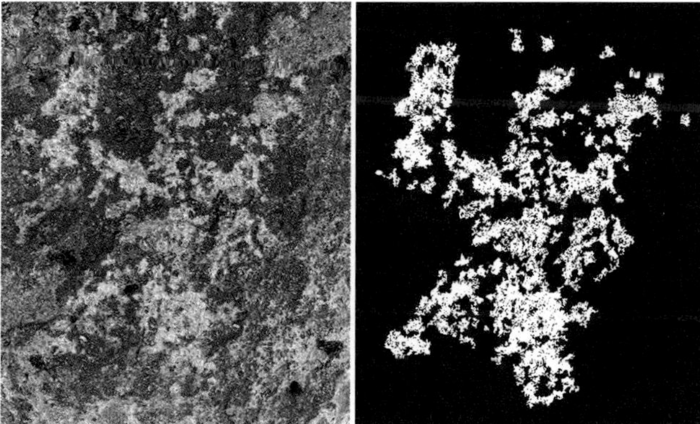

Figure 24. Panel 25 contains a single roughly pecked figure, an apparent anthropomorph with a horizontal line of pecks above its head (approx. 7.5 cm tall by 6.0 cm wide on a rock surface approx. 115 cm tall and 152 cm wide).

and their differentiation from mundane lizards eludes clarification via formal analysis of the imagery alone. The label "lizard man" presumably originated from the idea that this kind of figure represents the human form in a previous world, which included a tail, based on traditional Pueblo stories of humanity's movement through a series of tiered realms (Newsome 2005). In the case of the Zuni, Wright and Hopkins (2016:140)

explain, "members of ZCRAT [Zuni Cultural Resources Advisory Team] said that the A:shiwi, Zuni ancestors, are sometimes represented in petroglyphs as anthropomorphic figures with webbed hands and a tail, which is what they looked like after they first emerged from Chimik'yana'kya Deya." Somewhat differently, from a Hopi perspective, Kuwanwisiwma and Koyiyumptewa (2018:29) explain that classic "lizard men," anthropomorphic figures "with arms and legs extending at 90-degree angles in opposite directions," sometimes have "a distinct round torso or belly and some have a long tail." The round belly marks females while "the 'tail' represents an umbilical cord that connects humans with the Earth" and can be found on both male and female figures (Kuwanwisiwma and Koyiyumptewa 2018:29). While the information presented by Newsome (2005) and Wright and Hopkins (2016) points to the possibility of depictions of "literally" tailed anthropomorphs, Kuwanwisiwma and Koyiyumptewa (2018) suggest a more metaphorical reading of the same kind of imagery. Regardless, neither is particularly helpful in distinguishing a lizard from an anthropomorph with either a literal tail or a symbolic umbilical cord.

Bernardini (2005:106) offers a perspective on the orientation of the appendages on such figures: "Corn symbols contain only downward-facing appendages, representing the bent leaves of a corn plant. Lizard symbols, in contrast, usually contain two upward-facing sets of appendages or one set of downward-facing appendages and one set of upward facing appendages, representing the reptile legs bent at the knee." However, two sets of out-and-down appendages (corn) or upper appendages that extend out and up combined with lower appendages that extend out and down (lizards) are also reasonable anthropomorphic configurations. The configurations that seem least likely but that cannot be universally ruled out for anthropomorphs are those that include lower appendages that extend out and up. One of the instances of this appendage variation, on Panel 6 (Figure 17), has rectilinear appendages and also lacks a tail, making it not a good fit for either a lizard or an anthropomorph and an outlier in the catalog of variations on the Basic Form (Table 3); one resolution of this seemingly confusing form is its resemblance to other rock drawings in the region identified as butterflies (Bernardini 2005:Figure 4.4; Hernbrode and Boyle 2016:Figure 4).

This still leaves five of the 30 instances of the Basic Form at the Rattlesnake site—all of those with no tails and upward curving lower appendages—as seemingly neither anthropomorphic nor reptilian. While not the only remaining alternative, many of these variants (as well as some others) could be interpreted as plants. The one tailed Basic Form with two sets of limbs that both extend out and up in a curvilinear form (on Panel 21) and the five instances without tails but with curving out-and-up lower limbs could be seen as resembling Bernardini's (2005:Figure 4.2) depiction of a petroglyph that is a possible symbol of the Tobacco clan. Indeed, the faint Basic Form image from Panel 21 (Figure 22) bears a striking resemblance to Bernardini's Tobacco clan symbol, which has curving branches, not rectilinear limbs (presumably bent at the knee/elbow), and similar examples exist in nearby Youngs Canyon (Rogers 2021). The Panel 21 example has a "tail," which can be seen as the bottom stalk or trunk of a plant. The five other cases of curving lower limbs discussed above do not have such a tail, but could still be depictions of plants with a central stalk and upward curving branches. I am not arguing that they are plants, but that we should not assume that all variations of the Basic Form are zoomorphs (be it anthropomorphs, lizard-like figures, or other animals).

A second issue in sorting out variations of the Basic Form is the degree to which seemingly small differences in form are significant, at least in and of themselves, without the aid of informed (emic, inside) perspectives. While not offering a "solution" to the mystery of what each variation on the Basic Form represents, I am arguing that these differences are most likely significant— that is, they likely mark different referents or meanings of a symbol. I am in no way claiming to have "cracked the code" as to what these various figures represent, but I am convinced that our ability to figure that out is partially dependent on paying attention to the differences instead of lumping them all together, as has been done in previous efforts documenting Northern Sinagua rock drawings (Rogers 2021; Weaver 1994; Weaver and Slominski 1992). These differences were choices made by the artist (or, more broadly, their culture and its symbolic systems)—they were not random. At least two sets of reasons support this claim.

First, my tabulation (Table 3) and observations at other Northern Sinagua sites indicate that certain patterns are far more common than others, the most common being the classic figure often described as a "lizard man": a stick figure with a "tail," a "head," upper appendages extending out then up at a generally right angle, and lower appendages extending out then down at a generally right angle. This lack of randomness is further supported by patterns in the co-occurrence of various traits. For example, most variants of the Basic Form with curved lower appendages have no "tails," and most with rectilinear lower appendages have "tails." In the case of the Rattlesnake site at least, the clearest "penis" (a tail so short as to be questionable as a tail) is accompanied by the only case of a clearly semicircular head—if this same pattern is seen at other sites, then the co-occurrence of an apparent penis on an apparent anthropomorph with a semicircular head shows the operation of cultural codes, not the preference of an individual rock art producer or a purely random "choice."

Second, a basic principle of semiotics is the crucial role of difference in the material components of symbols. To use a linguistic analogy, the words *bat*, *cat*, and *rat* all share the "at" (the middle and ending), they all start with a consonant, and they all refer to types of mammals, but the difference in the initial consonant is absolutely key in marking the specific meaning of a symbol (Saussure 1959:119). The Basic Form also shares many key elements, but appendage shape and position, presence or absence of a tail, length of a tail, shape of head, and other characteristics more than likely affect the understanding of each variant's specific referent and symbolic meaning. Previous inventories of Northern Sinagua rock drawings, for example, have generally assumed that the presence of a rounded abdomen ("pot belly") marks a difference of some kind, be that sex (or gender), pregnancy, or the shape of the specific animal being depicted (e.g., a horned lizard as opposed to a collared lizard). The same type of significance, I would argue, likely holds true for head shape, limb shape, and limb orientation (although perhaps not equally for all of them).

But what do these differences mean? Absent informed and willing consultants with meaningful connections to the culture that produced the rock drawings—a valid approach that I hope to pursue as part of my ongoing research of the Sinagua petroglyphs in the southeastern San Francisco Mountain Volcanic Field—one approach is based on the assumption of visual realism, comparing, for example, limb positions of the figures with the visual shape of the real things (referents) we think they might represent, as demonstrated by Bernardini's (2005) general guide for distinguishing figures representing corn from those representing lizards (described above). Based on this kind of approach, one could argue that lower limbs extending out then up is not a likely representation of a human. However, even a visual and figurative symbol's form may not be a "literal" representation based on visual fidelity between the image and the thing being represented, instead guided by certain codes and conventions operating in a particular culture. Under a paradigm of visual realism and temporarily setting aside existing reports from Pueblo consultants that a figure that looks like a lizard is actually a human with a tail or a symbolic umbilical cord, the most common variant of the Basic Form would readily be interpreted as a lizard unless clear human-like (and not lizard-like) traits are present in the images themselves. Simply remove the tail, however, and the most common variant of the Basic Form is easily taken to be an anthropomorph.

In addition to the complexities introduced by the codes and conventions of particular cultures' visual systems of communication, another complication with the assumption of visual realism comes from the fact that not all rock drawings are representations of "empirical" things in the "mundane" world as defined and perceived by contemporary Westerners. A Southwestern example is serpents ("mythical" figures) versus snakes (the "actual" critters in the landscapes we traverse). While some snake-like figures may have clear horns, arms, or wings that mark them as something different from the mundane snake we might encounter on our way to see some rock art, in other cases they may not be so marked, or the roughness of a particular petroglyph may obscure such marks, or we simply may not know what we need to pay attention to in the imagery or its context to make the distinction between the two—we lack the "code," much of which would only be available through informed approaches rooted in ethnography and consultations with informed and affiliated indigenous peoples. The same may hold true for a Basic Form lizard versus a Basic Form tailed anthropomorph.

There are significant limitations to a purely formal approach, especially the one I have employed here, which only pays attention to certain kinds of differences, mostly related to certain aspects of the shape of the figures. In creating a model for the Basic Form, I selected certain features and not others, and that has directed (and continues to direct) my analysis of the imagery. A good example of the limitations of my particular taxonomy is that it ignored various other differences between elements that have the same basic shape, such as the most frequent one at the Rattlesnake site with a head, tail, upper limbs extending out then up, and lower limbs extending out then down. Panel 1 (Figure 13) has four examples of this common form, all of which have roughly similar tail lengths (when compared to the lowest point of the lower limb) and similar

proportions in terms of length of torso to length of tail and overall height versus width. Panel 23 (Figure 23), however, has a lizard-like figure with the same variations on the Basic Form but that is visually very different than the cases on Panel 1. Its tail is proportionally far longer compared to the lowest point of its lower limbs and its head is almost as wide as the overall width of the upper limbs, whereas three of the four examples of the same form on Panel 1 have heads that are roughly one-quarter the overall width of the upper limbs (Figure 13). The Panel 23 lizard-like figure is approximately 23 cm tall/long and 7 cm wide, a roughly 3.3:1 ratio. The Panel 1 instances have height-to-width ratios of 1.3:1, 1.3:1, 1.4:1, and 1.5:1 and are all between 10.0 and 10.5 cm tall/long. The Panel 23 instance (Figure 23) is over twice the overall length of the four on Panel 1, and is proportionally 2.5 times as "skinny" as the four on Panel 1. Visually, as a gestalt, the Panel 23 lizard-like glyph is simply not the same as those on Panel 1 with the same Basic Form, a difference clarified by comparison not just to the four instances of the same variation of the Basic Form on Panel 1, but every other instance of that form at the site (also found on Panels 4 and 15).

My limited perceptual schemas—both intentional and unconscious—are in full operation in my "description" of the site and its petroglyphs. However, having spent substantial time observing and analyzing Northern Sinagua rock drawings, include documenting over 440 elements in Youngs Canyon (Rogers 2021), I have noticed other patterns and characteristics in the imagery itself, although their significance and relevance to the Northern Sinagua and other ancestral Puebloan cultures is still uncertain. Building on my discussion of the Panel 23 lizard-like figure and one of the distinctions noted through years of observation, I turn to a discussion of potentially "special" lizard-like images.

"Special" Lizards

Close examination of the Rattlesnake Petroglyphs made me more conscious of a pattern I have seen elsewhere in Northern Sinagua petroglyphs relating to variations in the production of lizard-like glyphs. Certain lizard-like images appear to be "special," particularly in terms of their mode of manufacture, characterized by being more finely pecked with clear edges and more solidly pecked within those edges than most other instances of variations of the Basic Form (and many other element types). There is one especially clear and a second less clear instance of "special" lizards at the Rattlesnake site; these not only stand out because of their distinctiveness within the site's inventory, but also because of similar images in nearby Youngs Canyon and elsewhere.

The central part of Panel 3 in Figure 14 contains, among other things, three figures that are variations on the Basic Form, one of which (second from the left in the top row) is different in multiple ways related to its shape: it has a proportionally larger head, it has a proportionally longer tail, the end of its tail distinctly bends to the left at a roughly right angle, it is the only case of a tailed variant of the Basic Form at this site with all four limbs extending out then up, and it displays the most visually prominent of only two instances of a circular abdomen at the site (the other being the faint figure to its right, whose rounded abdomen is ambiguous and not visually prominent). In addition to these morphological differences, it is also the most finely and solidly pecked figure on Panel 3 (possibly at the whole site), it is the tallest figure on the panel (and one of the tallest at the whole site at 23 cm), and its solidly pecked body has the most surface area of any figure on the panel. It therefore presents visually as the dominant figure on the panel: taller, more solid, brighter, more carefully crafted, and more uniquely shaped.

In Youngs Canyon, on Panel 4 at site AR-03-04-02-4966 (Figure 25), is a figure that, while morphologically different in some ways from the Panel 3 "special" lizard at the Rattlesnake site, is nonetheless strikingly similar. It has a similar proportionally large head, proportionally long tail, and a possible bend or "hook" at the end of its tail (to the right in this case). However, it lacks a rounded abdomen, all four of its limbs extend out then down (as opposed to the less common out then up on the Rattlesnake Panel 3 case), and it has a finely pecked "spray" seemingly coming from each side

of its head about where its eyes would presumably be (Rogers 2021), which the Rattlesnake Panel 3 figure lacks. It is 20 cm tall, larger than the average Northern Sinagua petroglyph and close to the 23 cm height of the Rattlesnake Panel 3 figure. The Panel 4 lizard-like figure is finely and densely pecked, is the most visually prominent petroglyph at the site, and is paired with another image that is very roughly pecked (indeed, barely detectable), all traits similar to the Panel 3 lizard-like figure at the Rattlesnake site.

Also in nearby Youngs Canyon, Panel 5 at site AR-03-04-02-4980 contains two variations on the Basic Form (Figure 26), one of which manifests traits of a

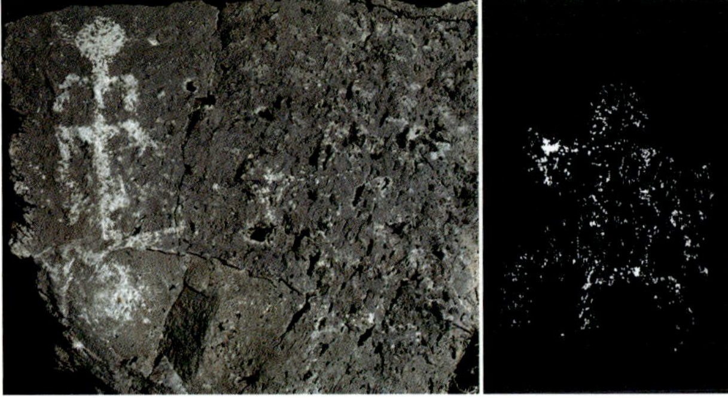

Figure 25. *Panel 4 at site AR-03-04-02-4966 in nearby Youngs Canyon contains a finely and solidly pecked 20 cm tall lizard-like figure comparable to the largest figure on Panel 3 at the Rattlesnake site (see Figure 14); a very roughly pecked, almost undetectable variation of the Basic Form is on the right.*

Figure 26. *Panel 5 at site AR-03-04-02-4980 in Youngs Canyon features paired variations on the Basic Form, a finely pecked lizard-like figure with a rounded abdomen and a roughly pecked figure with the same basic limb orientation.*

"special" lizard-like figure. The figure on the left side shows a clear contrast to the one on the right. The left figure has all four limbs extending out then up, a clear tail, a proportionally large head, and a circular abdomen, and is finely and solidly pecked. While not exactly the same, this glyph is strikingly similar to the "special" lizard-like figure on Panel 3 at the Rattlesnake site (Figure 14), albeit without a "hook" on the bottom of its tail. At 17 cm tall, this figure is also relatively large for a typical Northern Sinagua petroglyph. Also like the Panel 3 "special" lizard from the Rattlesnake site, it is next to a different variation on the Basic Form that is much more roughly pecked. These paired figures on Panel 5 in Youngs Canyon were the instigation for my early thinking about "special" lizards, especially in terms of being more finely and solidly pecked than most Northern Sinagua petroglyphs, with the contrast to less-well-pecked figures in their proximity suggesting their "specialness"—or, at least, their difference.

A second possible "special" lizard-like figure at the Rattlesnake site is the one from Panel 23 discussed above as an "outlier" in the Rattlesnake site's inventory of tailed, round-headed, out-then-up upper limbs and out-then-down lower limbs variations on the Basic Form (Figure 23). While not as finely and solidly pecked as the above examples from both the Rattlesnake site and Youngs Canyon, it is nonetheless more "solid" than many other petroglyphs at the Rattlesnake site, is 23 cm high (the same height as the "special" lizard on Panel 3 and quite large for Northern Sinagua petroglyphs), and, except for the lack of a rounded abdomen, a different orientation for the lower limbs (down instead of up), and lacking lizard-like companions on its panel, is strikingly similar in its style and form to the "special" lizard on Panel 5 at AR-03-04-02-4980 (Figure 26), including its proportionally large and round head and its proportional narrowness compared to most other instances of the Basic Form. It is positioned high on the eastern side of the site and is the only figure on Panel 23 visible from a distance, highlighting its visual (and perhaps symbolic) dominance.

Aside from the specific variations on the Basic Form involved with "special" and not-so-special lizards (or whatever else they may be), the overall visual contrast raises the question of whether the investment of time, energy, and skill necessary to produce these much more finely and solidly pecked lizard-like figures points to potential symbolic dimensions of finely and solidly pecked versus roughly pecked figures. For example, perhaps "special" lizard-like figures are not just generic lizards (or tailed anthropomorphs, or whatever) but specific figures such as those from traditional stories ("myths") or, more generally, they are distinct from mundane lizards in being more symbolic than "literal." In more practical terms, I do not think that these "special" lizards should necessarily be lumped together with the more common Basic Form images that may have some similar traits but that are very different in terms of their visual impression and visual dominance.

Bell Rocks

Finally, on a very different note, the Rattlesnake Petroglyphs site shows strong evidence for the existence of several "bell rocks," rocks that show signs of use-wear from striking and produce a ringing sound when struck (Hedges 1993; Hernbrode and Boyle 2016). Inspired by Janine Hernbrode's presentation at the 2021 virtual ARARA conference on bell rocks in the Tucson (Hohokam) area (Hernbrode 2022), I took the project of documenting the Rattlesnake Petroglyphs as an opportunity to look for signs of wear from frequent striking. I found several rocks on the outcrop with signs of use-wear, and minimally tested some of them that have no petroglyphs using a wooden mallet. Not all of them rang, which could be due to movement, cracking, or other changes to the rocks over time, or because of other causes of the visible use-wear. However, some of them definitely ring, including two stacked rocks on the west side of the southern part of the outcrop (Figure 27), three stacked rocks at the top of the southwestern corner of the outcrop just west of Panel 8 and just above Panel 15 (Figure 28), another near Panels 13 and 21 near the top of the outcrop's southeastern corner, and at least one north of the part of the outcrop that contains the petroglyphs. The top surface of the uppermost of the three bell rocks near Panel 8 (Figure 28) has a smooth, rounded basin presumably created by repeated grinding with a mano as well as repeated striking. This top surface has two areas of pecking that I initially examined as possible petroglyphs. Instead, the pecked areas seem to mark spots that produce stronger rings than other places on the rock (cf. Hedges 1993:124). On the left side of the top of the bottom rock in Figure 28, signs of use-wear are particularly clear, as they are on the bottom rock in Figure 27, presumably created by repeated striking. Panel 15, which has two petroglyphs, also shows signs of use-wear (Figure 20) consistent with that on other confirmed bell rocks without petroglyphs at the site. The rocks without petroglyphs that rang when tested

Figure 27. *Two rocks low on the west side of the outcrop, a few meters from most of the petroglyphs, show signs of use-wear, presumably from repeated striking, as they ring when struck.*

Figure 28. *These three rocks at the top of the outcrop, close to many petroglyphs, all show signs of use-wear and ring when struck. The top surface of the top rock has a smoothed, ground basin and two heavily pecked areas that seem to indicate areas that create stronger rings when struck.*

produced a range of different pitches depending on the rock and where the rock was struck (cf. Hernbrode and Boyle 2016:99–100).

The existence of multiple bell rocks combined with extensive flat areas on the east and west sides of the outcrop suggest a potential public and ceremonial function of the site, but the relationships between the bell rocks and the petroglyphs is unclear except for their proximity. More systematic survey of the entire outcrop for signs of use-wear and subsequent systematic testing for ringing are needed, as are surveying and testing the nearby Youngs Canyon petroglyph sites, where a few bell rocks have also been identified.

Conclusion

In many ways, the Rattlesnake Petroglyphs are consistent with previously documented Northern Sinagua petroglyphs from the PII–PIII period in terms of traits such as size, quality, style, and subject matter. However, the site has a higher concentration of spirals than Turkey Tanks and the Youngs Canyon sites, several complex spiral variations not present at other documented sites, a potentially higher concentration of feet than Lizard Man Village and the Youngs Canyon sites, and a distinctive linear element that possibly represents a trail or route, all of which point to a possible symbolic focus on migration. The Rattlesnake site also has a higher concentration of Basic Form images, providing a compact opportunity to analyze variations in these images, the insights from which can be applied to the analysis of similar imagery at other Northern Sinagua petroglyph sites. Finally, the Rattlesnake site contains one of the highest concentrations of petroglyphs in a very small area, as 96 of the 97 elements at the site are within less than 6 m of each other.

The presence of multiple bell rocks and this high concentration of petroglyphs enhance the possibility that this site marks a powerful place on the landscape (Hedges 1993) and point to possible ceremonial and public functions of the site. Somewhat removed from nearby habitation sites, perhaps the Rattlesnake site served as a gathering place for multiple small settlements scattered across the surrounding landscape, different but perhaps in some ways similar to the plazas, ball courts, and kivas at nearby, very large (in local terms), and architecturally distinctive centralized habitation sites such as Ridge Ruin and Two Kivas pueblos (Downum 1992; O'Hara 2015).

Acknowledgments. The Rattlesnake Petroglyphs site is on the ancestral lands of, among others, multiple contemporary Pueblo groups, and the petroglyphs specifically are part of the heritage of Pueblo peoples such as the Hopi. I thank the Pueblo peoples, past and present, for the opportunity to experience, document, and study these and other footprints of their ancestors. I also wish to thank Mark Neumann for his assistance with audio recordings of the bell rocks, as well as Christine Stephenson and Bern Carey for their work on the Angell Survey and Recording Project, which provided a broad, systematic picture of the archaeological context of sites such as the Rattlesnake Petroglyphs. All photographs and drawings are by the author.

References Cited

Anonymous
n.d. Turkey Tanks Historic Site, included in the Turkey Tanks site file (AR-03-04-02-252), unpublished manuscript on file at the Flagstaff Ranger District, Coconino National Forest, Flagstaff, Arizona.

Bernardini, Wesley
2005 *Hopi Oral Tradition and the Archaeology of Identity.* University of Arizona Press, Tucson.

Bernardini, Wesley, and Severin Fowles
2010 Becoming Hopi, Becoming Tiwa: Two Pueblo Histories of Movement. In *Movement, Connectivity, and Landscape Change in the Ancient Southwest,* edited by Margaret Nelson and Colleen Strawhacker, pp. 253–274. University Press of Colorado, Boulder, Colorado.

Colwell-Chanthaphonh, Chip, and T. J. Ferguson
2006 Memory Pieces and Footprints: Multivocality and the Meanings of Ancient Times and Ancestral Places among the Hopi and Zuni. *American Anthropologist* 108(1):148–162.

Colton, Harold S.
1946 "Fools Names Like Fools Faces–." *Plateau* 19(1):1–8.

1960 *Black Sand: Prehistory in Northern Arizona.* University of New Mexico Press, Albuquerque.

D'Amico, Diane H.
1977 *Rock Art of the Northern Sinagua Area.* Master's Thesis, Northern Arizona University.

Downum, Christian E.
1992 The Sinagua: Prehistoric People of the San Francisco Mountains. *Plateau* 63(1):1–32.

Downum, Christian E., and Daniel Garcia
2012 Peoples of the Sierra Sin Agua. In *Hisat'sinom: Ancient Peoples in a Land Without Water,* edited by Christian E. Downum, pp. 69–77. School for Advanced Research Press, Santa Fe, New Mexico.

Downum, Christian E., Ellen Brennan, and James P. Holmlund
2012 Wupatki Pueblo: Red House in Black Sand. In *Hisat'sinom: Ancient Peoples in a Land Without Water,* edited by Christian E. Downum, pp. 79–86. School for Advanced Research Press, Santa Fe, New Mexico.

Elson, Mark D., and Michael H. Ort
2012 Fire in the Sky: The Eruption of Sunset Crater Volcano. In *Hisat'sinom: Ancient Peoples in a Land Without Water,* edited by Christian E. Downum, pp. 27–33. School for Advanced Research Press, Santa Fe, New Mexico.

Ferguson, T. J., and Chip Colwell-Chanthaphonh
2006 *History is in the Land: Multivocal Tribal Traditions in Arizona's San Pedro Valley.* University of Arizona Press, Tucson.

Gearty, Erin, and David E. Purcell
2018 Sinagua Rock Art of Walnut Canyon. *Plateau—The Land and People of the Colorado Plateau* 10(1):68–72.

Hays-Gilpin, Kelley, and Christian E. Downum
2012 Pottery of the Sierra Sin Agua. In *Hisat'sinom: Ancient Peoples in a Land Without Water,* edited by Christian E. Downum, pp. 125–131. School for Advanced Research Press, Santa Fe, New Mexico.

Hays-Gilpin, Kelley, and Donald E. Weaver
2012 Marks on the Land: Rock Art of the Sierra Sin Agua. In *Hisat'sinom: Ancient Peoples in a Land Without Water,* edited by Christian E. Downum, pp. 17–25. School for Advanced Research Press, Santa Fe, New Mexico.

Hedges, Ken
1993 Places to See and Places to Hear: Rock Art and Features of the Sacred Landscape. In *Time and Space: Dating and Spatial Considerations in Rock Art Research,* edited by Jack Steinbring, Alan Watchman, Paul Faulstich, and Paul S. C. Taçon, pp. 121–127. Occasional AURA Publication No. 8. Australian Rock Art Research Association, Melbourne.

Hedquist, Saul L.
2012 Exotic Goods in the Sierra Sin Agua. In *Hisat'sinom: Ancient Peoples in a Land Without Water,* edited by Christian E. Downum, pp. 141–147. School for Advanced Research Press, Santa Fe, New Mexico.

Hernbrode, Janine
2022 Rings and Roars: Voices of Bell Rocks in Ancestral O'odham (Hohokam) Ritual. In *American Indian Rock Art, Volume 48,* edited by Amy Gilreath, Ken Hedges, and Anne McConnell, pp. 71–84. American Rock Art Research Association, Orem, Utah.

Hernbrode, Janine, and Peter Boyle
2016 Petroglyphs and Bell Rocks at Cocoraque Butte: Further Evidence of the Flower World Belief among the Hohokam. In *American Indian Rock Art, Volume 42,* edited by Ken Hedges, pp. 91–105. American Rock Art Research Association, San Jose, California.

Kuwanwisiwma, Leigh J., and Stewart B. Koyiyumptewa
2018 Hopi Footprints at the Crack-in-Rock Community. *Plateau—The Land and People of the Colorado Plateau* 10(1):29–32.

Kuwanwisiwma, Leigh J., Stewart B. Koyiyumptewa, and Anita Poleahla
2012 Pasiwvi: Place of Deliberations. In *Hisat'sinom: Ancient Peoples in a Land Without Water,* edited by Christian E. Downum, pp. 7–9. School for Advanced Research Press, Santa Fe, New Mexico.

Newsome, Elizabeth
2005 Weaving the Sky: The Cliff Palace Painted Tower. *Plateau* 2(2):28–41.

O'Hara, F. Michael
2012 Hohokam and Chaco in the Sierra Sin Agua. In *Hisat'sinom: Ancient Peoples in a Land Without Water,* edited by Christian E. Downum, pp. 59–67. School for Advanced Research Press, Santa Fe, New Mexico.

2015 Suyanisqatsi/Koyaanisqatsi: *Creating Balance in a Land of Little Water and Burning Rock: Cooperation, Competition, and Climate in the Flagstaff Region of the U.S. Southwest A.D. 1100–1300.* Ph.D. Dissertation, University of Arizona.

Pilles, Peter J.
2017 Flagstaff's Ancient Connections. Archaeology Café, February 28, 2017. Archaeology Southwest, Tucson, Arizona. Electronic Document, https://www.youtube.com/watch?v=QXkSG2K6boc, accessed June 22, 2020.

Rogers, Richard A.
2021 The Northern Sinagua Petroglyphs of Youngs Canyon. In *American Indian Rock Art, Volume 47*, edited by David A. Kaiser, Mavis Greer, and James D. Keyser, pp. 83 103. American Rock Art Research Association, Orem, Utah.

Saussure, Ferdinand de
1959 *Course in General Linguistics*. The Philosophical Library, New York.

Schindler, Kevin, and Michael Kitt
2019 *Historic Tales of Flagstaff*. The History Press, Charleston, South Carolina.

Waters, Frank
1963 *Book of the Hopi*. The Viking Press, New York.

Weaver, Donald E.
1994 Sinagua Rock Art: Petroglyphs at Lizard Man Village. In *American Indian Rock Art, Volumes 13 and 14*, edited by A. J. Bock, pp. 83–114. American Rock Art Research Association, San Miguel, California.

2014-2015 Picture Canyon's Petroglyphs and Ancient People. *Plateau—The Land and People of the Colorado Plateau* 8(1–2):38–47.

Weaver, Donald E., and Nancy Slominski
1992 Turkey Tanks: A Prehistoric Wayfarer Rest Stop? In *American Indian Rock Art, Volume 15*, edited by Kay K. Sanger, pp. 80–103. American Rock Art Research Association, Ridgecrest, California.

Wright, Aaron M., and Maren P. Hopkins
2016 *The Great Bend of the Gila: Contemporary Native American Connections to an Ancestral Landscape*. Archaeology Southwest, Tucson, Arizona.

Red Cliffs Incised: A Distinctive Style of Fine Line Art at Arizona's Palatki Heritage Site

Peter Anick, Spence Gustav, and Walter van Roggen

Although the presence of fine incised art has long been noted at the Palatki Heritage Site and nearby sites within central Arizona's Verde Valley, little systematic study has been done to characterize or quantify the phenomenon. In this survey focused on four sites open to the public along Palatki's Red Cliffs corridor, we examine a complex of features that we believe defines a distinct and significant local style. We present prototypical examples of Red Cliffs Incised panels and explore what superimpositions—with respect to other cultural features on the walls such as pictographs, pecked petroglyphs, gouges, and scratches—suggest regarding their relative chronology and cultural affiliation. We hope that focusing more attention on this hard-to-see but surprisingly pervasive practice at Palatki will encourage further local discoveries and lead to a better understanding of their cultural significance, as well as their possible relationship to other manifestations of scratched and incised geometric art in the American West.

Red Cliffs is a 700-meter-long stretch of box canyon wall within the Palatki Heritage Site (PHS) near Sedona, Arizona (Figure 1). Archaeological evidence in the form of lithics, roasting pits, and masonry structures attests to human presence in the region from Paleoindian through historic times. Four sites with alcoves within the section of Red Cliffs open to the public are decorated with abundant pictographs. Most of these painted images have been associated by style with three cultures: Archaic hunter-gatherers, Southern Sinagua farmers, and a subsequent hunter-gatherer population, the Yavapai (Pilles 2014).

Peter Anick
*Brandeis University,
Waltham, Massachusetts*

Spence Gustav
*Sedona Friends of the Forest,
Sedona, Arizona*

Walter van Roggen
*Northwoods Software Corporation,
Nashua, New Hampshire*

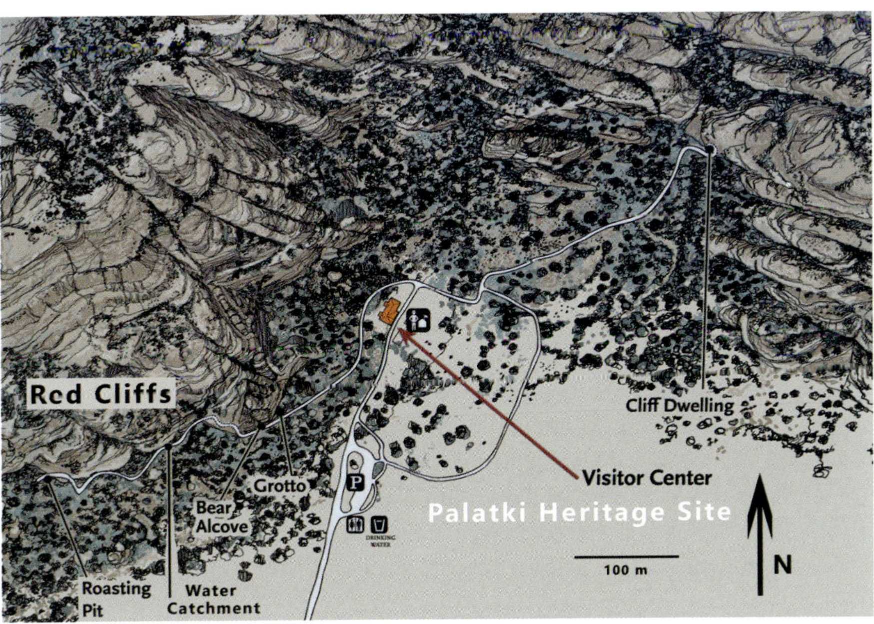

Figure 1. The trails and main archaeological sites at the Palatki Heritage Site, near Sedona Arizona. Base map courtesy of the U.S. Forest Service.

American Indian Rock Art, Volume 49. Amy Gilreath, Ken Hedges, and Anne McConnell, Editors. American Rock Art Research Association, 2023, pp. 117–134.

Lawrence Loendorf (1994) did a statistical analysis of paint color superimpositions at two of the public alcoves and used that along with stylistic features to propose a tentative chronology for the pictographs:

- Archaic hunter-gatherers were likely responsible for abstract designs painted in red, deep maroon, black, and buff white. These include long, ghostlike figures, rake symbols, and clusters of vertical zigzags.
- Farming came to the area around A.D. 600 with a culture known as the Southern Sinagua. This ancestral Puebloan population remained in the area till around 1350. At Palatki, their rock art includes primarily white zoomorphs and anthropomorphs, multicolored shields, and white horizontal zigzags, usually interpreted as snake symbols.
- From at least A.D. 1300 and well into historic times, the area was used by the Yavapai, a nomadic hunter-gatherer culture who harvested and roasted agave in large stone pits. Their rock art consists of black charcoal sketches of animals, horses, and riders, as well as multicolored anthropomorphs with long thin bodies and feathered headdresses.

While these pictographs attract the attention of today's visitors to PHS, the cliff walls also host a gallery of more esoteric designs formed not by paint but by incising. Composed of shallow lines barely half a millimeter wide, these are often nearly invisible unless viewed up close and with favorable lighting conditions. Coconino National Forest archaeologist Peter Pilles has conjectured, on the basis of repatination and stylistic similarity to archaeologically dated mobiliary paleoart from Texas (Lemke et al. 2015), that some of the finely incised designs may date back as far as Paleoindian times (Pilles 2014).

In 2019, we initiated a project to test the antiquity of incised art at Palatki (Anick et al. 2022). We selected two panels on which fine incised lines share panel space with pictographs that had been proposed by Loendorf to be among the oldest Archaic images at Red Cliffs (Loendorf 1994:2.7). Using high-resolution photography with raked (obliquely angled) lighting, we were able to document thousands of faint incised lines on the panels. Incisions that intersected the early pictographs consistently showed evidence of superimposition by the paint. This would date the incised designs lying beneath the Archaic pictographs as some of the oldest rock art on Red Cliffs.

The incised motifs—particularly parallel lines and crosshatched checkerboard and diamond patterns—are similar to scratched art found throughout the Desert West. But the density and complexity of the subpanels we examined at PHS were a good order of magnitude greater than most of what has been reported at other sites. We recognized a need to better understand the nature and extent of the incised art along the Red Cliffs. By enlarging the scope of our study to cover all of the panels at the four public archaeological sites within PHS, we hope to address a number of questions raised during our initial research:

- How pervasive is incised art at Red Cliffs?
- Where and under what conditions does it occur?
- How was it produced?
- How do incisions relate chronologically to each other and to other rock art (both painted and pecked)?
- Are there consistent elements and motifs across the four sites?
- Are there recognizable compositional principles or cultural styles?

In this paper, we present the results of our four-site survey. We recognize a recurring pattern of motifs and compositional conventions which appear to define a significant local style of fine-line rock art, referred to here as Red Cliffs Incised (RCI). After introducing its basic components—line types and motifs—we review summary statistics describing their presence and position on panels throughout PHS. We then introduce each of the four public archaeological sites along Red Cliffs and present details of specific panels that contributed to our stylistic characterization and relative dating of RCI. We briefly consider possible interpretations for the art and conclude with opportunities for further research.

Line Types

Although they are often lumped together (e.g., Woody and Quinlan 2008:139), we distinguish incised from scratched lines (Figure 2). *Scratches* abrade the surface of the rock, typically creating very shallow lines with discontinuities. By contrast, *incised* lines cut through the surface enough to create precise, continuous lines. *Fine lines*, the primary focus of our study, are typically around a half millimeter in width and, while also shallow, cut deep enough to cast a distinct shadow in raked light.

Many panels with fine lines also contain *gouges*. Gouges are deeper and wider cuts with widths typically greater than 1.5 mm. Many appear to have been created by repeated strokes of a fine engraving tool similar to that used for producing fine lines. Gouges

Figure 2. Line types: gouge, fine incised, groove, and scratch, shown at the same scale.

often have a rough and ragged appearance, tapered at the ends, which may trail off into single or multiple individual incisions. Traces of one or more individual incisions may be detected within the wide line. In some cases, the interior of the wide line appears to have been smoothed by abrading or planing, resulting in a more refined **U**- or **V**-shaped groove. We refer to these more refined gouges as *grooves*.

Motifs

As with descriptions of geometric scratched/incised art elsewhere (e.g., Ritter 1994), it is useful to describe the panels at Red Cliffs in terms of recurring motifs. The most commonly observed patterns are parallel and regularly spaced vertical, horizontal, or diagonal lines (Figure 3a). One special case involves a group of vertical lines that run for a long distance along the straight edge of a panel. When horizontal and vertical lines cross in a regular fashion, we refer to the pattern as a *checkerboard* motif (Figure 3b), even when the sections are more rectangular than square due to spacing differences between the horizontal and vertical lines. We refer to the pattern created by crossed ascending (left to right) and descending diagonals as *diamonds* (Figure 3c). *Micro-patterns* are very small-scale, local-

ized designs that contrast with a larger-scale incised background. For example, Figure 3d shows a small group of short parallel lines arranged into a striped rectangle within more widely spaced verticals and diagonals. *Vertical zigzags* occasionally occur both as sin-

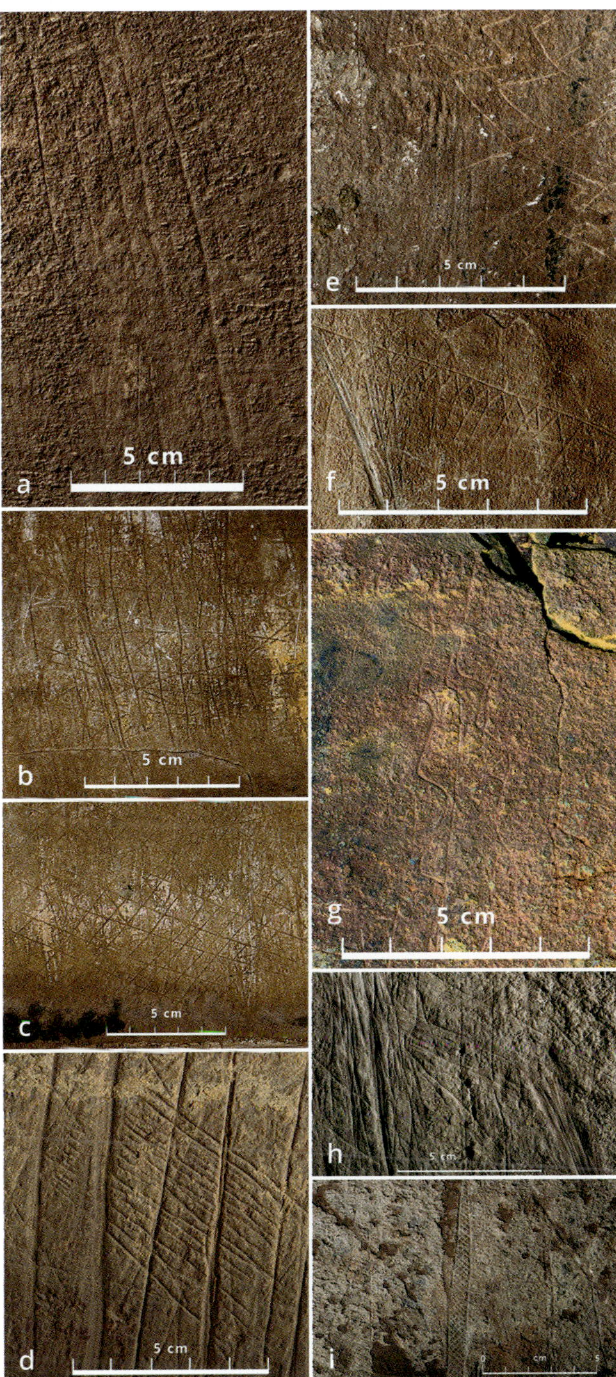

Figure 3. Motif examples: (a) parallel fine lines, (b) checkerboard, (c) diamonds, (d) micro-pattern, (e) vertical zigzags, (f) chain of Vs with linear extensions and bounded by a horizontal line, (g) curved and wavy lines, enhanced with DStretch LBK, (h) bundles, and (i) bounded figures.

gletons and side by side in clusters (Figure 3e). Rows of *chained* **V**s, resembling horizontal zigzags, also occur, usually accompanied by a horizontal boundary line or lines (Figure 3f).

Given the predominance of rectilinear patterns, we initially assumed that curved lines were graffiti (and some are). But a closer look revealed them to be an integral and fascinating component of the fine-line repertoire. Their most common form is a long, wavy line oriented vertically (Figure 3g), but they occasionally take on more elaborate shapes, even incorporating loops. They tend to appear on the more complex panels and where one meandering line occurs, there are often other curved lines in close proximity.

Several other incised effects recur often enough to merit ascribing to distinct categories. These all consist of a cluster of very closely crowded lines of varying depth, usually not exactly straight, that have an organic, flowing appearance (Figure 3h). We call these clusters a *bundle* if the lines remain roughly parallel, a *splay* if they tend to fray apart at one or both ends, and a *fan* if they remain close to straight but appear to disperse from a single point to create a **V**-shaped arc of rays.

We occasionally find artificially bounded designs, such as a rounded triangular outline containing parallel lines or a thin, tapered form filled in with fine diamond crosshatching (Figure 3i). The latter design we refer to mnemonically as a snake figure (following Loendorf 1994:4.10–11), but we generally assign such instances to the category *bounded figures*.

It is important to acknowledge that in defining motifs, we are imposing an interpretation on the incised features for the sake of describing and relating panels. We do not know how the designs were conceptualized by the artists themselves. For example, overlapping checkerboard and diamonds may have been interpreted as a single object.

Survey Statistics

Along most of the Red Cliffs trail, the cliff walls consist of three distinct strata of sandstone—a hard layer forming a lower ledge (Figure 4, label a), a softer, highly fragmented layer with highly variable (lateral and vertical) sedimentary layering (Figure 4, label b) and an overlying, more resistive, massive layer (Figure 4, label c). The overlying massive layer is consistently greater than 10 meters in thickness. The underlying hard layer is mostly covered by eroded material but is also on the order of 10 meters or greater in thickness. Geologically, the middle, softer zone (Figure 4, label b)

Figure 4. *Cliff face at the Water Catchment site, showing multiple layers of sandstone: (a) hard, lower ledge, (b) fragmented intermediate layer, and (c) harder, overlying massive layer. White scale bar = approx. 3.3 meters.*

has absorbed stress deformation which is not seen in the more massive sandstone levels above and below. As a result, there is a much greater quantity and variety of fracture planes within this zone, leading to its greater susceptibility to erosion and structural collapse. This has resulted in the formation of alcoves containing numerous rock faces, frequently capped by overhangs of the more massive sandstone. It is in this intermediate zone, typically varying between 3 to 4 meters high, that most of the rock art appears. The white vertical scale in Figure 4 represents approximately 3.3 meters.

The 700-meter-long stretch of sandstone cliffs in our study has 132 numbered panel areas. Each numbered panel roughly corresponds to a well-defined section of the fragmented cliff face, separated from its neighbors by some natural feature, such as a fissure or a marked change in the orientation of the wall. Our survey located incised art on 54 of the 132 panels, nearly 40%. In Table 1, we show the number of panels on which we observed various designs, attributes, and motifs. The overall totals are in the column labeled "Incised." The other columns give totals for incised panels that also contain pictographs stylistically classified as Archaic, Sinagua, and/or Yavapai. Because incised lines are so difficult to see and some panels are extremely weathered, these numbers very likely represent undercounts.

The occurrence of incised designs is highly correlated with the presence of clastic fracture fill on the cliff surface. Fracture fill consists of one thin layer or more of typically clay-like material that had filled thin fractures in the native sandstone while the stone was still deep underground. Compared to the native sandstone, fine-grained fracture fill provides a much less brittle surface for cutting extremely fine incisions. Loendorf

Table 1. Distribution of incised motifs and presence of culturally attributed rock art on the same panels.

Feature	Incised	Incised and Archaic	Incised and Sinagua	Incised and Yavapai
any incision	54	19	27	27
Bundle	11	7	11	5
Checkerboard	14	3	5	8
Curve	7	3	4	3
Diamonds	21	7	9	9
Gouge	12	6	11	4
Parallel Diagonal	20	6	10	5
Parallel Horizontal	6	1	3	1
Parallel Vertical	25	10	14	10
Parallel to Edge	4	2	4	3
Zigzag	11	4	4	4
Intersection: Line with Gouge	10	5	9	3
Intersection: Line with Paint	16	11	15	9
Intersection: Line with Pecked	2	0	2	0

(1994:1.2) noted that the hardness and consistency of surfaces varied widely across panels. Artists likely sought out and tested panels for their texture before initiating a design.

We recorded whether art on a panel consisted of isolated images, such as a checkerboard surrounded by empty space, or more dense incising extending out to some of the panel's natural edges. At least 22 of the panels containing incised lines had evidence of dense and/or overlapping motifs filling a working surface out to some natural boundaries.

The height of incised art on the cliff face, measured from where someone could stand today, varied across the panels (Figure 5) and was likely a function of both the availability of suitable carving surfaces and what was within reach at the time. On complex panels, incised art often continued to the very tops of panels, requiring not only reaching high up but, in a number of cases, using a ladder or something to stand on. Stone was collected and utilized for building during the Sinagua and historic periods, so it is possible that more rock and rubble may have once existed at the foot of the cliff. This

may have previously made some panel areas reachable that are well beyond standing reach today. Many pictographs attributed to each culture are also located at heights unreachable today without assistance.

On each panel, we also measured the length of the longest continuous fine line observed. Figure 6 shows the results, ordered by their length on the x axis. The longest lines tend to be oriented vertically. Their median length, about 30 cm, likely reflects the mechanics of incising. It is the distance that corresponds to moving the arm from a partially raised position to nearly straight ahead, the range in which an artist would have the most control.

Weathering

The cliff walls have been subjected to many types of weathering. Although most panels are in protected alcoves, wind and rain can dull the incised lines and dust can adhere to the surface. More damaging is water seeping from the cliff itself, which accelerates exfoliation of the thin, clayey, fracture-fill layers. Sandstone diagenesis may lead to bulging and overgrowths. In some alcoves, smoke from fire pits has left surfaces coated with black soot. Finally, rock falls along weakened fracture lines can remove previously decorated sections of the wall, leaving behind freshly exposed patches of smooth sandstone (Figure 4). Among the latest to occupy the area, the Yavapai often took advantage of these more recently exposed subpanels to add charcoal images of

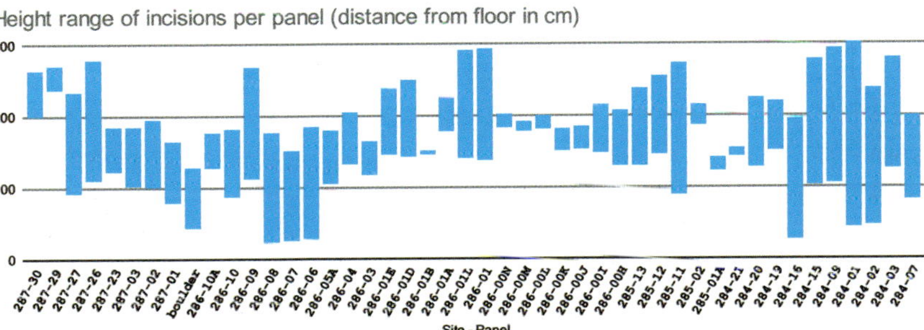

Figure 5. Height range of incised art on panels, ordered from southwest to northeast.

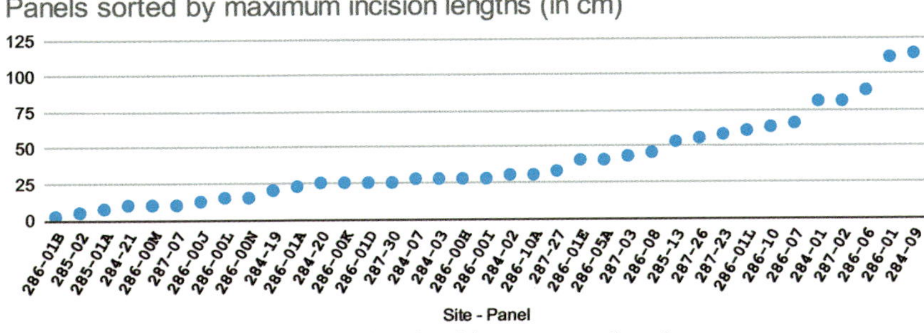

Figure 6. Longest incision per panel, ordered by increasing length.

zoomorphs and horseback riders.

The various weathering effects, along with natural color differences between very thin layers of fracture fill, complicate using repatination and erosion to gauge the relative age of incised motifs. However, some complex panels with multiple overlapping motifs appear to show differential weathering of lines. While not easily quantifiable, such differences suggest long periods of time between incising episodes.

Distribution of Rock Art Across Sites

The four archaeological sites open to the public along the Red Cliffs show evidence of extensive utilization beyond the production of rock art. They contain the remains of roasting pits where agave was prepared, as well as alcoves which would have provided shelter and water seeps. In this section, we provide a brief overview of the general appearance and rock art within each of the four sites we studied.

Roasting Pit
(Forest Service site AR-03-04-06-0287)

This site gets its name from a very large mound of stones and debris from an agave roasting pit used by both Sinagua and Yavapai. Among its 36 primary panels, there are two loci where fine lines are found. Weathering, soot from a smaller roasting pit, and geology (surface texture and fragmentation) appear to account for the bimodal distribution of incised panels. An abundance of Archaic pictographs, but fewer Sinagua and Yavapai pictographs, appears in direct association with fine lines at the southern locus. These include at least five red ghostlike images considered Archaic (Panels 26, 27, and 34), reminiscent of Barrier Canyon anthropomorphs with long torsos and short arms and legs (Loendorf 1994:4.20–23; Schaafsma 1980:61–72). On the northern panels with fine lines, most of the co-occurring painted images are believed to be Sinagua and Yavapai. One long slab leaning against the cliff face contains a number of small cupules and several pecked petroglyphs in Sinagua style (Panel 8a). No fine lines were observed on this slab.

Water Catchment
(Forest Service site AR-03-04-06-0286)

This site is named for a prehistoric/historic reservoir fed by a natural spring and seasonal waterfalls. The alcove has 16 primary panels with many subpanels. Towards the center of the site (Panels 3 and 4), there is a cluster of mixed incised/scratched/painted Yavapai

images depicting *akaka*, spirits with thin rectangular bodies and feathered headdresses (Figure 7). To the right, beyond a series of highly weathered panels, a group of relatively well-preserved subpanels contains very complex incised designs that completely cover the workable areas. Most of these are on hanging sections roughly at eye level and show little evidence of paint. One large, densely incised rectangular area within Panel 1, extending nearly three meters high, contains a distinct black rake-like Archaic pictograph (Figure 8) and highly eroded vestiges of other paintings.

To the left of the central Yavapai cluster are boulders with fine lines, cliff panels with Sinagua and Yavapai

Figure 7. *Yavapai incised/scratched* akaka *with headdress on Water Catchment Panel 4, with enhancement to clarify design.*

Figure 8. *Archaic painted rake symbol on Water Catchment Panel 1.*

pictographs, and a number of scratched images. Most of the scratched images are presumed to be Yavapai and include radiating headdresses and a series of vertical zigzags. One panel with a rough surface (Panel 16g) contains a deeply engraved diamond motif at an unusually large scale (10–12 cm between parallel diagonals.)

Bear Alcove
(Forest Service site AR-03-04-06-0285)

The Bear Alcove, named for a charcoal Yavapai bear image on its wall, once hosted a Sinagua stone structure. Dismantled in the 1920s, only some floor plaster remains today. It contains 13 primary panels and multiple subpanels. Some of the central alcove is soot-covered, but several panels to the left contain not only densely incised lines and gouges but also Sinagua pecked petroglyphs and cupules (Panels 11–13). To the right, there is an abundance of Sinagua, Yavapai, and Archaic pictographs, as well as historic graffiti, but very few incised lines. Many of the panels here have far less fracture fill. This likely made them less attractive for incising. But it is also possible that incised art once existed here that has since weathered or fractured off. A scratched grid graces the top of one highly decorated panel (4) but does not extend out to the natural boundaries of the panel like the incised designs on the panels to the left of the alcove.

Grotto (Forest Service site AR-03-04-06-0284)

The Grotto site includes a large alcove with a seasonal waterfall which creates a small pool that reflects sunlight against the cliff walls. A smaller alcove to the right has Sinagua pictographs impacted by smoke from a roasting pit. Further to the right is a historic structure built in the 1920s utilizing stone likely recycled from the Sinagua structure in the Bear Alcove. The Grotto holds 17 primary panels. Some of the most densely incised fine line panels at Red Cliffs are found at the right corner of the large alcove, along with complex layers of Archaic, Sinagua, and Yavapai pictographs (Panels 1, 9, and 15).

Complex Panels

Ritter's documentation of scratched panels in Nevada includes a subjective measure of panel complexity, in which *simple* panels with "single or several simple motifs on a panel with a low number of lines" are contrasted with *complex* panels of "multiple motifs of larger size with numerous lines" (Ritter 1994:58). A distinctive feature of the line art at Red Cliffs is the large number of very complex panels which, as a cor-

pus, exhibit recurring and nuanced design features that appear to reflect a long-running cultural tradition (Figure 9). Below we list some of the shared traits observed among complex panels.

- They are composed of a relatively small number of primarily rectilinear motifs, with a predominance of parallel lines.
- Motifs rarely appear in isolation or with empty space between them. They are contiguous or overlapping, filling all space on a panel up to a natural boundary, such as a fissure or change in the wall's orientation.
- Incising often runs from the lower boundary of a panel to the ceiling, even when the top of the panel is beyond arm's reach given the current floor level. Density may diminish in high sections and in a few cases, incising appears to cease at a height just out of arm's reach.
- The distance between parallel lines within motifs typically varies between one and two centimeters, with verticals often spaced closer than horizontals when they co-occur within checkerboard patterns.
- Crosshatched patterns are often superimposed; checkerboards may share space with other checkerboards of a different scale; diamonds may share space with other diamonds at a different orientation. Parallel diagonals are sometimes observed without any crosshatching.
- Patterns tend to vary across a panel. Variations include grids at different line angles or scales, changes in the density/complexity of lines, and changes in the depth/width of fine lines. Transitions between motifs often appear fluid, with one pattern overlapping the next, rather than terminating at precise boundaries.
- Panels vary in the degree of overlapping patterns. Subjectively, some appear to be the result of a single drawing event, while others appear to have multiple generations of overlaid patterns.
- Artificial boundaries, such as an inscribed oval, rectangle, or straight line, occasionally demarcate patterned areas within a larger inscribed area. A double line or a line scored multiple times may serve as an artificial boundary where a series of perpendicular parallel lines or a row of connected **V**s might terminate.
- "Micro-patterns," such as a localized cluster of parallel lines forming a small parallelogram shape or a minute area containing crosshatching, may occur embedded within larger motifs.

Figure 9. Section of Water Catchment Panel 1L, showing compositional complexity across the entire workable surface.

- The most common curvilinear elements are wavy lines oriented vertically. These tend to occur in clusters of two or three. Proximal lines have unique meandering shapes that may come close to each other at points and even occasionally cross. More complex curves, including loops, are rare but do occur.

Towards a Chronology

The presence of fine incised art on panels that also contain pictographs and petroglyphs attributable to specific cultures offers an opportunity to tease out chronological relationships among parietal features. In this section we review the evidence for temporal orderings using superimposition. We begin with a review of panels that contain Archaic-style pictographs that intersect incised designs. Superimpositions on these panels were examined to determine which motifs and compositional styles can be directly associated with the Archaic period. We then turn to panels that lack Archaic paint but have painted Sinagua elements that overlap with fine lines. We focus on a relatively well-preserved and multifeatured panel in the Bear Alcove to show examples of superimposition analysis not only between lines, paint, and pecked petroglyphs, but also between different types of lines and fine-line motifs. Finally, we discuss incised, gouged, and scratched lines in the context of figures associated with the Yavapai.

Seriation with Respect to Archaic Pictographs

In a previous study (Anick et al. 2022), we found evidence on two panels that parallel and crosshatched incised motifs preceded the painting of Archaic pictographs. Our current survey identified an additional seven panels where pictographs ascribed to the Archaic intersected fine lines, for a total of nine: five in the Grotto, two in the Roasting Pit, and one each at the Water Catchment and Bear Alcove sites. Inspection of the intersections of lines and paint consistently showed evidence of superimposition of lines by paint. Below we summarize the findings, moving southwest to northeast along the cliff walls.

Roasting Pit Panel 27

Much of the panel is highly weathered, with some exfoliation of the outer fracture-fill layer revealing an iron-rich layer below. The Archaic art includes a red outlined ghostlike figure superimposed in part over wavy vertical lines in alternating black and buff white paint. A second, smaller ghostlike figure below it is also outlined in red. In this lower section of the panel, there is evidence of what may be a single episode of checkerboard and diamond crosshatching across the right side. Faint remnants on the left side hint that the entire naturally bounded panel may have been incised at least up to arm's reach from the current ground level. The upper ghostlike figure continues far above the apparent top of the incised area (Anick et al. 2022:Figure 6).

Many incised line fragments at various orientations are scattered across the panel. Some may be remnants of earlier motifs. There is a group of intersecting bundles in the lower right. Where these overlap with a red leg of the lower ghostlike figure, the red paint appears to be above the lines. Several small, incised arcs suggest there may have been longer curved lines here, but weathering has obscured them.

Four small vertical "snake" figures, executed with extremely fine crosshatching within narrow, double tapered outlines, appear on the left, superimposed over faint horizontal lines (Figure 3i). Their relation to the Archaic paint to the right is indeterminate but all except one of the snake designs exhibit weathering similar to lines found running under Archaic paint.

Roasting Pit Panel 26

The Archaic pictographs include three faint red ghostlike figures, one completely filled with red paint and two drawn as outlines, the leftmost showing vertical rows of dots inside. As seen in Figure 10a, enhanced using DStretch (Harman 2008), these figures extend across most of the lower portion of the panel. The incised art here is dominated by long, narrowly spaced verticals which terminate at a thin horizontal natural fracture on the right but continue beyond it on the left

Figure 10. (a) Three ghostlike Archaic figures on Roasting Pit Panel 26, enhanced with DStretch LDS. (b) Close-up of two overlapping red ghostlike figures, with vertical and diagonal fine lines underneath, enhanced with DStretch CRGB. (c) Vertical parallel and wavy fine lines under the right ghostlike figure, enhanced with DStretch LRD.

125

(well beyond arm's reach). There are also widely spaced horizontals and diagonals; long, paired, parallel lines at slightly off-vertical orientations; and some descending fans. The density, possibly reflecting multiple episodes of incising, increases towards the lower portion of the panel. The majority of lines on the panel intersect Archaic red paint and all show evidence of paint over the lines (Figure 10b). The close-up in Figure 10c reveals several wavy lines among a group of parallel vertical lines.

Water Catchment Panel 1

A single black, rake-like figure (17 x 13 cm) stands out near the upper center of this 2.2 x 2.7 m panel, over-lying a profusion of incised lines (Figure 8). Faint remnants of white, beige, and black paint survive elsewhere on the panel. This is an extremely dense panel with fine lines extending to the panel's natural boundaries, likely representing multiple generations of incising. A cluster of gouges sits to the left of the black pictograph. The gouges appear to be more recent than cospatial fine-line motifs, as does a horizontal zigzag and a diagonal groove carved to the right of the pictograph.

Checkerboards and diamonds are the most common identifiable incised motifs, exhibiting many transitions which involve angle changes between partially overlapping patterns. A long, narrow subpanel near the base of the panel area has been better preserved than the larger upper section and clearly shows at least seven motif transitions along its 265-cm span. Figure 11 illustrates several of these transitions.

Bear Alcove Panel 9

The panel contains Yavapai charcoal zoomorphs superimposed over red and black Archaic geometric figures. The surface is highly weathered, making iden-

tification of incised motifs very speculative but several line segments can be recognized underneath one red Archaic figure.

Grotto Panel 20

This panel at the rear of the large grotto for which the site is named displays a white horizontal zigzag and disk design that is believed to be a Sinagua calendar. Although the surface here in the upper area of the panel is very worn, many vertical lines can be detected running down the panel under the white paint. Faint horizontals imply this area may have been covered with a checkerboard pattern. Moving down the panel, diagonals begin to appear crossing the verticals. The complexity of lines continues to increase with many areas of miniature crosshatching and clusters of superimposed lines in seemingly random orientations. Approaching the very bottom of the panel, several overlapping crosshatched patterns are superimposed by an unusually thick fan of tightly packed lines converging downwards (Figure 12).

The only distinct Archaic paint in this section of the Grotto is on a physically separated subpanel below the main panel. Here, a few faint traces of incised lines can be detected under the strokes of a complex red geometric design.

Grotto Panel 19

Portions of an extremely weathered checkerboard pattern can be seen running under a red indeterminate shape believed to be Archaic.

Grotto Panel 15

This panel lies at the northern corner of the large grotto. Because the panel is highly decorated with mul-

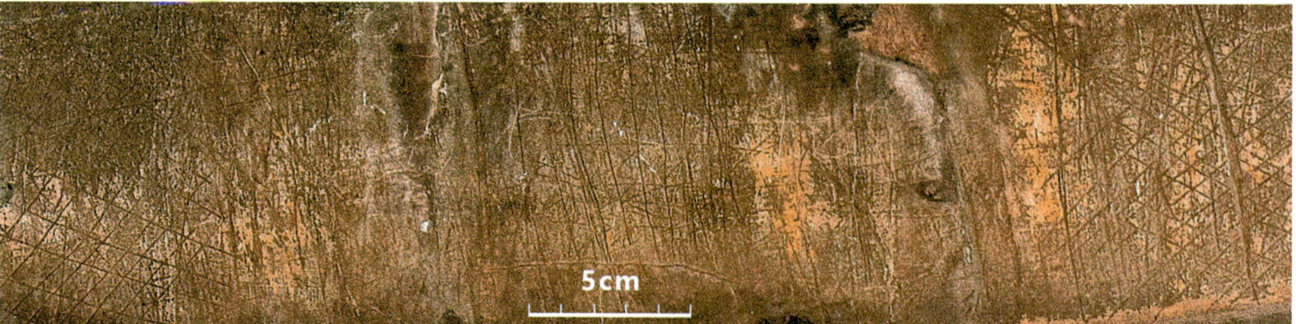

*Figure 11. A 42-cm span of a longer subpanel near the bottom of Water Catchment Panel 1. On the left is a diamond grid with 160- and 50-degree diagonals. Near the top of this section, a pair of slightly ascending diagonals intrudes, providing the base for a row of inverted **V** shapes. To the right, after a slight dip in the surface in which the design thins out to a scattering of off-vertical and off-horizontal lines, a checkerboard pattern emerges, crossed by ascending diagonals and several vertically oriented wavy lines. After another slight depression in the panel surface, a strong diamond pattern emerges at the right edge, cut by a number of closely spaced vertical lines, including a deep gouge.*

Figure 12. A broad fan overlying crosshatched patterns on Grotto Panel 20. Photo by Peter Anick.

tiple layers of both painted and incised designs, we divided it into several arbitrary regions for an earlier study detailed in Anick et al. (2022).

Subarea A1 is high up on the rock face with most of the area well beyond arm's reach without a ladder or other support. Most of this section is covered by a figure composed of alternating vertical wavy and straight lines in buff white and black paint, interpreted as a possible water symbol. The figure is nearly identical to one superimposed by the upper ghostlike pictograph on Roasting Pit Panel 27, indicating it is probably also Archaic in origin. Several white Sinagua pictographs are superimposed over the Archaic images.

Fine incised lines, superimposed by the Archaic paint, extend all the way up to the top of the subarea and cover most of the surface. Many parallel diagonals at different angles give the impression of multiple episodes. Some clusters of diagonals fan out slightly in upward or downward directions. In the central section, cross hatching and checkerboards are more definitive. Several long deep gouges with **U**-shaped incisions run down a rougher section on the lower left, appearing to cut through remnants of Archaic buff white paint.

Subarea A3, directly below A1, encompasses two separate concave surfaces side by side. The left-hand section has primarily vertical white and buff white wavy pictographs running the full height of the workable area. The buff paint, interpreted to be Archaic, is superimposed over fine diamond patterns with spacing typically less than 1 cm amid an abundance of vertical lines. Horizontal lines are much fainter but may be integral to a checkerboard type motif. On the right portion of this section are very closely spaced vertical lines that in parts resemble bundles or splays.

The right side of subarea A3 has a rake type pictograph in Archaic buff white paint superimposed by white Sinagua paint that in part traces the rake symbol. The area is covered with multiple incised diamond and checkerboard patterns with a typical spacing of about 1.5 cm between parallel lines. There is also a prominent series of vertical gouges that show clear evidence of being older than paint, although distinguishing between the shades of Archaic and Sinagua paint within the lines, particularly in the presence of iron staining, is difficult. There are distinct bundle and splay motifs superimposed by buff white vertical wavy pictographs.

Grotto Panel 9a

High up, well beyond arm's length, are Archaic black, buff white, and red descending zigzags painted over diamond and checkerboard fine-line motifs. Long vertical lines run parallel to the straight right edge of the panel. Lower down, the complexity of the fine lines increases significantly where an estimated 5000 lines fill the panel with multiple layers of crosshatching under multiple layers of indistinct paint.

Grotto Panel 9

Possible Archaic painted buff white and black vertical zigzags descending from the top of the panel cover long vertically incised lines running parallel to the panel's straight vertical edge. The lower portion of the panel includes a distinct concave subsection with an extremely complex crosshatched design incorporating many curved lines. This section contains only one culturally recognizable pictograph, a red Sinagua maiden, painted over the lines.

Grotto Panel 3

Grotto Panel 3 has abundant Yavapai and Sinagua pictographs. It also contains several small-scale, not very distinct ghostlike pictographs in dark red paint and, nearby, a white rake symbol. Several "random" fine lines are superimposed by the red paint.

Seriation with Respect to Sinagua Features

To illustrate the relationship of incised art to Sinagua rock art, we present details from a study of the upper subpanel of Bear Alcove Panel 11 (Figure 13). This panel contains large white Sinagua pictographs, some small, lightly pecked Sinagua petroglyphs, and several zigzag and circular marks made by a red crayon (assumed to be historic Yavapai marks). It also contains many incised lines, gouges, and grooves, some of which extend to the very top of the panel.

Figure 13. Upper section of Panel 11 in the Bear Alcove.

The upper portion of the panel is a 1.5 m wide by 1.3 m tall section of the cliff with a relatively smooth planar surface uninterrupted by any major natural fractures. The bottom of this subpanel lies about a meter above the current floor level. A second incised subpanel hangs just below it, separated by a large fracture (Figure 14). The top of Panel 11 is about three meters above the present ground surface, well above the reach of a person standing on the current floor. The entire panel is recessed under an overhang which provides some protection from the elements, although the upper region shows significant degradation due to moisture.

To do detailed documentation of the panel, a comprehensive collection of high-resolution photos was shot at multiple lighting angles and imported into an online tool developed by Walter van Roggen called the Fine Line Analyzer (Figure 15). Several volunteers painstakingly transferred the line information from the photos into the tool (Figure 16), yielding a count of nearly 4000 lines.

As the line diagram shows, nearly the entire available space was utilized, with the possible exception of the extreme upper right, which, along with the upper left, has suffered the most weathering. The top section is less dense overall, probably due to its height, but we do find both vertical lines and diamond crosshatching here.

Figure 14. Walter van Roggen standing in front of Bear Alcove Panel 11 at current ground level, holding a two-meter scale placed where artists may have stood. Photo by Peter Anick.

About a third of the way down, perhaps at a more convenient height for the artist(s), the line density markedly increases. As is typical in complex panels at Palatki, no single pattern fills the entire space. Instead, partially overlapping regions present localized grids and diamonds at different scales and orientations. The extent of

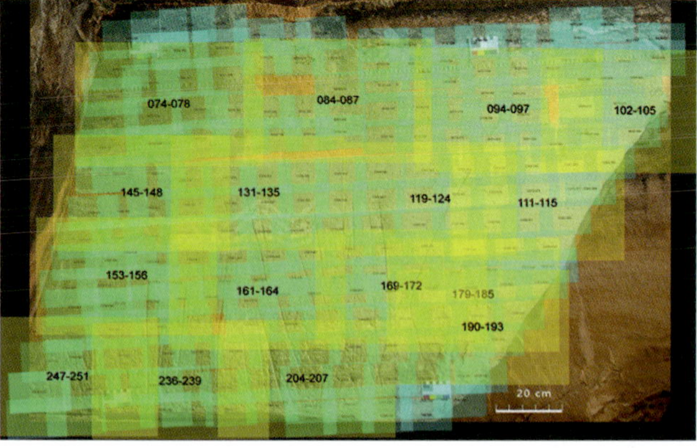

Figure 15. Screenshot of the Fine Line Analyzer of upper section of Bear Alcove Panel 11, previously shown in Figure 13. Yellow areas show coverage of small area photos (12–15 pixel/mm). Blue areas show coverage of detail photos (40–60 pixel/mm.) The full reference photo (Figure 13) seen behind the colored areas has a photographic scale of 3.1 pixels/mm. There were nearly 1000 high-resolution photos taken for this one panel.

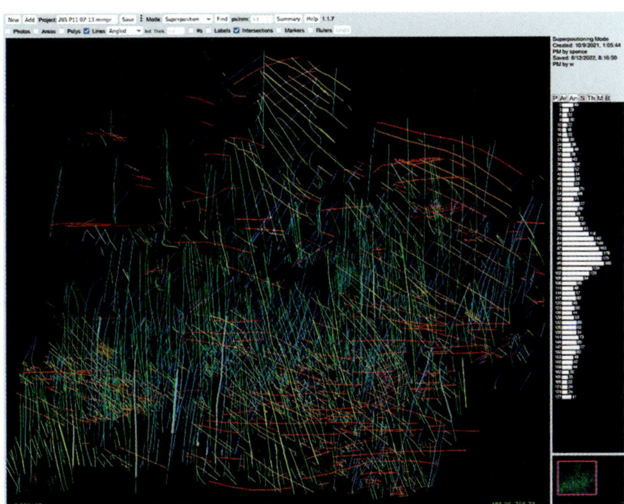

Figure 16. Approximately 4000 incised lines were recorded in the Fine Line Analyzer. The bar chart shows the distribution of the line angles. The area covered by fine lines is 2.614 by 1.589 m.

a motif may itself be a function of physical mechanics—it may represent the size of a region that can be conveniently drawn while standing in one spot. This is a topic worthy of further study. Diagonals are prominent in the central section, whereas verticals, including many deep gouges and grooves dominate the lower portion.

As in other complex panels, curved lines are relatively rare but present. Here one starts at the top center of the panel and winds all the way down to the bottom. There are several others nearby. They resemble the long meandering lines descending from the top of Grotto Panel 3, shown earlier in Figure 3g.

To determine the chronological relationship between incisions and paint on Bear Alcove Panel 11, we examined the intersections of lines/gouges with painted images. All of the pictographs on this panel are believed to be Sinagua. In every case, we found evidence of paint within the fine lines (Figure 17, label a). By contrast, the deep gouges often gave an initial impression of cutting through the paint, since a number of intersections showed no evidence of paint within the gouge. However, in all such cases, closer inspection revealed remnants of paint within some other portion of each gouge, indicating that paint must have been applied after the gouges were cut (Figure 17, labels b and c). According to a local artist

who has experimented with traditional pigments, depending on the consistency and manner of application of the paint, it can skip over deeper incisions entirely or adhere poorly and weather off (Nori Thorne, personal communication 2021). This likely accounts for the lack of paint in many portions of the gouges. As we assume that all of the white pictographs on this panel are Sinagua in origin, their superimposition over intersecting incisions dates both fine lines and thicker gouges on this panel to Sinagua or earlier. The same relationship of Sinagua paint to incisions was observed on all the other panels we examined at Red Cliffs.

Several lightly pecked Sinagua petroglyphs with distinct shapes can be seen on this panel—an anthropomorph with raised arms bent at the elbows and a sinuous form suggesting a snake. The anthropomorph intersects both paint and fine lines, affording us the opportunity to examine superimpositions. As seen in Figure 17 at label d, dints are clearly covered by paint. In some cases, dints have fully eradicated parts of incised lines (label e, in the head of the anthropomorph), while in other cases there is evidence of a line remaining visible through a dint mark (label f, in the left hand of the anthropomorph). The latter observation suggests that the line was incised after the pecking. However, in all such cases, the line width appears narrower where it traverses a dint. This narrowing would be expected if the depth of the dint was shallower than a preexisting line. The surviving portion of a **V**-shaped incision would appear thinner than the original width of the

Figure 17. Examples of superimpositions on Bear Alcove Panel 11: (a) paint over fine lines, (b) paint in gouge, (c) paint over gouge, (d) paint over dint, (e) dints completely obliterating section of line, (f) shallow dint partially impacting line, and (g) dint impacting gouge.

line as incised into the wall's surface (Figure 18). We noted similar obliteration and thinning of intersecting lines within the **S**-shaped petroglyph in a paint-free zone to the right, as well as within several additional pecked figures on a neighboring panel. Petroglyphs rarely intersected gouges, but at least one dint can be seen impacting a gouge in the same manner (Figure 17, label g). Based on these observations, we believe that all of the pecked petroglyphs were produced after the lines that they intersect were already on the panel.

Figure 18. *Close-up showing dints impacting lines at intersections (f) and (e) in Figure 17.*

We next turn to the relationships among types of incisions. As noted earlier, the panel contains many deep vertical gouges. Most of these are found in the lower section of the panel, within arm's reach of the current floor. The distribution of the gouges and the fact that few traces of fine lines could be observed impacting the gouges made us suspect that they represent a later, intrusive cultural phenomenon unrelated to the fine line designs they cut through. However, several ambiguous intersections are arguably interpretable as lines traversing gouges (Figure 19, label a), raising the possibility that augmenting the panel with fine lines may have continued to some small extent after the gouges were added. We also noticed that some gouges tapered into fine lines at the top and bottom, and that these continuations sometimes appear to be part of larger finely incised motifs. It is possible, then, that some grooves were cut to amplify fine lines already on the panel, not to override them.

With respect to relationships among the fine lines, we had hoped to use superimposition analysis to model the overall sequence of motif creation on the panel. The Fine Line Analyzer tool allows us to examine photos of intersections taken with multiple raked-lighting angles and to record which line was produced later by add-

Figure 19. *Examples of superimpositions on Bear Alcove Panel 11: (a) gouge possibly cut by thin diagonal, (b) curve cut by many intersecting lines and gouges, (c) diagonal cutting curved line (b), (d–d') highly weathered descending diagonal line, (e) faint horizontal line.*

ing a "bridge" icon to our line diagrams. However, even on this relatively uneroded panel, we were not able to determine the sequence of many superimpositions due to the graininess of the surface, the relative depth of the lines, or weathering or paint obscuring intersections. We had to settle for a more piecemeal analysis.

Figure 19 illustrates a number of intersections of fine lines of varying thickness, depth, and weathering within a 5 x 5 cm area. The curved line just below label b is cut by every straight line in the photo, with the exception of one diagonal at label c, making the curved line one of the earliest drawn in this small area. Similarly, the faint diagonal marked by the two d labels is cut by all the lines that intersect it. Its worn edges give it a very weathered appearance, suggesting a relatively early episode of incising, perhaps even predating the curved line, although their intersection is obscured by paint. A thin horizontal line at label e (barely visible in the photo) shows evidence of cutting faint verticals while being cut by several deeper verticals, placing it at an intermediate age.

Figure 20 shows a close-up view of an area near the lower right section of Figure 17. The 30-degree ascending diagonal just above label a is impacted by a dint to the left but otherwise appears to be more recent than all the lines it intersects. Notice how the width of the curved line to the left of label b varies as the line bends, likely due to a change in the angle of the cutting tool.

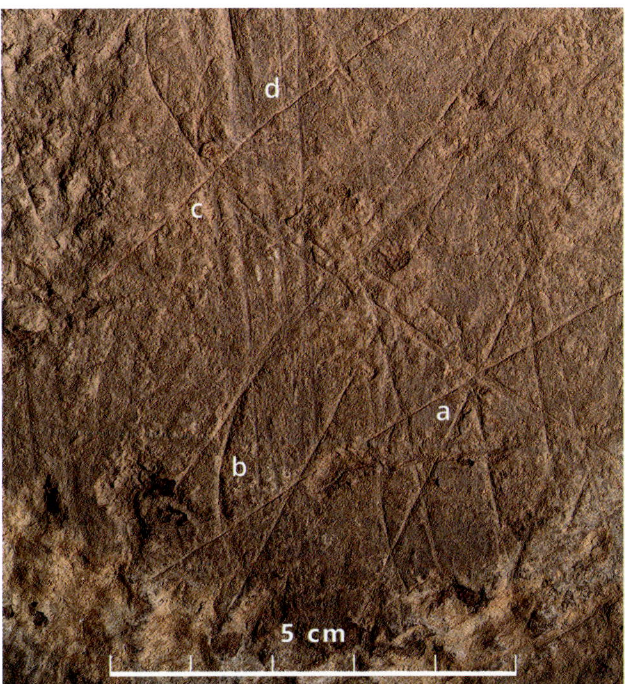

Figure 20. *Close up near the lower right corner of Figure 17: (a) 30-degree ascending line impacted by dint at left, (b) curve with varying thickness, (c) ascending line similar to line (a), (d) bundled vertical lines.*

This arc is part of the long meandering line that runs from the top center of the panel. It is impacted by the cluster of vertical lines in the bundle to the right of label b. Further up the panel (out of the photo), it continues to be cut by nearly all intersecting diagonals, confirming its status as one of the earlier lines to have been drawn on the panel. By contrast, the ascending diagonal near label c may be a contemporary of the similar looking, nearly parallel diagonal just to the right of label a. It clearly cuts both the curved line and the bundle of lines at label d.

By examining numerous sections of a panel in this way, it is possible to formulate partial models of a panel's evolution. These can eventually be compared with observations from other panels to probe for common behaviors.

Seriation with Respect to Yavapai Features

Most of the Yavapai art at Red Cliffs consists of charcoal zoomorphs with banana-shaped bodies. However, the cluster of hybrid painted/scratched/incised *akakas* in the Water Catchment site (Panels 3 and 4) indicate that the Yavapai also produced some scratched and lightly incised designs. Vertical zigzags appear within the body of the *akaka* in Figure 7 as well as in Yavapai pictographs elsewhere in the Verde Valley, leading us to believe that the less-weathered zigzags incised over fine

lines in Grotto Panel 3 (Figure 3e) have a Yavapai origin. Groups of scratched verticals and diagonals (Water Catchment Boulder 1) and several scratched grids that do not extend to panel boundaries or interact with other incised motifs (Figure 21) are also presumed to be Yavapai (Roasting Pit Panel 3, Bear Alcove Panel 4).

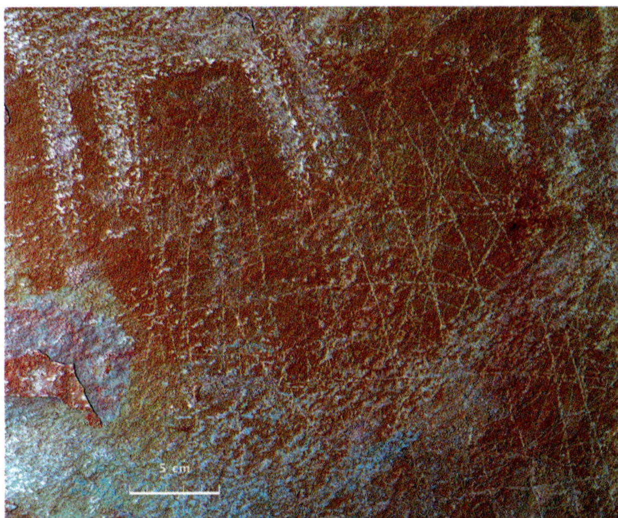

Figure 21. *Scratched checkerboard and diagonals in Roasting Pit Panel 3, enhanced with DStretch* LRD, *are presumed to be Yavapai.*

Discussion

Assuming that we attribute the cospatial pictographs to their correct cultures, instances of superimposition of lines by Archaic and Sinagua paint provide a terminal date for the creation of a fair number of the fine-line panels at Red Cliffs. Unfortunately, some of the best-preserved incised panels lack culturally diagnostic paint and cannot be dated in this manner. This leaves open the possibility that the RCI style continued relatively unchanged from the Archaic (or earlier) through the Sinagua period and into historic times. We find this unlikely. The family resemblances among so many of these panels, in terms of scale, motifs, surface utilization, and composition, not to mention weathering, strongly suggest an Archaic origin, perhaps restricted to specific intervals within the long timespan of preagricultural use of the area. Major changes in lifeways would likely have been reflected in incised art, just as it was in pictograph and petroglyph styles. Representational petroglyphs using percussion arrived with the Sinagua, while the Yavapai favored a more scratched style that included motifs such as akaka, rayed headdresses, and vertical zigzags that were not found in the prototypical Archaic panels. Even so, both Sinagua and Yavapai may have added lines and figures to preexist-

131

ing panels, such as the row of zigzags on Grotto Panel 3 (Figure 3e), or some of the grooves and splays that deeply score areas of some panels (e.g., Bear Alcove Panel 11, Figures 13–17).

Over the last 10,000 years, the Red Cliffs themselves underwent constant change. In addition to the erosive effects of wind and water, rock falls would have changed the face of the cliffs, removing engraved panels and exposing new blank canvas. Extensive fragmentation can be seen in the rock layer just above the current floor level (Figure 4). This breakage may have led not only to the loss of rock art on the lower register but also to the loss of platforms or ledges that may have extended the upper reach of early artists. As such, a geoarchaeological analysis of the Red Cliffs might shed further light on the chronology. Excavation for incised fragments that may have been redeposited in the valley floor might even yield dates on when the remains were deposited.

Many researchers have speculated on the purpose of abstract scratched/incised art in the American West. Bettinger and Baumhoff (1982:494) proposed that scratching over pecked petroglyphs at some Great Basin sites was intended to obliterate earlier art from a different culture. Since fine lines are the earliest art at Red Cliffs, such an interpretation does not fit the data here. However, the fact that many of the deeper gouges appear to be relatively late in the sequence of incising leaves open the possibility that they may have been an attempt to either retire or draw power from the underlying designs.

One popular explanation for the widespread distribution of certain abstract motifs such as cross-hatching and parallel lines is that they represent universal entoptic visions that shamans encounter in trance (Ritter 1994:64; Whitley 1994). With its fissures, seeps, seasonal waterfalls and pools, Red Cliffs may well have been perceived as a place of power by shamans. However, the large protective alcoves and water sources may have made the sites more attractive for use as public spaces rather than as secluded spots for vision-seeking. Furthermore, the limited set of motif types on RCI panels includes only a small fraction of the many entoptic images shamans were likely to encounter.

An alternative hypothesis draws upon the analogs between rectilinear patterns and textile and basketry designs (Ritter 1994:62). Recent radiocarbon dates have revealed that very sophisticated textiles, likely even requiring some form of loom, were being produced as early as 10,000 years ago in the Great Basin (Fowler and Hattori 2008). Ethnographic accounts describe woven patterns such as diagonals and diamonds being used to indicate gender on cradle boards (Fowler and Dawson 1986:710,714). Finger (2012) explores the relationship between basketry and scratched art designs around Little Lake, California, and uses their association to speculate that the artists may well have been women. Inspiration from weaving could also explain the minute scale of incised designs, as well as the tendency to fully cover panels out to their natural borders.

One notable difference between woven designs and incised panel compositions is the latter's tendency to juxtapose motifs that vary in their orientation and/or scale. As described earlier in our Water Catchment example (Figure 11), the orientation, distance between lines, or number of intersecting line angles is rarely constant for more than 10 or 15 centimeters. This patchwork quilt style of arranging motifs also appears on complex scratched panels in Nevada (Ritter 2006:Figures 20, 21), California (Reed 2012:Figure 5.4), elsewhere in Arizona (Christensen 1992:Figure 6b), and even on portable art, such as incised limestone slabs from Nevada's Gatecliff Shelter dating to 1550–1365 B.C. (Thomas 2019:Figure 6). While some of the motif types used in these other regions differ from those found on Red Cliffs, their arrangement into partially overlapping sections, including superimposed motifs, suggests that common design principles may have been widespread. Perhaps, like a quilt, some adjacent designs were contributed by different individuals working together in a contemporaneous episode of incising. A study of differences in line thickness, depth, and care of execution might offer clues to multiple vs. individual authorship.

Thomas (2019:2) has argued that the locations where some styles of incised portable art have been found in the Great Basin is consistent with a votive role for the incised stones. They were "deliberately emplaced in areas of known spiritual power, accompanying prayers for personal power to become healers, for success in hunting and gambling, and to give thanks for safe passage." The Red Cliffs, with its water seeps, seasonal waterfalls, and explosive rock falls would no doubt have been recognized as a place of power. Its fracture-filled panels may have served as a natural blackboard for leaving incised votive offerings.

Conclusions and Future Work

The RCI style consists of a small set of primarily rectilinear motifs featuring fine (roughly half millimeter wide) lines in parallel and crosshatched relationships.

Complex panels tend to completely fill naturally bounded spaces with dense overlapping and superimposed motifs drawn at different scales and angles, many likely added in multiple episodes over a long period of time. Although the amount of care taken to execute the lines varies, many compositions display great precision in terms of straightness, termination points, and distance between parallel lines, producing stunning "abstract" designs. The presence of a few wavy lines on a panel, usually drawn in a vertical orientation, is not uncommon.

Based on strong evidence for superimposition of fine lines by both Archaic and Sinagua paint, we propose that the RCI rock art is primarily an Archaic artifact. Some deep gouges may have been added later by the early Sinagua, and some isolated geometric motifs such as zigzags and scratched grids appear to be associated with protohistoric Yavapai. Weathering and repatination, while unreliable indicators, suggest that this Archaic practice may have spanned many thousands of years. Dates proposed by Loendorf (1994:2.6) for Archaic pictographs painted over incised panels would push the RCI tradition to at least 3000–5000 years ago. Portable incised stones with stylistically related designs have been dated as far back as 10,000 years ago in Texas (Lemke et al. 2015).

Ken Hedges lamented in 1989 that "Designs lightly scratched into the surface or sketched with dry pigment represent some of our least understood and most frequently ignored rock art" (Hedges 1989:91). His observation remains nearly as true today. If our effort to survey the incised rock art at Palatki Heritage Site has taught us anything, it is how easily this art can hide in plain sight. On more than one occasion, we discovered a new panel only because we happened to be there just as the sun hit it at the right angle. And it often took a major effort with a strong flashlight and magnifying camera lens to tease highly weathered lines out of an exfoliating or paint-speckled cliff wall. We encourage more rock art researchers to make an effort to look for fine-incised lines when visiting sites, especially on sandstone surfaces with evidence of fracture fill.

A better understanding of the geographical extent of incised traditions such as that found at Red Cliffs would contribute to our knowledge of southwest Archaic cultures, complementing evidence from lithics and basketry. We are aware of the presence of very similar rock art at several other sites within the Verde Valley, but there is likely much more yet to be discovered. Comparisons with the well-documented panels at Little Lake Ranch (Reed 2012) and Massacre Bench (Ritter 2006) would make an interesting research project. Ferg (1979) and Wright and Bostwick (2010) document "scratched" abstract art in south and south-central Arizona, which in some cases appears both above and below pecked petroglyphs (Wright and Bostwick 2010:Figure 10). With a larger geographical database of rock art to work with, distinctions between localized and more globally shared motif sets and design principles will likely emerge, as well as opportunities to corroborate, refute, or refine conclusions drawn from the Palatki corpus.

Even within the boundaries of Palatki's Red Cliffs, we have barely scratched the surface of the rich trove of incised art. Its many complex panels offer a rare opportunity to delve deep into the minds of the artists, applying analytical approaches such as design grammar (Klimowicz 1988). Further research directions include identifying subtle motif types we may not have recognized yet; probing for conventions of composition, including interactions with natural panel features and earlier drawings; evaluating the use of weathering/erosion/repatination for more detailed seriation; and exploring possible analogs with pictograph and textile/basketry designs.

Acknowledgments. This project could not have been achieved without the abundant assistance of volunteers from the Sedona Friends of the Forest. The following volunteers were instrumental in doing much of the data acquisition and interpretation for this study:

Cultural Heritage Photo Documentation Team volunteers Jon Petrescu, Terri Petrescu, Ed Hodges, Brian Painchaud, Marilyn Painchaud, Vicky Garrard, David Irvine, Robert Elliott, Mike Vitek, Frank Wirkus, and Kerri Simonian spent many hours acquiring photo coverage of the various areas of study. Credit for all photos goes to the Sedona Friends of the Forest volunteers, unless otherwise attributed.

Cultural Heritage volunteers Annie Glickstein, Rosalie O'Donnell, Jerry Walters, and Vicky Hill put in many hours of computer-based line interpretation via the Fine Line Analyzer software.

Scott Newth provided information and guided us to a number of sites potentially related to the Red Cliffs area for comparative analysis. Professor Kennard Bork provided confirmation and additional interpretation of the nature of the cliff face rock surface and fracture-fill issues. Alan Cornell provided various examples of prehistoric style stone tools and methods of their employment to emulate the incised lines studied. Nori

Thorne provided insight and examples of pictograph and petroglyph methods to assist in the interpretation of how such methods might be identified in the archaeological record. Dr. Bonnie Gustav provided information and input as to archaeological and anthropological concepts, methods, and practices.

Kerri Simonian and Mark Bales very generously lent scaffolding equipment to the photo team to allow us to do detailed imagery on the higher areas of multiple rock art panels. This equipment was carried up to and from the alcoves and was set up and taken down by the Friends of the Forest Trail Construction Team.

The support of the Coconino Forest Service staff was instrumental. Peter Pilles (Coconino Forest Archaeologist), Dr. Anne Dowd (Coconino Forest Red Rock District Archaeologist), Bruce Carlson (Coconino Forest Red Rock District Heritage Site Manager), and Michele Chvapil (Coconino Forest Heritage Site Assistant) provided information and access to the site during and after the Covid pandemic shutdown and allowed work to continue during periods when the site was open to the public.

References Cited

Anick, Peter, Spence Gustav, and Walter van Roggen
2022 A Close Look at the Fine-lined Engravings at Palatki Heritage Site. In *American Indian Rock Art, Volume 48*, edited by Amy Gilreath, Ken Hedges, and Anne McConnell, pp. 85–98. American Rock Art Research Association, Orem, Utah.

Bettinger, Robert L., and Martin A. Baumhoff
1982 The Numic Spread: Great Basin Cultures in Competition. *American Antiquity* 47(3):485–503.

Christensen, Don D.
1992 Scratched Glyphs in Arizona: A Reevaluation. In *Rock Art Papers, Volume 9*, edited by Ken Hedges, pp. 101–110. San Diego Museum Papers 28. San Diego Museum of Man, San Diego.

Ferg, Alan
1979 The Petroglyphs of Tumamoc Hill. *Kiva* 45(1–2):95–118.

Finger, Judith W.
2012 Woven Identities: The Aesthetics of Native American Basketry. *American Indian Art Magazine* 37(4):66–77.

Fowler, Catherine S., and L. E. Dawson
1986 Ethnographic Basketry. In *Handbook of North American Indians, Volume 11: Great Basin*, edited by Warren d'Azevedo, pp. 705–737. Smithsonian Institution, Washington, D.C.

Fowler, Catherine S., and Eugene M. Hattori
2008 The Great Basin's Oldest Textiles. In *The Great Basin: People and Place in Ancient Times*, edited by Catherine S. Fowler and Don D. Fowler, pp. 60–67. School for Advanced Research Press, Santa Fe, New Mexico.

Harman, Jon
2008 Using Decorrelation Stretch to Enhance Rock Art Images. Electronic document, https://dstretch.com/AlgorithmDescription.html, accessed August 12, 2021.

Hedges, Ken
1989 Sketches and Scratches. In *Rock Art Papers, Volume 6*, edited by Ken Hedges, pp. 91–99. San Diego Museum Papers 24. San Diego Museum of Man, San Diego.

Klimowicz, Janis Rose
1988 *A Structural Analysis of Prehistoric Incised Stones from Southern Nevada*. M.A. Thesis, University of Nevada, Reno.

Lemke, Ashley K., Daniel C. Wernicke, and Michael B. Collins
2015 Early Art in North America: Clovis and Later Paleoindian Incised Artifacts from the Gault Site, Texas. *American Antiquity* 80(1):113–133.

Loendorf, Lawrence L.
1994 *Rock Art at Red Cliffs*. Report #43-8167-3-0501 prepared for USDA Forest Service, Coconino National Forest.

Pilles Jr., Peter J.
2014 Ancient Rock Art of the Verde Valley. *Archaeology Southwest Magazine* 28(2):15–17.

Reed, Rebekah M.
2012 Scratched Rock Art at Little Lake Ranch. In *Rock Art at Little Lake: An Ancient Crossroads in the California Desert*, edited by Jo Anne Van Tilburg, Gordon E. Hull, and John C. Bretney, pp. 106–117. Cotsen Institute of Archaeology, University of California, Los Angeles.

Ritter, Eric W.
1994 Scratched Rock Art Complexes in the Desert West: Symbols for Socio-Religious Communication. In *New Light on Old Art: Recent Advances in Hunter-Gatherer Rock Art Research*, edited by David S. Whitley and Lawrence L. Loendorf, pp. 51–66. Monograph 36. Institute of Archaeology, University of California, Los Angeles.

2006 Archaeological Context and Explanation for Nevada's Massacre Bench Scratched Rock Art. In *American Indian Rock Art, Volume 21*, compiled by Peggy Whitehead, pp. 463–484. 1994 IRAC Proceedings, Rock Art—World Heritage. American Rock Art Research Association, Phoenix, Arizona.

Schaafsma, Polly
1980 *Indian Rock Art of the Southwest*. School of American Research, Santa Fe, and Museum of New Mexico Press, Albuquerque.

Thomas, David Hurst
2019 A Shoshonean Prayerstone Hypothesis: Ritual Cartographies of Great Basic Incised Stones. *American Antiquity* 84(1):1–25.

Whitley, David S.
1994 Shamanism, Natural Modeling and the Rock Art of Far Western North American Hunter-Gatherers. In *Shamanism and Rock Art in North America*, edited by Solveig A. Turpin, pp. 1–43. Special Publication 1. Rock Art Foundation, San Antonio.

Woody, Alanah, and Angus Quinlan
2008 Rock Art in the Western Great Basin. In *The Great Basin: People and Place in Ancient Times*, edited by Catherine S. Fowler and Don D. Fowler, pp. 137–144, School for Advanced Research Press, Santa Fe, New Mexico.

Wright, Aaron M., and Todd W. Bostwick
2010 Technological Styles of Hohokam Rock Art Production in the South Mountains, South Central Arizona. In *American Indian Rock Art, Volume 35*, edited by James D. Keyser, David A. Kaiser, George Poetschat, and Michael W. Taylor, pp. 61–78. American Rock Art Research Association, Phoenix, Arizona.

The Hearthstone Project: Applying Archaeological Science, Formal Art Analysis, and Indigenous Knowledge to Rock Art Research

Carolyn E. Boyd, J. Phil Dering, and Karen L. Steelman

The Hearthstone Project, a collaboration between Texas State University and Shumla Archaeological Research & Education Center, is a study of Pecos River style rock art in the Lower Pecos Canyonlands of southwest Texas. The project synthesizes expertise from archaeological science, formal art analysis, and Indigenous consultants. It is comprised of two complementary research designs with shared baselines goals: (1) unravel the technical history of Pecos River style murals and decode the symbols contained therein; and (2) build a chronological model of Pecos River style rock art. To provide a balanced, complete review of both research designs, we necessarily touch on a few topics twice. However, as you will see, the thrust of the research methods and the information generated are distinctive. The sites we visit, the data we gather, and the methods we use are conditioned by specific goals. We present our research designs as an example of best practices for radiocarbon dating pictographs within a multidisciplinary research and documentation program.

Archaeologists have reported over 300 rock art sites near the confluence of the Rio Grande and Pecos rivers in southwest Texas. Our research focuses on the most prevalent paintings in the region, Pecos River style pictographs, which were created with multicolored paints in many shades of red, yellow, black, and white. We do not know the exact age or time span of Pecos River style (PRS) pictograph production. We have a small suite of radiocarbon dates showing that some of the murals were produced as early as 4000 years ago and some as recent as 1300 years ago (Steelman et al. 2021b), during the Archaic period.[1] Our goal is to digitally preserve the art and study the information it contains, including the temporal history of the paintings—when production of the style began, developed, and ended. Understanding the chronology of the pictographs will connect the trajectory of Pecos River style murals to the environmental and cultural conditions that triggered and ended its production.

Researchers have found strong parallels between cosmological concepts portrayed in Pecos River style art and the myths and cosmologies of later Mesoamerican agriculturalists (Kelley 1974), most notably the ancient Nahua (Aztec) and present-day Huichol (Boyd 2003, 2010, 2021; Boyd and Cox 2016). These parallels inform hypotheses about the origin, distribution, and tenacity of myth in North America. Many scholars maintain that the beliefs and worldviews underlying Mesoamerican cosmovision are hunter-gatherer in origin, perhaps from the earliest migrations into the Americas (Flannery 2003; Gossen 1986; Joralemon 1976; López Austin 1997; Rice 2020). They suggest that aspects of this pan-Mesoamerican belief system, such as a multilayered and quadripartite universe, complementary dualism, and cyclical time, reflect an Archaic core of cosmological concepts found throughout the West-

Carolyn E. Boyd
*Shumla Archaeological Research &
Education Center,
Comstock, Texas
Texas State University, San Marcos*

J. Phil Dering
*Shumla Archaeological Research &
Education Center,
Comstock, Texas*

Karen L. Steelman
*Shumla Archaeological Research &
Education Center,
Comstock, Texas*

ern Hemisphere. It is essential to understand the timing of Pecos River style pictography in the context of the hypothesized pan-Mesoamerican (or western North American) Archaic core belief system. The Hearthstone Project is designed to identify graphic components of the Archaic core in Pecos River style and generate a chronological model to establish the inception, variation, and cessation of Pecos River style production. Pecos River style pictography may represent the oldest extant example of this Archaic core cosmology.

The Hearthstone Project

The Hearthstone Project is named for the fire hearth, a focus of domestic life and food preparation in Native American culture. Centered in the household and a part of daily activities, the fireplace was not only functional, but also powerful and symbolic at many levels. In Mesoamerican households, the hearth was made with three stones supporting a clay griddle or *comal* on which food was cooked. Three stones or pillars comprise the most stable arrangement of any support system. The hearth fire represented the center of the universe and the source of all knowledge and wisdom. Like a *comal*, our research effort is supported by three pillars of inquiry: (1) archaeological science, (2) formal art analysis, and (3) Indigenous knowledge.

The Hearthstone Project is a collaboration between Texas State University and Shumla Archaeological Research & Education Center. The project team includes the authors of this paper, as well as anthropology graduate students from Texas State University and other staff at the Shumla Archaeological Research & Education Center. The project is anchored in both science and the humanities and is partially funded by the National Endowment for the Humanities (NEH) and the National Science Foundation (NSF). The research designs of the two grants have different, yet complementary goals: (1) unravel the technical history of Pecos River style murals and decode the symbols contained therein; and (2) build a chronological model of Pecos River style rock art. The sites we visit, the data we gather, and the methods we use are conditioned by the specific goals of each research design.

The NEH research, led by Carolyn Boyd and Phil Dering, is titled "Origins and Tenacity of Myth, Ritual, and Cosmology in Archaic Period Rock Art of Southwest Texas and Northern Mexico." This work combines archaeological and ethnographic fieldwork to decode the message in the medium. At its core, it examines the technical history of the murals (the materials, techniques, and methods used to create the art) and studies the graphic signs and symbols embodying Pecos River style iconography. We are analyzing three Pecos River style murals using digital microscopy to determine the murals' painting sequence. Boyd uses this information, in conjunction with GigaPanoramas, to create digital reconstructions of the murals and to identify recurring patterns in Pecos River style pictography. Boyd and Dering will share these mural reconstructions with contemporary Native Americans to obtain their perspective rooted in generations of knowledge, understanding, and practice.

The NSF research, led by Karen Steelman and Carolyn Boyd, is titled "Layers of Meaning: Pictograph Stratigraphy and Chronological Modeling." The goal of this work is to produce a temporal history or chronology of Pecos River style paintings. We focus our study on anthropomorphic figures with diagnostic Pecos River style attributes distributed across ten sites in the region. During fieldwork, the team conducts digital microscopy to analyze paint stratigraphy of selected anthropomorphs and their mural context (relationship with superimposed figures). In the computer laboratory, archaeologists examine the photomicrographs to determine the painting sequence of the figures included in the study. The results inform us on the best locations for collecting paint samples for radiocarbon dating. This novel approach allows us to apply dates from a single figure to figures interwoven with it, thereby dating much larger areas of a mural with the least destructive analyses. In the chemistry laboratory, paint samples are processed using plasma oxidation followed by accelerator mass spectrometry (AMS) isotope measurement. These age results will be analyzed using Bayesian statistics to create a chronological model for the style.

Lower Pecos Canyonlands

The Lower Pecos Canyonlands are situated on the southwestern edge of the Edwards Plateau, near the eastern edge of the Chihuahuan Desert (Griffith et al. 2007:8; Van Devender 1990:109). The northern half of the region lies in southwestern Texas, U.S.A., and the southern half in Coahuila, Mexico (Figure 1). Near the region's center, the Pecos and Devils rivers converge with the Rio Grande. Deep and narrow canyons sustain desert ash, live oak, and mountain laurel trees. On the adjacent uplands, semiarid vegetation includes a mix of C4 grasses (warm-season grasses); woody shrubs such as desert hackberry and several species of acacias; and yucca, prickly pear, lechuguilla (a small agave), and sotol (Dering 1999).

Hundreds of rockshelters in the region contain a deeply stratified and well-preserved record of hunting and gathering lifeways spanning at least 13,000 years (Kilby et al. 2020; McCuistion 2019; Shafer 2013; Turpin 2004a). Preserved within these dry rockshelters are deposits holding an assemblage of stone and bone tools, perishable artifacts, and the debris left from plant and animal processing activities (Shafer 2013). The Lower Pecos Archaic period lasted from 9500 cal B.P. to 1300 cal B.P., ending with the introduction of the bow and arrow (Shafer 1986; Turpin 2004a). Evidence exists for residential occupation at both open and sheltered sites (Dering 2002). Hypotheses addressing residential mobility and labor organization have ranged from highly mobile foragers to semisedentary, rockshelter-dwelling collectors with explicit territorial limits (Dering 1999; Shafer 1986; Turpin 2018).

Lower Pecos rockshelters contain pictographs that are categorized as: Historic (Turpin 1989); Red Monochrome (Turpin 1984); Bold Line Geometric (Turpin 1986); Red Linear (Boyd et al. 2013); and Pecos River (Boyd and Cox 2016; Harrison Macrae 2018; Turpin 1990). Pecos River style, however, is by far the most abundant, complex, and data rich rock art in the region. It is the defining archaeological phenomenon of the Lower Pecos Canyonlands and the subject of the Hearthstone Project.

Pecos River Style

More than 200 sites containing Pecos River style (PRS) imagery are north of the Rio Grande in Val Verde County and, to a lesser degree, Terrell County, Texas (Figure 1). South of the Rio Grande in Coahuila, Mexico, 35 murals have been identified, but there are likely far more in the secluded canyons of the Serranías de Burro (Turpin 2010:41). Across the region, PRS is stylistically homogenous, with universal themes, a conventionalized graphic vocabulary, and similar artistic expression (Boyd 2003; Gebhard 1960; Kirkland and Newcomb 1967; Turpin 2004b). Within that homogeneity, however, there is variation.

PRS panels range considerably in size and complexity. Some are quite small, less than a meter in length and

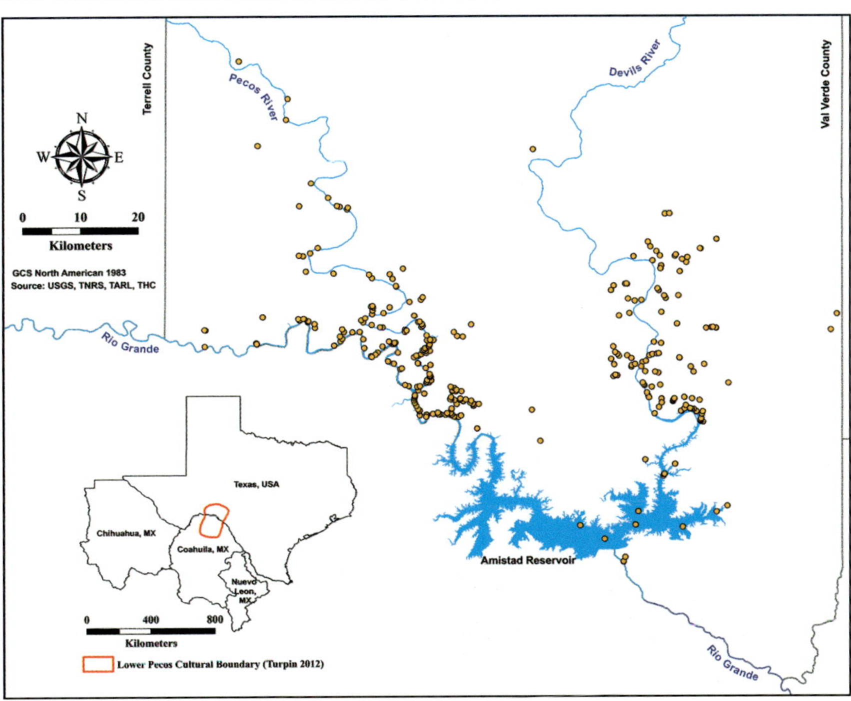

Figure 1. The Lower Pecos Canyonlands archaeological region showing known rock art sites.

height, and contain only a few figures. Others span as much as 150 meters long, 15 meters tall, and contain hundreds of figures. Pictographic elements in these PRS murals are based on human (anthropomorphic) and animal forms (zoomorphic), as well as enigmatic figures that are not identifiable as human or animal. Figures often are elaborately executed in red, yellow, black, and white paint, and at other times plainly painted in only one color. Anthropomorphs are the most frequently depicted element and the focal point in many PRS murals (Figure 2). Although these figures share many characteristics, such as elongated, rectangular bodies with disproportionally short arms and legs, among them there is diversity. They typically average in size between 1 to 2 meters; however, some are monumental, towering more than 7 meters in height, while others are pocket-sized standing only 10 centimeters tall.

Human and animal forms provided a framework upon which artists added or packed on semantically charged visual attributes, such as headdresses of varying types; adornments attached at the wrist, elbow, waist, or hip; and paraphernalia including atlatls (spear-throwers), darts, staffs, and rabbit sticks. Attributes such as these function like a graphic vocabulary and their arrangement in the mural, not unlike syntax, conveys meaning. Selecting from within this wide range of meaning-filled pictographic elements, PRS artists constructed messages that related myths, prescribed

Figure 2. Researchers documenting a variety of Pecos River style anthropomorphs with differing sizes, paraphernalia, adornments, and headdresses. PRS artists needed scaffolding or ladders to paint the upper registers of the murals.

rituals, and provided social cohesion (Boyd 2003; Boyd and Cox 2016; Turpin 1990). Recent interpretations of these complex, polychromatic murals are challenging previous knowledge about hunter-gatherer complexity and the origins and tenacity of myth (Boyd and Cox 2016).

Not only is there variability in the forms and colors used, but also in the accoutrements and paraphernalia. Headdresses of varying types, clusters of feathers at the waist, and wrist or elbow tassels often adorn these humanlike figures. Generally, the artists portrayed anthropomorphs wielding paraphernalia such

as atlatls and darts in their right hand. In the left hand, they hold staffs, feathered darts, and rabbit sticks. In some examples, these items are not present or they are associated with the opposite hand.

Considerable variation exists within categories of paraphernalia and accoutrements associated with anthropomorphs. For example, PRS artists represented atlatls as single lines or as lines with finger loops, weights, or spurs. Some incorporate all of these attributes. Likewise, they represented atlatl darts as single lines or as lines with fletching, stylized dart tips, or both. Perhaps the most frequently encountered and most diagnostic paraphernalia associated with PRS anthropomorphs are "power bundles." This term applies to objects attached to the end of a line or a series of lines extending outward from the hands of anthropomorphs (Figure 3). Power bundles often are found associated with the left hand of anthropomorphs, but sometimes they are associated with the right hand, and in rare cases, both hands. The shape and color of the distal end of power bundles varies significantly, ranging from monochromatic and simple to polychromatic and highly elaborate. Often, they resemble thorny seedpods, but sometimes they possess human or animal attributes (Boyd and Dering 1996; Harrison 2011). Variation among anthropomorphs and associated pictographic elements led early researchers to suggest an

Figure 3. Pecos River style anthropomorphs are commonly depicted with an atlatl in one hand and a power-bundle associated with the other hand. The term power-bundle refers to shapes, often ovoid with spiny protrusions, attached to the distal end of long lines. The proximal end of the lines connects to a perpendicular staff-like object wielded, most often, in the left hand of an anthropomorph.

internal development in the paintings (Gebhard 1965; Kirkland and Newcomb 1967).

In the 1930s, Forrest Kirkland and his wife, Lula, both professional artists, produced accurate watercolor renderings of 43 rock art panels in the Lower Pecos. Kirkland recognized the compositional nature of the paintings and maintained that many of the PRS murals illustrated mythologies, rather than "individual ideas of the art" (Kirkland 1939:71).

> These firmly fixed mythological ideas and the highly conventionalized forms with which they are illustrated, along with *the extremely individual style of painting seem to point to a very long period of development*. The question naturally arises: was this culture with its elaborate paintings slowly evolved around the mouth of the Pecos, or was it evolved elsewhere and brought in fully developed? [Kirkland 1939:72, emphasis added].

Kirkland's (1939:72) close examination of the murals and his inability to identify internal development led him to suggest that "the present evidence…points to an outside development." He argued that if this is the case, we should be able to find the "pictures from whence it came" in areas outside the Lower Pecos. Although there is inadequate data to satisfactorily answer Kirkland's questions of origins and affiliations, researchers have related patterns in PRS attributes to patterns in Mesoamerican myth and iconography (Boyd and Cox 2016; Kelley 1974).

Gebhard (1965) proposed a typological and chronological framework that subdivided the art into "Types" and "Phases" based on stylistic variation among PRS anthropomorphs, their attributes, and associated imagery. Although he recognized variation within PRS, Gebhard (1960:32–33) concluded that within the style there was such homogeneity that it must have been produced over a short period of time, perhaps only spanning one or two generations.

In the 1960s, W. W. Newcomb speculated PRS emerged during the Archaic period, and continued in production for several millennia, increasing in sophistication until running its course by A.D. 1000 (Kirkland and Newcomb 1967:60). He based this estimate on similarities between PRS imagery and artifacts, most notably the atlatl. Newcomb (Kirkland and Newcomb 1967:46) also proposed the existence of substyles or "Periods" within PRS. Based on patterns among attributes, such as color, paraphernalia, body adornments, scale, and superimposition of figures, he maintained that the substyles represented a developmental and chronological sequence, transitioning from crude beginnings into "highly evolved figures" (Kirkland and Newcomb 1967:48).

Turpin (1990, 2004b) defined the art as shamanistic in origin, execution, and application. She discussed the art as a mechanism of social control, both as a reaction to scalar stress and as a focal point for ritual performances in the context of seasonal gatherings in a space delineated by art (Turpin 1990:110-111, 2004b). These interpretations are based on the assessment that population density increased along the rivers in response to the long period of dry Middle Holocene maximum temperatures. The higher density resulted in larger aggregations and group size due to environmental constraints. The larger social units likely developed expedient hierarchies, ritual activities, and leaders such as shamans (Turpin 1990:111, 2004a). Turpin asserted that shamans are represented as anthropomorphs in the PRS panels.

Mesoamerican Connections

J. Charles Kelley saw evidence of Mesoamerican symbolism in PRS iconography, north of the accepted Mesoamerican geographical boundary. In 1974, he suggested that the pictographs were produced by a Chichimec Archaic culture in response to cultural emanations originating in Mesoamerica (Kelley 1974:51). He identified parallels between PRS portrayals of anthropomorphs with their distinctive attributes and accoutrements, and the elaborate codex depictions of Mesoamerican warrior-hunter-deities. Based on these parallels, he suggested that PRS anthropomorphs represent deities, or their deity surrogates, and, further, that the Lower Pecos was "an island enclave of dilute Mesoamerican culture, developed by Chichimecs far out in the Chichimec sea under the influence from the great civilizations to the south" (Kelley 1974:52).

Boyd has also identified evidence of Mesoamerican symbolism in PRS iconography (Boyd 1996, 1998, 2003, 2010, 2021; Boyd and Busby 2021; Boyd and Cox 2016). She has focused on a formal and iconographic analysis of the art. This research reveals that patterns in PRS imagery have common themes with the myths and rituals of Uto-Aztecan-speaking peoples, most notably the ancient Aztec (Nahua) and the present-day Huichol (Boyd 2003; Boyd and Cox 2016). Unlike Kelley, who attributed these parallels to the diffusion of ideas from Mesoamerica to the Lower Pecos, Boyd ascribes the parallels to the existence of an ancient, highly complex, and widely shared cosmovision. Scholars have long argued that the concepts expressed in Mesoamerican religious traditions persisted across time and across cultural, linguistic, and geographical boundaries (Gossen 1986). López Austin (1997) and Rice (2020) argue that these perceptions of reality came out of an earlier Archaic core of belief, perhaps as old as the earliest migrations into North America. While Boyd does not suggest that the canyons of southwest Texas and northern Mexico are the birthplace of these ideas, she does suggest that the Lower Pecos Canyonlands may house the oldest surviving and documented graphic expressions of them.

NEH Research Design: Origins and Tenacity of Myth, Ritual, and Cosmology in Pecos River Style Rock Art

The function of PRS art and its relationship to the Archaic core will become clear only when the rock art corpus is considered as a whole. The NEH component of Hearthstone examines the message in the medium, tapping into a large dataset of unanalyzed PRS pictographs to answer the following research questions:

- Are PRS murals compositional in structure and narrative in function?
- Are there consistent rules in paint application order?
- What do patterns in the production of these complex murals—the image-making process—tell us about the artists, their worldview, and the organization of labor needed to produce the murals?
- What pictographic elements recur in specific patterns and associations?
- What do patterns in the geographic distribution of PRS rock art tell us about territoriality and social interaction within the region?
- Are these patterns recognizable to modern Indigenous societies?

Mining an expanded dataset to address these questions, we will reveal graphic components of the Archaic core beyond those previously identified. If there are consistent patterns in the association of these elements, we may be able to find underlying rules governing the arrangement of pictographic elements, much like rules of syntax. If contemporary Native Americans in the U.S. and Mexico recognize the patterns and similarly attribute them to their cosmologies, then the patterns may represent components of an enduring and widely shared ideological universe—the Archaic core.

We have organized the NEH work into two phases: (1) formal analysis and mural reproductions, and (2) consultation with Indigenous communities. We designed a protocol for data collection and analysis necessary for detecting patterns within, between, and among pictographic figures at three rock art sites: Panther Cave (41VV83), Fate Bell Shelter (41VV74), and Halo Shelter (41VV1230).

Formal Analysis and Mural Reproductions

We are conducting a formal analysis of three sites to make connections within and among figures and to reconstruct the chain of operations used by the artists to produce the murals. The immediate objective of this analysis is to examine the technical history of these murals and the graphic signs and symbols they contain. If not generated during previous documentation efforts, we begin by creating GigaPans of the mural. These gigapixel composite photographs are created using a robotic camera mount, which enables DSLR cameras to produce gigapixel (one billion pixel) images. The GigaPans serve as the foundation for each subsequent step in the mural documentation and analysis process.

Figure Identification and Site Maps. We use the GigaPans to identify and describe individual figures in the murals. We categorize figures as anthropomorph, zoomorph, or enigmatic based on the presence or absence of predetermined attributes. We assign a unique reference code and write a description for each figure. With the GigaPan serving as the base layer in Adobe Photoshop, we insert a new layer for each figure ID. In another Photoshop layer, we note locations of intersecting paint layers within and among figures. These are potential locations for digital field microscopy and stratigraphic analysis. A printed scroll is generated from the labeled and annotated GigaPan, which serves as a site map for use in the field (Figures 4 and 5). The digital version provides the first layers of what will become an extensive graphic database.

Mural Stratification. Determining the order in which artists applied the paint layers is critical to understanding the mechanics of mural production and the relationship between and among pictographic elements. The principle of superposition establishes that layers at an archaeological site are deposited in chronological order. In a rock art panel, layers located closest to the rock surface were painted prior to those overlying them. Figures painted both over and under other figures can be used to identify the compositional structure of murals. Interwoven figures are part of the same painting episode.[2]

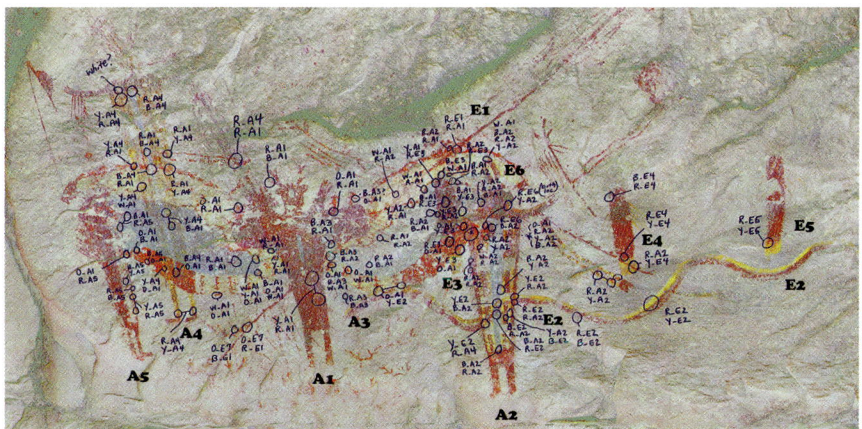

Figure 4. *An annotated site map of a panel showing locations of intersecting paint layers requiring digital field microscopy. The site map is constructed in the computer laboratory prior to fieldwork using a GigaPan image (DStretch* YRD*) and printed as large scrolls on oversized paper.*

Figure 5. *Field crew using a printed site map to find microscopy locations for analysis.*

represent. Descriptions of individual figures in a rock art panel, just like analysis of artifacts from any other archaeological site, provide data for inter- and intra-site patterning. Patterns in attribute data coupled with ethnographic and ethnohistoric texts facilitated Boyd and her collaborators' previous interpretations of PRS pictography (Boyd and Busby 2021; Boyd and Cox 2016; Boyd and Dering 1996). We record attribute data for each figure, such as size, shape, color, paraphernalia, and body adornments, then enter these data into Shumla's searchable rock art database. We run database queries to identify patterns in the geographic distribution of figures and attributes, and to identify motifs or patterns in the association of figures and attributes.

Compositional Analysis. Decoding the meaning of PRS rock art requires that we find the compositional systems within which the artists worked. Working alongside the archaeologists, artist Ashley Busby evaluates the murals' compositional elements through a formal analysis of the art. According to Busby (personal communication August 12, 2022), studying these internal systems reveals "how the

We use a handheld, digital microscope to take photomicrographs of intersecting paint layers to determine color stratigraphy within individual elements and among multiple figures (Figure 6). We take a series of photographs to document the context of each analysis location. The photomicrographs are analyzed in the computer laboratory. To avoid subjective bias, different researchers make independent stratigraphic determinations for each analysis location. We enter results into Harris Matrix Composer software to manage and graphically diagram paint-layer stratigraphy.

Figure Attribute Data. Figures in PRS murals are portrayed with distinctive attributes. These attributes provide clues about what the figures

Figure 6. *(a) A digital microscope is connected to a laptop via USB to view and photograph paint layer stratigraphy. The microscope is placed at the locations of intersecting paint layers indicated on the site map. Photomicrographs at X50 (b) and at X200 (c) reveal the stratigraphy of red paint over black.*

141

painters conceptualized space, utilized surface as a physical site as well as a visual plane, and organized line, color, and form as a vehicle for expressing and activating narrative."

Busby produces a field sketch map, measuring figures and the distance between figures across the mural. She examines lines, shapes, use of space, color, and texture, and analyzes the artists' use of balance, proportion, patterning, and unity. Busby uses this information to identify figures painted by the same hand, images painted from the same paint pot, the use of framing techniques to define the composition, and the use of visual planes to establish depth or proximity to the viewer. These results will be incorporated as a separate layer into each mural's graphic database.

Full Panel Renderings. We produce digital, layered illustrations of the murals in Adobe Photoshop using an interactive pen display. As discussed above, the high-resolution GigaPans serve as the base layer for the graphic database. We digitally apply the paint, color layer by color layer, reproducing the painting sequence used by the original artist. The layered composite represents the final illustration (Figure 7).

Through the production of these digital illustrations, we identify artistic similarities and variations in graphic expressions of PRS pictography. This is a critical step. As noted by Frederick Franck (1973:6), "I have learned that what I have not drawn I have never really seen." Through the illustration process, we identify relationships among figures and the techniques used by artists to produce images, such as dry brushing, underpainting, blocking in, building texture, and stenciling. We also identify possible tools used by the artists, such as feathers, brushes, plant fibers, stencils, straight edges, and fingers.

Ethnographic Fieldwork and Laboratory Analysis

Our final line of inquiry will be to consult with contemporary Native Americans to obtain their perspective, rooted in generations of knowledge, understanding, and practice. Our first consultation will be with members of a Huichol community living in the Sierra Madre Occidental mountains of Mexico. Boyd and Dering will travel with anthropologists Stacy Schaefer and Jim Bauml to a Huichol community to interview five Huichol shaman/artists. Schaefer and Bauml's work with Huichol communities has spanned more than 40 years and resulted in enduring friendships and numerous publications.

Boyd and Dering will share the wide-format scrolls of the PRS GigaPans and panel illustrations with Huichol shaman/artists and other knowledgeable community members to elicit discussion and the identification of recognizable pictographic elements. After obtaining signed consent forms, the team will digitally record open-ended interviews that document how the consultants relate the PRS imagery to their cosmology. Huichol consultants will be encouraged to illustrate their thoughts/stories/myths. Copies of their illustrations and the recorded interviews will remain with the community.

NSF Research Design: Pictograph Stratigraphy and Chronological Modeling

According to McDonald and Veth (2013:68), stylistic homogeneity within arid-lands rock art indicates open social networks, such as shared language, kinship, and territory, and provides "broad scale intergroup cohesion." Given the homogeneity of PRS rock art, therefore, one can assume an open social network throughout its production. However, within that homogeneity, there is variation. Building a chronological

Figure 7. A digital illustration of a Pecos River style mural created in Adobe Photoshop based on GigaPan photographs. A separate layer is created for every color of paint within each individual figure. This illustration is a composite of 647 individual layers. The layers are arranged according to the results of the stratigraphic analysis. Illustration © Carolyn E. Boyd.

model of PRS rock art production is a necessary first step toward understanding the timing of PRS pictography—its origin, variability, and duration—within the context of material culture, socioeconomic reorganization, climate change, and extra-regional influences, particularly those emanating from Mesoamerica. Research questions include:

- When did PRS rock art production begin and end?
- Were there pulses in PRS rock art production?
- Is there temporal variation in the type, elaboration, and geographic distribution of anthropomorphs and their attributes?
- What is the timing of PRS pictography attributed to the Archaic core?
- Is there temporal variation in the technical history of the images (materials, techniques, and production methods)?
- Do changes in mural production or iconography align with social and economic changes at the beginning and end of the Late Archaic 1 (mesic) period (3200–2500 cal B.P.)?
- Does PRS iconography change during the terminal Late Archaic 2 period (2500–1200 cal B.P.), a time corresponding to the establishment of Teotihuacan and other major developments in Mesoamerica?

To address these questions, our research design involves: (1) conducting a formal analysis of the art to document and describe diagnostic PRS pictographs selected for dating; (2) examining mural stratigraphy using digital microscopy and the construction of Harris matrices for superimposed figures; and (3) obtaining 60 radiocarbon dates for PRS pictographs using plasma oxidation and accelerator mass spectrometry (AMS). We are selecting anthropomorphs that display diagnostic attributes of PRS rock art from ten sites across the region. We then use digital microscopy to examine the stratigraphic relationship of selected anthropomorphs with other imagery in the murals to identify the extent of the composition. Based on the results of the stratigraphic study, we select six paint sampling locations within each of the ten murals. The paint samples are processed using plasma oxidation and submitted for AMS radiocarbon dating.

Rock Art Site and Figure Selection

In 2016, Shumla began conducting baseline documentation of PRS rock art sites north of the Rio Grande. Baseline documentation includes 3D models produced using Structure from Motion (SfM) photogrammetry, high-resolution GigaPans of the murals, and a georeferenced, searchable iconographic database (Koenig et al. 2019). The iconographic database reports the presence or absence of recurring figures and figure attributes across the region. These data provide an unparalleled textual, spatial, and graphic inventory of Lower Pecos rock art. We use the baseline data collected by Shumla at 235 sites, as well as current project data, to select anthropomorphs and associated imagery from ten PRS murals for dating and analysis. The murals range between 10 to 65 meters in length and contain 25 to greater than 300 figures. They are located north of and along the Rio Grande and east and west of the Pecos and Devils rivers. As discussed above, variation among anthropomorphs led early researchers to propose a developmental and chronological sequence within PRS rock art. Accordingly, we select anthropomorphs from ten sites across the region that display at least three diagnostic attributes of PRS rock art, including:

- Head shapes—**U**-form, snouted or round with open mouth, headless
- Headdresses—antlered with dots on tines, dual or single "rabbit-ear"
- Body adornments—hip or waist adornment, wrist or elbow adornment
- Accoutrements—atlatl, darts, rabbit sticks, staff, power bundle
- Associated motifs—crenellated arch with portal, impaled dots, single-pole ladders, box with legs

We study the GigaPans to identify figures intersecting or in direct association with the selected anthropomorphs. We assign a unique identification number, describe, and document attribute data for each figure. These data will be used to determine the number, complexity, type, and geographic distribution of selected anthropomorphs and associated figures.

Stratigraphic Analyses

Using digital microscopy, we determine the paint application order for anthropomorphs selected for dating, as well as for all intersecting figures. This requires collecting photomicrographs from approximately 25 to 50 locations for each anthropomorph and associated figures, for a total of 50 to 100 photomicrographs per site. To avoid bias, at least two researchers make independent determinations for each analysis location. This data is entered into Harris Matrix Composer software to manage the hundreds of data points and to digitally diagram paint stratigraphy, the proxy for painting sequence (Figure 8).

Paint Sample Collection

Informed by the stratigraphic data, we collect six or more paint samples from each mural for plasma oxidation and AMS radiocarbon dating. We select paint sample locations from the bottom layer (first applied), middle layer, and top layer (last applied) in the painting sequence. By establishing the layering of figures, in combination with obtaining direct dates for each layer, we not only directly date specific figures but ascertain ages for imagery in stratigraphic relationships with the dated figure. In this manner, we can infer ages for a larger part of the mural, expanding the information obtained with the least destructive analyses. (See "Best Practices for Radiocarbon Dating Pictographs" below for an expanded discussion on recommendations for collecting paint samples for radiocarbon dating pictographs.)

Plasma Oxidation and Radiocarbon Dating

Steelman's laboratory at Shumla employs two independent methods to date pictographs. The first method uses plasma oxidation to obtain direct radiocarbon dates on organic constituents in paint samples. The second method isolates overlying and underlying oxalate mineral accretions for radiocarbon dating to constrain the age of paint layers with minimum and maximum ages. Using two independent methods ensures the accuracy and reliability of results (Steelman et al. 2021a).

Paint is comprised of three primary components: (1) pigment, which is the material that provides color; (2) binder, the component that holds the pigment together; and (3) vehicle or emulsifier to carry or disperse the pigment particles. Most rock art assemblages, including PRS, were created with mineral pigment (Rowe 2001). While inorganic pigments cannot be radiocarbon dated, extant organic materials used as binders or vehicles can be extracted using plasma oxidation to obtain accurate and reliable dates.

Plasma oxidation has been used to extract organic constituents from paint for radiocarbon dating in over 300 pictographs worldwide (Rowe 2012). At operating temperatures below the decomposition temperature of carbon-containing minerals (such as limestone/carbonate and whewellite/oxalate), oxygen plasma discharges convert organic matter in a paint sample to water and carbon dioxide. The carbon dioxide is collected for AMS radiocarbon dating. Only organic carbon is extracted, leaving the inorganic mineral portion of the paint sample intact as a solid in the reaction chamber. This is perhaps the most important advantage of plasma oxidation: extensive acid pretreatments used to remove carbonate and oxalate minerals are not necessary when plasma oxidation (instead of combustion) is used. This allows smaller sample sizes to be successfully analyzed, as a portion of samples is often lost during wet pretreatment steps. The technique has been verified by suc-

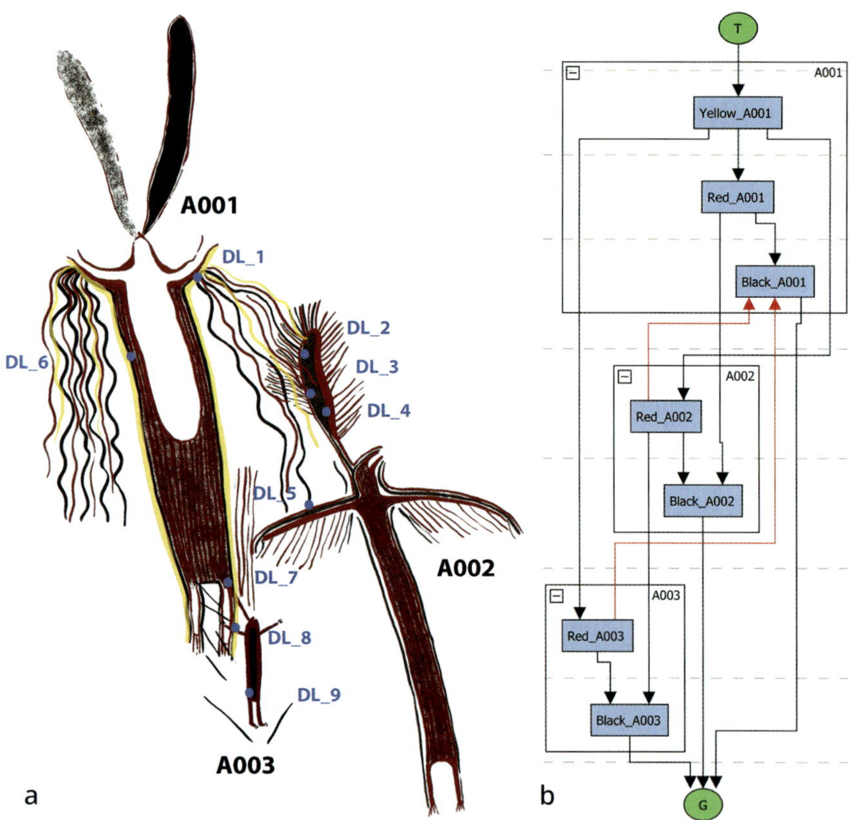

Figure 8. (a) Figure illustration of three anthropomorphs (A001-A003). Digital microscopy (DL) locations signified in blue. (b) Paint layers in a Harris Matrix are ordered top (T) to bottom (G). The principle of superposition establishes that layers located closest to the rock surface (G) were painted prior to those overlying them. The arrows in the matrix point from layers above to layers below. Red arrows in the matrix indicate figures with interwoven paint layers—figures that are both over and under other figures simultaneously. A001, A002, and A003 are woven together; therefore, obtaining a date anywhere within this composition will provide a date for all three figures.

cessfully dating materials of known age from radiocarbon laboratory intercomparisons (Steelman et al. 2004, 2017) and pictographs with archaeologically constrained ages (Armitage et al. 2001; Hyman and Rowe 1997).

Steelman's laboratory implements important protocols to improve the reliability and precision of paint dates. This includes the analysis of unpainted background samples to identify the presence or absence of contaminants in the rock substrate, and base pretreatments with NaOH to remove potential humic acid contamination. Preliminary results from Eagle Cave (41VV167) suggest an improved precision in replicate results with a ±70 RCYBP range or better (Steelman et al. 2021a).

Steelman also implements a second independent method to obtain minimum and maximum ages for the paintings by dating overlying and underlying oxalate accretion layers to constrain the ages of paint layers (Steelman et al. 2021a). During the formation of oxalate coatings, the prevailing hypothesis is that biological sources (bacteria, fungi, lichen, microbes, etc.) incorporate carbon from the atmosphere into oxalic acid, which is then precipitated onto the rock surface as calcium oxalate (Hess et al. 2008; Russ et al. 1995, 1996, 1999). Oxalate carbon is, thus, contemporary with the formation of the oxalate rock coating (Beazley et al. 2002; Russ et al. 2000). Numerous studies have utilized oxalate dating to provide indirect ages for pictographs around the world (e.g., Jones et al. 2017; Mazel and Watchman 2003; Pecchioni et al. 2019; Ruiz et al. 2012; Steelman et al. 2002). Radiocarbon assays obtained in preliminary studies in the Lower Pecos for the overlying accretion layers are younger than the painting they cover and the underlying accretion layers are older.

Steelman processes PRS paint and oxalate samples using a new NSF-supported multi-sample chamber plasma oxidation system at Shumla (Figure 9). Sampling and laboratory protocols and procedures implemented in our project are listed below.

Sample Collection Procedure. After determining the painting sequence using digital microscopy, we collect paint samples from actively spalling locations on the bottom (first applied), middle, and top (last applied) paint layers.

- Complete figure documentation and photography with scale and color-checker passport before sampling.
- Take macrophotographs of sampling locations before and after collection (Figure 10).
- Collect paint samples using sterile scalpel blades.

Figure 9. *NSF-supported plasma oxidation instrument with 10 sample chambers in Steelman's laboratory at Shumla.*

- Collect background samples of adjacent unpainted rock.
- Store samples in sterile, pre-baked (550°C) aluminum foil, and place in labeled plastic bags.

Plasma Oxidation Procedure. We dissect paint samples into overlying accretion, paint, and underlying accretion layers to employ two independent rock art dating methods.

- Paint and background samples
  - Remove any physical contaminants (plant fibers, rootlets, spider webs) under magnification using a stereoscope.
  - Chemically pretreat with base to remove potential humic acid contaminants, followed by filtration and drying.
  - Extract organic carbon from paint samples using plasma oxidation for AMS radiocarbon dating.
  - Measure amounts of organic material in background control samples to ensure negligible environmental contamination in the rock substrate.
- Oxalate accretion samples
  - Identify minerals (typically calcite, whewellite, gypsum) in accretions using Fourier transform

145

infrared (FTIR) and X-ray diffraction (XRD) spectroscopy.

- Treat accretion samples with weak acid washes (1 M H_3PO_4) to remove calcite.
- Use FTIR and/or XRD to demonstrate the complete removal of calcite and the remaining presence of whewellite (calcium oxalate, monohydrate).
- Remove any organic contaminants in oxalate samples using plasma oxidation.
- Combustion, graphitization, and AMS radiocarbon measurement of purified oxalate sample.

Analyses

Statistical Analysis Using OxCal Software. Statistical modeling will be applied to chronological data using Bayesian analysis to study start and end date ranges for PRS rock art production. If stratigraphic analyses demonstrate that dated paint samples were collected from a single composition, a weighted average and pooled standard deviation of radiocarbon ages can be calculated to obtain improved precision. Smaller error on ages will allow comparison of motifs and attributes across the landscape to test chronological development of the style.

Stratigraphic Analysis. Radiocarbon results are entered into Harris Matrix Composer metadata. This provides a textual and graphic diagram reflecting ages for figures engaged in a stratigraphic relationship with the directly dated painting. These dates will provide complete chronological information for compositions, with the least destructive sampling.

Spatial Analysis. Iconographic data and radiocarbon assays will be entered into Geographic Information Systems (GIS). These data will be analyzed for spatial and temporal relationships in iconography. These relationships will track and identify the use of specific iconographic attributes across the landscape and within a chronological framework.

Best Practices for Radiocarbon Dating Pictographs

The Hearthstone Project is the result of a decades-long collaboration between chemists, archaeologists, artists, site stewards, and members of Native American communities. Through this collaboration, we have gained different perspectives and shared knowledge that has informed, and will continue to inform, best practices in radiocarbon dating pictographs. Below we provide a brief review of preexisting best practices

and offer additional suggestions learned through this collaboration.

Guideline 1. Researchers must balance the potential for information gained through radiocarbon dating versus damage to the art through sampling. As stated by Clottes et al. (1992:128–129), "Direct dating [of rock art] must always be performed to check archaeological hypotheses and address particular problems. Aimless dating would only provide unrelated data that would have to wait until they could be corroborated by other methods." Prior to the initiation of a project, all participants (landowners/managers, site stewards, Indigenous groups, archaeologists, dating specialists, and other stakeholders) should have open communication to determine the research questions, understand the process, and recognize the challenges of obtaining radiocarbon dates.

Guideline 2. It is also important to remember that radiocarbon dating paint samples does not always work. Obtaining reliable radiocarbon dates for pictographs requires: (1) that prehistoric artists used organic materials in the paint recipe and enough of these have survived for accurate and reliable measurements and (2) there is negligible contamination in the rock surface that could affect results. It is crucial that control samples of unpainted rock substrate (backgrounds) are collected directly adjacent to paint samples and analyzed in a parallel fashion. Organic contaminants in the form of microbes, lichen, plant fibers, spider webs, and other matter can occur on the surface of and within the rock substrate. A project can be planned, fieldwork conducted, paint samples collected, weeks of laboratory work performed, and thousands of research dollars spent only to find out that radiocarbon dates cannot be obtained. Luckily, in the Lower Pecos region, we have observed that contamination is minimal and that prehistoric artists were using high-quality paint with organic binders/vehicles that allow us to obtain radiocarbon dates.

Guideline 3. A rock art panel is forever altered through the sampling process; therefore, full documentation of the art is essential prior to collecting paint samples. Researchers should document the art using high-resolution photography with and without a scale and color checker passport. This includes macrophotography of the sampling location before and after the paint is removed from the wall (Figure 10). This provides a precise context for the paint sample and facilitates pinpointing the location when researchers return to the site.

Figure 10. *Macrophotographs taken (a) before and (b) after collecting a paint sample from a Pecos River style pictograph. This black paint sample was collected from an area with a potential spall that was in the process of exfoliating. This rock fragment would have eventually been lost to natural weathering. We focus on minimizing sample sizes and the conservation of the panels.*

Guideline 4. Sampling for radiocarbon dating should be done in a manner that minimizes the impact of collection on painted images. PRS murals, like many rock art assemblages around the world, are a palimpsest of polychromatic, superimposed images. When figure superimposition is present, we have found that an analysis of paint stratigraphy using microscopy helps us to select the best sampling locations. By analyzing the painting sequence and constructing a Harris Matrix, we can collect paint samples from the first (bottom, oldest) and last (top, most recently) painted layers, thereby assigning an age range to figures sandwiched between directly dated figures. Further, by selecting figures that are in superimposition with other motifs, we can apply direct dates obtained from a single figure to those figures interwoven with it. This approach allows us to establish the mural's internal painting chronology with the least-destructive analyses.

Guideline 5. Careful choice of the sampling location within a figure is also important. Steelman prefers to collect a potential spall or rock flake that is actively exfoliating away from the rock surface for two reasons: (1) these are areas of paint that will eventually be lost due to natural weathering, and (2) samples can be dissected in the laboratory to obtain both direct paint and indirect oxalate dates. In some instances when there are no potential spall locations, paint samples are collected using a sterile surgical scalpel to remove paint material from the wall as a powder into an aluminum foil container. Typical sample sizes are on the order of 1–3 cm² of surface area and 10–100 mg by weight.

Guideline 6. Scientists who process the samples for radiocarbon dating should collect the paint samples themselves.[3] There is skill associated with delicately removing samples and minimizing the impact on the

rock art and the site. It is equally important that samples are collected from optimal locations to minimize environmental contamination from lichen, algae, insects, and other invasive substances.

Guideline 7. Archaeologists have to be aware that past methods of documentation such as applying kerosene or water for photo enhancement; using tape to mark panels or hold string grids; using adhesive putty to hold photography scales; and tracing may leave residues on the rock art that might impact future dating studies. With advances in photographic methods, these old strategies are often no longer necessary and should be discontinued. Even when these deleterious recording methods are used (or have been used) on unpainted walls, they could impact dating the control samples of unpainted rock, samples that are analyzed in tandem with paint samples.

Guideline 8. Steelman prefers to conduct blind studies, uninformed by archaeologists' expectations for the age of specific rock art motifs or panels. However, archaeology collaborators need some knowledge of what kind of information radiocarbon dating studies will give them. Most radiocarbon analyses will give ±40 RCYBP error, which corresponds to 200–400 cal B.P. or cal B.C./A.D. age ranges. This 200- to 400-year range may or may not be high enough resolution to answer specific research questions. There are plateaus in the radiocarbon calibration curve during certain time periods that result in even larger age-range estimates. For example, the Hallstatt plateau at 2450 RCYBP consistently calibrates to 800–400 cal B.C. no matter the measurement precision, which can make it difficult to resolve the radiocarbon dates of any samples whose true age lie between 400 and 800 B.C. And, radiocarbon dating anything with a true age after A.D. 1500 will mostly likely result in calibrated age ranges that span into the A.D. 1950s. Unfortunately, the Industrial Revolution and atomic bomb testing both altered the C-14 isotope concentration in the atmosphere, making calibration that converts radiocarbon measurements (RCYBP) to calendar years (cal A.D.) difficult. While there are some new Bayesian methods that can sometimes overcome these challenges, these statistical approaches often require numerous radiocarbon dates that are not available for rock art studies.

Summary

The Hearthstone Project's pair of research designs and best practices presented above embrace the following quote from Kubler's book *The Shape of Time*: "When we scan things for traces of the shape of the past, everything about them deserves our attention...Expression and form are equivalent challenges to the (art) historian; and that to neglect either meaning or being, either essence or existence, deforms our comprehension of both" (1962:126). PRS murals are technically complex, data rich, meaning-filled narratives relating a deeply rooted and widely shared ideological universe. Every brush stroke, choice of color, form, and placement on the wall and in the landscape carries information essential to our understanding of the message in the medium. Applying the best practices in radiocarbon dating helps us to establish the timing of these ancient and enduring messages. The artists of PRS murals communicated their messages through a complex tapestry of interwoven figures. Through the Hearthstone Project, we are weaving together archaeological science, art analysis, and Indigenous knowledge to unravel those messages and further our knowledge of the people who created these significant murals. With our studies, we strive to honor both past and living Indigenous peoples and their cultural heritage.

Acknowledgments. The Hearthstone Project is a collaboration between Texas State University and Shumla Archaeological Research & Education Center and is partially funded by the National Endowment for the Humanities (RFW-279507-21) and awards from the National Science Foundation Senior Archaeology (2113866 and 2113867). We thank our NEH partner investigators Stacy Schaefer and Jim Bauml, and Hearthstone Project team members Tim Murphy, Audrey Lindsay, Diana Radillo Rolón, Ashley Busby, Seamus Anderson, Katie Wilson, and Bennett Dampier. We thank our volunteers David Keim, Kelly Timmons, and the 2022 Senior Class of Comstock High School. We also appreciate the help provided by Tim Roberts, and the staff and volunteers of Texas Parks and Wildlife Department's Seminole Canyon State Park & Historic Site: Kassidy Stock, Julie Heineke, and Betty Shropshire. This research would not be possible without the collaboration and generosity of local landowners, Seminole Canyon State Park & Historic Site, and Amistad National Recreation Area. We especially thank Jack Johnson (Amistad National Recreation Area) for his endless support of our work in the Lower Pecos.

Notes

1. In the 1990s, the Lower Pecos Canyonlands was the first study area where the method of plasma oxidation was employed. This pioneering work conducted by Marvin Rowe's laboratory at Texas A&M University obtained 29 experimental radiocarbon dates for 16 PRS paintings. Reported assays range from 4200 to 1450 RCYBP, with a calibrated age range of approximately 5000 cal B.P. to 1150 cal B.P. (Bates et al. 2015; Hyman and Rowe 1997; Russ et al. 1990). Control experiments on unpainted rock substrate (backgrounds) to identify potential contaminants were not initially conducted and samples were often not pretreated with base to remove potential humic acid contamination. Reports were published with only site names and stylistic descriptions and did not include sampling locations or photographs of the sampled figures. These initial results successfully placed PRS paintings into the Archaic period. However, this data lacked precision for replicate analyses on the same painting with a ±250 RCYBP error range.

2. At the White Shaman site (41VV124), Boyd and her collaborators at Shumla used a handheld digital microscope to analyze 192 locations of intersecting paint layers (Boyd and Cox 2016). Ninety-nine percent of the locations follow a strict color order. Artists applied black paint first, followed by red, then yellow, and finally white. As a result, elements of one figure were painted over and under elements of another figure, indicating they were part of the same painting episode. Boyd and Cox (2016) demonstrate that this PRS mural is a visual narrative created in a single painting episode.

3. Steelman's laboratory does not accept random paint samples sent to her by others. This prevents undocumented sampling done without proper permissions and/or permits.

References Cited

Armitage, Ruth Ann, James E. Brady, Allan Cobb, John R. Southon, and Marvin W. Rowe
  2001 Mass Spectrometric Radiocarbon Dates from Three Rock Paintings of Known Age. *American Antiquity* 66:471–480.

Bates, Lennon N., Amanda M. Castañeda, Carolyn E. Boyd, and Karen L. Steelman
  2015 A Black Deer at Black Cave: New Pictograph Radiocarbon Date for the Lower Pecos, TX. *Journal of Texas Archeology and History* 2:45–57.

Beazley, Melanie J., Richard D. Rickman, Debra K. Ingram, Thomas W. Boutton, and Jon Russ

2002 Natural Abundances of Carbon Isotopes (14C, 13C) in Lichens and Calcium Oxalate Pruina: Implications for Archaeological and Paleoenvironmental Studies. *Radiocarbon* 44:675–683.

Boyd, Carolyn E.
1996 Shamanic Journeys into the Otherworld of the Archaic Chichimec. *Latin American Antiquity* 7:152–164.

1998 Pictograph Evidence of Peyotism in the Lower Pecos, Texas Archaic. In *The Archaeology of Rock-Art*, edited by Christopher Chippindale and Paul. C. Taçon, pp. 229–246. Cambridge University Press, Oxford.

2003 *Rock Art of the Lower Pecos*. Texas A&M Press, College Station.

2010 El Arte Ruprestre de Tejas: Análisis Contextual de Motivos Recurrentes en el Área de la Desembocadura del Rió Pecos. *Revista Iberoamericana de Lingüística* 5:5–42.

2021 Images in the Making: Process and Vivification in Pecos River Style Rock Art. In *Ontologies of Rock Art: Images, Relational Approaches and Indigenous Knowledge*, edited by Oscar Moro Abadía and Martin Porr. Routledge Press, London.

Boyd, Carolyn E., and Ashley Busby
2021 Speech-Breath: Mapping the Multisensory Experience in Pecos River Style Pictography. *Latin American Antiquity* 33:20–40.

Boyd, Carolyn E., Amanda M. Castañeda, and Charles W. Koenig
2013 A Reassessment of Red Linear Pictographs in the Lower Pecos Canyonlands of Texas. *American Antiquity* 78:456–482.

Boyd, Carolyn E., and Kim Cox
2016 *The White Shaman Mural: An Enduring Creation Narrative in the Rock Art of the Lower Pecos*. The University of Texas Press, Austin.

Boyd, Carolyn E., and J. Philip Dering
1996 Medicinal and Hallucinogenic Plants identified in the Sediments and Pictographs of the Lower Pecos, Texas Archaic. *Antiquity* 70:256–275.

Clottes, Jean, Jean Courtin, and Hélène Valladas
1992 A Well-Dated Palaeolithic Cave: The Cosquer Cave at Marseille. *Rock Art Research* 9:122–129.

Dering, J. Phil
1999 Earth-Oven Plant Processing in Archaic Period Economies: An Example from a Semi-Arid Savannah in South-Central North America. *American Antiquity* 64:659–674.

2002 *Amistad National Recreation Area: Archeological Survey and Cultural Resources Inventory*. Professional Paper No. 68. Intermountain Cultural Resources Management Anthropology Projects, National Park Service, Santa Fe.

Flannery, Kent V.
2003 Theoretical Framework: Divergent Evolution. In *The Cloud People: Divergent Evolution of the Zapotec and Mixtec Civilizations*, edited by Kent V. Flannery and Joyce Marcus, pp. 1–9. Originally published 1983. Percheron, Clinton Corners, New York.

Franck, Frederick
1973 *The Zen of Seeing: Seeing/Drawing as Meditation*. Vintage Books, London.

Gebhard, David
1960 Prehistoric Paintings of the Diablo Region of Western Texas—A Preliminary Report. Publications in Art and Science No. 3. Roswell Museum and Art Center, Roswell, New Mexico.

1965 Prehistoric Rock Paintings of the Seminole Canyon Area, Val Verde County, Texas. Report submitted to the National Park Service, Southwest Region.

Gossen, Gary
1986 Mesoamerican Ideas as a Foundation for Regional Synthesis. In *Symbol and Meaning beyond the Closed Community: Essays in Mesoamerican Ideas*, edited by Gary Gossen, pp. 1–8. Studies on Culture and Society, vol. 1. Institute for Mesoamerican Studies, State University of New York at Albany.

Griffith, Glenn, Sandy Bryce, James Omernik, and Anne Rogers
2007 *Ecoregions of Texas*. Report to Texas Commission on Environmental Quality.

Harrison, James B.
2011 An Argument for the Expanded Context of Dart-Headed Figures in Pecos River Style Pictographs. In *American Indian Rock Art*, Volume 37, edited by Mavis Greer, John Greer, and Peggy Whitehead, pp. 75–92. American Rock Art Research Association, San Jose, California.

Harrison Macrae, James B.
2018 *Pecos River Style Rock Art: A Prehistoric Iconography*. Texas A&M Press, College Station.

Hess, Darren, Dana Jo Coker, Jeannette M. Loutsch, and Jon Russ
2008 Production of Oxalates *In Vitro* by Microbes Isolated from Rock Surfaces with Prehistoric Paints in the Lower Pecos Region, Texas. *Geoarchaeology* 23:3–11.

Hyman, Marian, and Marvin W. Rowe
1997 Plasma Extraction and AMS 14C Dating of Rock Paintings. *Techne: Laboratoire de Recherché des Musées de France* 5:61–70.

Jones, Tristen, Vladimir A. Levchenko, Penelope L. King, Ulrike Troitzsch, Daryl Wesley, A. Alan Williams, and Alfred Nayingull
2017 Radiocarbon Age Constraints for a Pleistocene-Holocene Transition Rock Art Style: The Northern Running Figures of the East Alligator River Region, Western Arnhem Land, Australia. *Journal of Archaeological Science: Reports* 11:80–89.

Joralemon, Peter D.
1976 The Olmec Dragon: A Study in Pre-Columbian Iconography. In *Origins of Religious Art and Iconography in Preclassic Mesoamerica*, edited by Henry B. Nicholson, pp. 27–71. Latin American Center, University of California, Los Angeles.

Kelley, J. Charles
1974 Pictorial and Ceramic Art in the Mexican Cultural Littoral of the Chichimec Sea. In *Art and Environment in Native America*, edited by Mary E. King and Idris R. Traylor, Jr., pp. 23–54. Special Publications of the Museum No. 7. Texas Tech University, Lubbock.

Kilby, J. David, Sean P. Farrell, and Marcus J. Hamilton
2020 New Investigations at Bonfire Shelter, Texas, Examine Controversial Bison Jumps and Bone Beds. *Plains Anthropologist* 66:34–57.

Kirkland, Forrest
1939 Indian Pictures in the Dry Shelters of Val Verde County, Texas. *Bulletin of the Texas Archeological and Paleontological Society* 11:47–76.

Kirkland, Forrest, and William W. Newcomb, Jr.
1967 *The Rock Art of Texas Indians*. University of Texas Press, Austin.

Koenig, Charles W., Amanda M. Castañeda, Victoria L. Roberts, Jerod L. Roberts, Carolyn E. Boyd, and Karen L. Steelman
2019 Around the Lower Pecos in 1,095 Days: The Alexandria Project. In *American Indian Rock Art*, Volume 45, edited by Ken Hedges and Anne McConnell, pp. 147–160. American Rock Art Research Association, San Jose, California.

Kubler, George
1962 *The Shape of Time: Remarks on the History of Things*. Yale University Press, New Haven.

López Austin, Alfredo
  1997 *Tamoanchan, Tlalocan: Places of Mist.* Translated by Thelma Ortiz de Montellano and Bernard Ortiz de Montellano. University Press of Colorado, Boulder.

Mazel, Aron D., and Alan L. Watchman
  2003 Dating Rock Paintings in the uKhahlamba-Drakensberg and the Biggarsberg, KwaZulu-Natal, South Africa. *Southern African Humanities* 15:59–73.

McCuistion, Emily R.
  2019 *The Camel of Time: Radiocarbon Dating the Lower Pecos Canyonlands.* Master's Thesis, Texas State University, San Marcos.

McDonald, Jo, and Peter Veth
  2013 Rock Art in Arid Landscapes: Pilbara and Western Desert Petroglyphs. *Australian Archaeology* 77:66–81.

Pecchioni, Elena, Marilena Ricci, Orlando Vaselli, Cristiana Lofrumento, Vladamir Levchenko, Marco Giamello, Andrea Scala, Alastair Williams, and Barbara Turchetta
  2019 Chemical and Mineralogical Characterization and ^{14}C Dating of White and Red Pigments in the Rock Paintings from Nyero (Uganda). *Microchemical Journal* 144:329–338.

Rice, Prudence
  2020 In Search of Middle Preclassic Lowland Maya Ideologies. *Journal of Archaeological Research* 29:1–46.

Rowe, Marvin W.
  2001 Physical and Chemical Analysis. In *Handbook of Rock Art Research*, edited by David S. Whitley, pp. 190–220. Altamira Press, Walnut Creek, California.

  2012 Bibliography of Rock Art Dating. *Rock Art Research* 29:118–131.

Ruiz, Juan F., Antonio Hernanz, Ruth Ann Armitage, Marvin W. Rowe, Ramon Viñas, José M. Gavira-Vallejo, and Albert Rubio
  2012 Calcium Oxalate AMS ^{14}C Dating and Chronology of Post-Palaeolithic Rock Paintings in the Iberian Peninsula. Two Dates from Abrigo de los Oculados (Henarejos, Cuenca, Spain). *Journal of Archaeological Science* 39:2655–2667.

Russ, Jon, Marian Hyman, Harry J. Shafer, and Marvin W. Rowe
  1990 Radiocarbon Dating of Prehistoric Rock Paintings by Selective Oxidation of Organic Carbon. *Nature* 348:710–711.

Russ, Jon, Russell L. Palma, David H. Loyd, Dennis W. Farwell, Howell G.M. Edwards
  1995 Analysis of the Rock Accretions in the Lower Pecos Region of Southwest Texas. *Geoarchaeology* 10:43–63.

Russ, Jon, Russel L. Palma, David H. Loyd, Thomas W. Boutton, and Michael A. Coy
  1996 Origin of the Whewellite-Rich Rock Crust in the Lower Pecos Region of Southwest Texas and Its Significance to Paleoclimate Reconstructions. *Quaternary Research* 46:27–36.

Russ, Jon, Warna D. Kaluarachchi, Louise Drummond, and Howell G.M. Edwards
  1999 The Nature of a Whewellite-Rich Rock Crust Associated with Pictographs in Southwestern Texas. *Studies in Conservation* 44:91–103.

Russ, Jon, David H. Loyd, and Thomas W. Boutton
  2000 A Paleoclimate Reconstruction for Southwestern Texas using Oxalate Residue from Lichen as a Paleoclimate Proxy. *Quaternary International* 67:29–36.

Shafer, Harry
  1986 *Ancient Texans: Rock Art and Lifeways along the Lower Pecos.* Texas Monthly Press, Austin.

Shafer, Harry (editor)
  2013 *Painters in Prehistory: Archaeology and Art of the Lower Pecos Canyonlands.* Trinity University Press, San Antonio, Texas.

Steelman, Karen L., Carolyn E. Boyd, and Trinidy Allen
  2021a Two Independent Methods for Dating Rock Art: Age Determination of Paint and Oxalate Layers at Eagle Cave, TX. *Journal of Archaeological Science* 126: article 105315.

Steelman, Karen L., Carolyn E. Boyd, and Lennon N. Bates
  2021b Implications for Rock Art Dating from the Lower Pecos Canyonlands, TX: A Review. *Quaternary Geochronology* 63: article 101167.

Steelman, Karen L., Arturo de Lombera-Hermida, Ramón Viñas-Vallverdú, Xosé P. Rodríguez-Álvarez, Fernando Carrera-Ramírez, Albert Rubio-Mora, Ramon Fábregas-Valcarce
  2017 Cova Eirós: An Integrated Approach to Dating the Earliest Known Cave Art in NW Iberia. *Radiocarbon* 59:151–164.

Steelman, Karen L., Richard Rickman, Marvin W. Rowe, Thomas W. Boutton, Jon Russ, and Niède Guidon
  2002 Accelerator Mass Spectrometry Radiocarbon Ages of an Oxalate Accretion and Rock Paintings at Toca do Serrote da Bastiana, Brazil. In *Archaeological Chemistry VI*, edited by Katheryn Jakes, pp. 22–35. American Chemical Society Symposium Series, Washington, D.C.

Steelman, Karen L., Marvin W. Rowe, Solveig A. Turpin, Thomas P. Guilderson, Laura Nightengale
  2004 Non-Destructive Radiocarbon Dating: Naturally Mummified Infant Bundle from SW Texas. *American Antiquity* 69:741–750.

Turpin, Solveig A.
  1984 Pictographs of the Red Monochrome Style in the Lower Pecos River Region, Texas. *Bulletin of the Texas Archeological Society* 55:123–144.

  1986 Toward a Definition of a Pictograph Style: The Lower Pecos Bold Line Geometric. *Plains Anthropologist* 31:153–161.

  1989 The Iconography of Contact: Spanish Influences in the Rock Art of the Middle Rio Grande. In *Columbian Consequences Volume 1: Archaeological and Historical Perspectives on the Spanish Borderlands West*, edited by David H. Thomas, pp. 277–299. Smithsonian Institution Press, Washington, D.C.

  1990 Speculations on the Age and Origin of the Pecos River Style, Southwest Texas. In *American Indian Rock Art*, Volume 16, edited by Solveig A. Turpin, pp. 99–122. American Rock Art Research Association, San Antonio, Texas.

  2004a The Lower Pecos River Region of Texas and Northern Mexico. In *The Prehistory of Texas*, edited by Timothy K. Perttula, pp. 266–280. Texas A&M University Press, College Station.

  2004b Cyclical Nucleation and Sacred Space: Rock Art at the Center. In *New Perspectives on Prehistoric Art*, edited by Günter Berghaus, pp. 51–64. Bristol Lecture Series. Praeger, Westport, Connecticut.

  2010 *El Arte Indígena en Coahuila.* Universidad Autónoma de Coahuila, Mexico.

  2018 Buried Relations: Aspects of Late Archaic Social Configurations in the Lower Pecos Region of Texas Inferred from Genetic and Biological Clues in the Mortuary Population. *Bulletin of the Texas Archeological Society* 89:31–47.

Van Devender, Thomas R.
  1990 Late Quaternary Vegetation and Climate of the Chihuahuan Desert, United States and Mexico. In *Packrat Middens: The Last 40,000 Years of Biotic Change*, edited by Julio L. Betancourt, Thomas R. Van Devender, and Paul S. Martin, pp. 104–133. The University of Arizona, Tucson.

Near-field vs. Far-field Acoustic Study of White River Narrows Rock Art

Steven J. Waller

White River Narrows (WRN) in Lincoln County, Nevada, is a complex of sites with rock art clustered into discrete decorated locations separated by long stretches of non-decorated locations. Near-field study (sound source and recorder co-located) results of WRN show a statistically significant difference of 3.2 dB between the average sound pressure levels at decorated compared to non-decorated locations, i.e., the echoes are approximately 44 percent stronger at rock art locations. Far-field study (sound source located far from recorder's location) results show that very distant echoes can clearly be heard bouncing around within the canyon when loud sounds such as vocal yells are produced at the various rock art locations, demonstrating sound transmission between distant rock art sites. The general conclusion from the complementary studies presented here is that the artists apparently chose to decorate surfaces giving intrinsically strong local sound reflections that also help to gather and focus sounds from distant sources. The unusually strong sound reflection at each of the WRN rock art locations, and the acoustic interactions demonstrated for sound transmission between the various rock art sites within WRN, fit together into a possible concept of a cascade of sound flowing through the canyon that can be heard best at certain places of power.

This two-part acoustic study was conducted to document and analyze the auditory characteristics of the environments surrounding ten rock art locations (Table 1) in White River Narrows (WRN) in Lincoln County, Nevada (Figure 1).

This study was part of a larger project conducted and reported to the Bureau of Land Management (BLM) by Johannes Loubser (2021), and an earlier version of this acoustic portion of the project was included as Appendix II of that report. Rock art on BLM land affords unique opportunities for the agency to conserve and record the acoustic as well as visible aspects of these cultural resources, and to involve and educate the visiting public about their significance. To explore the possibility of presenting the WRN site complex as a multisensory experience, an instrument-based acoustic study was conducted, led by the author under the supervision of project director Dr. Johannes Loubser of Stratum Unlimited, together with the participation of volunteer Steve Dudrow as videographer.

Scientific instrument-based research at other rock art sites (e.g., Waller 1993) has demonstrated the existence of anomalous acoustic properties in the context of rock art. Those prior studies, together with ethnographic information on the cultural significance of echoes, strongly suggest that special auditory properties of rock art sites may be as important as their apparent visual ones.

The field of archaeoacoustics (Díaz-Andreu and Mattioli 2016; Waller 2005, 2006), also called acoustical archaeology, is a relatively recent and rapidly growing area of study. Methods and applications are still being developed and honed for application to the complex variety of archaeological sites, including rock art locations.

Steven J. Waller
Lemon Grove, California

American Indian Rock Art, Volume 49. Amy Gilreath, Ken Hedges, and Anne McConnell, Editors. American Rock Art Research Association, 2023, pp. 151–158.

Table 1. Rock art locations within the White River Narrows, with numbering per Loubser (2021).

Popular Name	NV State Site #	Locus
Cane	26LN6171	-
North of Cane	21424 (?)	-
Ash Hill	26LN4137	-
Calendar Fence	26LN4136	-
Martian Home	26LN6172	-
Amphitheater	26LN210	I
Red Pictograph	26LN210	II
Pink Rock	26LN210	III
Shoshone Frog	26LN210	IV
Signature Rock	26LN210	V

The WRN represents an area in which rock art is concentrated into discrete locations that are spaced out and separated by long stretches of locations without art that nonetheless visually appear to have rock surfaces equally suitable to the placement of art. This raises the motivational question of "why here, yet not there?" and thus WRN presents an excellent opportunity to investigate factors that influenced the selection of rock art locations.

An initial deliverable of the overall project was an acoustic study of the WRN site complex (dominated by 26LN210 with multiple loci), with its curving vertical cliff at Locus I resembling a giant parabola. Determining the special acoustics at the cliff and neighboring cliffs can help communicate the multisensory significance of the WRN to visitors, and foster respect for the location's physical integrity, thereby increasing its appeal to visitors and diminishing chances for vandalism. Researching the auditory component of site 26LN210 and other rock art sites within the WRN complex provides an underused management strategy to help specialists understand the placement of rock art locations and to make them more meaningful for visitors.

An acoustic analysis of the rock art of the WRN aimed to verify if acoustics were an essential element in the production and placement of rock art there. Specifically, the objectives were to investigate:

- The relationship between echoes or directive sound reflections and the placement of rock art.
- The possible connection between rock art and various places with exceptional acoustics in the WRN.
- The attenuation and/or enhanced propagation of distant sounds between rock art surfaces and the surroundings.

Methods

During fieldwork, the acoustical "signature" of the landscape was determined by taking impulse response (IR) measurements. For this, one needs a sound emitter that produces reproducible impulse sounds and a sound receiver capable of recording the sounds for quantitative analysis. As a sound emitter, a spring-loaded percussion device with loudness comparable to hand clapping was used for near-field studies. Various other sound emitters, including clapsticks, voice, and an automobile horn with loudness comparable to yelling, were used for far-field studies. Two different microphones were used as sound receivers: 1) an Edirol R-09 portable digital recorder with built-in stereo microphones, and 2) a DLSR Nikon D850 camera in video mode connected to an external mic.

In addition to subjective auditory perceptions, acoustic parameters were measured quantitatively as sound pressure levels in dB—the strength of reflected or propagated sounds. Results were anticipated to allow the following:

- Model the auditory perception at rock art sites according to two listener perspectives (in-audience, on-stage) and different territorial scales (site, adjacent areas, broad territory).
- Extract acoustic parameters.
- Model human echolocation.
- Investigate transmission loss for modeling the audibility of distant sounds.
- Measure sound reflection.

Experimental design and analysis of the results were guided by hypothesis testing:

- Hypothesis #0 (Null): Rock art site locations might have no relationship to sound.
- Hypothesis #1 (Near Field): Rock art site locations might have been chosen based on local acoustic properties of the site; thus, does data support that sound reflection is stronger at modified locations than at non-modified locations?
- Hypothesis #2 (Far Field): Rock art site locations might have been chosen based on interrelationships between distant locations; thus, does data

Figure 1. *White River Narrows canyon showing rock art site locations (courtesy of Johannes Loubser).*

ments in WRN as well as at nearby sites, including Mount Irish. On Day 2 systematic near-field tests were conducted throughout the WRN canyon, including measurements of sound reflection at both decorated and non-modified surfaces. On Day 3 a series of exploratory far-field experiments was conducted. Analysis of the recordings and a draft descriptive write-up of this study was completed within the subsequent five months.

In brief, for near-field acoustic analyses, the methods (see Waller 2000) consisted of systematically generating reproducible percussion noises (impulses of sound) with a spring-loaded device (a modified rat trap) in triplicate, spaced approximately 4 seconds apart at a consistent distance of approximately 30 meters from the test rock surface, and digitally recording the impulse responses (sound reflections) with an Edirol R-09 portable stereo digital recorder placed approximately one meter from the sound source, such that the sound emitter and receiver locations practically coincided in space. This represents hearing the echoes of one's own sounds, like what an individual hears with their own ears after making a percussion noise by their own hands.

A visual analogy is searching for the shiniest mirrors at night by looking for images of another "you" who is also holding a torch.

Rock art locations tested included all of the rock art sites within the WRN canyon known to, and pointed out by, the project director. Control locations without rock art were also tested for comparison. To avoid potential inadvertent bias, before actually testing for echoes, the non-modified control locations within the WRN canyon were preselected on a map by first measuring distances between the rock art locations, calculating either the mid-point between them, or a fixed distance from a rock art location, and then ensuring the control acoustic measurements took

support that rock art sites are exceptionally good places to hear sounds returned from elsewhere?

Fieldwork within the WRN by the acoustics crew of two people took three days to complete, excluding travel time. This work was supervised by the project director J. Loubser, including him pointing out where rock art was, and was not, present. The acoustic fieldwork was conducted June 16–18, 2020. Day 1 consisted of a familiarization period and preliminary informal scouting tests of both near-field and far-field experi-

place at a spot that has rock surfaces that are apparently suitable for rock art production.

Far-field experiments consisted of exploratory studies in which the sound emitter and receiver were in different locations in space, to represent the ability of a person to hear the propagation of sounds made by someone else far away. The audibility of sounds at various distances within the WRN canyon were determined and compared to an open field control.

A visual analogy is searching for shiny places where you can indirectly see light from a distant campfire bouncing around corners appearing as if there are additional campfires in other directions, sometimes brighter than expected for the direct line of sight.

There is an infinite number of combinations of emitter and receiver locations, so preliminary investigations began with the interrelationships of the rock art locations, with the receiver placed at a rock art site, and the emitter progressively placed at increasingly farther discrete distances toward an adjacent rock art site. The reproducible emitter in the quantitative far-field study included an automobile horn, which was measured to be of similar loudness to a human yell.

The acoustic studies were conducted during daylight hours from approximately 8 a.m. to 6:30 p.m., with temperatures ranging from approximately 20 to 30 degrees C, and low humidity with light winds. A challenge during our fieldwork was intermittent vehicular noise from irregularly spaced traffic traveling along State Route 318.

The recordings were later analyzed in the office via the computer acoustic software Sonic Visualiser, which quantifies the strength of sound pressure levels in decibel (dB) levels as a function of time and frequency, as well as rendering the dB levels visible in pseudo-color (reminiscent of weather maps that display temperatures). In lieu of formal calibration, the raw relative sound pressure levels derived from negative voltage readings were normalized by adding 100 dB so that the spring-loaded device gave an expected level of approximately 90 dB for the impulse sound. The reproducibility of the impulse sound had a 1.1 percent coefficient of variation (CV) for 99 replicates. In the case of near-

field measurements, sound pressure levels occurring greater than 0.1 seconds after impulse (representing distinct echoes audible to the human ear and distinguishable from the original sound) were compared to the background sound occurring before the impulse, to determine the strength of reflected sounds. The within-site reproducibility of the measured sound reflection dB levels for three replicates had a CV of less than 2 percent for locations with rock art (n=19) as well as for non-modified control locations (n=14), which allowed for homoscedastic (equal variance) statistical comparison.

Results

Near-field Test Results

At all of the rock art locations, sound reflection was objectively measured as well as subjectively clearly heard as distinct strong echoes. Of all the locations tested within WRN, the location with the strongest sound reflection level was at the rock art site named Pink Rock (26LN210, Locus III, see Figure 2), measured at 84.5 dB. In contrast, of all the locations tested within WRN, the six locations with the weakest sound reflection levels were all control non-modified locations, measured at 70.4 dB or less. Figure 3 displays the near-field quantitative measurements for the strength of sound reflection within WRN at rock art locations compared to non-modified locations. There was a statistically significant (p<0.010) difference of 3.2 dB between the means of the two populations: 76.9 dB

Figure 2. Pink Rock (26LN210, Locus III) overview and detail of rock art panel. This was the location found to have the strongest sound reflection result in the near-field tests. Also, far-field tests demonstrated that sounds produced at this site could be heard at Signature Rock (26LN210, Locus V), 0.7 miles away.

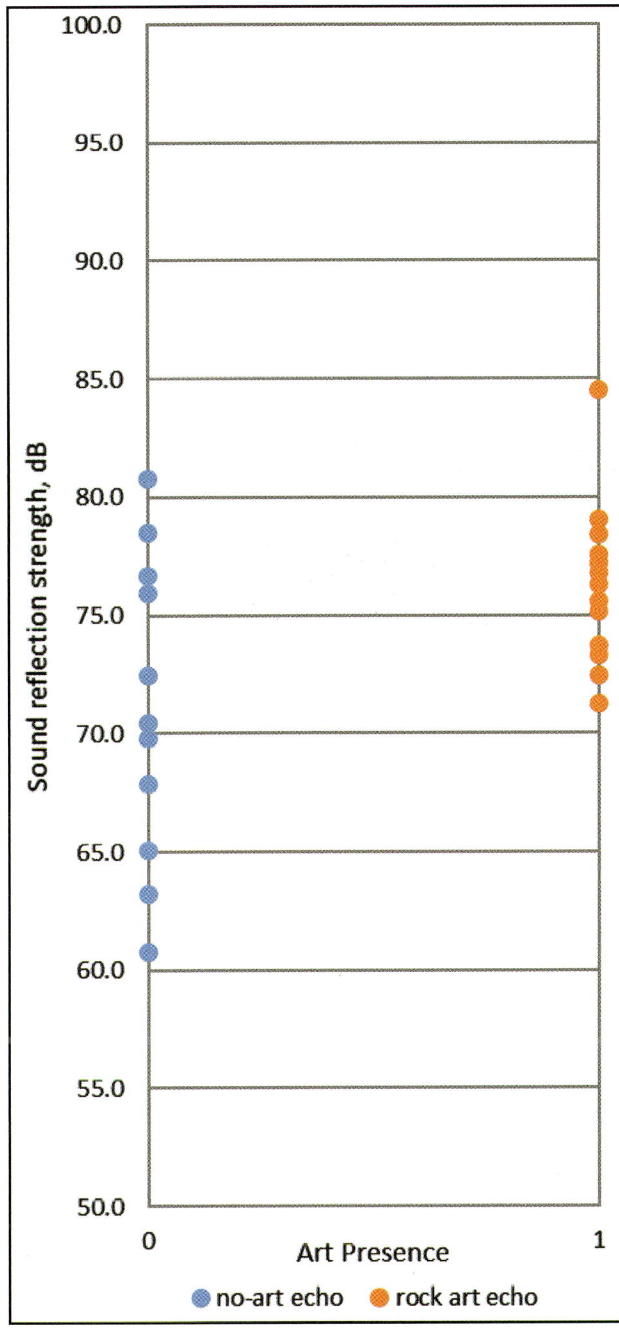

Figure 3. *Near-field acoustic measurements within WRN, showing a statistically significant (p<0.010) difference of the dB level of sound reflections (echoes) at rock art locations (orange symbols) compared to control locations within the canyon but without art (blue symbols).*

for locations with rock art vs. 73.8 dB for control locations without rock art within the canyon (non-paired, 1-tailed, homoscedastic t-test). Because the decibel scale is logarithmic, this 3.2 dB difference means that the test locations with rock art have on average a 44% stronger reflected sound pressure level than the test locations without rock art.

Far-field Test Results

Preliminary far-field studies demonstrated that when the receiver is at rock art locations within the WRN canyon, sounds can be heard from much greater distances than a control situation of a flat field outside of the canyon (Figure 4). While making very loud vocal sounds at WRN rock art sites in the canyon, echoes could be heard returning from remote locations, including from other rock art sites. For example, when an individual at the Amphitheater site (26LN210, Locus I, see Figure 5) yells, that same individual can hear the echo returned from the Red Pictograph site (26LN210, Locus II) approximately 0.4 miles away, a

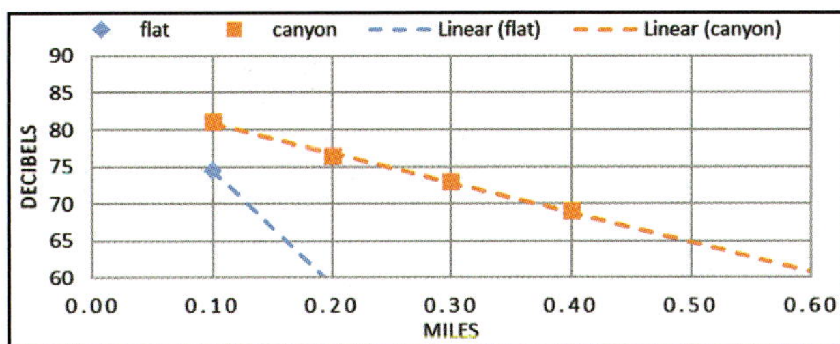

Figure 4. *Far-field acoustic measurements within WRN show that sound carries much farther within the canyon between rock art locations (orange symbols), compared to a flat, open field (blue symbols). Sounds produced at the Amphitheater site (26LN210, Locus I) could be heard and measured at the Martian Home rock art site (26LN6172) 0.6 miles away. In contrast, the same sounds produced in an open field could not be detected beyond 0.2 miles.*

Figure 5. *The Amphitheater site (26LN210, Locus I) with overview showing curvature of the cliff that focuses sound*

155

round trip path distance of approximately 0.8 miles. This implies that loud sounds produced by an individual at the Red Pictograph rock art site can be easily heard by a second individual at the Amphitheater rock art site (and vice versa); this ability to acoustically communicate between these two sites was confirmed by far-field experiments.

Interactions via acoustic communication were demonstrated by far-field testing between the following rock art locations (Figure 6) in the WRN area:

- Cane (26LN6171) to/from North of Cane (21424?)
- North of Cane (21424?) to/from Ash Hill (26LN4137)
- Ash Hill (26LN4137) to/from Cane (26LN6171)
- Calendar Fence (26LN4136) to Martian Home (26LN6172, see Figure 7)
- Amphitheater site (26LN210, Locus I) to Martian Home (26LN6172)
- Amphitheater site (26LN210, Locus I) to/from Red Pictograph site (26LN210, Locus II)

- Cane (26LN6171) to/from North of Cane (21424?)
- North of Cane (21424?) to/from Ash Hill (26LN4137)
- Ash Hill (26LN4137) to/from Cane (26LN6171)
- Calendar Fence (26LN4136) to Martian Home (26LN6172)
- Amphitheater site (26LN210, Locus I) to Martian Home (26LN6172)
- Amphitheater site (26LN210, Locus I) to/from Red Pictograph site (26LN210, Locus II)
- Pink Rock (26LN210, Locus III) to Signature Rock panel (26LN210, Locus V)

Figure 6. Schematic representation of acoustic interactions demonstrated between various rock art sites within WRN due to sound reflection, illustrating a cascade of sound bouncing through the canyon.

Figure 7. The Martian Home site (26LN6172).

- Pink Rock (26LN210, Locus III) to Signature Rock panel (26LN210, Locus V)

For example, when one individual produced loud sounds at the Pink Rock site (26LN210, Locus III) shown in Figure 2, a second individual at Signature Rock panel (26LN210, Locus V) could hear those sounds bouncing through the canyon from approximately 0.7 miles away, even though the two locations are not in the line of sight. Some of these interactions were found to be reciprocal between rock art locations, but there was not enough time to test all possible combinations of interactions.

Conclusions and Discussion

The statistically significant difference between means of 3.2 dB observed for the near-field study of WRN indicates that on average the sound pressure levels of the echoes are approximately 44 percent stronger at rock art locations than at non-modified locations. These results tend to refute the null hypothesis of no relationship between sound and rock art, and support Hypothesis #1 that rock art site locations might have been chosen based on local acoustic properties of the site. However, as Figure 3 shows, there was much overlap in the measured near-field sound reflection levels between the two data sets. While all the rock art locations gave strong echoes, several of the control non-modified locations gave echoes of comparable strength. Accordingly, the characteristic of sound reflection strength at 30 meters would not alone be able to distinguish between rock art locations versus non-modified control locations. It is concluded that a blind study using only near-field sound reflection strength could not have identified the exact locations of the rock art. It is accordingly unlikely that the only criteria used by artists for site selection was the ability to hear one's own percussive echoes returned loudly from a surface close by. Yet the documentation of strong echoes at all of the rock art locations, and the statistically significant difference of the echo strength at rock art locations versus locations without rock art—together with Indigenous ethnography revealing the mystical associations of echoes—provide tantalizing evidence suggesting that sound reflection was in some way important to the ancient artists. The results of this two-part study suggest that near-field echoing may have been a necessary characteristic for site selection, but not by itself sufficient. Other aspects may have been taken into consideration, such as the way in which the large-scale geometry of the terrain influenced sound propagation to facilitate long-range acoustic interactions.

The far-field study was conducted as an extension of the near-field study results. It was observed that very distant echoes could clearly be heard bouncing around within the canyon when loud sounds such as vocal yells were produced at the various rock art sites. This led to the plan of conducting the experiments that demonstrated sound transmission between distant rock art sites (Mattioli et al. 2017). The far-field results tend to support Hypothesis #2 that rock art site locations might have been chosen based on interrelationships of sound propagation between distant locations (facilitated by local sound reflective properties). This effect is reminiscent of—but on a much larger scale than—a science museum whisper gallery set-up consisting of two parabolic dishes that focus and gather sound waves so that two people can communicate across a surprisingly long distance.

One general conclusion from this two-part study is that the artists apparently did not simply choose to decorate nearby surfaces that give the intrinsically strongest sound reflections where they could hear echoes of themselves the best. However, the intrinsic sound reflection characteristics of a location—together with a favorable geometric configuration—help to gather and focus sounds from distant sources, to act like a commu-

nication device that enables hearing far away sounds that normally would be inaudible (Waller 2010).

A visual analogy with light reflection is that artists would not simply choose to decorate the shiniest mirrors where they could see a reflection of themselves the best. However, the shininess of mirrors at a location—together with a favorable geometric configuration—helps to gather and focus signals from distant sources, to act like a reflective telescope or periscope that enables seeing far away sights that normally would be invisible.

These results tend to confirm the theory that acoustics are an important part of rock art studies and documentation (Waller 1993). The preliminary results of this far-field study suggest that future more-detailed studies of sound propagation, under various conditions and combinations of locations, would be a fruitful endeavor. For example, when weather conditions form a thermal inversion, it is known that sound can reflect off the boundary layer between cool dense air underlying a warm air mass due to refraction, causing sound to carry much farther than usual. This suggests that sound propagation studies should also be conducted in the late evening or early morning, under conditions where the temperature inversion boundary layer sometimes acts like a lid or ceiling. This would effectively convert the canyon to act acoustically like an extensive cavern system to tunnel sound for long distances. Could this effect of weather be a clue that sound gave careful listeners at select locations the power to predict weather conditions, such as life-giving rain? And might this help explain the connection between rainmaking ceremonies, rock art, and thunderous reverberations?

The unusually strong sound reflection at each of the WRN rock art sites, and the acoustic interactions demonstrated for sound transmission between the various rock art sites within WRN, fit together into a possible concept of a cascade of sound flowing through the canyon, that can be heard best at certain places of power. This concept of certain locations where one is enabled to perceive the normally imperceptible is consistent with the manifestation of the spiritual concept of *puha*, which flows between sites in an interconnected landscape (Liwosz 2017; Whitley 2015).

The positive results from these preliminary studies serve as a basis for justifying the conservation and documentation of the acoustical properties as well as visual aspects of the rock art sites in the WRN, including the 26LN210 site complex, in Lincoln County, Nevada, and for presenting the site as a multisensory experience to involve and educate the visiting public about the significance of these cultural resources, for increased respect. These results are expected to be generalizable to a sizable portion of other rock art locations.

Acknowledgments. This acoustic study was conducted by invitation under the overall supervision of project director Dr. Johannes Loubser and was made financially possible by his company Stratum Unlimited. Volunteer Steve Dudrow documented the studies by video and participated as a source/receiver in the far-field studies. The author is grateful to both of these individuals and their invaluable contributions, without them this study would not have been possible. Appreciation is also extended to the BLM for enabling this project in general, particularly Jake Hickerson for guidance.

References Cited

Díaz-Andreu, Margarita, and Tommaso Mattioli
  2016 Archaeoacoustics of Rock Art: Quantitative Approaches to the Acoustics and Soundscape of Rock Art. In *CAA 2015. Keep the Revolution Going: Proceedings of the 43rd Annual Conference on Computer Applications and Quantitative Methods in Archaeology*, edited by Stefano Campana, Roberto Scopigno, Gabriella Carpentiero, and Marianna Cirillo, Volume 2, pp. 1049–1058. Archaeopress, Oxford.

Liwosz, Chester R.
  2017 Petroglyphs and Puha: how Multisensory Experiences Evidence Landscape Agency. *Time & Mind* 10(2):175–210.

Loubser, Johannes H. N.
  2021 *LCAI Round 11-Graffiti Mitigation and Rock Art Recording*, PO#140L3919P0070, Report Number 8111 CRR NV 040-FY-2240, submitted to BLM-NV, Caliente Field Office.

Mattioli, Tommaso, Angelo Farina, Enrico Armelloni, Philippe Hameau, and Margarita Díaz-Andreu
  2017 Echoing Landscapes: Echolocation and the Placement of Rock Art in the Central Mediterranean. *Journal of Archaeological Science* 83:12–25.

Waller, Steven J.
  1993 Sound Reflection as an Explanation for the Content and Context of Rock Art. *Rock Art Research* 10(2):91–101.

  2000 Spatial Correlation of Acoustics and Rock Art Exemplified in Horseshoe Canyon. In *American Indian Rock Art, Volume 24*, edited by Frank G. Bock, pp. 85–94. American Rock Art Research Association, Phoenix.

  2005 Archaeoacoustics: A Key Role of Echoes at Utah Rock Art Sites. In *Utah Rock Art, Volume 24*, edited by Carol B. Patterson, pp 43–50. Utah Rock Art Research Association, Salt Lake City.

  2006 Intentionality of Rock-art Placement Deduced from Acoustical Measurements and Echo Myths. In *Archaeoacoustics*, edited by Chris Scarre and Graeme Lawson, pp. 31–39. McDonald Institute for Archaeological Research, Cambridge.

  2010 Voices Carry: Whisper Galleries and X-Rated Echo Myths of Utah. In *Utah Rock Art, Volume 29*, edited by Anne McConnell and Elaine Holmes, pp. 31–35. Utah Rock Art Research Association, Salt Lake City.

Whitley, David S.
  2015 Ethnographic Interpretation of the Shooting Gallery, Mount Irish, and Pahroc Rock Art ACECs, ASM Affiliates, Inc., Carlsbad, California, Electronic document, https://www.researchgate.net/publication/280731566, accessed August 14, 2022.

Using retroReveal to Enhance Pictographs at Montana Sites

David L. Minick and James D. Keyser

Using the retroReveal enhancement technique suggested to us by Jack Brink, we analyzed pictographs at the Cut Bank Pictographs (24GL67) and Hidden Handprint Alcove (24GL1664) sites, both near Cut Bank, Montana, to determine whether additional pictographs could be identified at those sites. We were somewhat successful in both instances. At Cut Bank Pictographs we could discern additional minor details for the heraldic designs of two shield-bearing warriors. At Hidden Handprint Alcove our results were more noteworthy. At that site we were able to identify more than a dozen new characters in several horizontal rows of Vertical Series tradition imagery. The results of this research demonstrate that retroReveal is a valuable supplement to DStretch for rock art research.

In late 2021 Keyser was asked by Jack Brink to review a short paper introducing retroReveal, a photograph enhancement program similar to DStretch, that Brink and his co-author, Tom Andrews, believed would be a valuable addition to the toolkit that rock art researchers use (Andrews and Brink 2022). In that review, Keyser was immediately struck by the potential value of retroReveal to enhance a certain class of pictographs at sites where both of us had previously worked. After Minick used the technique on several different photographs, we were struck by the results at the two sites, and we contacted Brink to get his and Andrews's permission to publish our own results essentially concurrent with their research, since they were the first scholars to recognize and publicize the value of the technology for rock art research. They graciously gave us permission, and this article is the result.

Unfortunately, on June 1, 2022, retroReveal was removed from the servers at the University of Utah, and it is no longer available for public use. This caused Andrews and Brink to cancel their planned 2022 ARARA presentation, but we carried forward with our presentation and this subsequent publication because it has provided new information about two sites. We sincerely hope that someone picks up the pieces of retroReveal and resurrects the program since it shows such significant potential for rock art research.

As it existed before June 2022, retroReveal was a cloud-based software tool for the analysis of faint imagery, used mostly in the paper/ephemera collecting world to reveal faint underlying patterns like postmarks on stamps and faded signatures on documents. It had been hosted by the University of Utah's Marriott Library. Applying it to rock art research is a new idea, and the results were promising (Andrews and Brink 2022). The program as it was constructed had some quirks of operation that took a bit of getting used to, and that also limited its application compared to DStretch for analyzing large quantities of images, but it was very useful as a supplement to DStretch.

David L. Minick
*Oregon Archaeological Society,
Portland*

James D. Keyser
*Oregon Archaeological Society,
Portland*

American Indian Rock Art, Volume 49. Amy Gilreath, Ken Hedges, and Anne McConnell, Editors. American Rock Art Research Association, 2023, pp. 159–166.

Some Downsides of Using retroReveal

Given the uncertainty of whether or not retroReveal will be revived, we think it is appropriate to review its pitfalls before we turn to the satisfactory results that we achieved working with the application. When using retroReveal, there were file management issues that wasted time and slowed down the processing of photographic images. The software had a size limit for images of 6.5 megapixels. When using a pro-caliber DSLR camera, this required an approximate 50% size reduction for even a modest-sized jpeg file before processing could begin. Originals could be batch processed to match the restriction and streamline the process. The size requirement added a cumbersome extra step to photographic-image processing and raised a question about loss of data when compared to the original larger file. DStretch can process photographs of all sizes without too much effort, making it ideal for use on projects with large numbers of high-resolution photographs.

The file-size limitation in retroReveal was annoying, but the real impediment to quick operations in retroReveal was the naming and storage of the files it generated. In DStretch, original file names and metadata are not impacted by processing of photographs. They are retained and the chosen enhancement filter name is added. For example, an original file named " P33_45KL81" is renamed "P33_45KL81_LAB_AC" when processed using DStretch using "lab" enhancement and auto contrast, and the metadata is retained. In contrast, in retroReveal, "P33_45KL81" is renamed "0000078331_XYZ_z(norm_w_2pct,equalized,8-bit) _full" when processed, and the metadata is erased. The file names assigned by retroReveal are difficult to decipher. This renaming of files is a serious drawback on projects that require processing of large numbers of photographs with all their variants. When database numbering is used to date stamp original files, that information is lost when retroReveal is used, as well as the underlying metadata that may include GPS data and lens/exposure information.

retroReveal processing took place in the cloud. This would have severely limited the usefulness of retroReveal in the field in remote locations with spotty or nonexistent internet connections. Warnings about the time required to process a photograph abounded on the retroReveal website. We have found that processing time for a single 6-megapixel photographic image took about 25–30 seconds and produced a huge number of variants—312 options for each original. Downloading

processed files for future reference was overly complex and slow. The "Download Full tif" command could only be saved in the computer's "download" folder, not in a selected folder associated with a project. Files could not be renamed until after they were downloaded. There were also other usability issues with the retroReveal software that took some getting used to, but these were manageable when some experience was gained in using the program. When a researcher was in the middle of a huge project (or one that slowly gets huge over time) the time lost managing these issues and working around the clunky controls on retroReveal can be substantial.

Notwithstanding the potential unwieldiness associated with using retroReveal, when we first saw the results of using the enhancement program on pictographs in Alberta, both of us were struck by the possibility that the technology would be useful in identifying additional pictographic imagery, which prompted us to try the program on existing photographs from two pictograph sites in northern Montana, south of the city of Cut Bank (Figure 1). Spectacular pictographs from both sites have been previously reported (Greer and Greer 1994; Kaiser and Keyser 2019; Keyser 2017; Keyser and Poetschat 2014:56, 159), but each of these authors has noted that the paintings are badly faded and that DStretch has proven to be invaluable in reconstructing what we now know of the pictographs. Based on seeing the extra details Andrews and Brink (2022) were able to coax out of otherwise reasonably well-documented pictographs, our initial reaction was that retroReveal might yield important new data for both Cut Bank Pictographs and Hidden Handprint Alcove. To this end we subjected approximately a dozen on-file digital photographs of two extensive panels

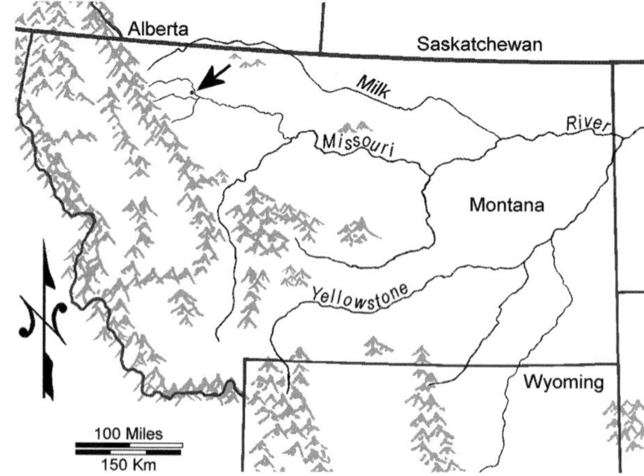

Figure 1. Location of Cut Bank Pictographs and Hidden Handprint Alcove in northern Montana indicated by arrow.

at these sites to enhancement analysis by retroReveal. The results were illuminating in several respects.

The Upside of Using retroReveal

The first digital photograph we analyzed using retroReveal was a close-up of two of four shield-bearing warriors in the well-known row of warriors at Cut Bank Pictographs (Figure 2c). These warriors are visible only under the best of conditions in natural light (Figure 2a) and they appear to have degraded somewhat since they were first professionally photographed (Greer and Greer 1994). Using DStretch in 2013 on

color slides taken in 1994 and digitized a few years later (Figure 2b), we were able to make a photo-tracing of all four warriors (Figure 3a), but the fine details were still missing in many areas. After visiting the site and rephotographing it in 2015 and 2016, we were able to make a much more accurate photo-tracing from those digital photographs when they were DStretched (Figure 3b). Finally, examining the retroReveal enhancement enabled us to see only very minimal additional detail. Specifically, it shows a small patch of smeared red pigment in the lower left[1] quadrant of the shield that is second from the right, a patch that is less noticeable in the DStretch image due to the very light color "bleeding" that characterizes DStretch enhancements, versus the cleaner retroReveal image (Figure 3c). retroReveal also accentuates the horizontal streaking in the upper and lower painted divisions of the shield carried by the right warrior. Both of these observations illustrate the technique used by the prehistoric artist to fill in the design on an outlined shield. In both cases the shield perimeter was carefully drawn with an approximately finger-width line after which the interior heraldic de-

Figure 2. *Two shield-bearing warriors at Cut Bank Pictographs. (a) Ambient lighting with contrast slightly enhanced; (b) DStretch* YWE; *(c) retroReveal* RGBW_G(*norm_w_2pct, equalized, 8-bit*).

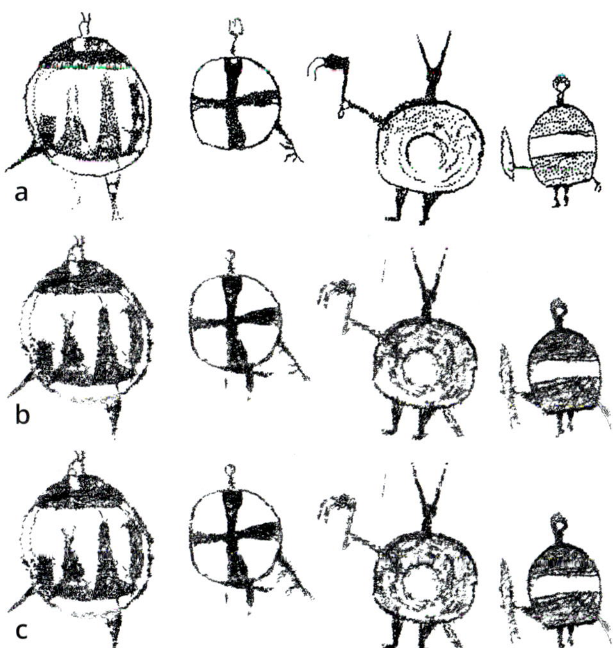

Figure 3. *Three versions of the shield-bearing warrior phalanx at Cut Bank Pictographs. (a) photo-tracing done for Keyser and Poetschat 2014 using DStretch on digitized 1994 color slide images from John and Mavis Greer; (b) photo-tracing using floodfill technique on DStretched 2015 digital image files taken by the authors; (c) added details include lower left quadrant of second shield from the right and more detail for the animal bundle attached to the third shield from the right resulting from retroReveal enhancement.*

sign was applied with slightly narrower lines with their pigment then smeared to fill in the desired spaces.

Following the discovery of minor additional details on these two shield-bearing warriors on the right, we did retroReveal enhancements of the two warriors on the left in that row and the three small rectangular-body style humans located above and slightly to the right of the shield bearers. Again, we found some small additional details for the row of three rectangular body figures (a head on the left one and added details on the bodies of two of them). The one significant discovery was that the bustle on the third warrior to the left in the row of shield bearers is actually a small animal bundle, with the front legs visible only by retroReveal (Figure 3c). In short, retroReveal provides a very small amount of additional detail for these figures, but this enables us to verify the techniques used in the manufacture of the designs of both warriors' shields, better identify the three small rectangular body humans, and identify a bundle tied to the shield of one shield bearer.

We analyzed a second group of digital photographs from Hidden Handprint Alcove, located just two km (1.25 miles) southeast of Cut Bank Pictographs. The Vertical Series tradition pictographs at Hidden Handprint Alcove have been the subject of two previous publications (Kaiser and Keyser 2019; Keyser 2017) but fading and abrasion of the paintings is severe (Kaiser and Keyser 2019:13–14). DStretch only enabled a partial reconstruction of what was obviously a more extensive composition comprising horizontal rows of symbols at Locus 5 on what is termed the fallen block panel (Figures 4 and 5a). Reconstruction of painted imagery on the fallen block is hampered by both animal abrasion and packrat urine flowing down across the panel's center. The result in many of the DStretch images is a colored "haze" that almost certainly results from pigment, packrat urine, and natural oils from animal hide and hair being smeared back and forth across the rock face by deer rubbing against it using it as a scratching post. The result is a "bio-varnish" coating much of the central section of the fallen block, and for many DStretch images, the colorspaces that ac-

Figure 4. *The fallen block at Hidden Handprint Alcove is indicated by the white arrow. The black arrow at rear indicates part of panel that remains in its original position.*

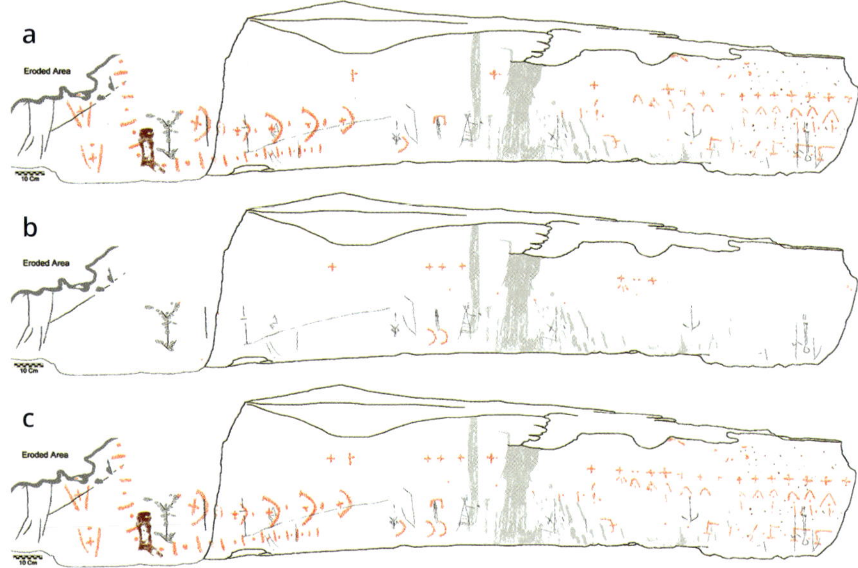

Figure 5. *Combined photo-tracing and direct tracing for the entire fallen block panel. The fallen block is the completely outlined area occupying the right three-quarters of the illustration. We have placed it as if it were not detached from the remainder of the panel (at left). (a) panel as documented from DStretch photo-tracing; (b) newly identified images from retroReveal analysis; (c) final tracing of the panel using both enhancements.*

centuate the faded and eroded pigment of the painted images also tend to recognize and amplify whatever pigment residue occurs in this bio-varnish. This effect is worse in some areas than in others on the fallen block and is also worse with some DStretch colorspaces than others (Figure 6). However, the DStretch colorspaces that best accentuate the faded red pigment naturally also pick up and highlight more of the "background noise" in the animal-smeared bio-varnish.

Examining the first retroReveal image it was apparent that this technology was better at filtering out the "background noise" coloration (Figure 7b) than

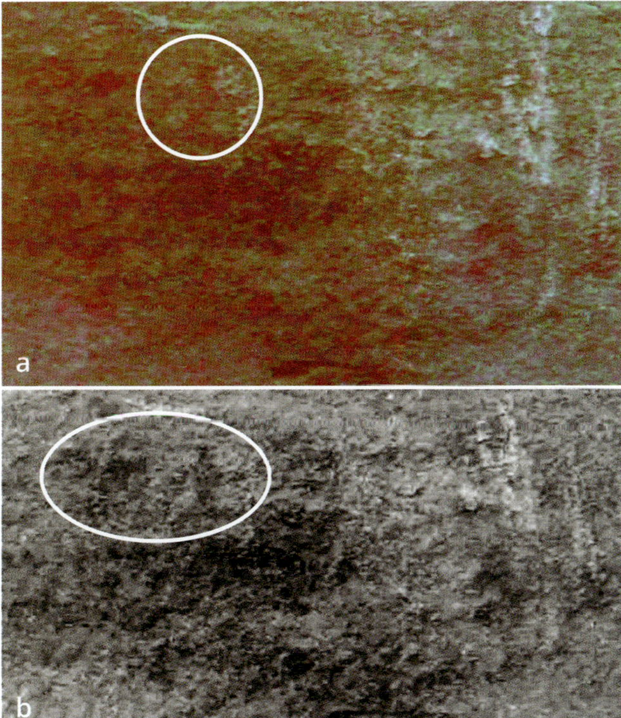

Figure 6. *Comparison of two DStretch colorspaces for the fallen block panel at Hidden Handprint Alcove. Note the red background coloration much more evident on (a) DStretch* YRD *than on (b) DStretch* YRE.

Figure 7. *Comparison of (a) DStretch* YWE; *with (b) retroReveal* RGBW_G(norm_w_2pct, equalized, 8-bit). *Note* ✚ *marks more visible in (b) at upper left. Once seen, the more-complete one can be located in (a).*

was DStretch (Figure 7a). This seems partly due to the fact that the retroReveal images are produced in greyscale, so the eye is not distracted by the myriad of other colors characteristic of the DStretch false-color images. But it is important to note that merely converting a DStretch image to greyscale does not equate it to a retroReveal image, since the many different gradations of color in a DStretch image tend to reduce the contrast of the greyscale version. This can be addressed to some degree by manipulating the resulting DStretch greyscale image to optimize the depiction of the rock art data. retroReveal does not require these adjustments because it creates its output as a greyscale image. The two programs, retroReveal and DStretch, perform different types of enhancement and analysis on photographic images and, thus, produce different results.

Using retroReveal imagery to analyze an array of photographs spanning the fallen block, we were able to identify an additional 16 pictographic characters in the Vertical Series tradition alignments in the bio-varnished center of the block (Figure 8) and augment one ✚ character at the far right end of the longest sequence painted on the block. For that row of ✚ marks, the seven we added amount to one-third of the total still visible in that sequence (Figure 5c). Perhaps more important,

Figure 8. *Comparison of (a) DStretch* YRE *with (b) retroReveal* Yuv_v(norm_w_2pct, equalized, 8-bit). *Encircled marks more visible in (b) once seen can then be easily located in (a).*

163

their revelation demonstrates that this alignment of **+** marks was originally a single row stretching more than 1.75 meters across this panel. In addition, we added two backward **C** shapes at the lower left center of the block to match a previously identified mark and create another horizontal row composed of three marks. We also added four dots and parts of two inverted **V** forms in two other horizontal rows.

For some of these marks, once we had identified them with retroReveal, we were able to find them in various DStretch images, but it was always easier to delineate the mark first with retroReveal and work backward onto a DStretch image. As noted above, we suggest that this is due to the ease with which the brain can interpret enhanced images in greyscale versus in false color. To check this, we tried converting several DStretch images to greyscale but found that the false-color signal in most of them muddied the greyscale to such an extent that these ephemeral shapes were no easier to identify than on the false-color DStretch image. As discussed above, the fact that retroReveal creates its output as a greyscale image helps preclude this muddiness.

Arroyo Del Tajo Site

After testing retroReveal on the pictographs from the two Montana sites, we were intrigued to see how the program would perform in recording and analyzing multicolored rock art images. A few years ago, Larry Loendorf showed us Arroyo Del Tajo, an unusual site in New Mexico. The site comprises a set of very small and beautifully realized pictographs of human figures and faces, painted on a very fragile rock surface by local Puebloan people—a panel that may be as much as 600 years old. Among the images was a human face with several colors—yellow, black, blue-green, and two shades of red (Figure 9). After resizing Minick's original visible light photo for retroReveal, we applied DStretch to generate a baseline of enhancements for comparison (Figures 9b and c).

When we applied retroReveal, we discovered several new results which showed some very useful effects pro-

duced using this program. The brush strokes apparent over the entire pictograph were greatly enhanced by the retroReveal program when compared to DStretch. This may be helpful for figuring out sequences of paint application and documenting pigment retouching episodes through time. Since retroReveal works by filtering and isolating colors, it also allows parts of a color palette to be analyzed individually. Figure 10 shows some of the isolated colors in the pictograph as they appear in various colorspaces. Finally, the most dramatic filtering in retroReveal pointed out only the red pigments (cf. Figure 11), and in doing so showed the artist's remarkable precision of line work in painting this pictograph.

Summary

So, what is the value of retroReveal in this study? Clearly it is not as easy to use as DStretch. It takes some getting used to and requires an accommodation of workflow quirks that can be challenging to manage. Its usefulness in large projects with many high-resolution

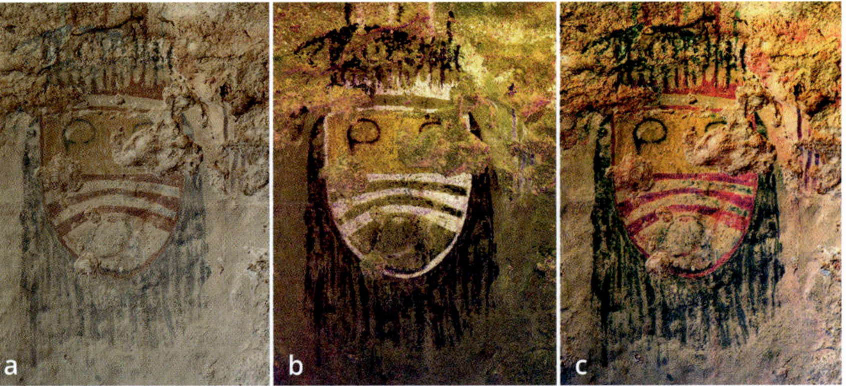

Figure 9. (a) Visible light photo from Arroyo Del Tajo, New Mexico; (b) DStretch LABI_AC *example and (c) DStretch* LBK_AC *example.*

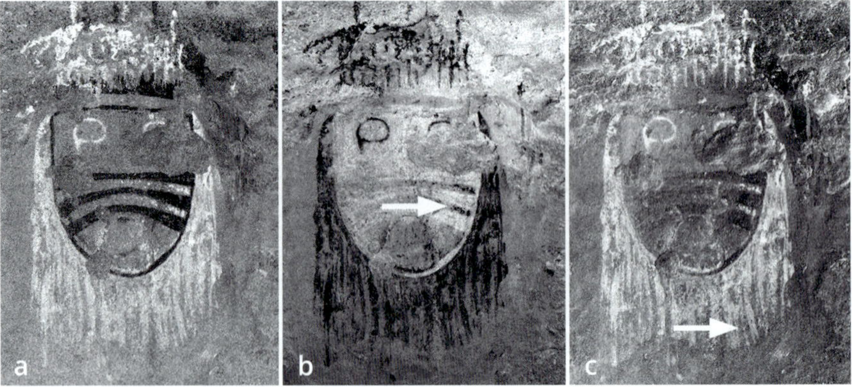

Figure 10. Three examples of retroReveal processed images, Arroyo Del Tajo, New Mexico. (a) 111213_13(norm_w_2pct,equalized,8-bit). *(b)* Luv_u(norm_w_2pct,equalized, 8-bit), *(c),* Yuv_v(norm_w_2pct,equalized,8-bit). *Arrows indicate brush strokes more evident in retroReveal than other enhancements (cf. Figure 9).*

Figure 11. Isolation of red image elements using retroReveal, HSV_V(norm_w_2pct,equalized,8-bit), at Arroyo Del Tajo, New Mexico.

original photographs is hampered by its clunky interface and serious file management issues. Additionally, its application in many instances provides only limited additional data—such as with the two shield-bearing warriors at Cut Bank Pictographs.

However, in other instances, retroReveal adds significantly to the recorded imagery. On the fallen block panel at Hidden Handprint, in the very central portion where animal abrasion and bio-varnish are most noticeable, we were able to add more than a dozen painted characters to the main Vertical Series tradition panel. By adding these, we showed that at least one row of Vertical Series tradition characters was apparently continuous, demonstrating that it is more than double the length that DStretch had shown it to be. In fact, given the length of this row as indicated by retroReveal and filling in the blanks with additional **+** marks spaced the same as the rest of those in the row, we suggest that the row originally contained at least 35 of the **+** marks. Likewise, we were able to transform a single freestanding reverse **C** shape into a horizontal row of three such marks. Again, this adds to the "vocabulary" of Vertical Series tradition imagery found at the site.

Conclusions

In conclusion, we echo the findings of Andrews and Brink (2022) in that we feel retroReveal has significant potential as a complementary analytical technique to DStretch. In specific situations it appears to show red pigment in ways that are easier for the brain to recognize and interpret. We found two things of importance. First, the technique works much better on close-up photographs than it does on ones taken some distance from the subject. While this is a bit of a "common sense" finding, it should encourage photographers in the field to be sure to capture close-up photographs of faded pictographs. This same suggestion is true for DStretch—our experience using it in a wide variety of situations has made it clear that it is always preferable to photograph rock art images as tightly cropped as possible to get the best result with the enhancement program. Thus, when using camera- or smartphone-based DStretch applications in the field, it is often beneficial to make sure that there is adequate photographic coverage so that faded pictographs and details can be enhanced with retroReveal. Second, red pictographs on iron-rich sandstones common to the northern Plains often are difficult to successfully enhance with DStretch precisely because the background red tends to mask the form of faded pictographs in the false-color images generated by DStretch. At Hidden Handprint Alcove we discovered another factor that caused the same sort of masking in DStretch, the bio-varnishing of a heavily animal-abraded painted surface. retroReveal resolves the "masking problem" to a greater or lesser degree depending on the particular surface and painted image. With this in mind, we suggest that retroReveal might be profitably employed on other sites such as the Vertical Series tradition/Foothills Abstract tradition panels at DgOv-2 (Turney et al. 2021), the Vertical Series tradition imagery on the Glenwood and Okotoks erratics[2] (Brink 2018), the Biographic tradition paintings at Crossfield Coulee (Klassen 2003:172), and the Foothills Abstract tradition imagery at No Bear (Keyser et al. 2021).

Sadly, we are forced to add a final paragraph to our conclusion in light of the demise of retroReveal in June 2022. Unless it is resurrected, no one will be able to use it. Thankfully, IT experts at the University of Utah's Marriott Library have expressed a willingness to show some of the steps necessary to remake the program and its website. We can only hope that this paper serves to encourage someone to invest the time needed to bring it back to life.

Acknowledgments. Thanks to Jack Brink and Thomas Andrews for bringing retroReveal to our attention with their paper that included testing of the program and a report on their results. Thanks to Anna Neatrour from the University of Utah's Marriott Library for her help and up-to-date information after retroReveal was removed from the library's servers.

Notes

1. Throughout the article, right and left are used from the perspective of the viewer.

2. We are aware that these erratics are Gog quartzite that is iron-rich, and DStretch images are often difficult to interpret for the same reasons that they are on many northern Plains sandstones.

References Cited

Andrews, Thomas D., and Jack W. Brink
2022 Using retroReveal as a Complement to DStretch for Enhancing Red Ochre Pictographs. *Canadian Journal of Archaeology* 46(1):1–15. Electronic Document, https://canadianarchaeology.com/caa/publications/canadian-journal-archaeology/46/1/001-015, accessed August 20, 2022.

Brink, Jack W.
2018 New VS Rock Art at the Glenwood Erratic, DiPi-42, Alberta. *Archaeological Survey of Alberta, Occasional Paper No.* 38:34–52

Greer, Mavis, and John Greer
1994 Addendum to Site 24GL67: Cut Bank Creek Pictographs. Site form on file with Montana State Historic Preservation Office, Helena.

Kaiser, David A., and James D. Keyser
2019 Looking North: The Origin of the Vertical Series Tradition. In *American Indian Rock Art, Volume 45*, edited by Ken Hedges and Anne McConnell, pp.1–19. American Rock Art Research Association, Glendale, Arizona.

Keyser, James D.
2017 The Cut Bank Creek Survey: New Sites in Central Montana (USA). *INORA The International Newsletter on Rock Art* 78:13–20.

Keyser, James D., Carl M. Davis, and Mark D. Willis
2021 Finding Another Way: Recording the No Bear Site by Pole-Assisted Photography. In *American Indian Rock Art, Volume 47*, edited by David A. Kaiser, Mavis Greer, and James D. Keyser, pp. 187–208. American Rock Art Research Association, Provo, Utah.

Keyser, James D., and George Poetschat
2014 *Northern Plains Shield Bearing Warriors: A Five Century Rock Art Record of Indian Warfare.* Publication No. 22. Oregon Archaeological Society Press, Portland.

Klassen, Michael
2003 Spirit Images, Medicine Rocks: The Rock Art of Alberta. In *Archaeology in Alberta: A View from the New Millennium*, edited by Jack W. Brink and John F. Dormaar, pp. 154–186. Archaeological Society of Alberta, Medicine Hat.

Turney, Michael, Landon Bendiak, and Jack W. Brink
2021 New Discoveries of Vertical Series and Foothills Abstract Rock Art at Writing-on-Stone, DgOv-2, Southern Alberta. *Plains Anthropologist* 66:179–216.